Speech Assessment
and
Speech Improvement
for the Hearing Impaired

Speech Assessment and Speech Improvement for the Hearing Impaired

Joanne D. Subtelny, Editor

First Edition

The materials herein were produced in the course of an agreement with the Department of Health, Education and Welfare. However, the content does not necessarily reflect the position or policy of that agency, and no official endorsement of these materials should be inferred.

Library of Congress Catalogue No. 80-6786
ISBN 0-88200-138-8

The Alexander Graham Bell Association for the Deaf
3417 Volta Place, N.W., Washington, D.C. 20007, U.S.A.

Preface

In some educational settings a very high percentage of hearing-impaired children achieve intelligible speech; however, on a national basis comparatively few children with severe to profound losses of hearing achieve intelligible speech by the time they have completed their education. This disappointing status in functional speech acquisition is partially explained by a failure to properly identify, refer, and educationally plan for children with impaired hearing. Although current shortage of personnel contributes to a high incidence of speech failure, other explanations have been projected. Recent surveys indicate quite clearly that the quantity and quality of speech training are largely responsible for failures in achieving intelligible speech. In fact, some professionals closely involved with the task of teaching speech to the hearing impaired contend that the training of personnel has not been adequate for the task—a task which, by Public Law mandate, will increase in complexity with time.

In May 1978, William Castle, the Dean and Director of the National Technical Institute for the Deaf, charged a committee with the responsibility to plan and implement a conference to address the problems related to speech training for the hearing impaired and problems related to professionally preparing people to undertake the task.

In initial planning sessions, it became very apparent that there was considerable heterogeneity in programs providing speech services and in programs training personnel to provide speech services. It also became very apparent that the committee did not have enough information to define concisely the content of the conference. This realization encouraged the development of two questionnaires. The first was addressed to the directors of programs and schools providing speech services for hearing-impaired children. The second was addressed to directors of personnel preparation programs in areas of education of the hearing impaired and in speech/language pathology.

The purpose of the first questionnaire was to identify obstacles encountered in speech training or areas in need of in-service training as identified by teachers and clinicians. To develop the questionnaire, members of the program committee met to select the 25 topics they considered most likely to represent problem areas. Each respondent was then requested to rate the current relevance of the topic using a 5-point scale, ranging from 1 (least or not needed) to 5 (most needed). Additional space was provided on the questionnaire to add topics other than those listed.

The questionnaires were disseminated to 59 directors of rehabilitation programs and schools for the deaf in New York, Michigan, Massachusetts, Kansas, California, Connecticut, Illinois, Missouri, Nebraska, Ohio, Texas, and Wyoming. Of this number, 42 responses were received. Analysis of these responses revealed that there were seven areas greatly in need of in-service training. They are listed in rank order as follows:

1. Demonstration Techniques in Speech Therapy
2. Optimal Use of Amplification in Speech Training and Within the Environment
3. Speech Diagnostic Procedures To Facilitate Planning of Therapy
4. In-service Training for Classroom Teachers in Mainstreamed Environments
5. Appropriate Test Material To Assess Speech Discrimination
6. Integration of Training To Improve Speech Perception and Production
7. Procedures To Evaluate Adequacy of Hearing Aids

This list of high priority needs was considered adequate to define content of the conference from the viewpoint of the speech teachers and clinicians currently providing services. However, additional content to present and discuss contemporary concepts and research was considered essential to round out the conference program and indicate areas in need of further study.

The purpose of the second questionnaire was to address the same content questions to 50 professionals currently involved in personnel preparation. In this instance, questions were framed to obtain estimates of teacher or clinician competence upon completion of a master's degree in Education of the Deaf or in Speech/Language Pathology, and to secure recommendations for improvement in personnel preparation. By securing half of the responses from programs in education of the deaf and half from programs in speech/language pathology, diversity in training could be identified to further tailor the conference to contemporary needs. Since the ultimate goal of the conference was to improve speech services for the hearing impaired, a conference audience consisting of teacher trainers was selected to produce the greatest impact on future training.

A summary of the questionnaire responses from teacher trainers is presented in Part VI of this text. In overview, the responses from members of personnel training programs were mostly consistent with the responses from personnel currently providing speech/language instruction. Since teachers and clinicians with many years of experience and university professors preparing students for future service identified essentially the same areas of strengths and weaknesses, there is reason to recommend some change at the level of personnel preparation.

In sum, analysis of questionnaire responses confirmed: a target audience of professionals involved in personnel preparation; and a title for the conference, "Institute on Speech Assessment and Speech Improvement for the Hearing Impaired," with broad objectives specified as follows:

1. To summarize what is known about the effectiveness of speech training;
2. To review the current status in speech diagnosis and training for the hearing impaired;
3. To present contemporary concepts pertinent to speech and language training;
4. To review current research with implications for training speech of the hearing impaired;
5. To critique current programs designed to educate teachers of the deaf and speech/language pathologists; and
6. To formulate recommendations to improve personnel training.

The chapters in this text present extended versions of papers presented at the Institute, June 21–23, 1979. Sponsored by the Communication Program of the National Technical Institute for the Deaf, Rochester Institute of Technology, the Institute brought together approximately 150 participants. This number included 42 speakers, 25 participants from personnel training programs in Education of the

Deaf, 25 participants from personnel training programs in Speech/ Language Pathology, and approximately 60 participants from other organizations and institutions involved in rehabilitative services for the hearing impaired.

This text is organized into six parts: Part I deals with speech and audiological assessments of the hearing impaired; Part II describes principles, objectives, and strategies employed in speech training for various levels of development; Part III presents several studies to evaluate the efficacy of speech training; Part IV covers five contemporary concepts pertinent to speech and language training; Part V discusses current research with implications for training speech of the hearing impaired; and Part VI covers personnel preparation for teaching speech to the hearing impaired and presents a summary of the recommendations to improve preparation which were submitted by participants in the Institute. As Dr. William Castle is a speech scientist and a speech/language pathologist by profession and also an educator of the hearing impaired by assimilation and continuing education, it is appropriate that he, who was responsible for the Institute, write the Introduction to these Proceedings.

Much of the content of this text reflects the viewpoint of the program committee that better gains in improving speech training for hearing-impaired children over the long term will be attained through free dialogue and cooperative efforts of professionally trained persons in areas of education of the hearing impaired, special education, audiology, linguistics, psychology, speech science, and speech/language pathology. Distinguished participants from each of these areas contributed to the Institute, which was designed to be a small interactive forum which would foster introspection of current training for the professionals who will direct the training programs tomorrow, research critical areas, and provide more effective procedures to improve the communication skills of the hearing impaired. After reviewing the current status of speech assessment and training procedures, contemporary concepts and research, it is hoped that professionals will be motivated to close the gaps in preparing teachers for tomorrow and open the doors for interdisciplinary exchanges and cooperative efforts to help hearing-impaired children reach their full potential in cognitive, linguistic, and communicative development.

Whatever benefits may accrue from the Institute are attributable to many people and to the U.S. Department of Health, Education and Welfare for its support of the National Technical Institute for the Deaf,

Rochester Institute of Technology. Members of the planning committee, which included Sister Joyce Buckler, Mary Campbell, William Castle, Helen Golf, Ann Lieberth, and Lee Murphy, are gratefully acknowledged for their assistance in designing the program and for their very tangible contributions to it. Despite our best planning efforts, the Institute would not have been successful without Lee Murphy's coordination and skill in making local arrangements.

We are most appreciative of the authors who have taken the time from busy schedules to share their thinking. The critical response of Institute participants to the problems addressed is also gratefully acknowledged as a major contribution.

I personally wish to thank Kathleen Crandall for her continued support in managing the Institute and for providing me the time and editorial assistance needed to complete the task. In particular, I want to thank Penelope Webster for assistance in editing all manuscripts. Jorge Samper, audiovisual specialist in the Media Production Department, is also gratefully acknowledged for processing most of the illustrations included in this text.

Finally, I wish to thank Donald Johnson, Julie Goldstein, and Monica Davis for their help as liaison and contract negotiators with the Alexander Graham Bell Association for the Deaf, which very generously has agreed to publish and disseminate the Proceedings of the Institute on Speech Assessment and Speech Improvement for the Hearing Impaired. Specifically, we thank Bettie Loux Donley in Silver Spring, Maryland, for her expertise in final editing and for sustained assistance in gaining closure on this project. We also appreciate the confidence in this work expressed by the A.G. Bell Association for the Deaf.

—Joanne D. Subtelny
Editor

Contents

Introduction

Dear Reader,

As one who is formally trained in the fields of speech pathology and experimental phonetics and as one who has been trained on-the-job over the last eleven and a half years in the field of education of the hearing impaired, I am, of course, extremely pleased that the conference for which these proceedings have been published took place. As the Director of the National Technical Institute for the Deaf (NTID), I am also extremely glad that the conference could be sponsored by NTID and that it took place at the Rochester Institute of Technology (RIT), the host institution for NTID. I wish to thank everyone who participated.

We at NTID are convinced that much more can be done today for the development of the spoken language skills of hearing-impaired people than might have been true earlier. This is allowed for by today's advances in technology and advances in the training of professionals who help such persons to develop those skills. We also believe that still more advances will occur in the future that will increase our capabilities for teaching better spoken language skills to hearing-impaired people. Hopefully, NTID can be one catalyst to those advances; and we will endeavor to make sure that these proceedings fill more needs than simply taking space on library shelves. We trust that you, as a reader, will help us with this endeavor.

Sincerely,

William E. Castle
Vice President of RIT and
Director of NTID

List of Contributors

Milo E. Bishop, Ph.D.
Dean
National Technical Institute for the Deaf
Rochester Institute of Technology
Rochester, New York 14623

Arthur Boothroyd, Ph.D.
Director, Research and Clinical Services
Clarke School for the Deaf
Northampton, Massachusetts 01060

Sister Joyce Buckler, Ed.D.
Director
St. Joseph Institute for the Deaf
St. Louis, Missouri 63132

Donald R. Calvert, Ph.D.
Director
Central Institute for the Deaf
St. Louis, Missouri 63110

Mary E. Campbell, Ph.D.
Supervisor, Special Education
Plymouth-Canton Community Schools
Plymouth, Michigan 48170

Kathleen E. Crandall, Ph.D.
Associate Dean and
Director, Communication Program
National Technical Institute for the Deaf
Rochester, New York 14623

Margot Cusack, M.A.
Assistant Speech Supervisor
Lexington School for the Deaf
Jackson Heights, New York 11370

Norman P. Erber, Ph.D.
Research Associate
Central Institute for the Deaf
St. Louis, Missouri 63110

Linda Rothman Freeman, M.S.
Speech and Hearing Institute
Institute for the Crippled and Disabled
New York, New York 10010

Donna S. Geffner, Ph.D.
Director, Speech and Hearing Center
St. John's University
Jamaica, New York 11439

Helen R. Golf, M.Ed.
Director, Sunshine Cottage School for the Deaf
Assistant Professor, Trinity College
San Antonio, Texas 78212

Marianne Streff Gustafson, M.S.
Assistant Professor,
Speech/Language Pathologist
National Technical Institute for the Deaf
Rochester, New York 14623

Katherine S. Harris, Ph.D.
Professor, Speech and Hearing Science
City University of New York Graduate School
New York, New York 10036

Sister James Lorene Hogan, Ed.S.
Director, Teacher Preparation Program for the Deaf
Fontbonne College
St. Louis, Missouri 63105

Robert A. Houde, Ph.D.
Director, Center for Communications Research
Rochester, New York 14623

Brenda K. Humphrey, M.A.
Speech/Language Pathologist
National Technical Institute for the Deaf
Rochester, New York 14623

Laura W. Kretschmer, Ed.D.
Associate Professor, Audiology
Program Director, Department of Speech Pathology and Audiology
University of Cincinnati
Cincinnati, Ohio 45221

Richard R. Kretschmer, Ed.D.
Associate Professor
Department of Special Education and School of Psychology
University of Cincinnati
Cincinnati, Ohio 45221

Harry Levitt, Ph.D.
Professor, Speech and Hearing Sciences
City University of New York Graduate School
New York, New York 10036

Ann K. Lieberth, M.A.
Assistant Professor, Speech/Language Pathologist
National Technical Institute for the Deaf
Rochester, New York 14623

Daniel Ling, Ph.D.
Professor, School of Human Communication Disorders
McGill University
Montreal, Canada H3G 1A8

Jean E. Maki, Ph.D.
Research Associate
National Technical Institute for the Deaf
Rochester, New York 14623

Noel D. Matkin, Ph.D.
Director, Language and Learning Center
Boys Town Institute for Communication Disorders in Children
Creighton University Medical Center
Omaha, Nebraska 68178

Nancy S. McGarr, Ph.D.
Research Associate
Haskins Laboratories
New Haven, Connecticut 06510

Eugene O. Mencke, Ph.D.
Professor
Department of Communication Disorders
University of Oklahoma Health Science Center
Oklahoma City, Oklahoma 73106

Dale E. Metz, Ph.D.
Research Associate
National Technical Institute for the Deaf
Rochester, New York 14623

Ann M. Mulholland, Ph.D.
Associate Professor, Director Teacher Preparation Program for the Deaf
Teachers College, Columbia University
New York, New York 10028

Lee C. Murphy, Ed.D.
Coordinator, Continuing Education
National Technical Institute for the Deaf
Rochester, New York 14623

Raymond S. Nickerson, Ph.D.
Vice President
Bolt, Beranek and Newman, Inc.
Cambridge, Massachusetts 02109

Nicholas A. Orlando, M.S.
Associate Professor
Assistant to the Associate Dean of Communication Program
National Technical Institute for the Deaf
Rochester, New York 14623

Linda J. Rowe, M.S.
Director of Education Services
John Tracy Clinic
Westminster, California 92683

Nicholas Schiavetti, Ph.D.
Department of Speech Pathology and Audiology
State University College of Arts and Science
Geneseo, New York 14454

Sister Roseanne Siebert, M. A.
Teacher, Primary Department
St. Joseph Institute for the Deaf
St. Louis, Missouri 63132

Ronald W. Sitler, Ph.D.
Chairman
Department of Speech Pathology and Audiology
State University College of Arts and Science
Geneseo, New York 14454

Clarissa R. Smith, Ph.D.
Associate Professor, Communication Science
Health Science
Hunter College
City University of New York
New York, New York 10036

Kenneth Stevens, Ph.D.
Professor
Research Laboratory of Electronics
Massachusetts Institute of Technology
Cambridge, Massachusetts 02139

Joanne D. Subtelny, Ph.D.
Professor
Communication Program
National Technical Institute for the Deaf
Rochester, New York 14623

Raymond J. Trybus, Ph.D.
Dean, Research Institute
Gallaudet College
Washington, D.C. 20002

Penelope E. Webster, M.A.
Speech/Language Pathologist
National Technnical Institute for the Deaf
Rochester, New York 14623

Harris Winitz, Ph.D.
Professor
Speech Science and Psychology
University of Missouri—Kansas City
Kansas City, Missouri 64110

PART I

Speech Assessment: Interpretation Relative to Training

1
Speech Assessment at the Primary Level: Interpretation Relative to Speech Training

Donna Geffner and Lisa Rothman Freeman

IT IS KNOWN THAT as peripheral hearing handicap increases, so do the related speech problems. The literature reveals that speech patterns of the deaf are typically characterized by excessive breath; slow, labored rhythm; weak quality; and substitutions, omissions, and distortions of syllables (Nober & Nober, 1977). Articulation is imprecise and ratios of vowels to consonants are different from that produced by normally hearing individuals. Syllable duration and features of voice are also affected. The speech of a deaf person presents many different parameters that have received extensive study (Hudgins & Numbers, 1942; Levitt & Smith, 1972; Nober, 1967; Smith, 1973).

The first quantitative study of the speech production of hearing-impaired children was carried out by Hudgins and Numbers in 1942. Their findings showed that the major consonant errors were nonfunction of the initial consonants, voiced-voiceless confusions, and consonant cluster errors. The major vowel errors were substitutions, errors in the production of diphthongs, and neutralization. The results of this and other studies, Levitt et al. (1976); Markides (1970); Nober (1967); and Smith (1973) are generally in agreement that the most frequent consonant errors involved are incorrect production of the palatal and alveolar fricatives, the affricates, and velar nasal. In addition, the results indicate better production of bilabials, glides, and labiodental fricatives. The most frequent vowel errors reported were those of neutralization (Markides, 1970; Smith, 1973), diphthongization (Boone, 1966; Markides, 1970) and nasalization (Mártony, 1965, 1966). Of the studies mentioned, only Nober tested children aged 6 years or younger. The children participating in the other studies ranged in age from 7 years to 15 years of age.

The test stimuli used varied from standard articulation tests such as the Templin-Darley (1969) word picture test to word and sentence material which the children were required to read. Many of the studies previously cited also measured the intelligibility of their subjects' speech. Hudgins and Numbers (1942), John and Howarth (1965), Markides (1970), Smith (1973), Gold (1978), and McGarr (1978) measured intelligibility either by percentage of words correctly understood as a function of all words produced and/or in percentage of complete sentences correctly understood. Other studies have used rating scales either exclusively (Levitt et al., 1976) or in conjunction with percentage of words understood (Gold, 1978; Smith, 1973). The majority of these studies utilize written material as stimuli. Only Markides elicited and analyzed the intelligibility of spontaneous speech samples.

The present investigators studied the speech production of 6-year-old deaf children within the framework of a larger effort to evaluate the speech, language, and communication skills of those children.[1] Sixty-seven children in state-supported or funded schools for the deaf were selected. As a rather extensive project conducted by Levitt et al. (1976) included children aged 8 through 12, and prior studies refer to children in primary grades, it was of interest to measure the speech performance of younger deaf children. Since an original longitudinal study was planned, age 6 appeared to be a reasonable beginning point to which subsequent years could be compared. In addition, these children would be enrolled in school and easily accessible for testing. Because of their young age, and inability to read, test materials utilizing written stimuli were inappropriate. Furthermore, no standardized articulation tests for deaf children were available. These investigators attempted to develop or adapt appropriate instruments with which to measure speech production.

Methodology

Subjects

Sixty-seven children in state-supported or funded schools for the deaf, ranging in age from 6.0 to 6.11 years, mean age 6.5 years, were tested. The average hearing loss for frequencies 250 Hz–4000 Hz (where obtainable) was 104 dB. Ranges for each frequency in the better ear can be found in Figure 1.1. The average age of onset of loss

[1]Language, Speech and Communication Skills Project conducted in 1977, supported by the Cooperative Research Endeavors in the Education of the Deaf (CREED) of the New York State Department of Education.

FIGURE 1.1
Range and mean hearing threshold levels for the better ear (N = 62).

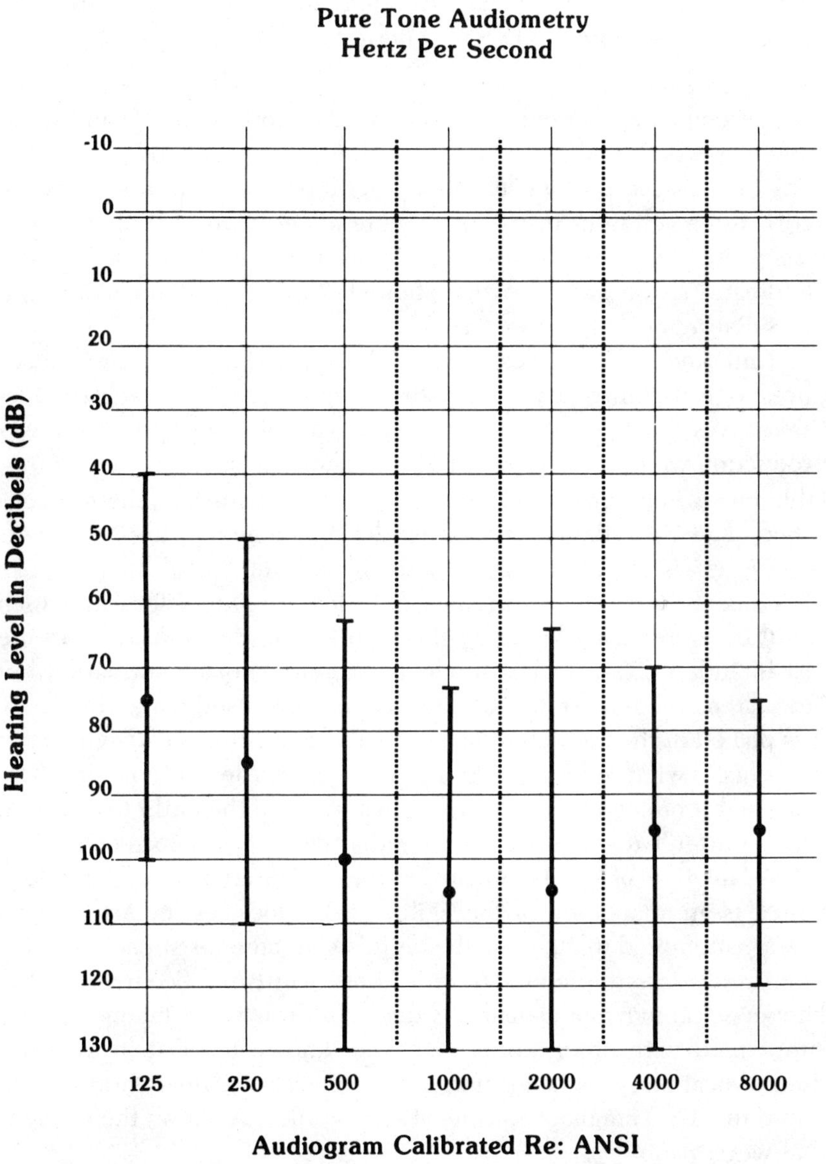

was 2.7 months with a range from 0 to 24 months. Because 50 percent of the losses were due to unknown causes, and 24 percent due to genetic factors, one may make an assumption that most of these children were prelingually deaf. For 62 of these children special education began at 3 years of age. English was the primary language spoken at home for 73 percent of the children, while sign language was the primary language for 17 percent. Another language used was Spanish. Of the parents, 18 percent were reported as deaf.

Instruments

An attempt was made to obtain samples of both imitative and spontaneous speech production. Because there were no known available tests to measure the speech of deaf children with limited reading skills, three different instruments were adapted and utilized. These tests were the Imitation Syllable Test (IST), an adaptation of the Goldman-Fristoe Test of Articulation (1972), and a Speech Intelligibility Rating Scale (Johnson, 1975).

Imitation Syllable Test. As syllable imitation is an elementary phonological skill that is precursory to spontaneous speech production, it was felt that requiring the children to imitate the examiner's production would determine whether or not the children were stimulable for various consonants and vowels in a CV cluster. The test consisted of 36 CV syllables containing the phoneme /b/ plus the vowels /a/, /u/, /ae/, /ɔ/, /ɪ/, /o/ and the diphthongs /eɪ/, /aʊ/, /oʊ/, /aɪ/, /ɔɪ/.[1] The phoneme /b/ was selected because of its low-frequency formant which could be more easily heard by these children. The remainder of the test included CV syllables in which the initial consonant varied but vowel remained constant. All consonants were used. In addition, /b/ was placed in the medial (əbə) and final (əb) positions of a syllable to determine what effect position might have on production. The examiner produced the target syllable and asked the child to repeat it. The children's responses were scored as correct or incorrect.

Adaptation of the Goldman-Fristoe Articulation Test. This test, which is an adaptation of the Goldman-Fristoe Test of Articulation (1972), attempted to measure the child's spontaneous speech production in response to picture stimuli. Those words not occurring in the known vocabulary of 6-year-old deaf children were taken out and supplanted with other words that were known to exist in the children's vocabulary, as heard in a preschool class for deaf children and found in a CID language outline (1950). Table 1.A shows the changes that were made.

[1]To expedite printing, all phonetic symbols in this text are enclosed by slashes rather than brackets.

Consonants, diphthongs, and vowels were tested. Consonant blends were eliminated due to their high level of difficulty. Colored pictures representing the word changes were placed in the test book, and as each picture was presented, the child was stimulated to say what it was. The examiner scored each error as either correct, omission, substitution, distortion, or addition.

TABLE 1.A
Modifications of the Goldman-Fristoe Test of Articulation for 6-year-old deaf children.

Words Omitted	Words Substituted or Added
telephone	elephant
vacuum	valentine
matches, feather	mother, catching
lamp	light
shovel	shoe, oven
church	chair, sandwich
bathtub	bib
ring	
plane	
blue	
brush	toothbrush
squirrel	girl
sleeping	
stove	glove
	book
	boy
	baby
	flower

Speech Intelligibility Rating. To assess the child's speech production ability in connected spontaneous discourse, the Speech Intelligibility Rating Scale, developed at the National Technical Institute for the Deaf, was used. Two pictures were used to stimulate spontaneous oral language. Each child was shown a large, brightly colored picture from the Peabody Pre-School Kit depicting a city street with activity. The child was asked to tell the examiner as much as possible about the picture. The child was then shown a series of four pictures in sequence, depicting a family preparing for and going on a picnic (Stuckless, 1966) and asked to tell a short story about it. A 5-point rating scale was used to evaluate the child's speech, as seen in Table

1.B. The rating ranges from totally unintelligible production (1) to completely intelligible speech (5). Two examiners conferred with one another prior to recording a rating for each picture stimulus. Because a rating was given for each picture, average ratings often fell between two categories. The classroom teacher was also asked to evaluate each child's speech intelligibility based on daily exposure to the children using the same rating scale.

TABLE 1.B
Speech intelligibility rating scale.

Rating	Description
1	Speech cannot be understood.
2	Speech is very difficult to understand—only isolated words or phrases are intelligible.
3	Speech is difficult to understand; however, the gist of the content can be understood.
4	Speech is intelligible with the exception of a few words or phrases.
5	Speech is completely intelligible.

Data Analysis

Particular procedures were designed to emphasize distinctive features as crucial phonemic parameters. Such features as manner, place, and voicing were recorded for each response. In addition, each phoneme was coded by its particular set of features (Smith, 1975). Another parameter considered was visibility.

Visibility was determined by administering a pre-test to a class of college students. The tester presented each phoneme in a CV context where the consonant varied and the vowel (ə) was constant. The c + ə cluster was presented silently. Each student was asked to record the consonant/or vowel visually received. A matrix of order of visibility was developed from most visible to least visible, dividing the order to establish three categories: visible, semivisible, nonvisible.

Each phoneme was analyzed as either a vowel, diphthong, or consonant. For vowels, features of frontness, height, rounding, tenseness, and also visibility were considered. For consonants, features of place (front, medial, back), manner (nasal, affricate, plosive), voice (voice, voiceless), in addition to visibility were evaluated. Diphthongs were analyzed by formant change from small to large change in second formant and by visibility.

From this analysis the percentage of consonant/vowel errors, error types (substitution, omission, distortion), rank of difficulty, and differences in initial, medial, and final positions were determined. Imitative versus spontaneous phoneme production was also compared.

Results

Imitative Syllable Test

The rank order of proportion correct is presented in Table 1.C. While vowels were produced correctly more often than consonants, the overall proportion correct for all phonemes is only .44. Vowel imitation ability corresponds to standard vowel charts, indicating that those having lowest second formants (F_2) are more easily recognized and produced (/a/, F_2 = 1370 Hz), than those with higher F_2 values (/i/, F_2 = 3200 Hz; /ɪ/, F_2 = 2730 Hz). The latter received lower ranking. Formant values for children were obtained from Peterson and Barney (1952). Children produced mid and low back vowels more accurately than mid and high front vowels.

According to Levitt (1978), the lowest two formants play a dominant role in identifying the vowels. Vowels are differentiated not on the basis of formant frequency, but rather by F_2/F_1 ratio (Peterson & Barney, 1952). It is therefore important to note that those vowels having smaller formant ratios were produced more correctly than those with larger ratios, e.g., /a/, F_2/F_1 = 1.33; /i/, F_2/F_1 = 8.65.

Consonants that were more visible were produced more accurately than those that were partially or not visible, e.g., /w/^{1}, /f/^{2}, /p/^{3} received higher rank than /ʃ/^{17}, /j/^{15}, /h/^{14}. No consistent relationships between distinctive features or even threshold of recognition of consonants (Fletcher, 1953) could be drawn.

Articulation Test

Data for the spontaneous production of phonemes can be found in Table 1.D. As expected, vowels were produced correctly more often than consonants; however, the overall proportion correct was only .42.

Proportions of .50 or greater were obtained for all vowels with the exception of /ɪ/ (.34). For consonants, only /p/, /b/, /f/ achieved proportions correct of .50 or greater. A feature that appears to be commonly shared by these consonants is front placement. An analysis of error types, omission, substitution, and distortion indicated that of the 3,290 errors, 91 percent (2,996) were omissions, 7 percent (241) substitutions, 1 percent (35) distortions, and .1 percent (18) additions. The

TABLE 1.C
Production of imitated syllables ranked in order of proportion correct.

Rank	Syllables	Proportion Correct
1	*a*	.91
2	u	.86
3	ɔ	.83
4	oU, æ	.82
5	aU	.78
6	w	.71
7	ɔɪ,o	.69
8	f, i, ɪ	.68
9	e	.63
10	aɪ	.62
11	p, b	.60
12	v	.55
13	l	.43
14	θ	.38
15	əb	.37
16	d, əbə	.34
17	m	.31
18	ð	.28
19	t	.26
20	n	.15
21	g	.11
22	r	.09
23	h	.07
24	tʃ, j	.06
25	k, ʒ, s	.05
26	ʃ	.02
27	z, dʒ	.00

propensity toward a greater number of omissions reflects early speech acquisition errors as seen in normal children.

The frequency of omission errors in all positions, as seen in Table 1.E, indicates that the velar consonants /g/, /k/, /ŋ/ which are not visible were omitted in greater proportion than the more visible front consonants /f/, /p/, /b/, and other bilabials and labiodentals. Vowels were omitted less often than consonants in general. Among consonants, those with the features of sonorance and frication were omitted more frequently.

Substitution errors, Table 1.F, comprised a small proportion of the

TABLE 1.D
Rank order in percent correct for phonemes produced in all positions on the articulation test.

Rank	Phoneme	Proportion Correct
1	e	.88
2	ʌ	.84
3	u	.83
4	aʊ, æ	.80
5	aɪ	.77
6	iʊ	.75
7	ɛ, *a*	.73
8	ɔ	.69
9	b	.60
10	ɔɪ	.59
11	p	.54
12	f	.51
13	oʊ	.50
14	w	.44
15	v	.43
16	l	.36
17	ɪ	.34
18	ð	.29
19	h	.28
20	m	.27
21	r	.26
22	d	.23
23	n	.22
24	j	.20
25	t	.17
26	θ	.15
27	ʃ	.14
28	s	.07
29	tʃ, k	.06
30	z, dʒ	.05
31	ŋ, g	.04

total number of errors (ranging from .00 to .23) and reflected a greater number of omissions rather than substitutions for those phonemes not yet acquired.

The proportion of errors for the distinctive features of manner, place, and voicing were interesting. For manner of production, the lateral and glide phonemes were elicited more accurately than were the affricates as displayed in Figure 1.2. For place of production, the

TABLE 1.E
Phonemic errors ranked in order of proportion of omission on the articulation test.

Rank	Phoneme	Proportion of Omission
1	ŋ	.95
2	g	.94
3	k	.93
4	z	.89
5	s	.88
6	dʒ, tʃ	.87
7	s	.81
8	t	.80
9	θ	.76
10	n	.75
11	d	.74
12	h	.70
13	r	.69
14	m	.66
15	j, ɪ	.63
16	ð	.59
17	l	.57
18	w	.53
19	v	.52
20	oʊ	.47
21	f	.42
22	p	.40
23	b	.32
24	i	.22
25	ɔ	.20
26	*a*	.19
27	ɔɪ, ɛ	.17
28	æ	.16
29	ʊ, aʊ, aɪ	.14
30	ʌ,u	.11
31	e	.09

labiodental and bilabial consonants were correctly produced more often than velar consonants (Figure 1.3). The voicing feature differed minimally, with a greater proportion correct for voiced (.25) rather than voiceless (.22) consonants.

In comparing phoneme positions, the data indicate that initial consonants were produced more correctly (.30) than those in the medial position (.22), which were produced more correctly than those in the final position (.19). Further analysis indicates that errors of omission

TABLE 1.F

Phonemic errors ranked in order of proportion of substitution on the articulation test.

Rank	Phoneme	Proportion
1	ɔɪ	.23
2	j	.16
3	ð	.12
4	ʊ	.11
5	ɛ, ɔ	.04
6	aɪ, *a*	.08
7	θ,m	.07
8	f, dʒ, aʊ	.06
9	z, r, v, u, æ	.05
10	l, ʃ, v, s	.05
11	tʃ,p	.04
12	w, ɪ, oʊ, t, b, d	.03
13	n, g, e, i	.02
14	k	.01
15	ŋ, h	.00

were greater for final position consonants (.77) than initial position (.61). Errors of substitution, while constituting a minimal percentage, were greater for initial position (.08) than final position (.02).

Production of vowels can best be analyzed by comparing the features of tongue height and place of constriction. Figure 1.4 gives the proportion correct for each vowel according to the standard vowel chart. While no definitive statement can be made from this data, one can make the observation that low vowels were more accurately produced than high vowels.

Comparison between spontaneous speech production and imitative speech indicates differences in ranked order correct for phonemes. On the imitation tests, vowels produced correctly more often (i.e., /a/, /ʊ/, /ɔ/) were different from those produced and ranked most correctly on the articulation test (i.e., /e/, /v/, /ʊ/). Differences may be attributed to a visibility factor that was inherent in the Imitative Syllable Test as well as other coarticulatory factors present in the articulation test. For consonants, the six phonemes produced correctly were the same for both spontaneous and imitative tests (/w/, /f/, /p/, /b/, /v/, /1/), all sharing front placement. Those phonemes ranked among the lowest in production (/k/, / ʒ /, /s/, /ʃ/, /z/, / dʒ /) were the same for both tests, sharing the manner feature of frication. This finding is similar to what is

FIGURE 1.2
Proportion correct for manner *of production on the articulation test.*

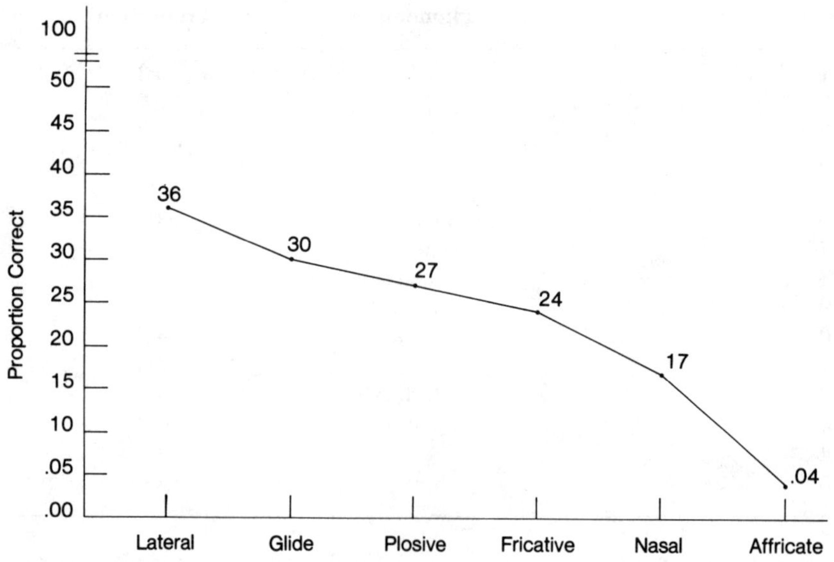

FIGURE 1.3
Proportion correct for place *of production on the articulation test.*

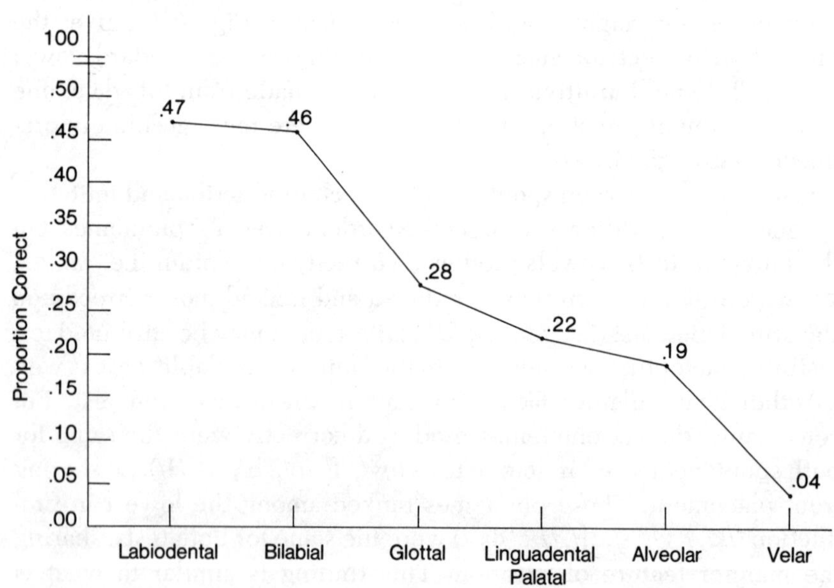

FIGURE 1.4
Vowel production by features as elicited by the articulation test (in proportion correct).

	Front	Central	Back
High	i = .75 I = .34		u = .83 U = .75
Mid	e = .88 ε = .73	ɔ = .69	o = .50
Low	æ = .83	ʌ = .84	a = .73

known about speech development in normally hearing children, that phonemes / ð /, /z/, / ʒ /, / dʒ / are the last to emerge.

Speech Intelligibility Rating

The examiners rated 49 percent of the children in category 1, producing no intelligible speech. Twenty-seven percent of the children were found extremely difficult to understand, category 2, producing only a few intelligible words. Category 3 included 2.5 percent of the children who were found to produce enough intelligible speech to transmit the main idea to the listener. For the remainder of the group, 3 percent attained a rating of 4, and 1.5 percent received a rating between 4 and 5. The mean rating given by the examiners was 1.7.

In comparison, the teachers rated the children higher, with a mean rating of 2.3. The majority of the children received ratings in levels 1, 2, and 3, but 7.5 percent received a rating of 4, and 3 percent received a rating of 5. Despite these differences, the correlation between teacher and examiner ratings was statistically significant at the 0.001 level. It should be noted that examiners were trained listeners of deaf speech. Figure 1.5 compares the examiners' ratings to the teachers' ratings across each category.

FIGURE 1.5
Speech intelligibility ratings by classroom teacher and examiner.

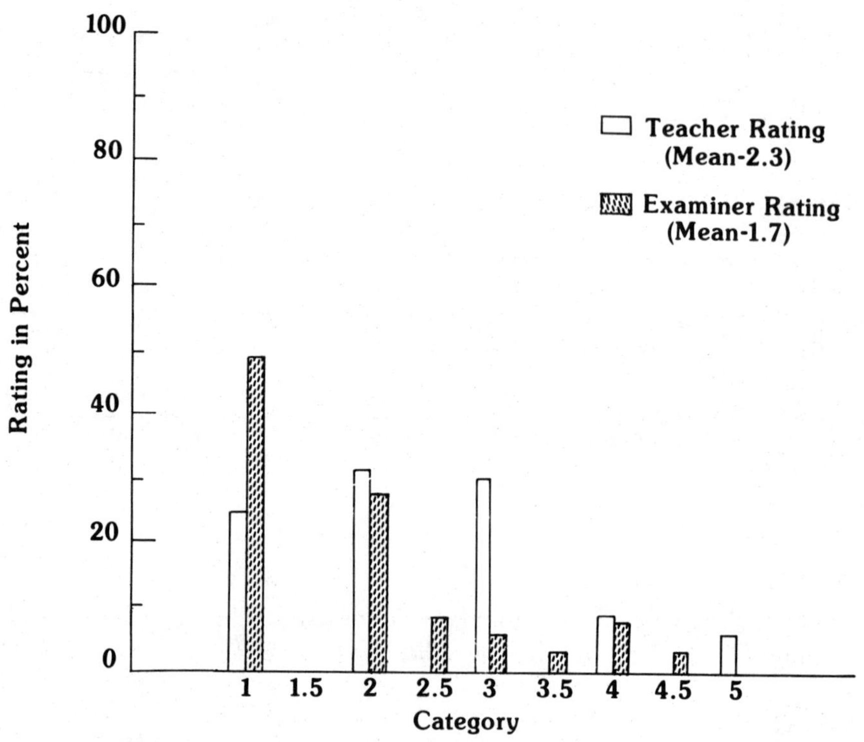

Key
1. Not Understood
2. Difficult to Understand
3. Gist Understood
4. Some Errors
5. Completely Intelligible

Discussion

The results of this investigation indicate that for the imitative and spontaneous tests, the proportions correct were .44 and .42 respectively. These values indicate that less than half of the phonemes tested were produced correctly, reflecting a proficiency level of younger normally hearing children. Such a finding is consistent with the low intelligibility rating achieved.

Findings were consistent with other studies, indicating that bilabials, glides, and labiodentals were produced more correctly than palatal and alveolar fricatives, affricates, and glottals (Markides, 1970; Nober, 1967; Smith, 1973). The most common error type was omission (Hudgins & Numbers, 1942; Levitt et al., 1976; Markides, 1970; Nober, 1967; Smith, 1973). Omission of initial consonant was more frequent than that in the final position, a finding which is in agreement with that of Hudgins and Numbers (1942). In contrast, Nober (1967) found that the order of consonant errors increased from initial to medial to final position. Smith (1973) also found errors in final position to be more numerous. Perhaps this difference in error analysis may be explained by differences in the age of subjects studied and/or by differences in stimuli employed.

Visibility of phonemes proved to be an important factor in both the imitative and spontaneous ability to produce speech. Bilabials and labiodentals were more accurately produced.

Findings for vowel production are also in agreement with other studies, indicating that vowels with low tongue position are correct more often than those produced with mid or high tongue position (Nober, 1967; Smith, 1973). Boone in 1966 hypothesized that because the deaf tended to keep their tongues too far back and too low in the mouth, the resonance patterns were affected, further interfering with production of front and high vowels. In general, vowels were produced more accurately than consonants, which would be attributed to their phonetic power and visibility. Consonants, because of their high-frequency components and inherently weaker intensity, were more affected. This is further substantiated by the fact that voiced consonants were produced more accurately than voiceless consonants.

Results reported, although not totally conclusive, contribute to our body of knowledge of *younger* deaf children. What we see is that speech production patterns characteristic of the deaf have already emerged by *age 6*.

Implications for Training

Vowel production in deaf children has been known to reflect a low, posterior tongue position. This low back position creates a contour of the oral cavity that will affect the resonance quality. Because deaf children produce these low back vowels, there is a need to train them to utilize more front, high, and central positions. Perhaps lingua tracking utilizing visual display units could be implemented to train these children to reposition their tongue. An education of the oral cavity and vault with visual displays may assist in altering the resonance quality from the predominantly nasal one to a more oral tone.

Emphasis should be placed on consonant training whereby those phonemes containing higher frequencies may be transferred to lower formant frequencies and identified. An individual should be trained to utilize his residual hearing to discriminate those consonants that are less visible and powerful. Perhaps training that utilized a hierarchy of phonemes with increasing F_2/F_1 ratios may assist the child to identify and produce more difficult phonemes. The ordering of phonemes for training by acoustic and frequency ratio cues is suggested.

Furthermore, an analysis of distinctive features reveals that frication is the most difficult feature to produce and is the last feature that normally hearing children master. Thus acquisition of this feature may require coordination and refinement of respiratory control of the breath stream for speech. Training in control of expired vocalized breath should be considered.

It appears that because visibility and intensity are important factors in the deaf child's ability to produce phonemes, and since each phoneme is affected by the phonetic context, one should be inclined to train the child to identify and produce *words* rather than isolated phonemes. The coarticulatory influence of vowels in CV syllables may help in the identification and subsequent production of consonants, particularly voiceless ones. The relatively similar scores obtained on the imitative vs. spontaneous articulation tests indicate that these children are no more proficient at producing isolated phonemes/syllables by imitation than they are at producing words, and are even less proficient at two- to three-word utterances as substantiated by the Speech Intelligibility Rating. Much emphasis needs to be placed on production of words and words in context if one is to be committed to teaching speech to deaf children. Surely additional aids such as sensory devices, tonal modulators, and visual cues should not be ruled out in the speech training process.

REFERENCES

Boone, D. R. Modification of the voices of deaf children. *Volta Rev.*, 1966, *68*, 686–692.

Fletcher, H. *Speech and hearing in communication.* Princeton, N.J.: D. Van Nostrand, 1953.

Gold, T. *Speech and hearing skills: A comparison between hard-of-hearing and deaf children.* Doctoral dissertation, City University of New York, Graduate Center, 1978.

Goldman, R., & Fristoe, M. *Goldman-Fristoe test of articulation.* Circle Pines, Minn.: American Guidance Service, Inc., 1972.

Hudgins, C. V., & Numbers, G. C. An investigation of the intelligibility of speech of the deaf. *Genet. Psych. Mono.*, 1942, *25*, 289–392.

John, J. E. J., & Howarth, J. N. The effect of time distortions on the intelligiblity of deaf children's speech. *Lang. Speech*, 1965, *8*, 127–134.

Johnson, D. Communication characteristics of NTID students. *J. Acad. Rehab. Audiol.*, 1975, *8*, 17–32.

Language outline prepared by a committee of teachers at the Central Institute for the Deaf. *Am. Ann. Deaf*, 1950, *95*, 353–378.

Levitt, H. The acoustics of speech production. In M. Ross & T. Giolas (Eds.), *Auditory management of hearing impaired children.* Baltimore: University Park Press, 1978.

Levitt, H., & Smith, C. R. Errors of articulation in the speech of profoundly hearing-impaired children. *J. Acoust. Soc. Am.*, 1972, *51*, 102 (A).

Levitt, H., et al. *Language communication skills of deaf children, 1973-1975.* Albany, N.Y.: Bureau for Physically Handicapped Children, State Education Department, 1976.

Markides, A. The speech of deaf and partially hearing children with special reference to factors affecting intelligibility. *Brit. J. Dis. Comm.*, 1970, *5*, 126–140.

Mârtony, J. Studies on the speech of the deaf. *I. Speech Trans. Lab. - Quart. Prog. Status Rep.*, Royal Insti. Tech., Stockholm, 1965.

Mârtony, J. Studies on the speech of the deaf. *Speech Trans. Lab. Rep.*, Royal Insti. Tech., Stockholm, 1966.

McGarr, N. S. *Differences between experienced and inexperienced listeners in understanding the speech of the deaf.* Doctoral dissertation, City University of New York, Graduate Center, 1978.

Nober, E. H. Articulation of the deaf. *Excep. Child*, 1967, *33*, 611–621.

Nober, E. H., & Nober, L. Effects of hearing loss on speech and language in the post-babbling stage. In B. Jaffe (Ed.), *Hearing loss in children.* Baltimore: University Park Press, 1977.

Peterson, G. E., & Barney, H. L. Control methods used in a study of the vowels. *J. Acoust. Soc. Am.*, 1952, *24*, 175–184.

Smith, C. Residual hearing and speech production in deaf children. *Comm. Sc. Lab. Res. Rep. No. 4*, City University of New York, 1973.

Smith, C. Residual hearing and speech production in deaf children. *J. Speech Hear. Res.*, 1975, *18*, 795–811.

Stuckless, E. R., & Marks, C. *Assessment of the written language of deaf students.* H.E.W. Cooperative Research Proj. 2544, Dept. Spec. Ed. and Rehab.; University of Pittsburgh, 1966.

Templin, M. C., & Darley, F. L. *Templin-Darley tests of articulation.* Iowa City: University of Iowa, Bureau of Educational Research and Service, 1969.

2
Speech Assessment at the Elementary Level: Interpretation Relative to Speech Training

Clarissa R. Smith

BETWEEN 1973 AND 1975 a study of communication skills of deaf children (Levitt et al., 1978) was carried out under the auspices of the Cooperative Research Endeavors in the Education of the Deaf program, New York State Education Department. More than 100 children from 10 different schools who were all 10 years old at the outset, were assessed repeatedly on a number of different skills. The findings were not encouraging. For each of the three years during which assessments were made, more than 70 percent of the children were rated difficult or impossible to understand. Ratings of speech intelligibility also were found to indicate very slight improvement over that time.

The same kind of information, on a one-time basis, is found in the Office of Demographic Studies report by Jensema, Karchmer, and Trybus (1978) on the rated speech intelligibility of hearing-impaired children in special education programs of all types. In that nationwide survey, some 1,300 children were divided into age groups of under 7 years, 8 to 11 years, 12 to 15, and over 16. The very youngest children were represented in the very intelligible group by a smaller percentage than the other age groups. Otherwise, in each category of rated intelligibility, the several age groups did not differ from each other by more than a few percentage points. Excluding children who would not speak in the 8–11 year grouping, 45.5 percent were barely intelligible or not intelligible.

From data presented in these two studies, it appears that deaf children stopped getting easier to understand, at least by age 10, and perhaps even earlier than that. It is the premise of this Institute that perhaps the situation can be improved.

Many people here have engaged in intense research efforts toward building our knowledge of the problems of deaf children's speech. But little time is devoted to those same problems in many master's training programs for speech/language pathologists. Likewise, little time and practical help have been given to classroom teachers to help them make speech training a constant part of the children's activities.

Speech Characteristics of Deaf Children

It seems appropriate to begin by reviewing what has been learned from a number of studies about the errors characterizing the speech of deaf children. Hudgins and Numbers (1942), in their pioneering investigation, found the most common consonant errors to be: (a) nonfunction of the releasing or initiating consonant, resulting from improper closure of the vocal tract; (b) voiced-voiceless confusions; (c) errors in clusters, abutting consonants, and nasality. For vowels, the most frequent errors were substitution; failure of diphthongs, usually involving loss of the second component; and neutralization.

Mártony (1966) noted the lack of synchrony between articulation and phonation at the junction between a consonant and the following vowel; prominent errors in velar function involving abnormal and misplaced nasalization of vowels; and a super-stationary form of vowels, wherein transitions are often missing, or, if present, are too short, indicating overly abrupt articulatory movements.

Markides (1970b) observed that vowel substitutions were not limited to adjacent positions in the vowel space, nor to vowels of a similar type of tongue formation. Among consonants, omissions were found to be the most prominent error, especially for velar sounds. Substitutions for all consonant types most often involved an error in manner of articulation.

Various analyses of a large amount of data in the Communication Sciences Laboratory of the City University of New York Graduate School have substantiated some earlier findings, qualified others, and added new information. For example, Smith (1975a) also found omission to be the most common error in consonant sounds, but with far greater occurrences in final rather than in initial position. Omission of a final consonant is by itself not a great obstacle to intelligibility but, unfortunately, it is most likely to be found in children who make a great many other errors.

The most common substitutions include glottal stops for almost anything, voiced for voiceless sounds (and the reverse of this), voiced stops for nasal sounds, and stops for fricatives. However, a number of fricatives can be heard which are perfectly acceptable in languages other than English, i.e., the voiced bilabial, voiceless velar, and palatal.

Because place of articulation is the visible aspect of speech, most substitutions, except for the glottal stop, are produced in approximately the same place as the intended sound. Predominant errors in manner and voicing involve timing, failure to reach the target accurately, and failure in control of the velum or of phonation.

Smith's (1975a) order of consonants correctly produced is similar to the order reported in previous studies. Bilabial sounds, glides, and labiodental fricatives are most commonly produced correctly; affricates and final *ng* are most commonly produced incorrectly. Affricates seldom contain both their intended components. Final *ng* is almost never produced; the preceding vowel is nasalized instead. In general, identifiable consonant errors remain in much the same proportion from one level of intelligibility to the next; however, voiced and diphthong errors, omissions, and unidentifiable substitutions decrease quite systematically from the poorest to the best speakers.

Levitt (1976) has proposed a mathematical model for specifying the segmental errors of a given child. The central assumptions in this model are that for each population of hearing-impaired children, there is a common set of error patterns; and that the primary difference between children is the overall frequency of production errors.

Intrusive Sounds

It has been frequently observed that errors in deaf children's speech are associated with deviant movements of the articulators from one position to another. For example, Calvert (1961) found that deaf speakers—to be identified as such—had to produce at least a diphthong or a CVC syllable. Identification could not be made on the basis of sustained vowel production, which did not require movement. Brannon (1966) made physiological measurements to compare tongue movements of normally hearing and deaf children. The latter group was described as showing extremely slow lingual movement, associated with a number of unnecessary movements.

Lack of lingual control during speech results in omitted or inaccurate production of one element in consonant blends or in abutting consonants, distortion of diphthongs, and in a variety of sound interjected in the speech pattern. Smith (1975b) examined these intrusive sounds and found that they may occur either during the formation of a consonant, while the tongue is moving toward its target, or during the release. Intrusive sounds may be produced in all positions in the mouth; however, in producing velar consonants, the extra sound is more likely to be produced following the intended phoneme rather than preceding it.

Mistiming of articulatory movements may cause a stop plosive to be produced after a nasal sound because the oral constriction is held while the velum is raised. In other instances, a fricative noise may be produced in the formation or release of a stop plosive because the articulatory movements are extremely slow. Slow lingual movements may also be responsible for the intrusion of a neutral vowel at syllable boundaries, between elements in abutting or blended consonants, and after final sounds in words.

Other interjected sounds appear to result from a greater than normal degree of constriction and an overshoot of the intended target which produces an added stop during the formation of glide and fricative sounds. Sounds produced in normal speech affect each other because of the continual movement of the articulators from one position to another. These constant changes in the oral cavity produce the complex encoding of the acoustic signal. In the deaf child, the effects of mistiming and undershoot or overshoot of targets produce a scrambled acoustic code.

Factors Influencing Intelligibility

What accounts for a word's intelligibility or the lack of it within sentence context? Is intelligibility determined by the particular sounds in the word? Data analyzed at the City University of New York indicate a negative answer to this question. To illustrate, there are words that differ by 20 percentage points in correct identification by listeners, yet these words contain individual phonemes that are about equal in overall correct production.

Does practice make perfect? Data again suggest it does not. Words like *school* and *book* have a very high frequency of usage in sentences produced by children. Yet these words were found to be correctly understood only about 20 percent of the time. Words like *red*, *fall*, and *good* also have a very high frequency of usage, yet these words were correctly identified less than 20 percent of the time. The particular word *fall* is made up of sounds which have high rank orders for correct production. It is probable that most deaf children could produce the word *fall* in isolation acceptably, but they cannot achieve intelligible production in sentence context. This probability may offer one possible explanation for the lack of improvement shown by many children who have had speech training for long periods. Speech training limited to single-word utterances does not prepare the deaf child for intelligible discourse. These same single words, produced acceptably on many speech evaluations, cannot be used in sentences. Without evaluations of speech in context, the evaluator cannot reliably estimate the intelligibility of conversational speech.

The correlation between segmental production and intelligibility is about $r = .80$ as determined by most investigators (Brannon, 1966; Markides, 1970b; Smith, 1975a). It has been observed, however, that children with about the same frequency of segmental errors can have speech intelligibility scores that differ by as much as 30 percentage points in correct word identification (Smith, 1975a). In the opinion of the author, these differences are related to the child's competence in use of nonphonemic or suprasegmental aspects of speech. Usually, the suprasegmental features which carry meaning are classified as intonation, stress, and pause or juncture. Suprasegmental characteristics are commonly described as voice pitch and quality, loudness, and appropriateness of rate. Although the latter characteristics do not affect meaning very directly, they do give information about the speaker, helping to indicate the speaker's attitude toward the utterance. This may be considered an important part of meaning in the broad sense.

Suprasegmental Characteristics

The deaf child's performance at the suprasegmental level of speech has been described in most of the studies previously referenced. Phrasing suffers from the child's tendency to use short, irregular breath groups, which are not related to meaning. Often these consist of a single word or single syllable. A child may break up a longer sentence as though not organizing a whole utterance at all.

Stress is often placed randomly, partly because of faulty breath control. If a child takes breath on almost every word and makes no concomitant adjustments to control subglottal pressure or vocal fold tension, upward shifts in fundamental frequency will occur continually. As a consequence, an utterance that should have a terminal fall often ends in a rising shout. Another basis for abnormality in stress and pitch has been suggested by Angelocci, Kopp, and Holbrook (1964). These authors contend deaf children attempt to achieve vowel differentiation by varying intensity and fundamental frequency.

Duration, a component of stress, is also deviant in the speech of many deaf children. Durations of sounds and syllables are not controlled, as in normal speech, by requirements of stress and maintenance of rhythm. Rather, durations seem to be controlled by the inefficiency of articulatory movements which cause distortion in duration and miscellaneous pauses.

When inappropriate pauses and prolongations in speech produced by deaf children were acoustically measured and compared to measures of speech produced by hearing children (Levitt et al., 1974), a highly consistent reduction in intelligibility was found to occur as these deviations increased. This finding provides objective evidence that aberrations in timing adversely impact upon the intelligibility of the signal produced.

Unpleasant voice quality, particularly when it is associated with an abnormally high pitch, is often a further deterrent to the intelligibility of the speech. Many uncomplimentary adjectives have been used to describe the deaf child's voice. Without adjectives, it appears appropriate to comment that the effort and strain accompanying many children's attempts at speech make listening a genuinely uncomfortable experience.

What is the source of suprasegmental errors? There are at least two possibilities. Obviously, one source of error is hearing which may be too poor, even in the low frequencies, to transmit natural speech patterns. A second source of error may relate to methodologies employed in attempting to teach speech. In the writer's opinion, the flow of speech often has been crippled by over-zealous efforts to keep the child thinking about where the tongue is supposed to be at every moment. Some of the extraneous sounds in deaf children's speech may have been trained into the speech patterns in this manner.

Although some minimum articulatory competence must co-exist with natural intonation and good voice pitch, this minimum appears to be poorly defined at present. The relative contribution of nonphonemic aspects to satisfactory message reception is a major question of clinical and research importance. Although this question cannot be answered at present, both phonemic and nonphonemic aspects of speech must be assessed to implement individualized education plans for deaf children.

Assessment Procedures

Asp (1973) recommended an evaluation procedure which is applicable for the assessment of both phonemic and nonphonemic aspects of speech, which may range from poor to excellent. In this procedure a similarity scale is used by listeners who judge the closeness of a child's response to a teacher's stimulus on a 9-point scale. Judgments of suprasegmental features are included. A second group of listeners contributes an intelligibility score. Phoneme counts are obtained for each point on the scale, and physical measures of the speech also may be carried out. These data permitted comparisons of a number of measures for various levels of intelligibility. Whereas this testing procedure has advantages, it also has one disadvantage. Since the imitation is used as stimulus to production, a variable of unknown weight is introduced in the testing situation.

A common practice with school-age populations is to perform a screening test to examine the most commonly misarticulated sounds. As pointed out by Rotunno (1980), such a test is inadequate for deaf children because they misarticulate many sounds which are easily produced by the normally hearing child. On the other hand, diagnostic tests used with normally hearing children usually examine a very complete list of sounds in all word positions (Templin & Darley, 1979; McDonald, 1968). These are not applicable to the young deaf child either, since the necessary skills are simply beyond the child's range of competence. Such tests are time-consuming, ineffective, and frustrating for the deaf child.

Many articulation tests do not have adequate normative data even for hearing children. Adequate data to establish norms for the "average" speech of a deaf child at a given age have not been accumulated. Such norms would be useful in facilitating a broad comparison with other children of the same age, with the same relative degree of hearing loss.

Rotunno (1980) has examined a large number of existing speech measures and considered their applicability to the deaf child. A few of these will illustrate those aspects to consider.

The Photo Articulation Test (Pendergast, Dicky, Selmar, & Sodir, 1969) has been designed for ages 3–12 and was, in fact, used in the CREED project (Levitt et al., 1978) with 10-year-olds. However, some of the 72 pictures included may be unidentifiable for the younger deaf child in a situation which requires absolute familiarity of vocabulary. The last three pictures are suggested for assessing intelligibility, voice, and fluency by storytelling, but with most young deaf children this stimulus would provide at best a very limited speech sample for assessment.

The Goldman-Fristoe Test of Articulation (Goldman & Fristoe, 1972) examines phoneme production both in words and in sentences, which is essential in determining if the deaf child can produce sounds in context. Considering the number of substitutions typically produced by the deaf child, it is questionable if this test can be readily scored during administration to a deaf child, because more than one phoneme is tested in each stimulus word.

The Ohio Test of Articulation and Perception of Sounds (Irwin, 1974) is adequate and includes a very good sound sample, with a subtest for self-monitoring. The nonsense word subtests, however, may be confusing to the young deaf child.

Ling's tests (1976) of phonetic and phonologic level speech skills have become very popular since their appearance. Basic articulation skills are measured at the phonetic level. At the phonologic level these skills are evaluated in the context of spontaneous speech. The effectiveness of these measures has not been formally studied to date. It may be important to note that Ling's evaluation methods require considerable expertise for proper administration.

There are few tests specifically designed for examination of suprasegmental aspects of speech produced by deaf children. One of these is the Preschool Connected Speech Inventory (DiJohnson, 1971), which contains phrases and short sentences, with picture clues. This test was designed to evaluate intonation and intelligibility in connected speech. The Markides Rating Scales (Markides, 1970a) provide normative data for comparison of a child's voice quality, intonation, loudness, pitch, rate of speech, and speech intelligibility. Administration requires a panel of experienced raters.

Another measure requiring experienced raters is the Prosodic Feature Production Test (Stark & Levitt, 1974). In this test the child is asked to produce sentences of three or five syllables as a statement, as a question with rising contour, with stress on particular words, and, finally, with a pause at an indicated position. In another subtest, the reception of the same features is examined.

In the Communication Sciences Laboratory at City University of New York, procedures to assess suprasegmental aspects of speech have been re-examined in a variety of ways. Initially, three skilled raters, working independently, made binary judgments of presence or absence of error on 19 aspects of voice quality, pitch control, phonatory control, intonation, stress, fluency, and rate. These judgments were time-consuming and quite unreliable; however, those judgments on which the raters did show substantial agreement were consistent with physical measures of the speech. Later, the panel was expanded to six well-trained judges who received initial practice and briefing on rating criteria. The number of error items was expanded to

26. This increased reliability, although it also increased time consumption. Furthermore, binary judgments of presence or absence of a given error do not provide an adequate profile, and do not allow for any quantitative measures of improvement.

In these judgments, the most common problems identified were: inappropriate pauses between words, improper control of stress and intonation, breathiness, and hypernasality. Inappropriate pauses and inappropriate stress had a frequency of occurrence of greater than 50 percent, which is important since either of these errors can change the meaning of an utterance, or make it meaningless altogether. A factor analysis showed that four factors accounted for 70 percent of the variance. These were identified as: (1) improper control of stress and intonation; (2) breaks in fluency; (3) improper stress and timing; (4) improper rate. Since the components of stress are increased fundamental frequency, duration, and intensity, it is logical that stress combines with intonation in Factor 1 and with improper timing in Factor 3. Intensity appears as a high loading on Factor 1 for inappropriate variations in loudness.

The research group at City University has recently devised a Fundamental Speech Skills Test (Levitt et al., 1979) which attempts to examine separate components of the speech act as they relate to suprasegmental features and characteristics. The intent, as in any measurement instrument, is a direct indication of manageable steps in remediation that can be understood by both evaluator and child. A checklist format has been used so that findings can be recorded during testing and rechecked from the tape recording only as needed.

Breath control and adequacy of breath support are examined first by imitation of a sustained vowel, and then by spontaneous counting, sequentially and in groups of five numbers. This yields a measure of duration of phonation, as well as graded judgments of loudness, breathiness, and nasality. During the counting task, the degree of movement of the articulators, degree of pressure build-up for stop consonants, and the presence of hypernasality, glottalization, and intrusive sounds are observed. These judgments are then repeated for CV syllables, using initial stop consonants, nasal sounds, and glides.

At this point, the evaluator has information about the child's control of fundamental mechanics: intra-oral pressure, velar closure, phonatory control, and the coordination of these with respiration. These skills are then examined in key words, selected to require maximum variation in articulator movements to reach the vowel targets. A pitch judgment is made for each key word, using the following descriptions: too low, acceptable, too high, pitch break, and falsetto. After assessing these fundamental mechanics, it is possible to examine the child's management of these mechanics in two-syllable words, and in phrases increasing in length from two to five words. In these contexts, intonation contour, correctness of juncture, and stress pattern are assessed. The word and phrase contours are judged for discontinuity, for presence or absence of terminal fall, and for appropriateness of intensity.

At present, data on this test are being analyzed for 100 children. The aim is to provide a measure that can be used without elaborate equipment. The analysis of preliminary data will proceed in three ways. First, two persons—the tester and another teacher—will make independent observations in the presence of the child. Two raters then make another set of judgments from tape recordings. Concurrently, pitch control, fundamental frequency, and nasalization will be instrumentally measured. The inter-judge reliability for the two listening conditions will be examined, as well as the relationships between subjective judgment and instrumental measures. From these data, rater reliability will be determined. Finally, the clinical utility of the test will be evaluated.

The problem of evaluating the deaf child's speech is that the deaf child does not have one speech problem. The speech problems exist in bunches or, more accurately, in stacks. A bunch has the possibility of being taken apart so that one part can be tidied up at a time. A stack has one error built on another in some unknown order. This order may differ from one child to another, but each error is fastened to another. The complexity and interrelatedness of speech errors make evaluations extremely difficult.

Despite the difficulty, speech evaluations are prerequisite to realistic planning for deaf children, yet we must also be realistic in our recommendations. No evaluations will be made with any regularity if they require extensive equipment, phonetic transcriptions of tapes, or large time commitments. Long protocols for speech evaluations should be studied only for the purpose of making them shorter.

This author does not believe that any assessment procedure intended for general use should be designed to require a panel of skilled raters. In the real world, a teacher or speech pathologist cannot find these people, especially in a school with only one or two classrooms for hearing-impaired children. Furthermore, as reported previously, inter-rater reliability of judgments for suprasegmental characteristics was poor, even between speech pathologists, when they worked independently. If groups of skilled raters were to be found everywhere, it is unlikely that they would find time to practice together.

The intelligibility score and the intelligibility rating are another matter. These can be obtained from any raters, provided that the mix of experienced and inexperienced is kept fairly constant. The intelligibility ratings correlate highly with intelligibility percentage scores (Smith, 1975a), but in this writer's opinion the intelligibility rating really relates to whether or not the child sounds as if he were speaking the right language; whether the suprasegmental aspects of speech match the listener's expectations. A frequent comment by those unfamiliar with deaf children's speech is that it sounds like Dutch, Russian, or other unfamiliar languages. When the expected patterns are not present, the listener cannot participate in the communication act. Knowledge of one's own language, which can provide closure through synthesis in many situations, is useless if the patterns are foreign or unrecognizable.

Must so many deaf children go on year after year, making minimal or no improvement in their speech? We have seen that most evaluation instruments used in the past have not been adequate even to delineate the problems for clinician, teacher, or child. Current research and the sharing of it in institutes like this one give us some hope for an improvement in that situation.

REFERENCES

Angelocci, A., Kopp, G., & Holbrook, A. The vowel formants of deaf and normal hearing eleven- to fourteen-year-old boys. *J. Speech Hear. Dis.*, 1964, *29*, 156–170.

Asp. C., et. al. A *similarity scale to evaluate the intelligibility and the segmental and suprasegmental patterns of young deaf children.* Paper presented to the Am. Speech Hear. Assoc. Convention, 1973.

Brannon, J. B. The speech production and spoken language of the deaf. *Lang. Speech,* 1966, *9*, 127–136.

Calvert, D. *Some acoustic characteristics of the speech of profoundly deaf individuals.* Doctoral dissertation, Stanford University, 1961.

DiJohnson, A. *Preschool connected speech inventory.* Harrisburg: State Department of Education, 1971.

Goldman, R., & Fristoe, M. *Goldman-Fristoe test of articulation.* Circle Pines, Minnesota: American Guidance Service, 1972.

Hudgins, C., & Numbers, F. An investigation of the intelligibility of the speech of the deaf. *Genet. Psych. Mono.*, 1942, *25*, 289–392.

Irwin, R. B. Evaluating the perception and articulation of phonemes of children, ages 5–8. *J. Comm. Dis.*, 1974, *7*, 45–63.

Jensema, C., Karchmer, M., & Trybus, R. *The rated speech intelligibility of hearing impaired children.* Washington, D.C.: Office of Demographic Studies, Gallaudet College, 1978.

Levitt, H. *Progress report,* Graduate School and University Center, City University of New York, 1976.

Levitt, H., Rotunno, R., Sullivan, J., & Head, J. *Fundamental speech skills test.* New York: Lexington School for the Deaf, 1979.

Levitt, H., Smith, C., & Strombert, H. *Acoustic, perceptual and articulatory characteristics of the speech of deaf children.* Speech Comm. Sem., Stockholm, 1974.

Levitt, H., et al. Language communication skills of deaf children 1973–1975. *Working papers in speech and hearing sciences,* Graduate School and University Center, City University of New York, 1978, *3*, 31–56.

Ling, D. *Speech and the hearing-impaired child: Theory and practice.* Washington, D.C.: A.G. Bell Association for the Deaf, 1976.

Markides, A. Ratings relating to the speech of deaf and partially hearing children. *Teacher Deaf,* 1970a, *68*, 323–330.

Markides, A. The speech of deaf and partially hearing children with special reference to factors affecting intelligibility. *Brit. J. Dis. Comm.*, 1970b, *5*, 126–140.

Mártony, J. Studies on the speech of the deaf. *Speech Trans. Lab. Quart. Prog. Status Rep.*, Royal Insti. Tech., Stockholm, 1966.

McDonald, E. T. *A deep test of articulation (DTA).* Pittsburgh: Stanwix House, 1968.

Pendergast, K., Dickey, S. E., Selmar, J. W., & Sodir, A. L. *The photo articulation test.* Interstate Printers and Publishers, 1969.

Rotunno, R. Tests of speech production and reception in deaf children. In D. Johnson (Ed.), *Communication performance evaluation with deaf students: A review.* Springfield, Virginia: National Technical Information Service, 1980.

Smith C. Residual hearing and speech production in deaf children. *J. Speech Hear. Res.*, 1975a, *18*, 795–811.

Smith, C. Interjected sounds in deaf children's speech. *J. Comm. Dis.*, 1975b, *8*, 123–128.

Stark, R., & Levitt, H. Prosodic feature reception and production in deaf children. *J. Acoust. Soc. Am.*, 1974, *55*, S63.

Templin, M. O., & Darley, F. L. *The Templin-Darley tests of articulation.* Bureau of Education Research and Service, Iowa City: University of Iowa, Bureau of Education Research and Service, 1969.

3

Speech Assessment: Intermediate and Secondary Levels

Harry Levitt

THE ASSESSMENT OF SPEECH PRODUCTION in deaf children is a many-faceted problem. Among the many factors to be considered are:

1. Whether measurements of performance or diagnostic information are required;
2. The specific speech-production skills to be measured and their interpretation relative to speech training;
3. The language and cognitive skills of the children and how they may affect the test procedures;
4. The skills required of the tester;
5. Psychometric considerations, e.g., validity, reliability, normative data; and
6. Logistical considerations, such as test duration, number of children that can be tested simultaneously, scoring methods, mode of stimulus presentation, special equipment and/or facilities required for administering the tests.

In addition to the above, it is important to bear in mind the historical development of speech testing. Every test has its limitations. In some cases the limitations are basic to the measurement problem, while in other cases the limitations are imposed in that the test may have been developed initially for purposes other than its present application.

The purpose of this paper is to discuss the issues cited above with special reference to the assessment of speech production in deaf children at the intermediate and secondary levels.

Performance vs. Diagnostic Measures

Although it is possible for a test to provide both performance and diagnostic information, such a test seldom serves both functions efficiently. For this reason, tests are usually designed to serve one or the other function directly, but without disregarding ancillary information on other aspects of speech production. Thus, for example, a speech-diagnostic test may be very effective in identifying specific speech problems for a given child. The results of this test could also be used to predict how well the child is likely to perform in everyday oral communication. It is important to recognize, however, that these predictions of performance are unlikely to be as accurate or as reliable as direct measurement of overall performance.

The measurement of overall oral-communication ability is, unfortunately, a very difficult task. First, there is no general agreement as to what should be measured. Several possibilities have been discussed:

1. The accuracy with which a specific set of information can be communicated;
2. The ability to interact effectively in communicating (this includes turn-taking, establishing a topic, maintaining the flow of meaning, correcting misinformation or errors of communication);
3. The time taken to communicate a specific set of information correctly;
4. The relative frequency with which basic units of speech (syllables, words, phrases or sentences) are correctly understood, i.e., the *percent intelligibility* of the speech.

In practice, the percent intelligibility of a deaf child's speech is frequently used as a measure of overall performance. Although this measure represents a compromise between a direct measure of overall oral communication ability and a measure that can be obtained in practice under controlled conditions, it is nevertheless not an easy measurement to obtain. The usual approach to measuring speech intelligibility is to have the child produce speech either spontaneously, or in response to questions, or by reading prepared material. Recordings of the speech are then played to one or more listeners who are not familiar with the test material. The percentage of words identified correctly by the listeners is typically used as the measure of percent intelligibility.

The measurement of percent intelligibility is widely used in research studies on the speech of the deaf (Hudgins & Numbers, 1942;

Smith, 1975), but is not often used for routine evaluations of children's speech at schools for the deaf although a test for this purpose has been developed (Magner, 1972). The objective measurement of speech intelligibility presents major logistical problems: Good quality recordings need to be made, a steady supply of listeners is required, and a relatively large sample of speech is needed in order to obtain a reasonably reliable estimate of intelligibility.

An alternative approach to the objective measurement of speech intelligibility is to obtain ratings of intelligibility using a well-defined scale. One such scale is that developed at the National Technical Institute for the Deaf (Subtelny, 1975, 1977) and which has since been used quite effectively with deaf schoolchildren at the intermediate and secondary school levels (Levitt et al., 1976). A 5-point scale was used, as shown in Table 1.B (page 6).

A major problem with the use of rating scales is that of inter-rater reliability. In the study reported by Levitt et al. (1976), comparative data were obtained in which a common set of recordings was rated by several different raters. Although in the majority of cases the raters differed by no more than one point on the rating scale, there were several cases in which the ratings differed by two points on the scale and on a few occasions by as much as three points. Because of the problems of inter-rater variability, it is advisable to use an average of several ratings over several raters. This will help reduce the effects of inter- and intra-rater variability on the assessment procedures, but it will not eliminate the problem.

It is important to recognize that there are at least three major sources of variability in rating speech intelligibility: variations in the child's performance between ratings, variations in the rater's criterion between ratings, and differences between raters. The last is quite often the largest source of variability. The magnitude of between-rater differences can be reduced by training the raters on selected recordings of children's speech that are representative of each point on the rating scale. It is possible to develop, within a school for the deaf, a team of skilled raters who are reasonably consistent with each other with respect to their rating judgments. This approach represents, at least for the immediate future, one way in which a measure of overall intelligibility can be obtained routinely on large numbers of children in a school setting. As noted earlier, however, there are problems with this procedure and it is preferable to obtain objective measurements of intelligibility, if at all possible.

Diagnostic measurements of speech production are concerned typically with identifying specific speech problems. The results of a diagnostic test may be used to predict overall intelligibility, but the reliability of these predictions is limited by the accuracy of the extrapolation procedure used in going from measurements on individual sounds of speech to more global aspects of communication. Whereas it is clear that there is a high correlation between correct production of individual segments of speech and overall intelligibility (Smith, 1975), the nature of this relationship is quite complex (Stromberg & Levitt, 1979) and one should be extremely cautious in attempting to predict overall performance from a limited subset of diagnostic data.

Historically, the development of speech diagnostic tests began with a heavy emphasis on diagnosing articulatory errors on individual speech sounds, often in the context of a simple monosyllabic word. Most of these tests were developed for the diagnosis of speech disorders in normally hearing children. Many of these tests have also been used for the the diagnosis of articulatory problems in hearing-impaired children. Although useful data can be obtained in this way, it is not the most efficient way of obtaining diagnostic information on the hearing impaired. Tests developed for general screening purposes are invariably designed to identify a wide range of possible speech disorders and are not especially sensitive to identifying problems that are characteristic of the hearing impaired or that are particularly prevalent among the hearing impaired. A number of new tests have been developed in recent years that are designed specifically for the hearing impaired (Ling, 1976; Levitt et al., 1979). These tests are discussed in the next section.

Assessment of Specific Speech Production Skills and Implications for Training

As a general rule, in order to measure a quantity it is necessary to have some idea ahead of time of the properties or characteristics of the quantity to be measured. In scientific terms, this advance information usually takes the form of a model or theory based on previous research. If relatively little is known about the quantities to be measured, then a pilot study may be undertaken in order to obtain the necessary information for designing an effective experiment. As a corollary to this general principle, the more that is known in advance about the quantities to be measured, the more efficient the measurements are likely to be.

The above principles apply equally well to the assessment of speech production. A crucial factor in the development of speech tests is the model of the speech process that is assumed. Until recently, considerable importance was attached to the correct production of the individual sounds of speech. As a result, most of the older speech tests concentrated on the identification of errors in the production of individual sounds. Similarly, speech training strategies were concerned primarily with the correct articulation of individual sounds.

A modern view of the speech process is that the correct production of suprasegmental features of speech is of great importance; not only because correct stress, intonation, and rhythm are crucial to natural sounding, intelligible speech, but also because the articulatory maneuvers underlying the correct control of suprasegmental characteristics of speech have a direct effect on the correct production of the individual sounds of speech. Studies of normal speech development show that many important suprasegmental characteristics are acquired well before the acquisition of segmental characteristics. In view of these observations, modern speech training programs for the hearing impaired greatly emphasize the teaching of suprasegmental features and, consequently, there is a need for speech tests that provide relevant information on the production of suprasegmental features.

An early attempt at developing such a test is that of Stark and Levitt (1974). This test was subsequently revised (Levitt & Resnick, 1978) and has been used to assess the ability of hearing-impaired children (10 years of age or older) to control the placement of stress and pausal juncture, and to control intonation for simple yes-no questions. A problem that has been encountered in the administration of this test is that some children overemphasize the suprasegmental feature being tested. Techniques for avoiding this difficulty have been developed (Gold, 1978), but there is no substitute for care in the administration of this (or any other) test.

As is evident from the above, there is a close correspondence between teaching procedures and types of speech tests used. The link is particularly strong in the case of the two tests developed by Ling (1976). These two tests, referred to as the Phonetic Level and Phonologic Level evaluations, respectively, are designed specifically to assess progress on the Ling speech-training system (Ling, 1976). In essence, Ling has proposed a model of the speech-training process, developed a strategy for speech training based on this model and, in doing so, also developed appropriate tests for assessing each child's progress. A feature of these tests is that they provide information on carry-over of specific speech skills, i.e., data are obtained on the ability to produce both segmental and suprasegmental aspects of speech in a standard test format as well as in spontaneous speech. A limitation of these tests is that they are very closely tied to a specific method of speech training; it is not clear how useful the tests would be if used in conjunction with other speech-training methods.

A new test currently under development and scheduled for field trials during the Fall 1979 semester is the Fundamental Speech Skills Test (Levitt, Rotunno, Sullivan, & Head, 1979). In this test an attempt has been made to assess the speaker's ability to control those articulatory manuevers that are basic to a wide range of segmental and suprasegmental features. Although the development of the test draws on modern theories of speech production, the test itself is not linked to any specific speech-training method. The test is also applicable to a wide age range, including intermediate and secondary level schoolchildren. Additional information on the test is provided in the companion paper by Smith in this text.

In summary, the quantities measured in any given speech test are a reflection of the theories or models of the speech process that were current at the time the test was developed. In the case of performance measurements, a common practice is to use intelligibility as the key indicator of relative performance. An objective measure of relative intelligibility is the percent of items correctly understood by a normally hearing listener. Subjective measures of intelligibility involve the use of a rating scale or other judgmental procedure. Subjective measurements of intelligibility are much easier to obtain, but are also less reliable than the corresponding objective measurements. With respect to diagnostic measurements, almost all of the early tests were designed primarily to assess the production of the segmental aspects of speech. Many of these early tests were not designed specifically for the hearing impaired, but were more general in scope and were intended primarily for the identification of speech disorders in hearing children. In recent years there has been a trend toward speech diagnostic tests that tap both segmental and suprasegmental aspects of speech and which are designed to identify speech problems that are typical of the hearing impaired.

Language and Cognitive Skills: Implications for Speech Testing

Speech and language are closely intertwined. The assessment of speech production necessarily involves language and, in the early years of life, the assessment of language necessarily involves speech.

Because of this mutual interdependence, it is often the case that both speech and language are tested simultaneously, particularly with young deaf children (Geffner, Levitt, Freeman, & Gaffney, 1978). As a child grows older, it is possible to obtain more detailed information on specific aspects of oral-language communication skills. Even so, tests designed to assess speech production, *per se,* are not independent of the child's language (and cognitive) skills. Given the special problems that deaf children have in acquiring language and the wide range of levels of development between deaf children of the same chronological age, it is quite easy to use a test that is inappropriate for a given child in terms of that child's language and cognitive skills.

A key component in almost every speech-assessment procedure is obtaining a sample of spontaneous speech. Speech elicited in response to questions or as part of a conversation is a very powerful technique for obtaining samples of spontaneous speech. However, the effectiveness of the technique depends upon the ability of the person administering the test (i.e., the tester) to interact effectively with the child. If too little is expected of the child, then a limited, unrepresentative speech sample will be obtained. On the other hand, if the tester overestimates the child's level of linguistic and cognitive functioning, then the resulting speech sample will again be limited and not representative of the child's abilities—this time because the child has simply not understood the tester. It is important that the tester be sensitive to the amount and complexity of speech produced by the child in the test situation. The tester must modify the nature of the interaction with the child accordingly in order to obtain the most from the child. Certain testers will be better than others in eliciting speech samples, and this factor needs to be taken into account when assessing the speech produced by a deaf child in a test of this type.

An alternative approach to obtaining a sample of "spontaneous" speech that is less critically dependent on the ability of the tester to interact effectively with the child is to have the child describe an interesting picture or sequence of pictures. The pictures should depict objects and actions that are within the child's experience. In using such a test, longer and more revealing speech samples have consistently been obtained from a picture sequence depicting children (a boy and a girl), roughly the same age as the child being tested, doing something a child of that age enjoys doing.

A factor to be considered in the use of pictures or similar stimulus material for eliciting speech is that the length and content of the speech sample will depend on the pictures that are used. It is relatively easy, however, to control for this variable in a school setting; e.g., the same set of pictures can be used for all the children tested at a given time or, in the case of longitudinal testing, one or more pictures (or picture sequences) would be the same on at least two successive administrations of the test.

A difficulty with the use of spontaneous speech as test material is that there are large differences between children in terms of the amount and complexity of the speech that is produced; further, the speech samples are unlikely to include all of the important phonetic and phonologic aspects of speech. For children at the intermediate or secondary school level it is possible to obtain balanced samples of speech that are matched across children by having each child read a prepared set of material. In so doing, it is important that the linguistic complexity of the prepared material be well within the child's level of functioning. It is also recommended that the child read the material more than once to reduce reading errors as far as possible.

For children who cannot read, it is possible to obtain balanced, matched samples of speech by having each child imitate a prescribed set of utterances. Once again, the complexity of the test material must be at a level appropriate for the child.

There are, of course, important differences between speech produced spontaneously and that produced by reading or by imitation. The nature of these differences and their effect on the measurement of speech production skills are complex and, to compound the problem, are affected significantly by the child's level of linguistic and cognitive functioning (Osberger, Johnstone, Swarts, & Levitt, 1978; Smith, manuscript submitted, 1979).

Skill of Rater

The administration of speech tests often requires special skills on the part of the tester. Although there is a trend toward the greater use of objective measurements, it nevertheless remains a basic requirement of very many tests that the tester have a trained ear. The essential problem is that somebody, either in the clinic or in the classroom, has to make the decision as to whether a given utterance has been produced correctly or incorrectly. Ideally, one would like to base important decisions such as these on objective measurements that are both accurate and repeatable. Our knowledge of the speech process is limited, however, and although research on the problem is in progress (Monsen, 1978), for the present time considerable weight must be given to subjective judgments in assessing the speech of the deaf. This requires that the tester be trained in specific listening skills; and, if data from two or more testers are to be compared, then some mutual training to establish common judgmental criteria may be needed.

Because of the important role played by subjective judgments in many speech tests, particularly those involving rating scales or those depending on subjective assessments of correct and incorrect productions, it is important that the listening skills of the tester be specified as part of the test requirements. This is not always done. It would also be most helpful if training materials (e.g., recordings of specific error types) could be provided for the purpose of establishing common judgmental criteria in using a given test.

The importance of physical measurements should not be underestimated. Although not widely used, measurements of nasal airflow, fundamental frequency, and various aspects of the speech power spectrum can be extremely useful in identifying errors in speech production. Instruments that provide these measurements have recently become available commercially and, if properly utilized, may have a substantial impact on speech assessment procedures at schools and clinics. By fortunate coincidence, those aspects of speech that are difficult to judge by ear (e.g., nasalization, particularly of vowel sounds; control of fundamental frequency) can be measured relatively well by modern instruments. On the other hand, the identification of errors of articulation or the recognition of complex sound sequences are not handled at all well by machine, whereas listeners with only a moderate degree of training are remarkably sensitive at these tasks. The successful use of instruments in the speech assessment process is thus more likely to be one of supplementing rather than replacing human judgment.

Psychometric and Other Considerations

Two of the most important considerations in the development of any test are validity and reliability. In general terms, validity refers to the accuracy with which the test score is a measure of the quantity or quantities to be measured. Reliability means that separate applications of the same test will yield essentially the same information. Specific interpretations of these concepts vary between disciplines; there are also various aspects of validity and reliability which have been defined for specific applications. See, for example, the definitions in Johnson (1978).

It is very difficult to demonstrate adequately the validity of a test. In the case of speech testing it has become an accepted practice to use measurements of intelligibility as performance measures and judgments of articulatory errors (usually on single words) as diagnostic measures. The use of percent intelligibility has already been discussed (pages 31–33). Also, as indicated earlier, the use of diagnostic tests based on single-word utterances is subject to certain caveats regarding the validity of the results. It is quite possible for a child to do well on a single-word utterance but rather poorly for speech in context. This is not to negate the value of obtaining data on what a child is capable of doing under controlled conditions, but it is important to supplement this information with an assessment of the child's speech production in context.

Tables 3.A, 3.B, and 3.C contain a listing of published tests of speech production compiled by Rotunno (1980). As can be seen from this listing, the vast majority of these tests use single-word utterances only. The validity of these tests as diagnostic tools in assessing the speech of deaf children needs to be demonstrated. Another major shortcoming of virtually all the tests listed is that very little information is available on test reliability. Normative data are available on a few tests, but for none of the tests is there a substantive body of data indicating the scores to be expected for hearing-impaired children.

Logistical Considerations

In order for a test to be of practical value in a school setting, it must be in a form that can be administered efficiently with minimum interruption of the child's regular activities and without placing an excessive burden on the school budget. It should be recognized, however, that an effective speech-testing program does require a commitment from the school. Speech tests typically need to be administered individually by a trained professional (usually the speech teacher). For a school of any size, this adds up to a signficant investment of time by at least one member of the professional staff.

With respect to special facilities and equipment, it is recommended that testing be done in a quiet room with good acoustic damping; e.g., a room with carpeting on the floor, acoustic tiles on the ceiling and, if possible, draperies or acoustic tiles on the walls. A good quality tape recorder (including a good quality microphone) should also be available. Additional logistical information on individual speech tests is provided in Tables 3.A, 3.B, and 3.C.

TABLE 3.A

Speech production evaluation instruments; segmental tests.

Author	Test Name	Method Stimulus Presentation*	Speech Unit**	Administration Time (minutes)	Normative Data†	Age Range
Berko	English Test of Morphology	V	W	15	—	4–7
Bogle & Ingram	Edinburgh Articulation Test	V	W	—	—	3–6
Cooper	Old Dominion Developmental Articulation Test	V	W	—	—	10+
DiJohnson	Preschool Speech Production Test	LV	W	15	—	5–
Farquhar	Spontaneous Picture Articulation Test	V	W	—	N	5
Fundala	Arizona Articulation Proficiency Scale	V, WR	W,S	20–30	—	3–11
Goldman & Fristoe	Goldman-Fristoe Test of Articulation	V,LV	W,S	20 per subtest	N	2+
Haspiel & Bloomer	Maximum Auditory Perception Word List	WR	W	—	—	10+
Hejna	Developmental Articulation Test	V	W	—	N	3–8
Hutchinson	Screening Test of Articulation	V	W	—	—	5–8
Irwin	Compact Picture Articulation Test	V	W	—	—	4–8
Irwin	Ohio Test of Articulation & Perception of Sounds	LV	W,S	—	—	5–8
Ling	Phonetic and Phonologic Level of Speech Evaluation Test	V,LV	W	—	—	3+

McDonald	Deep Test of Articulation	V	W	variable	N	5+
Mecham	Screening Speech Articulation Test	V	W	30	—	3.5–8.5
Pendergast	Photo-Articulation Test	V	W,S	2–20	D/N	3–12
Templin & Darley	Templin-Darley Test of Articulation	V	W,S	30–60	N	3–8
Van Riper & Erikson	Predictive Screening Test of Articulation	V	W	10	—	6
Weidner & Fensch	Weidner-Fensch Speech Screening Test	V	W	10	N	5+

TABLE 3.B

Speech production evaluation instruments; intelligibility tests.

Author	Description	Method Stimulus Presentation	Speech Unit	Administration Time (minutes)	Normative Data	Age Range
Amcoff	Speech Intelligibility Test	V	W	—	—	7–13
Larr & Stockwell	Test of Speech Intelligibility	V	W	—	—	14–19
Magner	Intelligibility Test for Deaf Children	WR	S	—	—	7+
Markides	Rating Scales	V	S	—	—	3+

Note. Key for interpretation.
*Method Stimulus Presentation: A/V—audiovisual stimulus; LV—live voice; WR—written; V—visual.
**Speech Unit: S—sentence; W—single word.
†Normative Data: D—deaf; N—normal hearing; D/N—both deaf and normal hearing.

In summary, a good speech-testing program requires a commitment from the school in terms of time and facilities. However, such a commitment is an essential investment for any school for the deaf concerned with improving the speech of its children.

TABLE 3.C

Speech production evaluation instruments; suprasegmental tests.

Author	Test Name	Method Stim. Presentation	Speech Unit	Admin. Time	Norm. Data	Age Range
Davidson	Imitative Skills Test	A/V	S	—	—	5–
DiJohnson	Preschool Connected Speech Inventory	V	S	—	D	3+
Markides	Rating Scales	WR	S	—	D	7+
Stark & Levitt	Prosodic Feature Production Test	LV	S	—	—	5+

Note. Key for interpretation.
*Method Stimulus Presentation: A/V—audiovisual stimulus; LV—live voice; WR—written; V—visual.
**Speech Unit: S—sentence; W—single word.
†Normative Data: D—deaf; N—normal hearing; D/N—both deaf and normal hearing.

REFERENCES

Amcoff, S. *Intelligibility of the speech of deaf children.* Uppsala, Sweden: Uppsala University, Institute of Education, 1968.

Berko, J. The child's learning of English morphology. *Word,* 1958, *14,* 150–177.

Bogle, D., & Ingram, T. *The Edinburgh articulation test.* London: E. & S. Livingstone, 1971.

Cooper, R. A revised developmental articulation test. *J. Speech Hear. Assoc. Virginia,* 1967, *9,* 17–20.

Davidson, A. *Imitative skills test.* Internal Report. New York: Lexington School for the Deaf, 1975.

DiJohnson, A. *Preschool connected speech inventory.* Harrisburg: State Department of Education, 1971.

DiJohnson, A. *Preschool speech production test.* Harrisburg: State Department of Education, 1971.

Farquhar, H. S. Prognostic value of imitative and auditory discrimination tests. *J. Speech Hear. Dis.,* 1961, *26,* 342–347.

Fundala, J. B. *The Arizona articulation proficiency scale.* Tucson, Arizona: Western Psychological Services, 1970.

Geffner, D. S., Levitt, H., Freeman, L. R., & Gaffney, R. Speech and language assessment scales of deaf children. *J. Comm. Dis.,* 1978, *2,* 215–226.

Gold, T. *Speech and hearing skills: A comparison between hard-of-hearing and deaf children.* Doctoral dissertation, City University of New York, Graduate Center, 1978.

Goldman, R., & Fristoe, M. *Goldman-Fristoe test of articulation.* Circle Pines, Minn.: American Guidance Service, Inc., 1972.

Haspiel, G. S., & Bloomer, R. H. Maximum auditory perception (MAP) word list. *J. Speech Hear. Dis.,* 1961, *26,* 156–163.

Hejna, R. F. *Developmental articulation test.* Madison, Wisconsin: Madison College Typing Co., 1959.

Hudgins, C. V., & Numbers, F. C. An investigation of the intelligibility of the speech of the deaf. *Genet. Psychol. Mono.,* 1942, *25,* 284–392.

Hutchinson, B. Rationale and standardization for a combined speech articulation and auditory discrimination test. *Percept. Motor Skills,* 1971, *33,*(3), 715–721.

Irwin, R. B. A compact picture articulation test. *J. Speech Hear. Dis.,* 1962, *27,* 36–39.

Irwin, R. B. Evaluating the perception and articulation of phonemes of children, ages 5–8, *J. Comm. Dis.,* 1974, *7,* 45–63.

Johnson, D. D. *Test selection and development manual.* Rochester, New York: National Technical Institute for the Deaf, 1978.

Larr, A., & Stockwell, R. A test of speech intelligibility. *Volta Rev.,* 1959, *61,* 403–407.

Levitt, H., & Resnick, S. B. Speech reception by the hearing-impaired: Methods of testing and the development of new tests. In C. Ludvigsen & J. Barfod (Eds.), *Scand. Audiol. Suppl.,* 1978, *6,* 107–130.

Levitt, H., Rotunno, R., Sullivan, J., & Head, J. *Fundamental speech skills test.* New York: Lexington School for the Deaf, 1979.

Levitt, H., Stark, R. E., McGarr, N., Carp, J., Stromberg, M., Gaffney, R. H., Barry, C., Vilez, A., Osberger, M. J., Leiter, E., & Freeman, L. Language communication skills of deaf children, 1973–1975. In *Proceedings of language assessment for the hearing impaired, A work-study institute.* Rome, New York: New York State Education Department, New York State School for the Deaf, 1976.

Ling, D. *Speech and the hearing-impaired child: Theory and practice.* Washington, D.C.: A.G. Bell Assoc. for the Deaf, 1976.

Magner, M. E. *A speech intelligibility test for deaf children.* Northampton, Mass.: Clarke School for the Deaf, 1972.

Markides, A. Ratings relating to the speech of deaf and partially deaf children. *Teacher Deaf,* 1970, *68*, 323–330.

McDonald, E. T. *A deep test of articulation.* Pittsburgh: Stanwix House, 1968.

Mecham, M., Jex, J. L., & Jones, J. D. *Screening speech articulation test.* Salt Lake City, Utah: Communication Research Assoc., 1970.

Monsen, R. B. Toward measuring how well hearing-impaired children speak. *J. Speech Hear. Res.,* 1978, *21*, 197–219.

Osberger, M. J., Johnstone, A., Swarts, E., & Levitt, H. The evaluation of a model speech training program for deaf children. *J. Comm. Dis.,* 1978, *11*, 293–313.

Pendergast, K., Dickey, S. E., Selmar, J. W., & Sodir, A. L. *The photo articulation test.* Danville, Ill.: Interstate Printers, 1969.

Rotunno, R. Tests of speech production and reception in deaf children. In D. Johnson (Ed.), *Communication performance evaluation with deaf students: A review.* Springfield, Virginia: National Technical Information Service, 1980.

Smith, C. R. Residual hearing and speech production in deaf children. *J. Speech Hear. Res.,* 1975, *18*, 795–811.

Smith, C. R. Differences between read and spontaneous speech of deaf children. Manuscript submitted for publication, 1979.

Stark, R. E., & Levitt, H. Prosodic feature reception and production in deaf children. *J. Acoust. Soc. Am., 55,* 1974.

Stromberg, H., & Levitt, H. Multiple linear regression analysis of errors in deaf speech. In J. J. Wolf & D. H. Klatt (Eds.), *Speech communication papers, 97th Meeting of Acoustical Society of America.* New York: Acoust. Soc. of Am., 1979.

Subtelny, J. D. Speech assessment of the deaf adult. *J. Acad. Rehab. Audiol.* 1975, *8*, 110–116.

Subtelny, J. D. Assessment of speech with implications for training. In F. H. Bess (Ed.), *Childhood deafness: Causation, assessment, and management.* New York: Grune & Stratton, 1977.

Templin, M. C., & Darley, F. L. *Templin-Darley tests of articulation.* Iowa City: University of Iowa Bureau of Educational Research and Service, 1969.

Van Riper, C., & Erikson, R. L. *Predictive screening test of articulation (PSTA).* Western Michigan University: Continuing Education Office, 1968.

Weidner, W., & Fensch, E. A. *Weidner-Fensch speech screening test.* Munster, Indiana: Psychometric Affiliates, 1955.

4

Evaluation of Speech In Intermediate School-aged Deaf Children

Nancy S. McGarr

THIRTY YEARS AGO, at the annual meeting of the American Instructors of the Deaf, C. V. Hudgins (1949) presented a paper on evaluating the speech of the deaf. In it, he focused on three key factors in evaluation procedure: the speaker, the test materials, and the listener. This paper is, to some extent, a variation on the theme espoused by Hudgins. It will be argued that while there has been a great deal of effort to quantify typical production errors of deaf speakers, and also to develop reliable production measurements (although, as Rotunno [1980] reports, this latter work is far from satisfactory), very little data have been collected on the effect of listener experience on evaluation.

Several investigators (Brannon, 1964; Markides, 1970; Smith, 1972), concerned primarily with assessing speech production skills, have noted that roughly one word in every five produced by a deaf speaker is intelligible to a listener not familiar with the speech of the deaf. Indeed, the differences between an experienced listener—such as a teacher of the deaf—and an inexperienced listener are so widely accepted that the intelligibility of deaf speech has been rated according to how likely the speaker may be understood "by most trained teachers of the deaf, most people familiar with deaf speech, or almost everyone" (Thomas, 1963). Since one goal of a viable speech program is to provide the deaf child with functional speech skills which are intelligible to the hearing world, it would seem reasonable to examine those factors which make deaf speech so difficult for the naive listener to understand.

We will begin by first noting some relatively new data on segmental and suprasegmental production in deaf children and, at the same time, briefly comment on some experimental tests to evaluate production.

Then, the important role of the listener in evaluating speech intelligibility will be examined. Hopefully, in this manner, we may evaluate the progress of 30 years and also focus our attention on areas requiring future effort.

Assessing Speech Production Skills of Deaf Children

Segmental Production

By far, the greatest amount of effort these past years has been devoted to identifying typical segmental errors in deaf speech. Several investigators, beginning with Hudgins and Numbers (1942) and, more recently, Markides (1970) and Smith (1972), have identified very similar patterns of segmental errors in deaf speakers. These include errors of omission, substitution, and severe distortion of the intended phonemes. Among the more common error types are: voicing confusions, incorrect production of the palatals, fricatives, and affricates, and a more neutralized production of the vowels. In general, this work suggests that as the number of segmental errors increases, overall intelligibility decreases. Also, as shown by Boothroyd (1970) and Smith (1972), intelligibility is fairly well correlated with hearing level until about 90 dB, at which point the relationship is not linear.

Recently some educators have questioned if these error patterns may relate in part to a particular training procedure or may result from sampling the speech of only a small group of deaf children. Also, it has not been shown how segmental production may change in a large group of deaf children. Some of these questions have been addressed in a longitudinal study which assessed changes in the language and communication skills of deaf children (Levitt et al., 1976). All deaf children born in 1962, and enrolled in state-supported or state-operated schools for the deaf in New York State, participated in the study. There were approximately 125 children whose speech production, speech reception, and language skills were evaluated each year for a total of four years. Only the speech production data will be discussed in this paper.

The children's segmental production was assessed using a phoneme inventory especially developed for the project but not unlike the typical articulation tests often used. Although the 125 children were en-

FIGURE 4.1
Percentile plots for production of segmental features. ▶

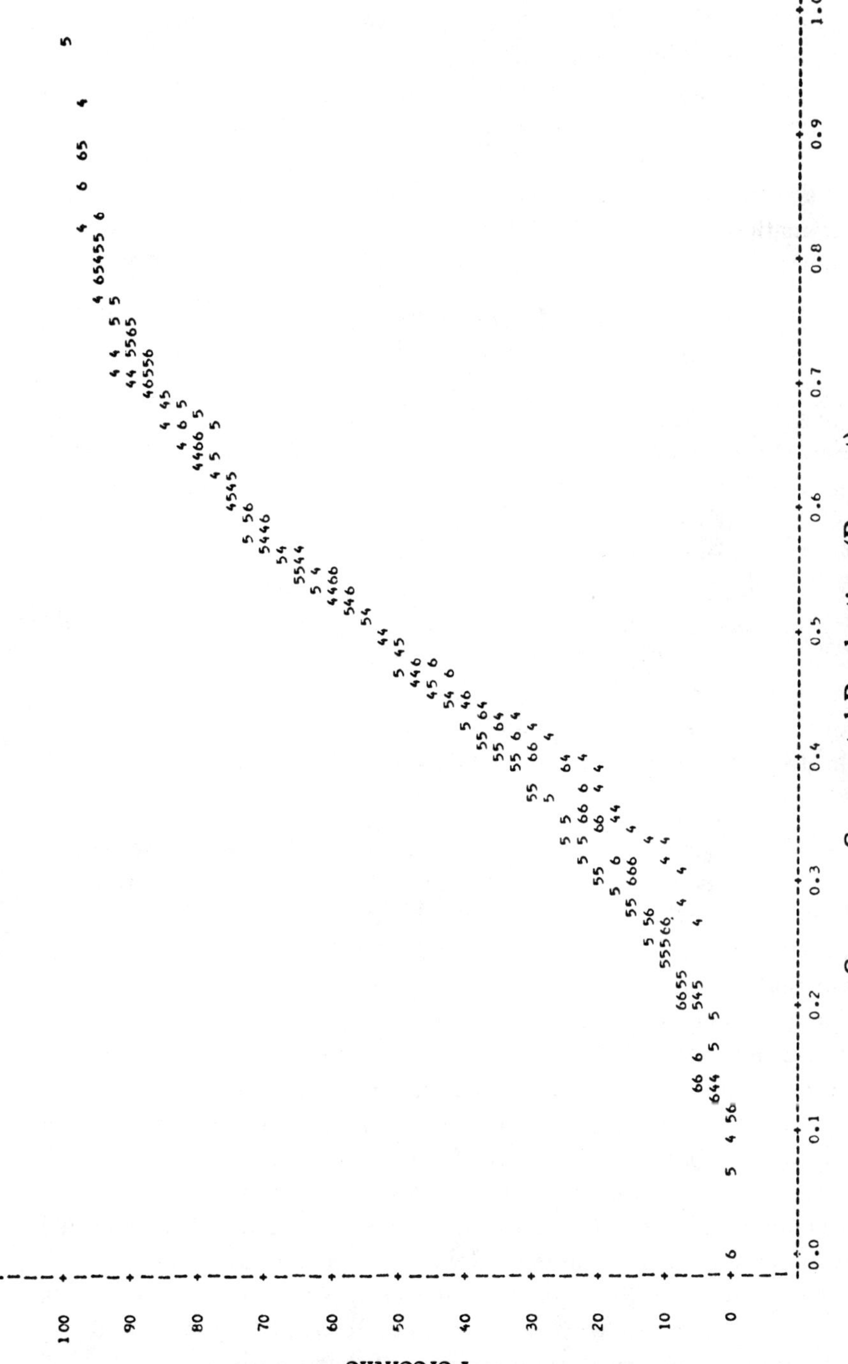
Percentile
0
10
20
30
40
50
60
70
80
90
100
0.0
0.1
0.2
0.3
0.4
0.5
0.6
0.7
0.8
0.9
1.0
Score on Segmental Production (Percent)

rolled in 13 different schools and received a wide variety of speech training, the error pattern was the same for these children as that reported in the literature. While the children showed some change in the production of a few phonemes over the years, the overall ranking of phonemic errors remained nearly the same each year. That is, the children were most successful in producing phonemes with a place of articulation at the front of the mouth, and least successful in producing phonemes in the middle or back of the mouth, respectively.

Figure 4.1 shows percentile plots illustrating overall change in segmental production for three years of data. Percentile plots were obtained each year by ranking the children in order of their test scores so that the top 1 percent of the children were ranked in the 99th percentile, the next 1 percent were ranked in the 98th percentile, and so on. Thus, two numbers represent the child's score: the actual test score (usually specified in percent correct), and the child's relative position in the ranking of all test scores (the percentile). Each year, percentile plots were obtained, and by comparing the plots, the relative amount of improvement for a skill may be seen. In Figure 4.1, the percentile plots for three years of data (1974, 1975, and 1976) are nearly superimposed. This suggests that most of the children showed very little relative improvement on phonemic production. If anything, children in the lower percentiles may actually have regressed slightly between 1974 and 1975.

Although these data do not compare different speech training programs *per se*, the results raise several important questions for training. First, one must ask if most of the children were enrolled in viable speech training programs. If so, was one type of training more effective than another? For example, does a particular speech teaching strategy such as proposed by Ling (1976) result in a pattern of phonemic errors which are significantly different from those found for most deaf children? The data from the children in the study by Levitt et al. (1976) do not speak to these points. However, it is certainly true that more data are needed which examine not only the effect of different training procedures but also the appropriateness of a given procedure for deaf children with different learning abilities. One such study conducted by Osberger, Johnstone, Swarts, and Levitt (1978) found differences in acquisition of speech skills in a group of deaf children trained in a program modeled after Ling's work, and also in the children's progress and carry-over of these skills.

Suprasegmental Production

A great deal of work has been conducted during the past 30 years to describe errors in suprasegmental production. However, the contribution of specific suprasegmental errors in reducing intelligibility is still unclear. Levitt, Smith, and Stromberg (1974) noted that deaf children with approximately the same frequency of segmental errors could have speech intelligibility scores that differed by as much as 30 percent. Of the 18 error types considered, errors such as intermittent phonation, spasmodic variation in pitch, and excessive variability in loudness correlated highest with differences in intelligibility. McGarr and Osberger (1978) also showed that most deaf children who could not sustain phonation had speech which was judged unintelligible. However, judgments of pitch deviancy were not as highly correlated with intelligibility as were measurements of phonemic production and prosodic feature production.

In addition to problems in pitch control, the timing of deaf speech is frequently described as prolonged because of inappropriate rate, inappropriate pauses between syllables and word boundaries, and also increased duration of phonemes—usually vowels. The recent work of Osberger (1976) and Reilly (1979) has indeed shown that while gross timing cues may be in error, the deaf do preserve some of the more subtle timing relations in their speech. These are not likely to have been taught during speech training programs.

While work continues to identify which typical suprasegmental errors interfere most with the intelligibility of deaf speech (Levitt, 1979; Stromberg & Levitt, 1979), one immediate need is a test to assess production of suprasegmental skills. Of course, assessing suprasegmental production is somewhat more complex than assessing segmental production, and we are still learning a great deal about suprasegmental production in both deaf and hearing speakers. Nonetheless, it would be appropriate to mention two tests which have been attempted to fulfill this need. One test, developed for the longitudinal study previously described, examined deaf children's production of three prosodic features. These were contrasting stress, intonation, and pause or juncture features derived from Bronstein's (1960) description of American English.

The prosodic feature production test may be considered experimental. Table 4.A shows the six sentences—either two or five syllables in length, and the methodological representation for each feature in the test. The feature of stress was indicated by capitalization and

TABLE 4.A
Sentences for the test of prosodic feature production.

Come here.
Oh boy.
Thank you.
He has one big dog.
I want to see it.
My new hat is blue.

Sample of test sentences.

Come . . . here.
COME here.
Come *HERE*.
Come here?

underlining, the feature of pause by three dots, the feature of intonation by a question mark. Each child tried several practice items in order to become familiar with the written cues. When it was felt that the child understood the concept, he/she was asked to read the randomized sentences while the utterances were recorded. Later, several experienced listeners, who were familiar with the stimuli, transcribed the recordings, indicating whether the feature was correct or—if not—what error type occurred. Examples of the error types included: pause in the wrong location, stress in the wrong location, inappropriate intonation (e.g., a statement instead of a question), staccato (equal stress and equal pause on all syllables), or an unintelligible utterance.

The children were most successful at producing the intended feature of pause. Scores well over 70 percent were obtained. The children did less well on production of stress. They seemed to be slightly better in producing a stressed form that occurred near the end of a sentence than one near the beginning. By far the most difficult form was the question. Only a small proportion of the children were able to control the intonation contour sufficiently well enough for it to be recognized as a question. The most common error type was production of the sentence with equal stress followed by equal pause for each syllable—that is, a staccato production.

FIGURE 4.2
Percentile plots for production of prosodic features. ▶

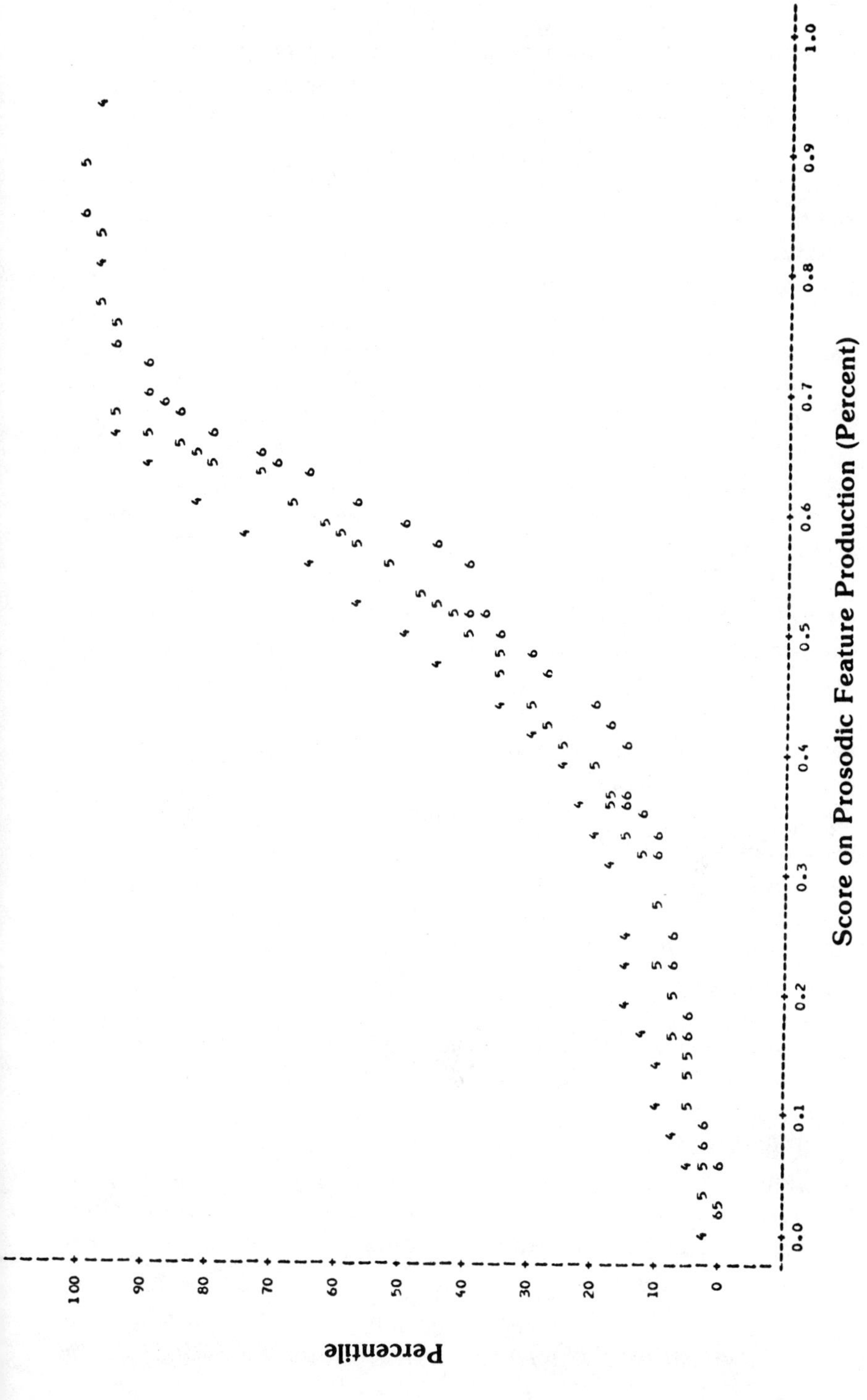

Percentile

0 10 20 30 40 50 60 70 80 90 100

0.0 0.1 0.2 0.3 0.4 0.5 0.6 0.7 0.8 0.9 1.0

Score on Prosodic Feature Production (Percent)

Figure 4.2 is the percentile plot for the test on prosodic feature production, again for three years of data. The curve for 1975 lies to the right of the 1974 curve by roughly a fixed amount. This indicates that, on average, all children's scores improved by approximately the same amount. Comparing progress for the next year (1975–1976), we note that the curve for 1976 lies to the right of the 1975 curve for approximately two-thirds of the children, thus indicating continued improvement. However, for the remaining one-third of the children, the data for 1975 and 1976 are nearly superimposed, indicating no improvement. It should be noted that this test assessed only the simplest prosodic contrasts, and intelligible speech is undoubtedly dependent on the control of many finer aspects of suprasegmental production.

Another test, designed by Gold (1978), attempted to assess production of stress, pause, and change in intonation in a more natural setting. The child was asked to produce the target features in response to a question prompt. For example: What color is the apple? The apple is *green.* Deaf and hard-of-hearing children enrolled in regular public schools in New York City were tested. The pattern of errors for the mainstreamed deaf and hard-of-hearing children were similar and not unlike the errors made by the children in schools for the deaf. However, Gold noted that the hard-of-hearing children were rated more natural in production and were less likely to exaggerate the intended prosodic feature than the other two groups of hearing-impaired children. While both these studies attempt to evaluate prosodic feature production in hearing-impaired children, these tests may be considered only experimental. There is still a tremendous need to learn more about suprasegmental production in deaf speakers and to develop appropriate instruments to assess these important skills.

Ratings of Overall Intelligibility

Since measurements of segmental and suprasegmental production are often quite tedious and time-consuming, many educators of the deaf use a rating procedure to obtain a quick assessment of overall intelligibility. While rating speech production is not without problems, such as the need for several raters to account for variability in listeners' scores, rating scales still represent a way to judge intelligibility without an inordinate investment in the listener's time or a need

FIGURE 4.3
Percentile plots for rating of overall intelligibility. ▶

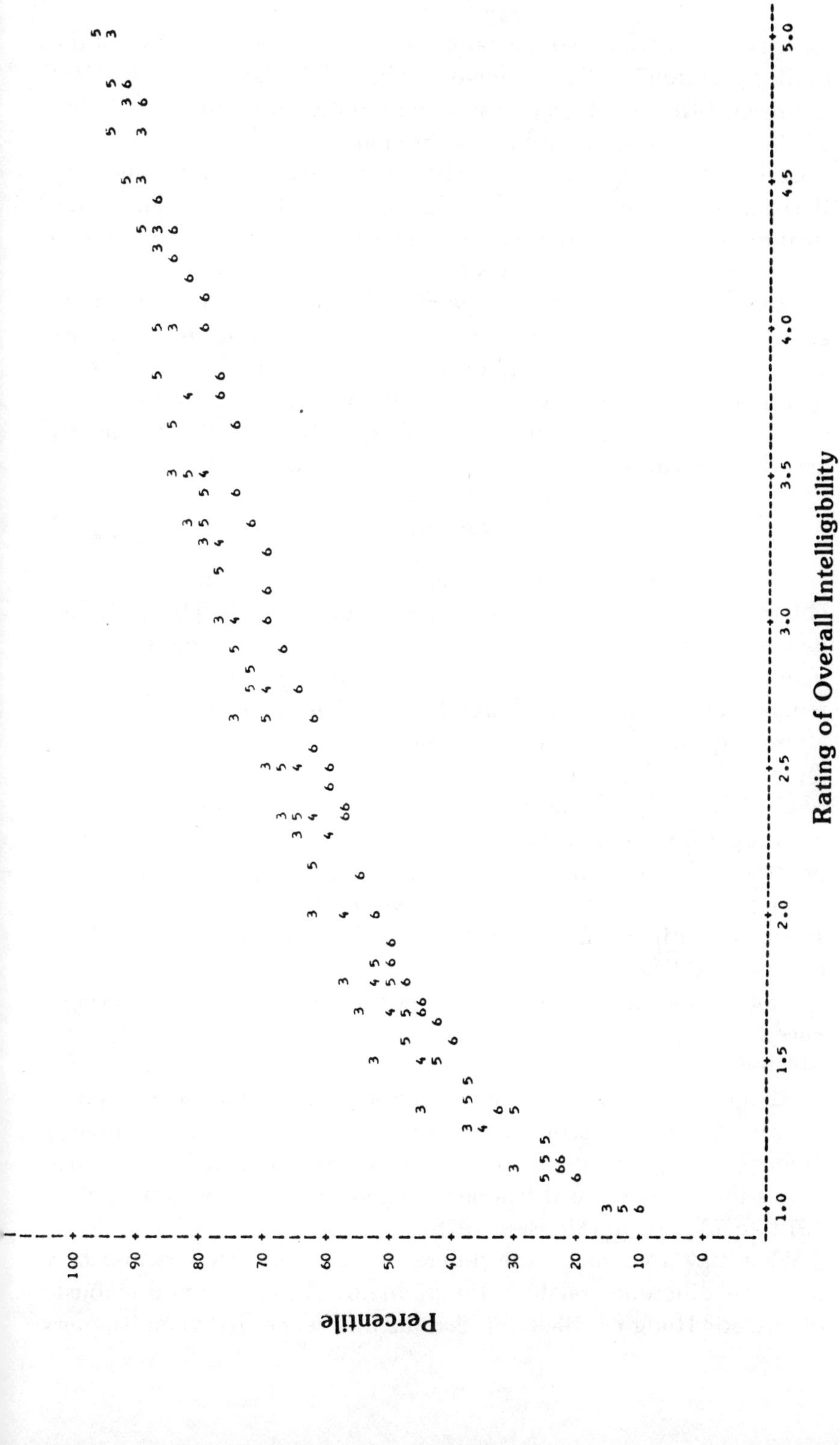

Rating of Overall Intelligibility

for specialized equipment. A rating scale has formed the basis of the profiling system at the National Technical Institute for the Deaf (Johnson, 1975) and the rating scale for intelligibility, shown in Table 1.B (page 6), was also used by Levitt et al. (1976).

Each child was required to describe two or more picture sequences. Recordings were made of each child's speech, which were later rated by three listeners familiar with the speech of the deaf, resulting in a total of six to nine observations for each child.

Figure 4.3 shows the percentile plots for the four years of the project. It is most discouraging to note that the data for all four years are essentially superimposed, indicating no improvement in overall intelligibility. Indeed, there were a large number of average ratings of 3.0 or poorer, indicating that the children's speech was difficult or nearly impossible to understand by listeners very familiar with the deaf.

Listeners

In all of the studies discussed above, the primary purpose was to obtain measurements of some aspect of deaf speech. These studies may have used either experienced or inexperienced listeners to evaluate the deaf speakers, but the reason for choosing one group of listeners over another was not carefully considered. Looking at this literature, summarized in Table 4.B, one is struck by the consistent difference in intelligibility scores reported for experienced and inexperienced listeners (Mangan, 1961; Thomas, 1963; Nickerson, 1973; Monsen, 1978). In general, the intelligibility scores decreased from experienced to semi-naive to naive listeners. While there may have been some overlap in scores for individual listeners, as a group the scores of the inexperienced listeners did not approach those of the experienced listeners.

Another noticeable point is that scores obtained by either experienced or inexperienced listeners are higher for sentences than for isolated words (Hudgins, 1949; Thomas, 1963; Subtelny, 1977). Indeed, there is a wider range of intelligibility scores for sentences than for words. Sentence scores for experienced listeners ranged from 31 percent (Markides, 1970) to 83 percent (Monsen, 1978); sentence scores for inexperienced listeners ranged from 18.7 percent (Smith, 1972) to 73 percent (Monsen, 1978).

What may account for the difference between listeners and how does this difference relate to the problems in production previously discussed? Hudgins (1949) felt that the differences between listeners

TABLE 4.B
Intelligibility scores obtained by experienced and inexperienced listeners in studies on the speech of the deaf.

Study	Percent Intelligibility for Experienced	Percent Intelligibility for Inexperienced
Isolated Words		
Hudgins, 1949	42%	—
Mangan, 1961	65%*	50%*
Thomas, 1963	37%	28%
	59%*	38%*
Brannon, 1964	—	17%
Subtelny, 1977	35%	—
McGarr, 1978	29%	23%
Sentences		
Hudgins, 1949	71%	—
Thomas, 1963	59%	50%
	92%*	68%*
Brannon, 1964	—	26%
John & Howarth, 1965	—	19%
Markides, 1970	31%	19%
Smith, 1972	—	18.7%
Nickerson, 1973	47% speech	28% speech
	59% reading	34% reading
Subtelny, 1977	66%	—
Monsen, 1978	83%	73%
McGarr, 1978	49% high context	38% high context
	33% low context	21% low context

*Auditory and Visual Cues

could be attributed to the experienced listener's knowledge of the typical production errors in deaf speech—many of which we described earlier in this paper. Since the inexperienced listener would not know the common errors, he/she would be unable to recode deaf speech to compensate for their effect on intelligibility. Hudgins and Numbers (1942) also felt that the experienced listener simply made better use of contextual information. On the other hand, both Brannon (1964) and Thomas (1963) concluded that naive listeners used context to increase intelligibility of sentences.

However, in many studies, the criteria of experience were not always clearly defined. In some instances, the experienced listeners were highly familiar with the children, the training procedures, or even the test material. In other studies, the listeners were not familiar with any of these factors. Many inexperienced listeners feel that it is personal knowledge of the deaf speaker that gives the experienced listener his advantage. But the extent to which any of these factors—knowledge of errors, context, familiarity with the speaker, etc.—account for the difference between listeners has not been systematically investigated.

Differences Between Experienced and Inexperienced Listeners

To resolve these questions, McGarr (1978) conducted a study in which groups of both experienced and inexperienced listeners were compared in their evaluation of deaf children's speech. Sixty experienced listeners had a minimum of one year's experience in listening to the speech of the deaf and did not know the child whose speech they heard or the school at which the child received training. Sixty listeners had no previous experience in hearing deaf speech.

Twenty congenitally deaf children, ranging from 8 to 15 years of age, were evaluated. The mean pure-tone average for the children was 98.6 dB (ISO) in the better ear. Each child recorded a list of 36 monosyllabic words and a list of 36 sentences. The 36 monosyllabic test words, selected from Smith (1972), were chosen to provide an estimate of *a priori* intelligibility of that word when produced by a deaf child. These words were all within the vocabulary of deaf children (Silverman-Dresner & Guilfoyle, 1972) and are likely to be found in many typical word or sentence intelligibility tests. Half were the 18 monosyllabic words which were ranked highest for intelligibility in the Smith study. These may be regarded as containing phonemes that deaf children were likely to produce correctly. Half of the words were the 18 monosyllabic words ranked lowest for intelligibility, and these contained phonemes that deaf children frequently misarticulate. Hereafter, these words are referred to as test words with high *a priori* intelligibility and low *a priori* intelligibility respectively. Thus, these test words were especially chosen to examine whether experienced and inexperienced listeners might differ in recoding typical segmental errors of deaf children.

In order to examine if listeners might use context differently, each of these 36 words was embedded in a sentence which varied with respect to the amount of overall contextual information. High or low context was defined empirically, using a standard word prediction technique. Table 4.C shows the 18 sentences that contain a high amount of contextual information. In nine of these sentences, the

TABLE 4.C

Sentences with high context containing test words with high or low a priori *intelligibility.*

High Context, High Intelligibility (Set A)	High Context, Low Intelligibility (Set B)
3 Syllables	*3 Syllables*
Read the book.*	*Keep* quiet.*
Come *with* me.	The *dog* barks.
That's no *good.**	Comb your *hair.*
5 Syllables	*5 Syllables*
My *name* is Nancy.	The *cat* chased the mouse.
Get your *coat* and hat.	Get your *ball* and bat.
Is there no *more* milk?	Did you brush your *teeth?*
7 Syllables	*7 Syllables*
That *man* is not my father.	I *wish* I had a pony.
The flag is *red,* white and blue.	We have *food* for the picnic.
May I have a *piece* of cake?	Can you dive in *deep* water?

*These sentences were defined as lower in context than others in the table.

TABLE 4.D

Sentences with low context containing test words with high or low a priori *intelligibility.*

Low Context, High Intelligibility (Set C)	Low Context, Low Intelligibility (Set D)
3 Syllables	*3 Syllables*
Have a lot.	*Feed* the dog.
I *need* it.	You *did* it.
Get the *cake.*	This is *his.*
5 Syllables	*5 Syllables*
They *will* come again.*	Is *that* the tall one?
Who wants *this* ice cream?	Mother *has* the car.
It's easy to *hear* her.†	He said he *could* go.
7 Syllables	*7 Syllables*
The *book* is on the table.	What *was* the name of that boy?
Is the *fat* baby crying?	If it's *cool* I cannot go.
It is nice on a *fall* day.	We will go to the *beach* today.†

*This sentence was defined as higher in context than others in the table.
†These sentences contain an additional syllable.

monosyllabic word in italics received a high intelligibility ranking; in the other nine sentences, the italic monosyllabic word received a low intelligibility ranking. Table 4.D shows the 18 sentences that contain a low amount of contextual information also balanced for *a priori* intelligibility of the monosyllabic word.

For hearing speakers, a word produced in isolation is known to differ from one produced in a sentence, both in perception and production. Thus, an additional set of stimuli were produced maintaining the same balance of context and *a priori* intelligibility. These test words were originally produced in sentences, but heard by the listeners in isolation. The segmented test words were obtained by processing the audio tape recordings of the sentences using a spectral and waveform editing system at Haskins Laboratories.

Thus, each experienced or inexperienced listener heard three types of stimuli produced by a single deaf child:

1. Test words produced in sentences and presented to the listener in sentences;
2. Test words produced in isolation and presented to the listener in isolation;
3. Test words produced in sentences, segmented from the sentences, and presented to the listeners in isolation (segmented test words).

Table 4.E summarizes the mean scores obtained by experienced and inexperienced listeners. Scores for experienced listeners were consistently higher than those for inexperienced listeners. For both groups, scores for test words in sentences were higher than those for isolated words, which were higher in turn than scores for segmented words. In fact, scores for test words in sentences were more than double the scores for the same words segmented from the sentence.

The greatest difference between listeners occurred on sentences. Scores for test words in sentences were 41 percent for the experienced and 30 percent for the inexperienced listeners, a difference of 11 percent. In contrast, the difference between listeners for isolated words was 6 percent and only 3 percent for segmented test words.

Figure 4.4 shows the scores obtained by experienced and inexperienced listeners for test words as a function of the *a priori* intelligibility of the test word. The percent intelligibility is plotted on the ordinate; the three types of stimuli are plotted on the abscissa. While the experienced listeners obtained higher scores than the inexperienced listeners for each type of stimuli, there was no evidence of an interac-

TABLE 4.E
Mean scores obtained by experienced and inexperienced listeners.

Type of Stimulus	Listeners	Mean Score % Correct
Test words produced and heard in sentences	Experienced	.41
	Inexperienced	.30
Test words produced and heard in isolation	Experienced	.29
	Inexperienced	.23
Test words produced in sentences and heard in isolation (i.e., segmented)	Experienced	.16
	Inexperienced	.13
All words produced and heard in sentences	Experienced	.49
	Inexperienced	.35

tion between listener experience and *a priori* intelligibility since the plots were essentially parallel.

For both groups of listeners, scores for test words with high *a priori* intelligibility were greater than for words with low *a priori* intelligibility. There was less of an effect on the scores for segmented words.

FIGURE 4.4
Mean scores obtained by experienced and inexperienced listeners as a function of a priori *intelligibility.*

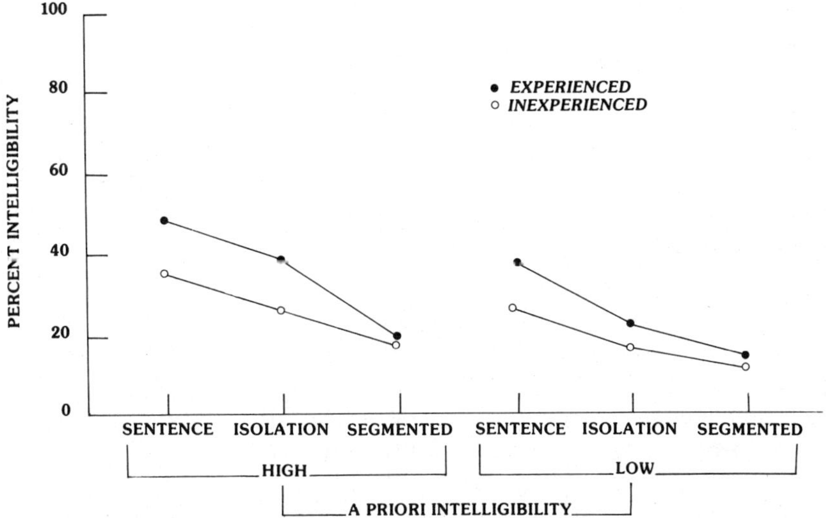

But for test words in sentences and in isolation, the effect of *a priori* intelligibility was most pronounced. In these conditions, scores obtained by experienced and inexperienced listeners were noticeably higher for test words with high *a priori* intelligibility than for those with low.

Figure 4.5 shows the scores obtained by experienced and inexperienced listeners for test words as a function of the amount of context. Intelligibility scores for test words in sentences are plotted at the left; the segmented test words originally produced in sentences are plotted at the right.

As before, the experienced listeners' scores were higher than those obtained by inexperienced listeners. However, there was no evidence of an interaction between listener experience and context since improvement due to experience was essentially the same for both high and low context words. This difference was about a 10 percent gain in intelligibility for sentences, and a 5 percent gain for segmented words.

The magnitude of the context effect is also evident from Figure 4.5. For test words in sentences, the effect of high context represents a gain of roughly 16 percent for either experienced or inexperienced listeners. The gain for segmented words is roughly 8 percent for either group of listeners.

Figure 4.6 shows that for both groups of listeners, the children were most intelligible when test words with high *a priori* intelligibility were produced in sentences with high context, and least intelligible for test words with low *a priori* intelligibility in sentences with low context.

Discussion

The results of this study on listener experience, taken together with the recent work on speech production of hearing-impaired speakers, have several implications for the evaluation of deaf children's speech. Turning attention once again to the speaker, the overwhelming fact is that a large number of deaf children showed little or no improvement in overall intelligibility, and also that the pattern of errors for these children was fairly typical of those reported in the literature. However, these results should certainly not be interpreted to diminish the importance of speech training. We have heard the reports at this conference from many fine speech training programs whose students are achieving intelligible deaf speech. But the salient characteristics of segmental and suprasegmental production in even the better deaf

FIGURE 4.5
Mean scores obtained by experienced and inexperienced listeners as a function of sentence context.

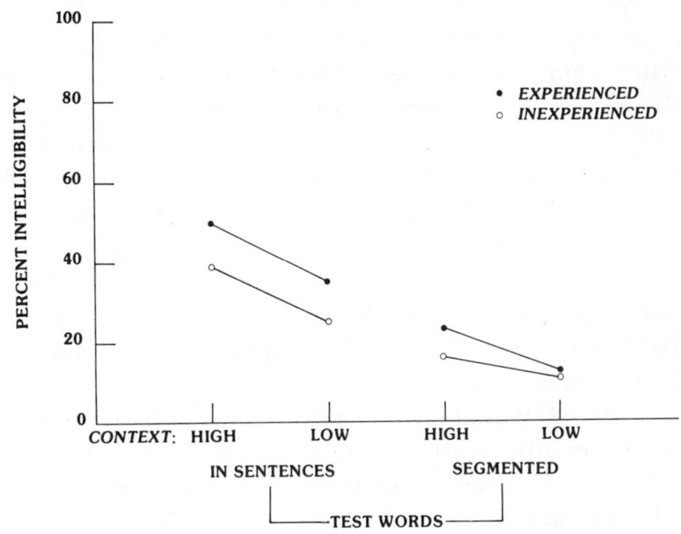

FIGURE 4.6
Mean scores obtained by experienced and inexperienced listeners as a function of a priori *intelligibility and sentence context.*

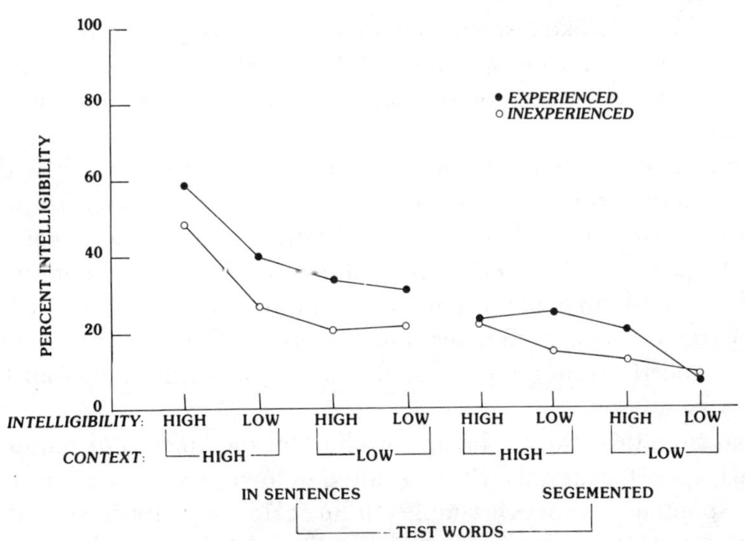

speakers suggest to many of us that our future efforts need to be focused on determining the underlying coordinative nature of speech production in the deaf. Harris and McGarr (1979) have outlined one such approach to this problem. It would also be of great value in developing speech training programs to know which errors, or more likely, which combination of errors, are most devastating to intelligibility. Of course, all this presumes that each deaf child will have the opportunity to participate in a viable speech training program.

The second factor affecting evaluation procedures is the choice of test materials. Many studies reviewed during these past 30 years have used large groups of speakers, large groups of listeners, an inordinate amount of the investigator's time, and often special equipment which is not entirely practical in many schools for the deaf. There is a need for a reliable and practical test to assess segmental and suprasegmental production in deaf speakers.

Educators faced with the need for evaluation in their schools today may find intelligibility scores quite different depending on the choice of some commonly used test materials. For example, the literature reports that the average score for experienced listeners on isolated words is about 38 percent, and for inexperienced listeners, about 22 percent. It is interesting to note that when scores for test words are examined as a function of *a priori* intelligibility, those with high *a priori* intelligibility fell essentially mid-range of the published data for either experienced or inexperienced listeners. This suggests that the phonetically balanced monosyllables commonly used in evaluation may be more like test words with high *a priori* intelligibility than like test words with low *a priori* intelligibility, and choice of these words to evaluate speech production will result in higher intelligibility scores.

Sentence scores reported in the literature covered a much wider range of intelligibility than scores for isolated words. McGarr showed that scores for test words in sentences with a high degree of context were 49 percent for experienced and 38 percent for inexperienced listeners—mid-range of those reported in the literature. Scores with a low degree of context (33 percent for experienced, and 21 percent for inexperienced listeners) fell near the lower end of the range for the respective groups.

Apart from this study, which controlled for the amount of sentence context, speech materials which resulted in lower scores were usually either spontaneous speech samples (John & Howarth, 1965; Markides, 1970) or sentences which varied in length and grammatical complexity (Smith, 1972). Speech materials which generally resulted in high intelligibility scores were those which contained words of common usage or were highly redundant (Thomas, 1963; Monsen, 1978). This wide variation in scores reported for deaf children with similar hearing losses, implies the necessity for a uniform set of speech materials, thus permitting more meaningful evaluation of intelligibility, and comparison between deaf speakers.

Finally, it is quite clear that intelligibility scores will vary considerably depending on whether an experienced or inexperienced listener is chosen to evaluate the speech. In all the studies reviewed, the scores for the experienced listeners were consistently higher than those of the inexperienced listeners. In spite of this difference, there were several common patterns observed in McGarr's data for both groups of listeners. The scores for test words in sentences were always higher than scores for isolated test words, which were higher in turn than those for segmented test words. Similarly, for both groups of listeners, test words with high *a priori* intelligibility were scored higher than those with low *a priori* intelligibility, and also test words in sentences with high context were more intelligible than test words in low context sentences.

These data do not support some possible explanations for the difference between experienced and inexperienced listeners. Recall the notion that suggests that experienced listeners obtain higher scores than inexperienced listeners because they are familiar with typical errors and recode these differently from inexperienced listeners. The data obtained in this study showed no evidence of an interaction between listener experience and *a priori* intelligibility. Also, the measured difference between test words with high *a priori* intelligibility was about the same as that for test words with low *a priori* intelligibility for both groups of listeners. This lack of an interaction between listener experience and *a priori* intelligibility does not mean that experienced listeners recode deaf speech in the same way as inexperienced listeners but suggests, should such an interaction exist, it is likely to be more subtle and less easily detected than previously supposed. We are presently analyzing the segmental error patterns of both experienced and inexperienced listeners to investigate this notion more thoroughly.

It was also suggested that experienced listeners simply make better use of contextual information, thereby increasing overall intelligibility. Recall that for both experienced and inexperienced listeners, scores were higher for sentences with high context than for those with low context, and that once again, the data showed no evidence of an interaction between listener experience and the degree of sentence context. Again, this does not rule out the possibility of such an effect, but suggests that should such an interaction exist, it is likely to be of a smaller magnitude than the literature suggests.

A final notion is that knowledge of a child or of a particular teaching strategy which results in a distinctive speech pattern particular to the child's school, enables the experienced listener to obtain higher intelligibility scores. This idea was also not supported. First, none of the listeners knew the child whose speech they heard. Second, in most cases, the experienced listeners did not know the school at which the child received his training. Teachers who served as listeners from the same school as the child scored no better or worse than experienced listeners from other schools. It would seem that once familiar with deaf speech, the experienced listeners were able to generate higher scores for deaf speakers in general.

To conclude, while evaluation of deaf children's speech is fairly routine in many schools for the deaf, there still is a need for research to quantify factors which affect evaluations of intelligibility. While we have not been idle in our research efforts in these 30 years since Hudgins first discussed assessment procedures, it is fairly obvious that we still have a good amount of work to keep us busy for at least 30 years more.

Acknowledgments

This research has been generously supported through grants from the Committee on Research Endeavors in Education of the Deaf (CREED), New York State Education Department, Bureau for Special School Supervision, Office for Education of Children with Handicap Conditions, and the National Institutes of Health (NH 09252), principal investigator, Harry Levitt. The research on the role of listener experience was conducted by the author in partial fulfillment of the requirements for the Ph.D. at the City University of New York. The author wishes to gratefully acknowledge the invaluable assistance of Harry Levitt and Kathrine S. Harris, who served as advisers to this latter work. Preparation of this manuscript was supported by grants NS 13870 and 13617 to Haskins Laboratories.

REFERENCES

Boothroyd, A. Distribution of hearing levels in the student population of the Clarke School for the Deaf. *SARP Report 3*, Northampton, Mass.: Clarke School for the Deaf, 1970.

Brannon, J. B. *Visual feedback of glossal motions and its influence on the speech of deaf children.* Doctoral dissertation, Northwestern University, 1964.

Bronstein, A. *The pronunciation of American English.* New York: Appleton-Century-Crofts, 1960.

Gold, T. *Speech and hearing skills: A comparison between hard-of-hearing and deaf children.* Doctoral dissertation, City University of New York, 1978.

Harris, K., & McGarr, N. *Relationships between speech perception and speech production in normal hearing and hearing impaired subjects: Implications for training speech of the hearing impaired.* Paper presented at the Institute on Speech Assessment and Speech Improvement, National Technical Institute for the Deaf, Rochester, N.Y., 1979.

Hudgins, C. V. A method of appraising the speech of the deaf. *Volta Rev.*, 1949, *51*, 597–638.

Hudgins, C. V., & Numbers, F. C. An investigation of the intelligibility of the speech of the deaf. *Genet. Psych. Mono.*, 1942, *25*, 289–392.

John, J. E. J., & Howarth, J. N. The effect of time distortions on the intelligibility of deaf children's speech. *Lang. Speech*, 1965, *8*, 127–134.

Johnson, D. Communication characteristics of NTID students. *J. Acad. Rehab. Audiol.*, 1975, *8*, 17–32.

Levitt, H., Smith, C. R., & Stromberg, H. Acoustic, articulatory, and perceptual characteristics of the speech of deaf children. In G. Fant (Ed.), *Proceedings of the speech communication seminar.* New York: John Wiley and Sons, 1974.

Levitt, H., Stark, R., McGarr, N. S., Carp, J., Stromberg, H., Gaffney, R. S., Barry, C., Velez, A., Osberger, M. J., Leiter, E., & Freeman, L. Language communication skills of deaf children, 1973–1976. In *Proceedings of language assessment for the hearing impaired: A work study institute.* Rome, N.Y.: New York State Education Department, New York State School for the Deaf, 1976.

Levitt, H. *Speech assessment: Secondary level.* Paper presented at the Institute on Speech Assessment and Speech Improvement, National Technical Institute for the Deaf, Rochester, N.Y., 1979.

Ling, D. *Speech and the hearing-impaired child: Theory and practice.* Washington, D.C.: A.G. Bell Association for the Deaf, 1976.

Mangan, K. Speech improvement through articulation testing. *Amer. Annals Deaf*, 1961, *106*, 391–396.

Markides, A. The speech of deaf and partially hearing children with special reference to factors affecting intelligibility. *Brit. J. Dis. Comm.*, 1970, *5*, 126–140.

McGarr, N. S. *The differences between experienced and inexperienced listeners in understanding the speech of the deaf.* Doctoral dissertation, City University of New York, 1978.

McGarr, N. S., & Osberger, M. J. Pitch deviancy and the intelligibility of deaf children's speech. *J. Comm. Dis.*, 1978, *11*, 237–247.

Monsen, R. B. Toward measuring how well hearing impaired children speak. *J. Speech Hear. Res.*, 1978, *21*, 197–219.

Nickerson, R. S. Computerized speech-training aids for the deaf. *Report No. 2366:* Bolt, Beraneck and Newman, Inc., 1973.

Osberger, M. J. *The effect of timing errors on the intelligibility of deaf children's speech.* Doctoral dissertation, City University of New York, 1978.

Osberger, M. J., Johnstone, A., Swarts, E., & Levitt, H. The evaluation of a model speech training program for deaf children. *J. Comm. Dis.*, 1978, *11*, 293–313.

Reilly, A. P. *Syllabic nucleus duration in the speech of hearing and deaf children.* Doctoral dissertation, City University of New York, 1979.

Rotunno, R. Speech production and speech perception: A review of the literature. In D. Johnson (Ed.), *Communication performance evaluation with deaf students: A review.* Springfield, Virginia: National Technical Information Service, 1980.

Silverman-Dresner, T., & Guilfoyle, G. *Vocabulary norms for deaf children.* Washington, D.C.: A.G. Bell Association for the Deaf, 1972.

Smith, C. R. *Residual hearing and speech production of deaf children.* Doctoral dissertation, City University of New York, 1972.

Stromberg, H., & Levitt, H. Multiple linear regression analysis of errors in deaf speech. In J. J. Wolf & D. H. Klatt (Eds.), *Speech communication papers, 97th meeting of Acoustical Society of America.* New York: Acoust. Soc. Am., 1979.

Subtelny, J. D. Assessment of speech with implication for training. In F. Bess (Ed.), *Childhood deafness: Causation, assessment and management.* New York: Grune and Stratton, 1977.

Thomas, W. Intelligibility of the speech of deaf children. *Proceedings of International Congress on the Education of the Deaf. Document No. 106*, 1963.

5
National Data on Rated Speech Intelligibility of Hearing-Impaired Children

Raymond J. Trybus

THERE CAN BE NO DOUBT that there is a continuing great need for the development and use of improved assessment devices which can measure continuous small increments in speech proficiency in hearing-impaired children. Such measurements are useful for plotting the increasing skill of individual children, and for assessing the relative success of a group of teachers or a method of training to achieve greater levels of speech proficiency and intelligibility. At the same time, however, there is an equally great continuing need for large-scale assessment in laymen's terms of the overall effectiveness of speech training provided across the nation.

The other speakers at this Institute are describing well a rich variety of activities in which they are engaged. The writer is not a speech scientist nor an educator of deaf children, and therefore is not in a position to advance that conversation. However, a variety of large-scale national data on the speech intelligibility of hearing-impaired children and youth in our special education programs can be reported from a layman's perspective. In this perspective, the overall ease of understanding of the deaf child's speech by naive listeners is reported. The purpose of this presentation is to summarize what we know from such national data, and to offer some comments and reflections on these findings. Since this presentation is based upon data which have already been published (Jensema, Karchmer, & Trybus, 1978; Jensema & Trybus, 1978; Karchmer & Trybus, 1977; Karchmer, Trybus, & Paquin, 1978) methodological descriptions will not receive emphasis. Instead, the writer will emphasize the overall findings and attempt to draw some conclusions from them, more in the form of a position paper than a research report.

While it is not appropriate to elaborate here, over the years of involvement with national studies of this sort, the writer has become increasingly aware of the very substantial power of simple methods used with large-scale data for the purpose of elucidating basic trends and relationships.

The data reported were obtained from the classroom teachers of a national stratified random sample of 978 hearing-impaired children in special education programs throughout the United States, in the Spring of 1974. The teacher was asked to rate the quality of the named child's speech as it would appear to a member of the general public who is unfamiliar with deafness and with the specific individual. The five possible responses and their explanations are as follows:

1. Very intelligible (similar to the speech of a hearing person of the same age);
2. Intelligible (somewhat difficult to understand);
3. Barely intelligible (can only understand after repetition and use of other cues);
4. Not intelligible;
5. Student would not ordinarily attempt to use speech.

The potential limitations of this procedure are quite apparent, and no claim is made regarding the usefulness of this procedure for clinical or individual child study purposes. The purpose of the study was simply to establish broad national evaluative information on the levels of speech intelligibility of hearing-impaired children, and to examine the relationships of rated speech intelligibility to other significant characteristics of the children.

The first finding is that rated speech intelligibility does not improve with age beyond age 7. The overall ratings for children above age 7 are somewhat higher than ratings for all children below age 7, but there are no other age trends in the data. Overall, the correlation between age and speech intelligibility ratings is −.04, a nonsignificant correlation. Regardless of the results produced in specific situations, therefore, there is no evidence for overall improvement with age in hearing-impaired children nationwide.

The second major finding is that probably the single most important variable which is related to speech intelligibility ratings is the degree of the child's hearing loss, as measured by pure-tone average threshold in the better ear. The correlation between hearing levels and speech intelligibility ratings was −.68. The proportion of children rated intelligible or very intelligible ranged from 90 percent for those children with a hearing loss of 55 dB or less in the better ear, down to 23 percent in those children with a hearing loss of 91 dB or greater in the better ear. The relationship is even more striking when only the "very intelligible" ratings are considered. In this situation, the proportion of children rated very intelligible declines from a high of 60 percent in the very mildest loss group, to only 3 percent in the group with a hearing loss greater than 91 dB in the better ear.

Another major finding is that the various major racial/ethnic groups vary considerably in the rated intelligibility of their speech. It is clear, of course, that speech intelligibility is in the ear of the listener as well as in the mouth of the speaker. Recent findings by Corbett (1979) indicate that 94 percent of all special education teachers of the hearing impaired are white, and 6 percent are black or of other racial or ethnic background. Within this context, the proportion of white hearing-impaired children rated intelligible was 51 percent. The comparable figures were 40 percent for Hispanic, and 21 percent for black children.

Family income, parental education, and parental occupations were also studied. Since each of these three measures produced comparable results, and because it was simplest, the socioeconomic data were analyzed in terms of annual family income. The results showed a clear relationship of rated speech intelligibility to these income figures. Of hearing-impaired children coming from families with less than $5,000 annual income, only 28 percent were reported to speak intelligibly or very intelligibly. The comparable figure for children in the $5,000 to $10,000 income category was 37 percent; in the $10,000 to $15,000 category, 51 percent; in the $15,000 to $20,000 category, 64 percent, and in the above $20,000 per year category, 52 percent. The differences among economic groups were most pronounced in the "would not speak" category, suggesting that cultural mores and motivations may be involved as well as differential ability levels. In any case, children from higher income families generally show greater willingness to speak and more intelligible results when they do speak.

Two other factors of major educational concern with respect to speech intelligibility outcomes are the child's use of hearing aids, and the type of educational program attended. There are clear differences between users and nonusers of hearing aids, and clear differences among the various types of educational placements in the rated intelligibility of the children's speech. Both of these results, however, are thoroughly confounded because of the differences in degree of hearing loss among these groups, as well as differences in other educationally significant factors. For example, Karchmer and Trybus (1977) showed clearly that hearing-impaired children in residential schools, day schools, full-time classes in local public schools, and in integrated programs differed significantly on degree of hearing loss, age of students, proportion of postlingually deafened children, racial/ethnic background, family income, parental education levels, proportion of children with deaf parents, and proportion of children who use hearing aids regularly. Similarly, Karchmer and Kirwin (1977) examined characteristics of users and nonusers of hearing aids, and determined that users differ from nonusers in degree of hearing loss, age, sex, family income, racial/ethnic background, hearing status of parents, and type of educational program in which the child is enrolled. As a result of these truly enormous educational and demographic differences, differences in speech intelligibility between users and nonusers of hearing aids, as well as intelligibility differences for children enrolled in differing educational programs, must be attributed to the entire complex of factors, and cannot be attributed to program placement or hearing aid use directly.

Overall, then, the national data on speech intelligibility of hearing-impaired children is very much like the national data of school achievement test scores of the same children. That is, the major differences among children in either of these educational outcomes—intelligibility or achievement scores—are associated with substantial complexes of relatively fixed and unchangeable factors such as degree of hearing loss, ethnic and economic factors. A major difference between speech intelligibility and achievement is that, with respect to achievement, various subgroups of hearing-impaired children begin their academic program at various unequal levels and, at the end of their academic program, are in approximately the same relative position with respect to each other. However, the overall level of achievement has clearly increased over the years of schooling. In the case of speech intelligibility, however, not only are there group-to-group inequalities at whatever age, but there is also no national evidence that the levels of speech intelligibility are any different at the end of schooling than they were approximately at the beginning.

It is very clear, then, that whatever it is we have been doing in the past has not been measurably successful at all in producing intelligible speech in our hearing-impaired children on a national scale. If the future is to be any different from the past, the clear message is that we must approach the problem and its solution in significantly different ways than from in the past.

REFERENCES

Corbett, E. *A descriptive study of teachers of the hearing impaired in the United States.* Doctoral dissertation, Gallaudet College, Washington, D.C., 1979.

Jensema, C., Karchmer, M., & Trybus, R. *The rated speech intelligibility of hearing impaired children: Basic relationships and a detailed analysis.* Washington, D.C.: Office of Demographic Studies, Gallaudet College, 1978.

Jensema, C., & Trybus, R. *Communication patterns and educational achievement of hearing impaired students.* Washington, D.C.: Office of Demographic Studies, Gallaudet College, 1978.

Karchmer, M., & Kirwin, L. *The use of hearing aids by hearing impaired students in the United States.* Washington, D.C.: Office of Demographic Studies, Gallaudet College, 1977.

Karchmer, M., & Trybus, R. *Who are the deaf children in "mainstream" programs?* Washington, D.C.: Office of Demographic Studies, Gallaudet College, 1977.

Karchmer, M., Trybus, R., & Paquin, M. *Early manual communication, parental hearing status, and the academic achievement of deaf students.* Paper presented to the Am. Ed. Res. Assoc., Toronto, 1978.

6

Toward an Objective Description of the Dependent and Independent Variables Associated With Intelligibility Assessments of Hearing-Impaired Adults

Dale E. Metz, Nicholas Schiavetti, Ronald W. Sitler

IN ATTEMPTING TO SET CRITERIA for the definition of speech disorders, Van Riper (1963, p. 16), suggested that speech is defective when it is "conspicuous, unintelligible or unpleasant." This definition uniformly applies to the speech produced by many hearing-impaired adults. Our mission for the next two days is to share insights, data, and perspectives regarding what we consider to be the most efficacious means to assess and modify the conspicuous, unintelligible, or unpleasant nature of the speech produced by some hearing-impaired individuals. We will be sharing information that has been derived from the science of speech analysis and from our equally important "hunches" regarding the clinical management of defective speech. In this sense we epitomize Bruner's notion, in his *Essays for the Left Hand,* that "reaching for knowledge with the right hand is science, yet to say only that much of science is to overlook one of its excitements, for the great hypotheses of science are the gifts carried in the left hand." These left-handed gifts are, of course, our hunches.

The present paper is a left-handed treatment of some issues regarding speech assessment. The basic assumption underlying the issues raised in this paper is that assessment and clinical management should be a data-oriented empirical approach with behavioral objectives. The most fundamental and desirable behavioral objective for the hearing-impaired adult is intelligible speech. This objective can only be achieved, however, when assessment procedures delineate the parameters of unintelligible speech and suggest specific remedial measures. In this sense, speech assessment can be conceptualized within the framework of multiple regression analysis where speech intelligibility as assessed by a listener is the *criterion* or *dependent variable* and the physical parameters of speech are the *predictor* or *independent variables.* Although this philosophy borders on being tautological, current assessment procedures typically do not delineate the parameters of unintelligible speech or suggest specific remedial procedures. The issues surrounding selection and measurement of speech parameters have not been resolved. A better understanding of how deaf adults produce unintelligible speech is needed.

Unfortunately, a clear understanding of the nature of unintelligible speech produced by hearing-impaired adults is not easily achieved. Monsen (1978) points out that even highly trained observers have difficulty determining the exact sources of speech errors that render a given speaker unintelligible. He further suggests, however, that knowledge of speech production abilities as they relate to a speaker's intelligibility is of potentially greater remedial value than knowledge of the speaker's hearing ability. Monsen's ideas are exemplified in a recent report by Stevens, Nickerson, and Rollins (1978). Stevens and his colleagues suggest that the fundamental problem of speech assessment is to quantify those aspects of speech that determine its intelligibility and to identify speech skills that could be useful in the specification of remedial procedures. These researchers proposed a tentative set of measurements that could be used to specify suprasegmental errors produced by hearing-impaired individuals with a future goal of incorporating these measures into a broader speech assessment profile.

The authors have initiated some research directed toward specifying some components of a broad speech assessment profile that considers both the underlying speech skills of hearing-impaired adults and the relationship of these skills to speech intelligibility as assessed by normally hearing listeners. However, there are several problems that, if left unresolved, could jeopardize the validity of such a profile. Specifically, the problems relate to measurement of the dependent variable (i.e., speech intelligibility as assessed by listeners) and measurement of the independent variables (i.e., the physical parameters of speech). We will discuss measurement of the dependent variable first.

Measurement of Speech Intelligibility: The Dependent Variable

Subtelny (1977) has commented on the importance of speech intelligibility measurement with the hearing-impaired population. She stated (p. 183):

> Intelligibility is considered the most practical single index to apply in assessing competence in oral communication. For many years the difficulties and limitations in evaluating the intelligibility of deaf speech have been recognized. This basic fact has necessitated considerable study to establish the validity and reliability of the intelligibility assessments and to define the variables influencing intelligibility. Without this effort, the term "intelligibility" cannot be used with confidence for research, academic, social, and vocational purposes.

It is crucial to recognize that any measure of speech intelligibility is a measure of an interaction between a speaker and a listener. Therefore, it is necessary to quantify the parameters of intelligibility that affect the listener's response as well as the parameters that affect the speaker's actual speech production. The basic algorithm for a measure of speech intelligibility includes three components: (1) the speaker; (2) the material to be spoken; and (3) the listener. Because of the speaker-listener interaction, speech material is a factor that affects both speech production and the listener's response and, as such, cannot be considered independently. Let us look first at what the listener is asked to do when assessing speech intelligibility.

There are basically two kinds of listener tasks that have been used for purposes of speech intelligibility assessment: (1) word identification tests (i.e., where the listener is required to write down what the speaker says) and (2) scaling (i.e., where the listener makes judgments about the speaker's intelligibility). Word identification tests appear to have more face validity than scaling procedures because the listener is required to demonstrate the degree to which he/she actually understood what was said. Additionally, word identification tests provide the opportunity for analysis of specific phonemes which are difficult for the listener to identify correctly and which may contribute to the overall degradation of the speaker's intelligibility. However, word identification tests are time-consuming and expensive because the listener is required to respond to every word he hears. Also, many listeners are needed as subjects because the same material is spoken by all the speakers. To prevent an order effect in which subsequent speakers appear more intelligible by virtue of the listener's familiarity with the material, individual listeners cannot hear more than one speaker. If different material is spoken by each speaker to prevent this order effect, problems may arise from the inability to adequately equate the speech material. For example, Giolas and Duffy (1973) reported rather poor inter-list correlations among the 10 CID sentence lists that they used in speech intelligibility assessments with normally hearing persons who were listening to filtered speech.

In contrast to word identification tests, scaling procedures are quick and easy because each listener typically judges several speakers. The listeners first hear the range of the continuum to be judged and must, of necessity, rate all the speakers saying the same materials. Familiarity with repeated material is of no consequence because the listeners do not have to write down each word. The listeners usually know the material prior to scaling the speakers' intelligibility. For example, the *Rainbow Passage,* committed to memory by every speech pathologist since Grant Fairbanks, is commonly used as the corpus for scaling speech intelligibility. Scaling procedures, however, lack the face validity of word identification tests and do not provide the opportunity for phonemic analysis of the listener's misidentifications of the speaker's intended words.

In summary, there appears to be a fairly even balance of advantages and disadvantages to both word identification tests and scaling procedures. In the past, personal preferences and pragmatic considerations, such as the amount of time or number of listeners available, have probably determined the method used by many researchers. Because various types of scaling procedures are frequently used to assess speech intelligibility, a major issue that needs resolution is the appropriateness of scaling methods used in this assessment.

Scaling Speech Intelligibility

If scaling procedures are used to assess speech intelligibility, the researcher or clinician is faced with the choice of using equal-appearing interval scales or direct magnitude estimation. Both scaling procedures have been employed in the past to scale many aspects of speech production. Direct magnitude estimation has been used, for example, by Martin (1965) to scale stuttering severity and by Zemlin, Daniloff, and Shriner (1968) to scale the difficulty of listening to time-compressed speech. Interval scaling has been used by Hoops and Curtis (1971) to rate the intelligibility of esophageal speech and by Jordan (1961) to rate defective articulation. Selection of direct magnitude estimation vs. equal-appearing interval scaling by previous researchers has probably been a matter of personal preference and/or practical considerations. For example, Martin (1965, p. 177) stated:

> As compared with the equal interval scaling procedure . . . the magnitude estimation method has distinct advantages in that it requires far less time for training and in that persons with little or no speech training seem to perform reliably as judges.

Others, however, have suggested similar pragmatic reasons for selecting interval scaling.

The selection of specific scaling procedures, however, can be easily determined by a more serious consideration of the appropriateness and validity of the equal-appearing interval and direct magnitude estimation procedures. Stevens (1974; 1975) has demonstrated that there are two kinds of continua that may be scaled and that the type of continuum has important implications for the appropriateness and validity of the particular scaling procedure employed. The two types of continua are called *prothetic* and *metathetic*. A prothetic continuum is additive whereas a metathetic continuum is substitutive. Stevens (1975, p. 13) stated:

> The prototypes of the two kinds of perceptual continua are exemplified by loudness and pitch. Loudness is an aspect of sound that has what can best be described as degrees of magnitude or quantity. Pitch does not. Pitch varies from high to low; it has a kind of position, and in a sense it is a qualitative continuum. Loudness may be called a prothetic continuum, and pitch a metathetic one. The criteria that define those two classes of continua reside wholly in how they behave in psychophysical experiments. . . .

Observers can easily partition a metathetic continuum such as pitch into equal intervals, and such judgments are linearly related to direct magnitude estimates of the same stimuli (Stevens, 1974). Thus, both equal-appearing interval and direct magnitude estimation scaling procedures could be appropriate for the scaling of a metathetic continuum. However, Stevens (1974) has demonstrated that interval scaling is inappropriate for use with a prothetic dimension like loudness. Experimental results have repeatedly shown that a linear partition is rarely, if ever, achieved when the dimension being scaled is on a prothetic continuum (Stevens, 1974). When observers try to partition a prothetic continuum into equal intervals there is typically a systematic bias toward subdividing the lower end of the continuum into smaller intervals than those at the upper end of the scale. Partitioning a prothetic continuum results in a nonlinear set of unequal intervals, casting doubt on the validity of interval scaling of prothetic dimensions.

On what kind of continuum does the dimension of speech intelligibility fall? Is it metathetic (i.e., substitutive like pitch) or prothetic (i.e., additive like loudness)? If speech intelligibility falls on a metathetic continuum, then either interval scaling or direct magnitude estimation may be appropriate and valid for scaling speech intelligibility. Therefore, decisions regarding the selection of one method over the other could be based on personal preference. If, however, the continuum of speech intelligibility is found to be prothetic, equal-appearing interval-scaled judgments would be inappropriate and direct magnitude estimation would be the better scaling procedure to employ.

How does one determine the kind of continuum on which the dimension of speech intelligibility falls? Stevens (1975) has outlined a reasonably simple method for this determination. First, direct magnitude estimations and equal-appearing interval scale judgments are made for a set of stimuli falling along the dimension in question. The interval scale scores are then plotted as a function of the direct magnitude estimation scores. If a linear relation obtains between the two sets of scaled judgments, the continuum is metathetic. If, however, the equal-appearing interval-scaled judgments form a negatively accelerating (downward bowed) curve when plotted as a function of the direct magnitude estimates, the continuum is prothetic. That is, the data exhibit the typical inequality of intervals associated with prothetic continua. The question of whether or not speech intelligibility falls on a prothetic continuum is intriguing because it is possible that intelligibility might grow in an additive fashion rather than in some substitutive fashion. If such is the case, interval scaling is probably inappropriate for measuring speech intelligibility. Our goal is to define a set of parameters that predict the speech intelligibility of hearing-impaired adults as assessed by normally hearing listeners. Therefore, one of our first considerations is to investigate the appropriateness of various types of scaling procedures as well as their relationship to word identification estimates of speech intelligibility.

The Listener Himself

The resolution of the continuum issue does not solve all the problems associated with measurement of the dependent variable, speech intelligibility. One must also consider the listener himself. Since the assessment of speech intelligibility is a measurement of a speaker-listener interaction, it is important to consider the variability among listeners. It is probably incorrect to assume that a given speaker, especially a hearing-impaired adult, demonstrates a certain degree of speech intelligibility to all listeners under all circumstances. Some listeners will understand more of what a given speaker says and others will understand less. In addition, the same listener may vary in his/her understanding of a given speaker if the test is conducted under different listening conditions. Except for the recent work of McGarr

(1978) and Monsen (1978), there has been little systematic research to isolate the parameters responsible for listener variability in speech intelligibility assessment with hearing-impaired individuals.

One variable of interest is the effect of short-term and long-term experience of the listener with the hearing-impaired individual. This issue was addressed by Monsen (1978) when he compared the responses of 49 naive and 21 experienced listeners to the speech of hearing-impaired adolescents. Overall, the experienced listeners understood about 9 percent more words in sentence contexts than did the naive listeners. However, both groups showed about a 15 to 20 percent improvement over four listening trials, with the naive listeners quickly approximating the performance of the experienced listeners. On the first trial the experienced listeners heard 14 percent more words than the naive listeners, but only 5 percent more on the fourth trial. One question not addressed by Monsen was whether this improvement resulted from exposure to the hearing-impaired individuals' speech *per se,* from exposure to the speech materials that were repeatedly presented, or from a combination of the two.

Long-term experience in listening to the speech of deaf individuals is probably a critical variable affecting listener performance in the assessment of speech intelligibility. However, at least five important questions regarding listener experience remain unanswered:

(1) How much listener improvement can be gained in how short a time?
(2) How much does speech material familiarity interact with practice to determine short-term improvement in the accurate identification of speech produced by hearing-impaired individuals?
(3) What baseline practice or familiarity criteria should be applied in selecting listeners to participate in speech assessment tasks? Should all naive listeners be used or should a standardized familiarity criterion be used to identify "experienced" listeners?
(4) Does the practice effect, as noted by Monsen (1978), generalize beyond the limiting case of the speech assessment task with a restricted group of hearing-impaired speakers to other hearing-impaired individuals?
(5) Is a real-world criterion for speech intelligibility of hearing-impaired individuals better defined as intelligibility to the experienced listener typically encountered in their families and schools for the deaf, or better defined as intelligibility to the naive listeners they will encounter daily in work and social environments?

At least one further important factor has not been addressed in the literature, the variability among listeners within a relatively "homogeneous" listening group. For example, hearing-impaired individuals are frequently evaluated by a group of five listeners in word identification tests, and their speech intelligibility is typically reported as the mean percent of words correctly identified by the five listeners. It seems, however, that attention needs to be paid to the variability among the listeners in their understanding of the speakers' intended words as well as to the central tendency of their responses. For example, the authors' preliminary data include two hearing-impaired adults who received mean word identification test intelligibility scores of 89 percent and 93 percent from naive listeners. Most people would consider these two individuals to be highly intelligible and essentially equivalent in terms of speech intelligibility. Yet the person with the 89 percent mean score had a narrow range of scores across the five naive listeners of 86 percent to 92 percent (i.e., a range of 6 percent), whereas the person with the 93 percent mean had a wider range of scores across the five listeners of 81 percent to 100 percent (i.e., a range of 19 percent). Can one really equate the speech intelligibility of these two hearing-impaired adults when one is understood about equally well by all five listeners and the other is not? How much variation among homogeneous listeners can be tolerated in assessing the speech intelligibility of hearing-impaired adults? Why is this variation present? Is it due to speaker factors, listener factors, material factors, or some interaction of the three factors?

The main point of the foregoing discussion is that hearing-impaired adults are frequently assigned some average speech intelligibility score by a group of listeners, but the variability of the listeners making these judgments is typically ignored. This treatment of speech intelligibility data appears to be based on the assumption that even under constant speaking and listening conditions, the hearing-impaired adult possesses a certain degree of speech intelligibility which can be easily characterized by a mean intelligibility score. The alternative position, however, rests on the premise that each hearing-impaired adult has a range of intelligibility to different listeners, and the central tendency of his/her speech intelligibility is only one way of expressing how well he/she can be understood. The dispersion among listeners' ratings of speech intelligibility may be as important as the central tendency of their responses when assessing an individual's speech intelligibility. Formal attempts to resolve some of these issues regarding listener variability appear to be a fruitful line of inquiry.

Speech Intelligibility: Potential Independent Variables

How might one go about identifying the most efficient predictor (independent) variables related to speech intelligibility for the hearing-impaired adult? If it can be done, the two most logical methods to employ for the search are multiple regression and discriminant analysis. One such attempt has already been made. Monsen (1978), using multiple regression analysis, found that the combination of three predictor variables, the VOT difference between /t/ and /d/, the second formant difference between /i/ and /ɔ/, and errors on liquids and glides bore a multiple correlation of r = 0.85 (73 percent of the total variance) to the speech intelligibility of a large number of hearing-impaired adolescents as assessed by experienced and inexperienced listeners. However, it is possible that the restricted set of predictor variables of speech intelligibility Monsen identified with regression analysis relates to certain methodological factors.

First, Monsen used extremely simple stimulus materials. The sentences read by his subjects averaged only 4.5 syllables in length. Also, each listener heard each sentence two times. It seems possible that these two factors contributed to the inordinately high speech intelligibility of his subjects. Monsen reported that the average speech intelligibility of his subjects (as rated by the listeners) was 76 percent as compared with previous research findings with comparable populations that found average speech intelligibility ranges between 19 and 21 percent (John & Howarth, 1965; Markides, 1970; Smith, 1973). The high average intelligibility of Monsen's subjects could have affected the contribution of his predictor variables in their relationship to speech intelligibility. As such, the predictor variables he identified may not stand the test of generalizability when different stimulus materials and/or estimates of speech intelligibility are used.

Second, Monsen initially subjected a very restricted set of predictor variables to the regression analysis. Although his variables were selected because of their probable relationship to speech intelligibility and their ability to be quantified, they do not exhaust all potential predictor variables.

Monsen's predictor variables do form a foundation for future building, however. We are employing Monsen's predictor variables in conjunction with the suprasegmental variables suggested by Stevens, Nickerson, and Rollins (1978) in our initial attempts to isolate critical speech parameters that contribute to the hearing-impaired adult's speech intelligibility.

In closing, it seems possible that speech intelligibility may be associated with different predictor variables or different combinations of predictor variables for speakers at different levels of intelligibility. If so, discriminant analysis could objectively determine these levels of intelligibility which, when considered in light of linguistic competence, speech discrimination ability and other communication skills, could have important implications for the type of instruction given to students at these various levels. Our current research addresses many of the issues and questions raised in this paper, relying heavily on strict psychophysical principles, the physical analysis of speech and, for a while, our hunches. Hopefully, the results of this research will reflect an appropriate balance between our right and left hands regarding the speech assessment of hearing-impaired adults.

REFERENCES

Bruner, J. *On knowing: Essays for the left hand.* New York: Atheneum, 1962.

Giolas, T. G., & Duffy, J. R. Equivalency of CID and revised CID sentence lists. *J. Speech Hear. Res.*, 1973, *16*, 549–555.

Hoops, H. R., & Curtis, J. F. Intelligibility of the esophageal speaker. *Arch. Otolaryn.*, 1971, *93*, 300–303.

John, J. E. J., & Howarth, J. N. The effect of time distortions on the intelligibility of deaf children's speech. *Lang. Speech*, 1965, *8*, 127–134.

Jordan, E. P. Articulation test measures and listener ratings of articulation defectiveness. *J. Speech Hear. Res.*, 1960, *3*, 303–319.

Markides, A. The speech of deaf and partially-hearing children with special reference to factors affecting intelligibility. *Brit. J. Comm. Dis.*, 1970, *5*, 126–140.

Martin, R. Direct magnitude-estimation judgments of stuttering severity using audible and audible-visible speech samples. *Speech Mono.*, 1965, *32*, 169–177.

McGarr, N. S. *Difference between experienced and inexperienced listeners in understanding deaf speech.* Paper presented at the Convention of Am. Speech Hear. Assoc., San Francisco, California, 1978.

Monsen, R. B. Toward measuring how well hearing-impaired children speak. *J. Speech Hear. Res.*, 1978, *21*, 197–219.

Smith, C. R. Residual hearing and speech production in deaf children. *Comm. Sc. Lab. Res. Rep. No. 4*, City University of New York, 1973.

Stevens, K. N., Nickerson, R. S., & Rollins, A. M. On describing the suprasegmental properties of the speech of deaf children. *Bolt, Beranek, and Newman Report Number 3955*, 1978.

Stevens, S. S. Perceptual magnitude and its measurement. In E. C. Carterette and M. P. Friedman (Eds.), *Handbook of perception (Vol. II).* New York: Academic Press, 1974.

Stevens, S. S. *Psychophysics.* New York: Wiley, 1975.

Subtelny, J. D. Assessment of speech with implications for training. In F. Bess (Ed.), *Childhood deafness: causation, assessment, and management.* New York: Grune and Stratton, 1977.

Van Riper, C. *Speech correction.* Englewood Cliffs, New Jersey: Prentice-Hall, 1963.

Zemlin, W. R., Daniloff, R. G., & Shriner, T. H. The difficulty of listening to time-compressed speech. *J. Speech Hear. Res.*, 1968, *11*, 875–881.

7
A Critical Assessment of Current Practices in the Audiologic Management of Preschool Children

Noel D. Matkin

THE PRIMARY PURPOSE of this presentation is to express a number of concerns with respect to the identification, evaluation, and habilitative strategies currently utilized by many audiologists while managing young children at risk for educationally significant hearing impairments. In this writer's judgment, there is a pressing need for pediatric audiologists both to modify the traditional service delivery model and to facilitate interdisciplinary communication. Therefore, recommendations based upon both a consideration of the current literature and clinical experience will be offered.

While some similarities do exist in the audiologic management of adults and children, significant differences must be recognized at the outset. The effects of a hearing loss in early childhood are pervasive, with habilitative and educational needs being complex, extensive, and long term. To complicate matters further, successful management of pediatric cases depends in large part upon the acceptance, understanding, and cooperation of the child's parents. For these reasons, the audiologic evaluation of children is most effective when undertaken as one facet of a team endeavor. Yet, far too frequently, the audiologist's contribution is limited in its effectiveness because services are often provided as a specialty assessment in isolation and then communicated to parents, clinicians, and educators in a lexicon which has limited meaning, at best.

Identification

A continuing concern is the relatively late identification of many children with hearing losses. Despite the efforts to develop neonatal and preschool screening programs, far too many youngsters are referred on account of a failure-based identification model: It is only after a child repeatedly fails to achieve major developmental milestones in communication that a referral is initiated. Even in instances of severe and profound bilateral impairments, there is often a 9- to 12-month delay from the first statement of concern by parents to the initial confirmatory evaluation (Malkin et al., 1976; Matkin, 1973). In milder degrees of hearing loss, a delay of one to two years is not uncommon. In fact, many high-frequency and unilateral impairments are not identified until the first pure-tone screening is undertaken in the public school.

Since the preschool years represent the prime period of oral language development, such delays in identification are clearly unacceptable. An aggressive educational program regarding the major milestones in receptive and expressive communication development must be initiated, not only for the general public, but also within the medical community. Far too often, a well-meaning physician allays initial parental concerns with a "wait and see if he/she outgrows it" response rather than aggressively referring to a speech and language center to determine whether or not the child is significantly delayed in communication skills as compared to normal development. As a profession, we should be concerned about the late identification of all communication disorders, whether related to a hearing loss or not.

Assessment of Residual Hearing

A second major shortcoming in the management of many young hearing-impaired children is the reliance upon the pure-tone audiogram as the definitive measure. A host of internal and external factors interact to influence the auditory function of each youngster with a hearing loss. Obtaining reliable and valid minimal response levels to pure tones across a variety of test frequencies is recognized as basic to any audiologic assessment. It is upon such information that the type, degree, configuration, and symmetry of the impairment between ears can be established. Further, generalizations regarding possible etiology, the need for amplification, and the probable effect upon communication development can be made. However, it must be recognized that two children with identical audiograms may function very differently. Thus, to assume homogeneity by grouping children for educational and habilitative purposes on the basis of audiograms is quite naive.

The focus, either when classifying the hearing losses among children or when planning individualized education programs, must be shifted from the loss of hearing to the potential for utilizing residual hearing. Such a shift in focus will require several major changes in the routine practice of pediatric audiology. First, while working within the child's receptive vocabulary knowledge, the same effort and emphasis must be placed upon the measurement of auditory discrimination as has been placed in the past upon the measurement of auditory sensitivity. With young children, this commitment, in the author's professional judgment, means that:

1. A developmental approach must be taken to select an appropriate auditory task, appropriate test materials, and an appropriate response mode, and
2. The audiologic evaluation must be an ongoing process during the preschool years so that with maturation and specialized training the emergence of auditory skills can be monitored.

Unfortunately, there has been limited research with respect to the development of appropriate test materials and techniques to permit the assessment of auditory discrimination among young children. The only pediatric test that has been widely used are the PB-K 50 lists of monosyllabic words developed by Haskins (1949). The lists were developed by utilizing vocabulary of kindergarten-aged children. Therefore, the use of these materials with a broad spectrum of hearing-impaired children with delayed language development often is inappropriate, resulting in depressed scores due to limitations in the child's receptive oral language, as well as in auditory discrimination.

Several discrimination tests have been developed that make it possible to examine a larger number of children having limited speech and language skills. The Word Intelligibility by Picture Identification test (Ross & Lerman, 1970) and the NU-Chips by Katz and Elliot (1978) are examples of materials that are appropriate for use with children who are delayed in receptive language. Further, these tests utilize a picture-pointing rather than a verbal response, so it is possible to accurately judge whether or not the child's response is correct.

As has been recommended when measuring auditory sensitivity, the pediatric audiologist must rely on a battery of materials that can be employed for testing auditory discrimination rather than on any one single test (Matkin, 1977a). In this way, the validity of the test procedure can be assured if one works within the child's level of language competence. Unfortunately, clinical and laboratory investigations suggest that none of the available measures can be appropriately applied with youngsters who are functioning at less than a three-year language level. For this reason, a pressing research need is to develop alternative procedures that will yield information with respect to the auditory function in the child with very limited language. While the tradition has been to use a single test, usually comprised of monosyllabic words, Erber and Alencewicz (1976) suggested that the audiologic assessment of residual hearing should include measures of detection, discrimination, recognition, and comprehension. In the professional opinion of this author, nonverbal stimuli, such as common environmental sounds, as well as verbal materials also should be utilized. The Sound Effects Recognition Test (SERT) developed by Hieber et al. (1975) can often be used to differentiate the level of auditory function even among nonverbal youngsters.

Recent publications suggest that the use of Visual Reinforcement Audiometry to assess speech sound discrimination abilities of children as young as 5 to 6 months of age may be feasible (Eilers, Wilson, & Moore, 1977). So far the procedure has been used primarily with normally hearing children and in a laboratory setting. However, research reports suggest that with certain modifications the basic principle and procedures may be quite adaptable to the clinical setting.

Analysis of Response Behavior

Failure to analyze each child's response behavior during audiologic testing is another major concern in relation to current practices in pediatric audiology. To explain, the audiologist traditionally has focused on careful control of stimulus parameters and recording a child's response level to a particular test signal. Yet, clinical experience suggests that a good deal of useful information is lost if the sole objective is an analysis of psycho-acoustic response data. Of equal importance is an analysis of each child's response behavior, even during routine threshold test procedures.

At present, there is growing interest among educators and clinicians in the assessment of central auditory processing. It is suggested that central processing problems, in addition to peripheral hearing loss, compound the effect of the handicapping condition in many children. Information from the Office of Demographic Studies indicates a high prevalence of multiple handicaps among hearing-impaired children (Gentile & McCartney, 1973). Yet, most audiologic tests designed to assess the integrity of the central auditory system require the presence of normal hearing sensitivity. In other words, it is not possible to administer many of the standard measures in a central auditory test battery once a peripheral hearing loss has been determined. Very often, observations regarding response behavior yield important clues to the possible presence of additional handicapping conditions. Such an analysis of response behavior often reveals that significantly more conditioning trials are needed to obtain stimulus-response control. A review of clinical records reveals that most children are conditioned successfully in six trials; often less are required, even with toddlers. Once a child is conditioned for behavioral testing, it then becomes important to assess the youngster's ability to generalize and transfer such conditioning across various test signals. Also, the rate of habituation is an important consideration; it often is more rapid in the case of the multihandicapped youngster. It must be kept in mind that even a simple operant conditioning procedure such as Visual Reinforcement Audiometry (suitable for use with infants as young as 6 months of age) taps basic cognitive and motor abilities. Further, visual and auditory attending abilities, as well as short-term memory, are required to maintain such behavioral conditioning during a test session.

Observation of aberrant reaction times during pure-tone and speech testing may be an additional clue to specific deficits in auditory reception and processing. As is the case with most auditory abilities, there is evidence that reaction time is developmental and becomes shorter with maturation. Further, in both children and adults, reaction time tends to become longer as one approaches absolute threshold. Finally, it has been noted that some young children respond to termination of the auditory signal rather than to its onset. Therefore, developmental age, the sensation level at which the stimuli are being presented, as well as the possibility of a "tone off" response, must be considered when analyzing reaction time. Focusing on the characteristics of a child's response behavior as well as upon the audiogram may facilitate early identification of additional handicapping conditions. Confirmation of such clinical impressions may be possible through a similar analysis of electro-physiological auditory activity obtained during brainstem evoked response audiometry.

In recent years, several conditioning techniques including visual reinforcement, tangible reinforcement, and conditioned play audiometry have been found to be effective with preschool children (Matkin, 1977a). Thus there is little basis for the continuing misconception, especially among allied health professionals, that youngsters cannot be reliably tested under the age of 5. Further, sufficient normative data are now available for the major techniques in the pediatric audiologic test battery to permit a judgment of the functional age range within which the particular child falls. For example, good success has been encountered in the audiologic testing of multi-handicapped school-aged children having quite limited cognitive abilities. Yet, the use of Visual Reinforcement Audiometry, which is typically appropriate for much younger children, was necessary. The point is that each audiologic report should include a comment on the conditioning technique utilized and the appropriateness of the approach relative to age.

Obviously, caution must be exercised to avoid overinterpretation of such observations of response behavior. However, it has been found productive to alert the clinician or teacher to the fact that the child's response behaviors during audiologic testing suggest that compounding problems may be present. Further evaluation and subsequent modification of remedial and educational strategies may result after sharing such concerns with respect to patterns of auditory behaviors.

Aided Testing

Far too frequently, the typical audiological report only stresses the degree, type, and configuration of the hearing loss. While such information is useful to the managing otologist, it often is of minimum utility to the educator. It is important to note that each of the behavioral conditioning techniques appropriate for use during the pediatric audiologic assessment also can be utilized while evaluating a young child's response with various hearing aids (Matkin, 1977b). In the case of the child with limited verbal abilities, educators and clinicians would be far better informed if audiologists routinely provided response data in the form of an aided audiogram which reflects the youngster's ability to perceive various auditory test signals across the frequency range while wearing the particular recommended hearing aid(s). It has been found that teachers often are far more realistic in establishing levels of expectation after being provided with an aided audiogram. With such information, it is possible at the outset to comprehend which segments of the acoustic spectrum of speech will and will not be audible while the child is wearing amplification.

As soon as the auditory discrimination tests can be reliably administered, aided scores obtained not only in a quiet listening environment but also in a background of competition should be available for education planning. It is well documented that the acoustic environment in which a hearing aid is used will determine in large part the benefits to be derived (Hieber & Tillman, 1978). Adult hearing aid users frequently complain about the adverse effects of the listening environment on their perception of speech. Yet, in the writer's experience, the limitations imposed by classroom acoustics are rarely discussed when the benefits and limitations of hearing aids for children are considered. With the current thrust toward mainstreaming of hearing-impaired children, the importance of providing information relative to a youngster's ability to understand speech in a background of noise cannot be overstated. Youngsters with excellent aided auditory potential are being placed in acoustic environments in regular classrooms which severely limit their auditory function. Since it is not reasonable to acoustically treat each classroom in a school, the use of a radio frequency auditory training system rather than a conventional hearing aid must be given careful consideration during individual educational programming.

Parent Management

As mentioned earlier, the successful management of preschool hearing-impaired children depends, in large part, upon the participation and cooperation of the parents. Since the audiologist often is the first member of the communicative disorders team to evaluate the child and confirm the presence of a hearing loss, the issue of parent management must be given primary consideration. Yet, few graduate training programs provide formal course work and practicum in the area of parent counseling. As a result, many audiologists feel they have fulfilled their role with parents when they have explained the child's audiogram, discussed the hearing aid, and referred for special education. Of even greater concern is the practice of excluding parents from observing the audiological testing. As a consequence, many parents, at best, have a limited understanding of the significance of the audiological results.

As indicated in a recent publication by Ling and Ling (1978), and previously by this writer (Matkin, 1976), the management of parents includes three endeavors: parent education, parent guidance, and parent counseling. It is readily acknowledged that each of these activities cannot be considered mutually exclusive. Yet, it has been quite helpful to organize clinical activities and to establish short-term goals for parents with these three endeavors in mind. To explain, parent education is viewed as an orientation through discussion, programmed materials, and selected readings to acquire the basic information (including terminology, concepts, and rationale) needed to understand the meaning of the audiological findings. Obviously, the content of a parent education program must be continuously expanded and extended as the child matures. Only through the development of an ongoing educational thrust for parents will the meaning and importance of many recommendations be understood and acted upon.

In contrast to parent education, parent guidance in this triad means assisting parents in their understanding of the various options that are available when planning for their child's future. In the author's judgment, this activity represents a critical step in fostering independence among parents and in assisting them to assume the role of parent advocate for their child. Too frequently, clinicians—whether audiologists, speech/language specialists, or teachers of the hearing impaired—assume that they must dictate the preferred program of management. Such a strategy suggests that the clinician knows both what is best for the family and what habilitative or educational approach will be most appropriate for the particular child under study. Unfortunately, our knowledge on such matters is not absolute. Further, such an approach fosters dependence rather than independence among parents.

Finally, it is suggested that the term "parent counseling" be utilized in a restrictive rather than general context. If the audiologist is willing to identify and describe the hearing impairment, it is imperative that he/she be prepared to support the parents in the inevitable emotional response that our findings initially elicit. There was a time when the author naively believed that the intensity and depth of the parents' emotional outcry would be reflected by the degree of the hearing impairment just identified. Unfortunately, there is no adequate way to predict the parents' level of expectation of their child or their ability to cope with adversity. It is not suggested that the audiologist attempt to assume the role of psychotherapist. However, it is recommended that the audiologist understand the grieving process and that there be a willingness to allot time for empathetic support of parents, which is considered mandatory.

Conclusion

A critical analysis of current practices in pediatric audiology indicates the need for significant modifications in the traditional service delivery model. Increased effectiveness of early identification programs to assure referral of all children with significant delays in communication development; the utilization of a developmental approach to evaluation of residual auditory potential as well as hearing loss; careful analysis of each child's response behavior during testing; detailed assessment of performance with amplification and the active involvement of parents in evaluation and remedial planning are all needed if the potential benefits of pediatric audiologic management are to be realized. Finally, involvement of the audiologist in the child study team as an active participant in multidisciplinary management is necessary if, as professionals, we honestly believe that maximal use of residual hearing is beneficial, regardless of the particular educational approach taken.

REFERENCES

Eilers, R. E., Wilson, W. R., & Moore, J. M. Developmental changes in speech discrimination in infants. *J. Speech Hear Res.*, 1977, *20*, 766–780.

Erber, N. P., & Alencewicz, C. M. Audiologic evaluation of deaf children. *J. Speech Hear Dis.*, 1976, *41*, 256–267.

Gentile, A., & McCartney, B. *Additional handicapping condition among hearing impaired students: U.S. 1971–1972.* Washington, D.C.: Office of Demographic Studies, Gallaudet College, 1973.

Haskins, H. A. *Phonetically balanced test of speech discrimination for children.* Master's thesis, Northwestern University, 1949.

Hieber, T. F., Matkin, N. D., & Skalka, E. *A preliminary investigation of a sound effect recognition task.* Paper presented at the Am. Speech Hear. Assoc. Convention, Washington, D.C., 1975.

Hieber, T. F., & Tillman, T. W. Room acoustic effects on monosyllabic word discrimination ability for normal and hearing-impaired children. *J. Speech Hear Res.*, 1978, *21*, 440–458.

Katz, D. R., & Elliott, L. L. *Development of a new children's speech discrimination test.* Paper presented at the Am. Speech Hear. Assoc. Convention, San Francisco, 1978.

Ling, D., & Ling, A. H. *Aural habilitation: The foundation of verbal learning in hearing-impaired children.* Washington, D.C.: A.G. Bell Association for the Deaf, 1978.

Malkin, S. F., Freeman, R. D., & Hasting, J. O. Psycho-social problems of deaf children and their families. A comparative study. *Audiol. Hear. Educ.*, 1976, *2*, 21–29.

Matkin, N. D. Some essential features of a pediatric audiological evaluation. In E. Kampp (Ed.), *Evaluation of hearing handicapped children.* 5th Danovox Symposium, Ebeltoff, Denmark: Danovox Corporation, 1973.

Matkin, N. D. The utilization of programmed instruction with parents of hearing impaired children. *Neb. Speech Hear. Assoc. J.*, 1976, *14*, 6–8.

Matkin, N. D. Assessment of hearing sensitivity during the preschool years. In F. H. Bess (Ed.), *Childhood deafness: Causation, assessment and management.* New York: Grune & Stratton, 1977a.

Matkin, N. D. Hearing aids for children. In W. R. Hodgson & P. H. Skinner (Ed.), *Hearing aid assessment and use in audiologic habilitation.* Baltimore: Williams & Wilkins, 1977b.

Ross, M., & Lerman, J. A. Picture identification test for hearing impaired children. *J. Speech Hear. Res.*, 1970, *13*, 44–53.

8
Audiologic Assessment: Interpretation Relative to Optimal Amplification and Speech Training

Derek Sanders

IN CONSIDERING THIS TOPIC, it is necessary first to clarify the meaning of the phrase "speech training." In this conference one cannot easily justify limiting the application of the phrase to stimulating production of speech. To do so would narrow too sharply current concepts of speech, and disassociate articulation training from receptive and expressive use of speech.

What is the audiologist required to do for the speech teacher? This can best be answered in the perceived goals of the teacher. The author suggests that major goals for teachers of speech at the primary and secondary levels are the improvement of oral communication and the improvement of the students' abilities to participate fully in oral communication. If these goals are accepted, then the teacher must be concerned not only with the pupils' amplification needs related to teaching of speech, but also their needs for amplification which permit conversation in academic and social activities.

Specifically, the speech teacher expects the audiologist to provide amplification to increase the student's ability:

1. To receive and decode the acoustic signal;
2. To internalize an acoustic image of sound patterns down to syllabic level;
3. To self-monitor attempts to generate an equivalent production model;
4. To improve the intelligibility of speech; and
5. To improve understanding of speech in various academic and social situations.

In providing appropriate amplification, the difference between the segmental and suprasegmental components of speech must be acknowledged. In this regard, the segmental components refer to the phonemic information derived from formants and transitions arising from articulation and coarticulation. The suprasegmental components refer to the melodic patterning arising from vocal inflection, stress, and duration. The development of articulated speech under normal circumstances is predicated upon the speaker's ability to effect vocal-articulatory behavior resulting in an acoustic signal which matches the model of the adult. This necessitates that speech be loud enough and have the full complement of frequencies when received. These, then, constitute three primary requirements of amplification for speech:

1. That it raise the intensity of speech into the pupil's range of residual hearing;
2. That it raise all frequencies important to speech to within the range of residual hearing except as deemed inappropriate; and
3. That the sound intensity will never exceed the student's loudness tolerance.

Two further considerations must influence the choice of amplification specification and, therefore, the assessment procedures. The first is the significant distortion which reverberation can exert on the acoustic speech signal. The second is the negative effect of environmental or speech noise upon discrimination. These requirements must be considered in the audiologic assessment as applied to speech processing.

Is diagnostic audiologic data sufficient to specify amplification? To answer this question, the difference between diagnostic and rehabilitative evaluations must be considered. The goal of diagnostic audiology is to assess the auditory system. In searching for objectivity, the diagnostician seeks to eliminate the client from the process as far as possible. One feels that ideally the diagnostic audiologist would say to the patient: "If you can drop your ears off by 9 a.m. tomorrow, we can have them all tested and fitted with an aid by 5 p.m." Rehabilitation assessment, by contrast, is concerned with the client's *functional* use of hearing. The rehabilitation audiologist seeks to determine the influence of the very factors which the diagnostic audiologist seeks to exclude. In rehabilitation, the audiologist must relate the audiologic assessment data to speech perception and production. To do this, parameters of residual hearing must be defined carefully to answer the following questions: What is the frequency range of residual hearing, and how much hearing remains within that range? That is to say,

"How intense does sound have to be in order to be audible?" How much intensity can be accepted? In other words, "What is the dynamic range of residual hearing between threshold and maximum acceptable comfort level?" Frequency range and tolerance limits represent the boundaries of residual hearing. This information relates to the selection of amplification, since amplified sound is expected to fill the area defined by these boundaries. As stated earlier in this paper: The sound must be made loud enough; it must amplify the full range of frequencies unless otherwise prescribed; and its loudest components must not exceed comfortable limits.

Gain

Making sound intense enough presents no problem to the hearing aid industry. The problem is to raise essential speech components sufficiently to make them clearly audible without exceeding comfort acceptability. This requires that the amplification unit used—personal hearing aid or auditory trainer—be set to a maximum power output appropriate to the student's maximum tolerance. McCandless (1976) has indicated that at some time loudness discomfort troubles 50 percent of hearing aid users. By limiting maximum power output, optimum use of the gain control is provided.

Currently, there is concern that audiologists are providing too much gain in the fitting of hearing aids. In this regard, a general guide proposed by McCandless (1976) specifies that user gain should be approximately 50 percent of the hearing deficit.

Gengel (1974) determined that user gain averaged 20–25 dB (at most 30 dB) above detection threshold, which was probably determined by the perceived loudness of the first formant. Maximum vowel discrimination occurred at 22 dB above speech detection threshold; however, maximum consonant discrimination occurred at 33 dB above speech detection threshold. This evidence suggests that adults (Gengel, 1974) and children (Byrne & Fitfield, 1974; Bess, 1976) with moderately severe to profound deficits tend to set the volume control lower than the position optimal for speech perception.

These reports also suggest that students should be encouraged to use a higher gain level for speech training than for general use. This suggestion receives further support from Gengel's demonstration that his subjects could become accustomed to a higher gain setting.

Frequency Response

Since frequency response in amplification should encompass the range of residual hearing, it is helpful to replot the pure-tone audiogram into sound pressure level (SPL) either by use of an equal loudness contour table (Sanders, 1971, p. 109) or by use of the Bragg SPL Converter (Bragg, 1977). This permits you to depict residual hearing levels in sound pressure level. The measured, or claimed, response curve of the hearing aid or auditory trainer then can be plotted on the same chart, allowing the teacher to see how well the amplification curve encompasses the residual hearing curve.

It should be stressed that low-frequency attenuation with associated high-frequency emphasis may prove beneficial in teaching or improving speech for students with residual high-tone sensitivity. Low-tone emphasis, however, is contraindicated for students with hearing at or above 500 Hz. For children who have only corner audiograms (response at 125, 250, 500 Hz only), extension of frequency amplification below the usual 400 Hz may prove of value in perceiving voicing components of speech sounds which may otherwise be inaudible.

Aided Frequency Response

The child's auditory reception with a hearing aid and with a particular auditory training unit is most important to the speech teacher. The speech teacher should have a pure-tone audiogram indicating both unaided and aided thresholds from 125–8000 including 750, 1500, 3000, and 6000 Hz. The audiologist can help by providing comparative aided audiograms for alternate frequency response settings. This information, together with the student's acoustic gain requirements and maximum output acceptance limits, should be converted into guidance about recommended control settings for auditory trainers.

Many teachers of speech choose to use the child's personal hearing aid for speech training because they do not understand how to set the controls on the auditory training unit to accommodate individual needs of different children. The audiologist should therefore be quite specific about the frequency response setting, gain, and maximum power output limits appropriate for each child. These should be written as a tentative prescription with trial modifications encouraged. The teacher will gain further insight into the effects of the child's hearing impairment on speech perception if the audiogram is plotted on a chart indicating the distribution of the formant energy F_1, F_2, F_3 for vowels, diphthongs, and voiced consonants and the energy concentrations for unvoiced consonants (Sanders, 1971, p. 100). This chart will give the teacher an indication of which sounds are inaudible, distorted, and/or confused for the student. The teacher needs audiologic data, therefore, which indicate the capabilities of the child wearing amplification:

1. To detect speech—to hear the vocal tone;
2. To discriminate among words of dissimilar phonetic structure;
3. To discriminate between words of similar phonetic structure;
4. To discriminate individual phonemes as a function of a wide range of phonetic contexts.

Room Acoustics—Speech Perception

Furthermore the teacher must be aware of the influence of room acoustics on speech perception (Börrild, 1978, Ross, 1978) and therefore on speech modeling and monitoring. This influence has been well documented. Tillman, Carhart, and Olsen (1970) showed that while normal-hearing subjects could achieve 40 percent discrimination even when the signal was 12 dB less intense than the noise, hearing-impaired subjects required the signal to be 18 dB greater than noise to achieve the same level of discrimination, a 30 dB difference. Under normal environmental conditions the effects of noise are compounded by room reverberation. While optimum classroom reverberation time should not exceed 1/2 sec., most rooms exceed 1 sec. The results of a number of studies confirm that discrimination decreases as reverberation time increases, and that persons with impaired hearing are far more adversely affected than those with normal hearing (Finitzo-Hieber, 1975; John, 1957; Nablek & Pickett, 1974a,b).

The implications of these findings for teaching speech are clear. If hearing-impaired children are to learn and improve speech production and comprehension, they must listen under optimal acoustic conditions. The simplest and most effective method of combating both noise and reverberation is to ensure that the input microphone for the teacher and the child's speech remain at a constant distance of 4 inches from the speaker's mouth. In the writer's opinion the mouth-to-microphone distance specification must apply to both student and teacher to provide the most favorable signal-to-noise ratio and minimize the effects of reverberation. Speech training using the child's aid with a nondirectional microphone picking up all sound including the sound echoes of reverberation is *not* acceptable.

Speech Discrimination

Speech discrimination in noise can be a helpful test administered as part of the rehabilitative audiologic assessment battery. Bode (1975, p. 293) has recommended that each audiologist "make arbitrary but tentative decisions" concerning the choice of noise and the manner in which it is used during testing. He urges the selection of noise representative of the environment in which the individual must function, and the collection of comparative normative data for that noise. The author believes the noise selected should include competing speech (cocktail party noise with simultaneous conversations) or speech-noise (equal intensity to 1000 Hz, then 6 to 12 dB drop-off in intensity per octave). Signal-to-noise test levels recommended by Berger and Millin (1971) are +10, +6, and 0 dB. This range encompasses the signal-to-noise ratios for a teacher's voice in the normal classroom specified as +5 dB (Sanders, 1965); and as +3 dB (Paul, 1967).

Rehabilitative Audiologic Assessment

What does the teacher of speech need from the rehabilitative audiologic assessment? Why is such assessment necessary? The process of speech acquisition and improvement is one of auditory and auditory visual modeling. Modeling involves:

1. Reconstructing as accurate an image as possible of the articulatory acoustic model presented;
2. Attempting to reproduce the acoustic pattern via articulatory behavior;
3. Comparing the actual output to the intended output; and
4. Using an external judge to determine the closeness of the actual output to the model presented.

The success of speech modeling depends primarily on the fidelity of the acoustic signal received, the success with which the pattern is internally represented, and, in spoken language, the determination of the phonemic categorization of the internal representation. The speech teacher needs to know, therefore, the extent to which the hearing impairment reduces the fidelity of the acoustic signals which represent the various speech sounds and speech sound combinations. The speech teacher needs to know:

1. Which sounds fall entirely within the range of the child's residual hearing?
2. Which sounds will be audible but distorted?
3. Which sounds will be indiscriminable from one or more other sounds?
4. In which combinations of phonemes are sounds most accurately discriminated?

This information has the potential to influence the teacher's approach to speech training. When it is known that a given speech sound falls fully within the range of residual hearing, heavy emphasis on auditory modeling will be justified. Those sounds which can be demonstrated to be audible but indiscriminable from other sounds will necessitate supplemental cues to auditory modeling, while those sounds not audible to the child must be taught exclusively through nonauditory monitoring.

The audiologic assessment must also address the child's ability to understand speech in the less than ideal conditions of the classroom. It is necessary that the audiologist become involved in ensuring that everything possible is done to provide the child with the type(s) of amplification which will minimize speech processing difficulties encountered in the learning environments. The audiologist must be prepared to investigate whether binaural aids will improve discrimination in noise, whether the use of an FM unit is advisable, and whether an FM-loop-telecoil system will overcome some of the child's difficulties, while reducing others.

At present, there is a need to identify a comprehensive battery of rehabilitative audiologic test procedures for widespread use. It is too easy to blame the inadequacy of present assessment practices on the audiologist. However, there is doubt that a large part of the problem rests in the audiologist's lack of understanding of the nature of speech, speech articulation, speech assessment, and speech teaching. The audiologist must learn what the speech teacher does and needs. Similarly, the speech teacher must recognize amplification as the most valuable aid in speech training. He/she must understand its capabilities and limitations and must be competent in its use.

Conclusion

The teaching of speech requires a team approach utilizing the knowledge and skills of the classroom teacher, speech teacher, and audiologist in a coordinated teaching plan. Coordination means an integrated, not parallel, process. These observations urge the author to argue for a modification in the training of audiologists and speech teachers. It is important to recognize our need for each other and the child's need for both of us. The nature of this conference should facilitate this recognition.

REFERENCES

Berger, K., & Millin, J. P. Hearing aids. In D. E. Rose (Ed.), *Audiological assessment.* Englewood Cliffs, N.J.: Prentice Hall, 1971.

Bess, F. H. *Characteristics of children's hearing aids in the public school.* Final report, Dept. H.E.W., U.S. Off. Educ., Grant and Procurement Management Div., 41, USC 252 (c)(d), 1976.

Bode, D. Speech signals and hearing aids. In M. Pollack (Ed.), *Amplification for the hearing impaired.* New York: Grune & Stratton, 1975.

Börrild, K. Classroom acoustics. In M. Ross & T. Giolas (Eds.), *Auditory management of hearing impaired children: Principles and prerequisites for intervention.* Baltimore: University Park Press, 1978.

Bragg, V. C. The Bragg SPL Converter: *A counseling guide teaching aid and hearing aid selector.* San Antonio, Texas: Hearing, Ltd., 1977.

Byrne, D., & Fitfield, D. Evaluation of hearing aid fittings for infants. *Brit. J. Aud.*, 1974, 8, 47–54.

Finitzo-Hieber, T. *The influence of reverberation and noise on the speech intelligibility of normal and hard of hearing children in classroom size listening environments.* Doctoral dissertation, Northwestern University, 1975.

Gengel, R. Discussion: Aided speech reception of hearing impaired children, perceptual and cognitive strategies. In R. E. Stark (Ed.), *Sensory capabilities of hearing impaired children.* Baltimore: University Park Press, 1974.

John, J. E. J. Acoustics and efficiency in the use of hearing aids. In A.G.W. Ewing (Ed.), *Educational guidance and the deaf child.* Manchester: Manchester University Press, 1957.

McCandless, G. A. Special consideration in evaluating children and the aging for hearing aids. In M. Rubin (Ed.), *Hearing aids: Current developments and concepts.* Baltimore: University Park Press, 1976.

Nablek, A. K., & Pickett, J. M. Reception of consonants in a classroom as affected by noise, reverberation and hearing aids. *J. Acoust. Soc. Am.*, 1974a, *56*, 628–639.

Nablek, A. K., & Pickett, J. M. Monaural and binaural speech perception through hearing aids under noise and reverberation with normal and hearing impaired listeners. *J. Speech Hear. Res.*, 1974b, *17*, 724–739.

Paul, R. L. *An investigation of the effectiveness of hearing aid amplification in regular and special classrooms under instructional conditions.* Doctoral dissertation, Wayne State University, 1967.

Ross, M. Classroom acoustics and speech intelligibility. In J. Katz, (Ed.), *Handbook of clinical audiology* (2nd ed.). Baltimore: Williams and Wilkins, 1978.

Sanders, D. A. *Aural rehabilitation.* Englewood Cliffs, N.J.: Prentice Hall, Inc., 1971.

Sanders, D. Noise conditions in normal school classrooms. *Excep. Child,* 1965, *31*, 344–353.

Tillman, T. W., Carhart, R., & Olsen, W. O. Hearing aid efficiency in a competing speech situation. *J. Speech Hear. Res.*, 1970, *13*, 789–811.

PART II

Speech Training for the Hearing Impaired: Principles, Objectives, and Strategies

9
Speech Training for the Hearing Impaired: Principles, Objectives, and Strategies for Preschool and Elementary Levels

Sister Roseanne Siebert

ALEXANDER GRAHAM BELL ONCE SAID, "One of the greatest achievements in the world is that of a child born deaf who learns to talk." (A.G. Bell Assn., 1979). Anyone who is involved in teaching speech to hearing-impaired children would agree wholeheartedly with this statement. Teaching a hearing-impaired child to talk is indeed a great achievement, and helping him speak with ease and intelligibility represents one of the greatest challenges facing educators of the deaf today. What are the basic principles upon which this goal is based? What objectives should guide our efforts in this direction? What strategies must be utilized to achieve success? This paper is an attempt to present some answers to these questions.

Teaching speech to hearing-impaired preschool and primary children is not only a challenging task, but also a rewarding experience. At St. Joseph Institute for the Deaf in St. Louis, Missouri, dedicated teachers have faced this challenge and have seen their efforts rewarded in the child who is eventually able to move out into society, confident and proud of his ability to communicate orally. In this writing, the principles and objectives of speech development are those currently in use at the St. Joseph Institute for the Deaf.

Principles of Speech Development

It is the belief of all who serve at St. Joseph's that *speech is the right of every child, regardless of the degree of hearing loss or additional handicap*. It is this principle that guides all interactions with hearing-impaired children. The Sisters of St. Joseph are dedicated to helping all children reach their highest potential as persons. For most hearing-impaired children, reaching their highest potential includes achieving the ability to speak intelligibly. With this skill, many of the limitations that might otherwise restrict personal-social growth are eliminated, and the possibility for a richer, fuller life experience is opened up.

Learning activities are directed by a basic principle of speech development, specifying that *the success of any program of speech instruction hinges on the skill of the person responsible for speech development. Each teacher in the preschool and primary classes is responsible for the speech development of the children she teaches.* It is her task to determine the skills needed by the children, to provide the necessary instruction, and to see that these skills are reinforced throughout the school day. It is also her task to keep all those who have contact with the child outside the classroom informed of progress and capability in speech, in order to assure that expectation levels are consistently realistic for all children.

Preschool and primary children have unique needs that must be taken into account when planning a program of speech instruction. These needs and their impact on the instructional program must be recognized to guide efforts in teaching speech. Some of the needs of the young hearing-impaired child that should be considered when planning programs of speech instruction are: the need to be actively involved in the process, not just verbally, but physically as well; the need for success and positive reinforcement; the need for love and support for all efforts; the need for personal, one-to-one attention, for egocentricity and for feelings of self-importance in all that is undertaken. These basic needs of the child may be incorporated in speech instruction for younger children in various ways. For example, lessons may include some kind of activity or game to keep the child actively involved and to stimulate interest. Practice items, which will give the child a feeling of success, as well as items involving the development of new skills, are part of every lesson. In addition, the teacher is constantly aware of praising and rewarding the child's efforts during the speech lesson. Rewards may include simple verbal expressions of approval, points, stars, or other tangible rewards. Lessons are conducted on a one-to-one basis, so the child is given the teacher's undivided attention during this period of the day. Every attempt is made to include material that is personal to the child. Such materials may consist of self-generated sentences or information known to have high interest value or to be within the child's experiential background.

In addition to recognizing these very basic needs, *each child's strengths and weaknesses should be determined.* The strengths should be capitalized upon in planning the instruction, and in determining specific techniques utilized to remediate weaknesses. If the weaknesses cannot be remediated, specific strategies should be used to teach the child how to compensate for these weaknesses. If adequate attention is given to the unique needs of the young hearing-impaired child, then speech instruction will be the exciting, rewarding experience it should be.

In his text, Ling (1976) has discussed speech development as an orderly process. Since speech develops in an orderly manner in the normal child, *the hearing-impaired child should also be taught in the same orderly manner.* Implementation of this basic principle is essential in planning an effective speech program.

Ling has described the orderly process of speech development and has suggested a model to be used in teaching speech to hearing-impaired children. This model has been adopted at the St. Joseph Institute for the Deaf and with some modifications is being used with the preschool and primary children. For the hearing-impaired child to move through the normal stages of speech development successfully, a number of additional components must support the process utilized to achieve the goal of satisfactory speech production.

Effective evaluation techniques should be employed, not only to determine need for further development, but also to discover those skills already mastered but not consistently used in meaningful speech. Each teacher in the preschool and primary departments is responsible for evaluating the speech of the children she teaches. Formal assessment is accomplished using Ling's phonetic evaluation instrument. Informal assessment is made by using either tape recordings of the child's running speech and/or by simply listening to the child's spontaneous utterances throughout the day, and then determining which skills have or have not been mastered. The results of these evaluations are then used as a basis for setting up specific targets to be developed on phonetic and phonologic levels.

Since speech is learned best through audition, maximum use of residual hearing should be part of all speech instruction and should be supplemented by the use of taction and vision when needed. All children are given extensive training in the utilization of residual hearing, with consistent and appropriate amplification being provided for each child. Great care is taken to see that no child is ever without proper amplification, and maintenance of both individual and group amplifying systems is given top priority at St. Joseph Institute.

Speech is a motor skill, and as such requires adequate motor control to be intelligible. It is probable that children having problems with gross motor control might also have difficulty with the fine motor control involved in speech. Recognizing this fact, the preschool and primary children, who give evidence of motor involvements, are given consistent regular training and practice in developing adequate skill.

Speech is a learned skill which must be taught to the hearing-impaired child. As a skill, speech requires sufficient practice for mastery. Daily individual speech training is the rule for preschool and primary children. This training includes the development of specific skills in addition to practicing skills already acquired.

The last principle of speech development relates to the type of atmosphere most conducive to growth in verbal skills. *Speech is developed most effectively in an environment that is relaxed yet demanding when it comes to the use of speech.* This principle should and does determine the atmosphere in the classrooms, hallways, dining rooms, dormitories, and play areas, where children are constantly encouraged to use the speech skills they have learned. In this setting, the child discovers that speaking satisfies his or her need to share thoughts and ideas with others. The child also learns that speech is a powerful tool for manipulating the environment.

Overview of the Speech Program

The principles of speech development and training discussed above have determined the character of the speech program. With this in mind, an overview of the structure of the program is presented before discussing the specific objectives and strategies employed to achieve intelligible speech—the primary goal of instruction.

In planning the individual child's speech program, the needs of that child are first considered. For some children, a structured, analytic approach to speech development is needed. This is especially true for children with severe memory problems or other deficits that make the learning of speech especially difficult. With other children, an unstructured, more spontaneous, synthetic approach is more effective.

Initially, when working with a child on speech skills, imitation is the primary technique employed. Later on, as the child develops reading skills, written material may be introduced if it is felt that such materials will aid the child's memory for speech.

Expectations with respect to speech production are very much determined by each child's stage of development. Exact articulation is expected if the child has all the skills necessary for precise articulation. However, if the child is lacking the necessary skills, an approximation is accepted.

There are four basic components to the preschool-primary speech program: tongue drills and breath control exercises, sound development and syllable drills, vocabulary and sentence work, and auditory development with utilization of visual and tactile clues when necessary. This program is supported by a number of other services offered outside the classroom. All children participate in a daily rhythm and music class where they are taught songs, dances, and rhythmical movement. Those children evidencing motor deficiencies are given special help in the learning center. The time spent in the center depends on the needs of the individual child. Those children with severe involvements receive help each day, while others may go two or three times a week for specialized training in perceptual-motor skills.

Every child in the preschool and primary departments receives 15 minutes of individual speech work every day. A very brief part of this time is spent developing tongue and breath control. The greater portion of the lesson is devoted to developing and practicing phonetic skills and encouraging carry-over of previously developed skills. Throughout a speech lesson, auditory clues are emphasized, but visual and tactile clues are provided when needed.

Objectives for Speech Development

The objectives of speech development and the strategies utilized in the process in the preschool and primary departments are as follows:

1. To vocalize and use voice meaningfully;
2. To develop a pleasant and relaxed voice quality;
3. To vocalize with proper pitch, intensity, and duration;
4. To develop imitative ability in respect to speech production;
5. To develop good tongue and breath control;
6. To make maximum use of residual hearing to improve reception and aid speech production;
7. To supplement auditory reception of speech with visual and tactile clues;
8. To correctly articulate the vowels and consonants of English in syllables, words, and sentences;

9. To use the skills mastered on the phonetic level in spontaneous speech;
10. To feel pleased and satisfied with communicative efforts, using speech; and
11. To recognize speech as an effective and valuable means of manipulating the environment to satisfy personal needs.

These are the objectives, but to think that all these objectives are accomplished with every child by the end of the preschool-primary years would be a false assumption. Some of these objectives are ongoing and receive attention throughout the child's academic years.

Strategies for Speech Development

Before any formal speech work is begun, it is imperative that some vocalization be present. All opportunities for encouraging vocalization are utilized by the teachers working with the young preschool child. The children are expected, encouraged, and helped to "ask" for what they want or need, to comment on or verbally react to the situations they encounter throughout the day, and to use speech in their interactions with one another and with the adults in their environment.

Since most children at 3½ or 4 years of age are already vocalizing and using their voices meaningfully, it is possible to begin formal speech training almost immediately. As previously mentioned, imitation is the primary technique used during the speech development period. Syllables, words, and sentences are spoken first by the teacher and then imitated by the child. With the young child who has difficulty in understanding the task of imitating speech, it is sometimes necessary to begin by imitating simple gross motor movements, and then move to imitation of lip movements and sound production. Part of the daily rhythm and music program is the imitation of movements and rhythm. This may be accomplished by using rhythm sticks or dance to establish patterns for imitation. These activities help develop imitative motoric skill which contributes to speech development.

Throughout the speech lessons the use of audition is emphasized. In the initial development of speech skills, group amplifiers are used because (1) they are generally more powerful and more consistent in terms of the auditory signal received by the child, and (2) they amplify a wider range of frequencies needed in receiving the speech signal. Individual aids are used in some speech work, particularly when children are practicing skills already acquired, and in all activities during rhythm and music periods.

Speech is a skill involving adequate control of tongue movements and the breath stream. The children in the preschool and primary departments spend a brief part of each lesson concentrating on these two skills. The tongue drills simply teach the child to control the tongue: to lift, point, flatten, etc. Usually a mirror is used during these drills, so that the child can compare his or her tongue movements with those of the teacher.

The purpose of the breath control exercises is to help the child maintain a continuous flow of speech without having to pause unnaturally for breath. To accomplish this, the child takes a deep breath and babbles continuously until he or she runs out of air. Blowing pinwheels and blowing up balloons are examples of other activities which help develop breath control. Although not all children need this type of training, it is recommended for those who have difficulty with tongue and breath control. Clinical experience indicates that such training improves the child's potential to use speech effectively.

Few children possess sufficient auditory capacity to learn speech utilizing only auditory clues. For most children, audition must be supplemented by visual and tactile clues. The approach most often used during speech training is to move from a visual-auditory (and tactile if needed) stimulus to an auditory-only stimulus. Once a child has developed a particular skill, the practice and drill of that skill is generally primarily auditory.

As previously mentioned, the development of the phonetic elements of speech with the preschool and primary children is carried out utilizing Ling's model. The subskills included in this model are taught utilizing many of the techniques suggested by Ling, as well as other techniques which have been used successfully in this educational setting for many years. For example, the piano and xylophone are used extensively to emphasize rhythmical speech and to gain approximation of pitch. These strategies are considered to play an important supportive role in the overall speech program.

According to Ling, speech patterns taught at the phonetic level do not need to be taught again at the phonologic level. While this statement is generally true, it is also true that most children with severe to profound hearing impairments cannot be expected to automatically use an acquired phonetic level skill on the phonologic level. Children need to be encouraged to correctly use speech patterns taught at the phonetic level in the broader, more demanding context of meaningful speech. Consequently, extensive work in fostering the use of phonetic skills in meaningful expression is a very important part of the speech program. At this stage, the child is taught to incorporate those skills acquired on the phonetic level into words and sentences. The vocabulary used may be based on a particular sound, or it may be centered around a particular category, such as foods, clothes, etc. In the first type of lesson, one particular sound may be reinforced in many different contexts, while in the second type of lesson, many sounds may be practiced. Both lessons will include some approximations for sounds the child has not yet mastered.

The goal of the sentence work is not only to encourage carry-over, but also to practice appropriate rhythm, intonation, and timing in speech. The sentences used may be programmed by the teacher, or they may be initiated by the child. The technique used depends upon the individual student. If the child initiates sentences, then these ideas can be incorporated in the sentences used during part of the speech lesson. On the other hand, it is sometimes necessary for the teacher to prepare sentences for the lesson. For example, nursery rhymes may be introduced for development of appropriate rhythm and intonation. Rhymes, which are enjoyable, may also be used to reinforce those skills.

The ultimate goal of the speech development program is to have the child use the skills he has mastered during the speech period in his spontaneous communications throughout the day. Accomplishing this goal is dependent upon the motivation of the child, but more importantly, in the beginning stages of speech development, upon the awareness and encouragement of those who are his speech monitors, namely his teachers, parents, and houseparents. The teacher must be constantly on the alert to help the child use the skills developed. She must be convinced that correction, modeling, and imitation will eventually result in improved speech production, and she must gradually move the responsibility for correct production to the child. At the same time, she must keep the parents and houseparents informed of the child's progress in acquiring speech skills, so that their expectation levels will be consistent with hers. Working together toward the goal of intelligible speech will eventually bring results well worth the time and effort.

The child's motivation to improve speech is also an important factor in bringing about successful carry-over. Parents and teachers play an important role here also. Basic to the desire to improve is the feeling that it is worth the effort. If parents and teachers let children know that their efforts at using speech are appreciated and valued, and if they provide children with experiences which help them realize the effectiveness of speech, then children will be motivated to use speech and to improve those aspects that interfere with effective communication.

Conclusion

Teaching a hearing-impaired child to speak with ease and intelligibility is a great achievement and an exciting challenge. Success in this endeavor is dependent upon a program of speech instruction based upon solid principles, guided by realistic and obtainable objectives, and achieved through the utilization of effective strategies. It is hoped that the ideas presented here will help those who teach speech meet the challenge and experience the joy of helping a child reach the goal of intelligible speech.

REFERENCES

Ling, D. *Speech and the hearing-impaired child: Theory and practice.* Washington, D.C.: A.G. Bell Association for the Deaf, 1976.

Statements on deafness. Washington, D.C.: A.G. Bell Association for the Deaf, 1979.

10
Speech Training for the Hearing Impaired: Principles, Objectives, and Strategies for the Intermediate Level

Sister Joyce Buckler

IF WE BELIEVE THAT SPEECH, as the accepted medium of human communication, is the right of every child, then no effort should be spared in order to give this gift to all hearing-impaired children. If the richness of verbal communication is to be enjoyed by hearing-impaired children, they have the right and we have the responsibility to equip them with the skills necessary for effective communication. Clear, intelligible speech makes this possible and is the challenge for those devoted to the full development of hearing-impaired children.

To be effective, speech programs for hearing-impaired children need to have solid principles upon which objectives are developed and strategies are applied. This presentation outlines key principles which may be considered basic in any program providing excellent quality in speech instruction. Objectives based upon these principles and strategies found to be most successful with schoolchildren 9 to 15 years of age are discussed.

Since this paper and the preceding one by R. Siebert were written by professional personnel from the same educational setting, St. Joseph Institute for the Deaf, the overall philosophy and most principles pertaining to speech development discussed by Siebert are applicable for children at elementary as well as intermediate levels of instruction. To avoid redundancy, this current discussion will address: teacher qualifications, student assessment, and speech instruction involving strategies particularly appropriate for children 9 to 15 years of age.

Teacher Qualifications

If Ling (1978, foreword) is correct when he says, "Faulty speech [of hearing-impaired children] is more frequently due to inadequate teaching than to impairment *per se*," then the teacher is the key to the success of any speech program and must possess basic qualities.

Since the objective is to provide quality speech instruction, a teacher must believe that hearing-impaired children can acquire intelligible speech. Unless the teacher has this conviction, the hard work necessary to aid hearing-impaired children in their speech development will be considered nonproductive. As a result, the consistent demand necessary for constant use of good speech will be lacking.

A teacher must have adequate and appropriate experience in the teaching of speech, for teaching speech is a skill perfected only with practice. Extensive experience in speech teaching must be provided by the teacher education program in cooperation with the laboratory school. To limit a student teacher in this area of skill development is to affect the speech development of hearing-impaired children for years to come.

A teacher must have knowledge of the physiology and neurology of the auditory and speech mechanisms in order to plan appropriate strategies in training speech. A teacher also must have the skills necessary to identify those factors which influence a child's speech production. To develop this skill, extensive practice in listening to the speech of hearing-impaired children is necessary. The ear must be trained to consistently monitor and discriminate acceptable versus unacceptable speech.

The teacher must be aware that speech is not an isolated entity. Speech interrelates with language, thought, and perception. A fundamental understanding of the interrelationships between cognition, language, and communication is needed if speech skills are to be integrated in the total educational plans. Provision for this integration must be part of the speech program if a successful transition from the phonetic to phonologic levels of speech is expected.

The teacher must be skilled in the use of both the formal and informal assessment of speech, knowledgeable about objectives of speech development, and experienced in the application of various approaches to successful speech development. A strength of any program is its well-trained, dedicated staff, and to assure satisfactory qualifications of the teaching staff, only those applicants with excellent teacher education backgrounds should be employed. Those teachers with years of successful experience in teaching speech to profoundly hearing-impaired children should serve as consultants to beginning teachers. Full-time supervisors also should be employed to monitor the teaching of speech. Such supervisors should be held responsible for the quality of daily speech instruction provided to each child in their respective departments.

Assessment and Programming

Assessment of the status of a child's speech skills is basic to planning a developmental speech program. In assessment and programming, each severely and profoundly hearing-impaired child is considered unique. This uniqueness goes beyond the fact that children enter strong programs at different ages and with differing backgrounds. The uniqueness reaches into the areas of intellect, auditory potential, personality, and overall motor intactness. These factors affect the child's ability to develop clear, intelligible speech and also may affect learning style and rate. In this respect, they exert a powerful influence upon the strategies utilized in instruction. Because intellect, auditory potential, personality, and overall motor intactness are highly important to academic planning, a careful analysis in these areas is a prerequisite to individualized education plans.

Intelligible speech is characterized by a normal rate of speed, appropriate use of breath stream, variation in pitch and appropriate rhythm, a pleasant voice, and correct articulation. Objectives flowing from this principle are: to develop the child's imitative ability; to encourage meaningful vocalization; to develop good tongue and breath control; to develop the nonsegmental aspects of speech—intensity, duration, and pitch; to develop the phonetic elements of speech emphasizing coarticulation and automaticity; and to assure the incorporation of phonetic skills in phonologic speech using proper rhythm, accent, intonation, and phrasing.

To accomplish these objectives, the following strategies are used: repetitive speech tasks to develop imitative ability; babbling to maintain a pleasant voice and to gain control of the breath stream; use of the xylophone, piano, songs, and rhymes to improve auditory perception for pitch and to develop and maintain control of pitch, duration, and intensity during speech; and phonetic skill development utilizing the techniques suggested by Ling (1976, 1978), and Sister Laurentine (Lorenz, 1970, 1971, 1974, 1978). In all instruction, consistent use of appropriate amplification is required. Though children benefit greatly from individual hearing aids, the auditory trainer has been found to be more effective in the development of speech skills. Both systems are used in the classroom setting.

As children move into the middle grades, work on the speech targets, delineated by Ling (1978), is continued if automaticity has not been achieved. To facilitate transfer of skill to the phonologic level, vocabulary from content subjects, songs, poems, prayers, and other controlled speech materials are used extensively.

Vocabulary development for comprehension and expression receive major emphasis. At approximately 9 years of age, or younger if appropriate, children are expected to know from memory all the sounds of the Northampton Charts and to be able to classify syllables and words under the correct spellings. One approach used by teachers is to dictate syllables or words with children responding by identifying the correct sounds on the chart and/or writing the syllables or words under appropriate headings. Before a child writes the syllables or words, the sound pattern must be repeated. Appropriate language in response is also required.

Other visual aids are used for frequent, quick review of the sounds. These aids provide practice for groups of sounds, e.g., *boo boo boo; foo fa(r) foo;* etc. Accent work is also practiced in this manner. At this age, children should learn the appropriate language model, e.g., "The accent is on the ____ syllable," "The ____ syllable is accented."

Children learn to express themselves in various ways. One strategy found very helpful in speech, as in other subjects, is teacher role playing. In this activity the child, acting as the teacher, is provided meaningful speech practice, and also practice in listening to and/or speechreading other children in class. Older children, 10 to 15, are taught to monitor the speech of their peers. They are responsible for challenging one another, e.g., "You left out the ____ sound," "You forgot to say the ____ sound in ____," "You accented the wrong syllable," "____ is a three-syllable word; you gave it only two," etc.

The developmental content of the speech program for children from fifth to eighth grade is presented in the speech books written by Sister Laurentine. These four books were designed for sequential speech and language development. For the fifth-grade children (Lorenz, 1970), definite procedures are explained, and practice materials provided to assist in mastery of consonant blends appearing in words taken from fifth- and sixth-grade content subjects. For the sixth-grade children (Lorenz, 1971), the speech program includes: teaching rules for syllabification, difficult consonant combinations, and unusual pronunciations of the "ch" sound. Specific components of the seventh-grade program (Lorenz, 1974) include: exercises for the "j" sound, rules and practice for pluralization, past tense, changing verbs to nouns; and work on homographs and similar-looking words which children find confusing. The eighth-grade speech curriculum (1978) includes words derived from Greek. This is particularly interesting since Greek mythology is part of the eighth-grade literature program. At this level, extensive practice is provided to change nouns to adjectives, to classify appropriately, to use analogies, to understand and use unusual words and words with unusual endings, e.g., *vogue, league,* etc. The speech training for older children continues to stress syllable drills, proper phrasing, syllabification of words, and daily practice for individually defined speech goals.

Using the speech books developed by Sister Laurentine, daily work on vocabulary is undertaken. A typical unit consists of definitions, accent work, exercises on phrasing, and sentences incorporating the vocabulary. For the 10- and 11-year-olds, definitions are provided; for the 12- to 15-year-olds, independent use of the dictionary is required. The children are also required to spell the word, tell the number of syllables in the word, identify similarities between words on a page, identify the accent, etc. These steps should be completed before studying the vocabulary to avoid meaningless, incorrect practice. All sentences in the speech curriculum for the 10- to 15-year-olds are discussed with the children to assure comprehension. The phrasing and accenting of the sentences are sometimes directed by the teacher, and at times directed by the child with the teacher as monitor.

More informal periods of speech training for our older children, as well as for younger children, may consist of work on common expressions or idioms which have come up spontaneously in conversation or in reading. Speech lessons may be built around incidental language needs for activities such as bowling, swimming, and the various school sports.

Supplementary listening and speech practice is provided for all children by means of Language Masters and tape recorders. Speech drills, vocabulary units, sentences, and stories are recorded by the individual teacher for respective classes. This material is listened to and orally practiced by the children at various periods throughout the week. Though not a replacement for the teacher, this practice has proven very beneficial for speech and vocabulary development, and for auditory training.

Once speech skills are mastered on the phonetic level and practiced on the phonologic level, all teachers are responsible for incorporating these skills in classroom communications and in daily conversations. Since speech production may be affected by tension, boredom, and lack of motivation, it is critical that the speech training periods be relaxing and enjoyable for the child, despite the hard work involved. Well-planned lessons at an appropriate level for success will reduce tension for both the teacher and the child. The teacher who not only recognizes errors, but immediately knows how to help the child correct the errors, increases motivation and the overall effectiveness of the training.

If the hearing-impaired child is expected to continue using good speech, he/she must experience a supportive speech environment and acquire skills for independent growth in verbal communication. A supportive environment can be assured provided all who are related to the child know his/her level of speech achievement and require constant use of the skills mastered. To make this possible, frequent observations in children's classes and frequent communication between teachers and parents and/or houseparents regarding speech skills are essential.

As children enter the middle grades, greater emphasis is placed upon helping them become more independent and more responsible for applying learned skills to new materials and new situations. Activities such as acting, reading, conducting class meetings, and choral speaking provide opportunities to use previously mastered speech skills in new situations beyond the academic setting.

Summary and Conclusions

It is difficult to develop clear, intelligible speech in children with severe hearing impairments. If intelligible speech is to be achieved, a speech program must be based on sound principles; it must have demanding yet attainable objectives, and must employ a variety of workable strategies. Skilled and talented teachers, knowledgeable and supportive parents, and an environment which encourages and requires oral communication are all essential components in a successful speech program.

The development of an organized, sequential speech program must be based on an appropriate assessment, using both formal and informal techniques to identify phonetic and phonologic speech targets, and to serve as a guide for determining strategies. Designing activities and situations for application of speech skills will assure the hearing-impaired child needed practice and growth in the independence necessary for continued success.

Speech success is not the right of a select few, but of every severely and profoundly hearing-impaired child in this country. The responsibility and challenge to help these children achieve success in communication is yours and mine!

REFERENCES

Ling, D. *Speech and the hearing-impaired child: Theory and practice.* Washington, D.C.: A.G. Bell Association for the Deaf, 1976.

Ling, D. *Teacher/clinician's planbook and guide to the development of speech skills.* Washington, D.C.: A.G. Bell Association for the Deaf, 1978.

Lorenz, Sister L. *Book V. Let's talk.* St. Louis: St. Joseph Institute for the Deaf, 1970.

Lorenz, Sister L. *Book VI. Let's talk more.* St. Louis: St. Joseph Institute for the Deaf, 1971.

Lorenz, Sister L. *Book VII. Let's talk more and more.* St. Louis: St. Joseph Institute for the Deaf, 1974.

Lorenz, Sister L. *Book VIII. Let's talk more and more and more.* St. Louis: St. Joseph Institute for the Deaf, 1978.

11

Speech Training for the Hearing Impaired: Principles, Objectives, and Strategies for the Secondary Level

Margot Cusack

SECONDARY SCHOOL EDUCATORS look upon hearing-impaired teenagers in a variety of different ways. Some educators see them as vibrant young people, struggling with internal conflicts, but eager to learn and grow. To other educators, adolescents are young people biding their time until they are guided by vocational counselors into the "real world" beyond high school. To still others, teenagers are already final products of their earlier years of education, too rigid to change.

Educators' views of their students have a great deal to do with the type of speech program, if any, that will be planned. Educators who recognize adolescent potential and motivation for growth, particularly in verbal communication, offer individual developmental speech tutoring and require speech in a wide range of situations. Educators who do not recognize potential for further growth may provide some monitoring for maintenance of acquired speech skills and perhaps some structured opportunities for speech practice in real life or simulated situations. Those who view adolescent speech as unalterable or unresponsive to change may not provide any program for verbal communication development.

The experienced teacher/clinician recognizes the potential for speech improvement in most hearing-impaired adolescents. Data presented by Donnelly (1964) and Lieberth and Subtelny (1978) support the concept that both receptive and expressive skills can be improved in hearing-impaired students of college age. Today, hearing-impaired students are guaranteed by law appropriate, individually planned educational programs. Teachers and clinicians, therefore, have a legislated obligation to evaluate each individual's needs in order to provide a speech program that will be effective. It is, of course, possible that for certain students, particularly those with multiple handicaps, priorities for the development of basic life skills may preclude developmental speech work. The decision to give precedence to basic life skills must be made after careful assessment. Educational planning should be based on student needs and potential rather than on existing program opportunities.

Pronovost (1978) has described a general program of communication development for hearing-impaired students at the secondary level. Other than this, relatively little has been written on the topic, and many specific questions about the nature of speech programs for secondary students remain to be answered. This paper will attempt to delineate some of the objectives, principles, and strategies that merit consideration in the formulation of such a program.

Objectives

Most educational programs aim to prepare people to function independently while seeking fulfillment of physical, psychological, and social needs. Programs for hearing-impaired adolescents are no exception. By virtue of their membership in a very specialized group, hearing-impaired teenagers have additional skills to master if they are to exercise options in the management of their lives.

Even if students are completely mainstreamed, they may choose to associate with other deaf teenagers (Cohen, 1978). In this case, these young people will need both oral and manual skills. They will also need to shift from one mode of communication to another, and to know when such a shift is needed. Regardless of close personal associations, all hearing-impaired people can be expected to have some contact with the hearing and speaking population. The climate in which this contact occurs is beginning to undergo significant change.

Public Law 94–142 emerges out of heightened sensitivity to the needs and rights of the handicapped. Section 504 of the Vocational Rehabilitation Act (P.L. 93–112) opens all programs and activities receiving federal assistance to qualified handicapped persons. Special adjustments in physical environments are being required in these facilities and in public buildings; funding also is being provided for interpreters and other support personnel. In recent months, movies and television have presented stories about handicapped people with successful lives. Newspaper and magazine articles on travel, hobbies, and other leisure activities for handicapped persons have appeared with increasing frequency. In specific response to the needs of hearing-impaired television viewers, technology for broadcasting closed captions has been developed, and home equipment will be available in 1980. As a result, hearing-impaired people will be brought into contact with new worlds of information and enjoyment. If media coverage and the passage of laws are a reflection of change in public attitudes, it follows that there is greater tolerance of individual differences and an expansion of the life arena for handicapped persons.

The task of educators of hearing-impaired young people is to prepare them to function more effectively in this expanded milieu. Skills which permit verbal interchange are highly important in this regard. Ease and confidence in speech reception and speech production may be important contributors to the hearing-impaired individual's ability to achieve satisfaction both socially and professionally. The choice of primary communication modality is a personal one that must be made by each hearing-impaired person. The unfortunate reality today is that inadequate speech training programs may compel many young people to choose manualism by default. It is the educator's responsibility to provide adequate training in speech development so that the hearing-impaired adolescent is afforded a realistic choice.

Principles and Strategies

The Adolescent

Life is a process of continual physical and psychological growth for all of us. But the adolescent is special because he or she is in a constant and dramatic state of flux. Adolescents often strive to become contributing members of a group, while simultaneously searching for unique identities and purposes in life. They often feel emotionally tied to their parents, but they are anxious to establish themselves as individuals. The carefree life of a child is appealing, but so are the rights and responsibilities of adulthood. The turmoil often created by these conflicting forces may affect, to some degree, the adolescent's participation in a speech training program.

The rapid physical growth in size and mass of the larynx, resulting in lowered fundamental pitch and altered dynamic range, may contribute to voice control problems. If the voice pitch does not stabilize appropriately and regain its normal variation by the time the growth spurt is completed, specific therapy may be advisable (Head, 1978).

Psychologically, the teenager may be in such turmoil that he or she is too distracted to concentrate on the developmental and carry-over activities required in a speech training program. Even if the disturbance is not severe enough to warrant psychotherapy, some modification of the speech program may be needed. Modification may include: ignoring or informally commenting on unacceptable behaviors; altering the program itself to include a bare minimum of drill while concentrating on linguistic application of skills; focusing on a speech activity specifically requested by the student; and/or building units around special interests. By adopting a flexible approach, teachers can maintain rapport and prevent escalation of simple issues into complicated problems. Speech work can thus continue, providing opportunities for additional harmonious work in the future.

For some hearing-impaired adolescents, alienation from parents, if the parents are normally hearing, may be especially intense (Cohen, 1978). In addition, these adolescents may transfer their alienation to hearing adults in general and to the oral mode of communication. In this case, the teacher may consider engaging the student in an earnest discussion of the present and future value of verbal communication abilities. The point emphasized is that work on these skills during the early teenage years will avoid later regret that communication was not given proper attention. This is exemplified by previously apathetic high school seniors who begin demanding speech services once they seek employment, and by graduates who have learned the value of spoken language skills from new perspectives in the "outside" world.

Some adolescents lack all discipline or motivation to work on speech because they have experienced actual failure and/or have come to perceive themselves as incapable of learning speech. In such cases, every effort should be made to encourage the young person to take advantage of available services. If such efforts fail, a speech training program may have to be abandoned.

Guiding hearing-impaired adolescents to make full use of a speech program requires sensitivity, integrity, and maturity on the part of the speech teacher. A teacher who tries to be a "pal" to an adolescent can no longer be an effective adult model (Mitchell, 1971). The teacher often loses the young person's respect and becomes unable to motivate him to work on speech skills which are valuable in adult life.

The Spoken Language Acquisition Task

Hearing-impaired adolescents may, depending on the status of their speech skills at the time of entry into a secondary program, need to go through the early stages and processes in acquiring spoken language. They still need to acquire the cumulative package of physical vocal skills and to develop an effective auditory kinesthetic feedback loop enabling them to reproduce vocal patterns reliably. They must have sufficient practice producing speech to acquire automaticity (Ling, 1976). The strategies for guiding hearing-impaired teenagers through this process of speech development must be specially tailored to the attitudes and interests of adolescents.

Use of Hearing. Since the efficient development of speech is based on sound, residual hearing must be fully utilized in hearing-impaired individuals. The value of amplification and training may be effectively presented to adolescents by offering an elective course on the science of hearing and hearing loss, the acoustics of speech, and other related topics. Such information may assist the adolescent in better understanding the nature of his or her handicap and the rationale and procedures employed in rehabilitation.

Adolescents need well-fitting, well-functioning hearing aids and convenient access to an audiological service for periodic testing, hearing aid evaluations, and minor repairs. A pool of loaner hearing aids can help provide consistency of amplification. A speech training unit which provides a high-quality extended frequency range signal is beneficial for students who can use extra auditory information during speech training sessions and when loaner aids are not available.

Students may reach adolescence without effective auditory speech decoding strategies; however, these strategies may be developed if students wear their aids consistently and participate in guided training activities (Hoversten et al., 1979). Improvement in auditory decoding of speech segments may be developed within the context of individual speech training.

Ling (1978) speculates that discriminations learned at the phonetic level may not necessarily transfer to discriminations of the same patterns in running speech. Listening exposure and discrimination practice on the phonologic level are, therefore, recommended.

Structure of Teaching/learning Activities. Hearing-impaired adolescents with minor articulation errors for consonants or blends, and with a functioning auditory kinesthetic feedback loop enabling them to learn new skills with relative ease, respond well to a variety of speech activities. In contrast, those with many automatized and resistant errors may require a more structured approach, such as the three-activity format developed at the Lexington School for the Deaf (Osberger et al., 1978). These three activities have been found to contribute to the establishment of an auditory kinesthetic feedback loop and to improved reception and production of speech.

1. *Imitation.* Students are asked to imitate the teacher's model through audition alone. If residual hearing or listening experience is limited, multisensory cues are added to the stimulus. These cues are then withdrawn so that attention is focused on the auditory pattern, and imitation follows.

2. *Production on demand.* Students are asked to generate the pattern without a spoken model. Students are asked to either recall a pattern practiced earlier in the session or to produce a pattern from a visual prompt. This activity weans students from dependence on a model and pushes them in the direction of spontaneous production.

3. *Discrimination.* Students are asked to discriminate between the target pattern and others. Within limits of residual hearing, students are asked to repeat what they hear and then to identify the pattern by pointing to one of several of the visual prompts. The conscious identification of the target ensures that the student is not simply parroting, but is cognitively aware of the characteristics that distinguish the target from other patterns.

There is no set order of presentation for these tasks within a single teaching session. There are, however, some guidelines for order of presentation over the course of training based on the abilities of the student. If, for example, a student can discriminate a target before it can be produced, a variety of discrimination activities can be presented first. If, on the other hand, the student learns to produce the pattern before it can be discriminated, imitation and production or demand activities should receive attention first. As reported by Lieberth and Subtelny (1978), abundant practice in production and exposure to auditory patterns result in concomitant improvement in auditory perception. If, of course, certain discriminations remain impossible for a student to make, the auditory task may be abandoned.

Evaluation of Speech and Formulation of Instructional Plan

Individual programming begins with individual evaluation. A variety of factors deserve consideration if the teacher is to develop a complete understanding of the student's speech behavior (Ling, 1976). In particular, knowledge of the student's language level is essential to the development of appropriate phonologic practice materials. Two tools are recommended for evaluation of hearing-impaired adolescents' speech: the Phonetic Level Speech Evaluation and the Phonologic Level Speech Evaluation, both formulated by Ling (1976). Administration of these tests will provide a clear picture of strengths and weaknesses in both production ability and usage. If the teenager's speech is highly intelligible, the phonologic measure may be administered first. Those patterns found to be faulty may then be checked phonetically to determine on which level the breakdown occurs. If the student's speech is not highly intelligible, the phonetic test may be given first through Step 4 consonants to determine all of the voice patterns, vowels and diphthongs, and consonants in the student's repertoire. These acquired patterns can then be used in varied combinations during practice on the four to six targets chosen for work. In this case, the phonologic assessment that follows need not be completed. Rather, the teacher need only determine whether phonetically acquired skills are, in effect, being used (Ling & Ling, 1978).

After the evaluations and analysis of results, a speech training plan for the adolescent can be formulated. A number of variables must be considered in this formulation. The teacher/clinician should try to determine the specific characteristics which, if changed, would contribute the most to intelligibility (Pronovost, 1978). The establishment of priorities in training on this basis is especially critical for adolescents who have few school years remaining in which to effect improvement. Other factors to consider in planning speech training include: the speech features which are most easily improved (Pronovost, 1978); the student's attitude toward a particular task (Raph, 1960); and the amount of time that can be devoted to speech work.

Ling's recommendation that speech work focus simultaneously on multiple targets at varying stages and levels of development is especially important for adolescents. If students have experienced previous failure, they will need to experience rapid success in some areas in order to sustain motivation to work.

A balance of phonetic and phonologic targets is necessary. In the author's experience, a confident teacher who understands the rationale for phonetic skill development is unlikely to meet resistance to vocal and syllable drills if the adolescent understands that drills are a necessary part of the program. An analogy can be used: Practicing the serve, forehand, and backhand is necessary before one can play a full game of tennis.

Activities to facilitate transfer of more advanced phonetic skills into usage are most effective if they are based on the interest and language level of the student. Such activities should proceed from easy to difficult phonetic contexts and from more structured to less structured linguistic contexts (Fleming, 1971; Winitz, 1975).

Carry-over

The time adolescents spend in speaking and listening activities on phonetic and phonologic levels will, indeed, result in improvement in skills. In general, the more time and attention given to the task, the greater degree of improvement realized. Although carry-over of the skills into consistent spontaneous use is not guaranteed, a number of strategies may be employed to assist it.

Only skills that reach an automatic level of production can be expected to carry over into spontaneous use. In working for carry-over, it is recommended that only one skill receive focus at a time. Sometimes verbal or written contracts made with students will help to focus attention on target behaviors. Such contracts are recommended, for in the process of setting realistic and responsible goals the student is directly involved in the planning (Hilgard, 1956).

Carry-over can begin with the teacher monitoring the target skill in spontaneous speech for short periods which are progressively lengthened. The teacher and the student can then move out of the physical setting of the tutorial session into new and unfamiliar surroundings. Gradually, situations containing an emotional overlay can be introduced in the form of competitive games or sensitive topics of conversation. Finally, the target skill can be monitored by people other than the speech teacher, beginning with one or two very supportive persons and expanding to the wider population (Winitz, 1975). Monitors may include parents, siblings, and other significant individuals in the student's life. The most important consideration in the choice of the monitors is their relationship with the teenager. If a personal relationship is undergoing stress, the additional task of monitoring a speech target should not be imposed upon it.

An environment in which adolescents are motivated to make themselves understood through speech provides the optimum condition for speech to continue to improve. Development of intelligible speech is one of the factors that allows students to communicate freely in this type of environment. Educators of the hearing impaired need to work to propel more students into this cycle of success.

Conclusion

If we as educators wish to encourage and inspire hearing-impaired adolescents to strive to reach their highest potential, we must work to improve the programs which will allow them to do this. In the area of speech, we will need commitment to the value of oral/aural communication and confidence in the student's potential to improve. We will also need funds and energies directed toward the implementation of well-designed programs, skilled and sensitive personnel to carry them out, and research to evaluate training programs and to provide direction for the future.

Acknowledgment

The author wishes to express special thanks to Janet M. Head, M.A., Speech Supervisor, Lexington School for the Deaf, for her guidance and assistance in the preparation of this manuscript.

REFERENCES

Cohen, O. P. The deaf adolescent: Who am I? In A. Neyhus & G. Austin (Eds.), *Deafness and adolescence.* Washington, D.C.: A.G. Bell Association for the Deaf, 1978.

Donnelly, K. *Hearing therapy for young deaf adults: An experimental study.* Washington, D.C.: Auditus Publications, 1964.

Fleming, K. J. Guidelines for choosing appropriate phonetic contexts for speech sound recognition and production practice. *J. Speech Hear. Dis.*, 1971, *36*, 356–367.

Head, J. *Adolescents with "new" voices.* Paper presented at a meeting of the A.G. Bell Association for the Deaf, St. Louis, June, 1978.

Hilgard, E. R. *Theories of learning.* New York: Appleton-Century-Crofts, 1956.

Hoversten, G., et al. *Auditory skills instructional planning systems.* Hollywood, Ca.: Foreworks, 1979.

Lieberth, A., & Subtelny, J. D. The effect of speech training on auditory phoneme identification. *Volta Rev.*, 1978, *80*, 410–417.

Ling, D. *Speech and the hearing-impaired child: Theory and practice.* Washington, D.C.: A.G. Bell Association for the Deaf, 1976.

Ling, D. Auditory coding and recoding: An analysis of auditory training procedures for hearing-impaired children. In M. Ross & T. G. Giolas (Eds.), *Auditory management of hearing-impaired children.* Baltimore: University Park Press, 1978.

Ling, D., & Ling, A. H. *Aural habilitation: The foundations of verbal learning in hearing-impaired children.* Washington, D.C.: A.G. Bell Association for the Deaf, 1978.

Mitchell, J. J. *Adolescence: Some critical issues.* Toronto: Holt, Rinehart & Winston of Canada, Ltd., 1971.

Osberger, M. J., Johnstone, A., Swarts, E., & Levitt, H. The evaluation of a model speech training program for deaf children. *J. Comm. Dis.*, 1978, *11*, 293–313.

Pronovost, W. L. Communicating with the world at large. In A. Neyhus & G. Austin (Eds.), *Deafness and adolescence.* Washington, D.C.: A.G. Bell Association for the Deaf, 1978.

Raph, J. B. Determinants of motivation in speech therapy. *J. Speech Hear. Dis.*, 1960, *25*, 13–17.

Winitz, H. *From syllable to conversation.* Baltimore: University Park Press, 1975.

12

Speech Training for the Hearing Impaired: Principles, Objectives, and Strategies for the Postsecondary Level

Brenda K. Humphrey, Marianne Streff Gustafson, and Ann K. Lieberth

THIS DISCUSSION OF SPEECH TRAINING at the postsecondary level for the hearing impaired is based upon clinical experience with students at the National Technical Institute for the Deaf (NTID). Young adults entering NTID come from varied educational backgrounds ranging from residential schools for the deaf to traditional public schools. Within this population, some have had extensive speech therapy, whereas others have had limited training. NTID students exhibit a broad range of competence and confidence in communication skills. Our mission becomes one of offering a variety of courses designed to accommodate specific needs for improving aural/oral communication.

For the purpose of this discussion, it is expedient to group the population into three general areas based on speech training needs, ignoring for the moment the interplay with hearing discrimination, speechreading, and language competence. The groups consist of students needing: 1) voice therapy; 2) remedial training in speech sound production; and 3) refinement or conservation of oral communication skills.

The first group generally consists of unintelligible speakers who display poor respiratory control, excessive vocal tension, and/or inappropriate pitch. They need training in coordination of respiration and phonation to produce an acceptable voice quality and to develop a speech sound system. These students generally receive individualized voice therapy as one of the initial steps in training. Materials have been written at NTID to aid the teacher in such training.

The second category of students generally are semi-intelligible to intelligible speakers who demonstrate reasonable proficiency in the basic parameters of voice production. However, they exhibit deviancies in segmental (phonemic) and suprasegmental (prosodic) aspects of speech. Research at NTID and elsewhere has shown that articulatory proficiency is highly correlated with speech intelligibility (Markides, 1970; Smith, C., 1975; Subtelny, 1977). The implication is that an improvement in phoneme production will result in improved intelligibility. Given this supposition, coupled with the time limitations at the postsecondary level, it seems logical to focus training efforts for this group on correcting articulation, with secondary emphasis on prosody. Since approximately 50 percent of the students who have entered NTID possess some discrimination for speech (Johnson, 1976), materials for speech production training have been designed to make maximal use of residual hearing in conjunction with speechreading skill. While optimally used with students who demonstrate an ability to auditorily discriminate speech sounds, they are adaptable for students with more limited perceptual skills. These materials will be described in greater detail in this paper.

The third group of students generally are intelligible speakers who demonstrate adequate respiratory, phonatory, and articulatory skills. They need refinement and maintenance of aural/oral communication skills, which can be accomplished through group instruction. Several courses have been designed for speech and listening practice while focusing on pronunciation, vocabulary development, and conversational dialogues.

Descriptions of the design and evaluation of most of the materials and curricula mentioned above have been presented and/or published elsewhere (Humphrey et al., 1979; Lieberth & Subtelny, 1978; Maki & Streff, 1978; McMahon & Subtelny, 1976; Nutter, 1975; Orlando, 1975; Smith, J., 1975; Spector et al., 1979). The purpose of this paper is to describe the Speech and Auditory Training (SAT) program, an approach used in speech training for students who have some hearing discrimination for speech and are candidates for individualized articulation training. The theoretical framework, objectives, principles, and strategies will be discussed.

Theoretical Framework

Procedures in teaching speech to the deaf generally have been influenced by the results of auditory testing. Oyer (1966) and Ewing and Ewing (1967) have concluded that the quality of speech produced by hearing-impaired individuals is directly influenced by their abilities to perceive their own speech and the speech of others. Speech pathologists and audiologists have recognized the primacy of the auditory channel in the development, correction, and refinement of the phonologic and language systems (Fry, 1978; Ling, 1978; Magner, 1971). The strong influence of the auditory feedback systems is dramatically reflected in the speech disorders of the deaf (Black, 1971). Ling (1976) states that audition provides both proprioceptive and exteroceptive cues and therefore is superior to both vision and touch in teaching speech to the deaf. Because of the close relationship of production and auditory perception, training in either skill probably should not be treated as a separate, independent activity, at least in remediation of the speech problems of the hearing-impaired young adult. Auditory training often is recommended to improve perception, which ultimately results in improvement of speech production (Asp, 1975; Winitz, 1975). It follows, therefore, that effective and efficient aural rehabilitation should utilize and improve both expressive and receptive skills.

Objectives

Using the above information as a base, the general objective of the SAT program is to maximize the use of residual hearing as a conceptual and perceptual base for correction of deviant articulation in both structured and spontaneous speaking situations. Auditory discrimination and speech training materials were written to achieve the following specific objectives: 1) to develop auditory perception of a selected target by contrasting that phoneme with its substitution; 2) to further develop perception by contrasting the target with phonetically similar phonemes in the student's repertoire; 3) to train correct speech production of a target, simultaneously shaping the cognate; 4) to stimulate other deviant phonemes within the manner category; 5) to develop active and accurate self-monitoring skills; and 6) to reinforce appropriate prosodic features. Secondary objectives of this program are to achieve consistent production of phonemes previously noted as correct, to reinforce and/or improve speechreading skills, and to model and encourage correct English usage.

Principles of Program Design

In order to meet these objectives, a number of basic principles were incorporated in the design of the SAT materials. These principles are drawn mainly from research and theories related to auditory training and correction of articulation.

Training Principle 1: *Discrimination training, when used in production training, is most effective and efficient if it is based on the error patterns as evidenced on discrimination and articulation tests.*

Auditory discrimination and articulation testing should be completed before production training begins. The results of testing may indicate consistent error patterns on phonemes that are identified auditorily but are not produced correctly, or vice versa. The tests may also reveal features of the error sound that are present in the student's repertoire and can be used in training . Thus, by identifying response patterns, a base for discrimination and production training can be established using skills available to the student to develop those skills that are absent or in error.

Training Principle 2: *Speech production is enhanced if the student can discriminate between the standard and error productions of a phoneme before production training begins.*

After the response patterns have been identified and the target for correction has been selected, discrimination training should begin. The starting point in auditory training is perception of some difference between two units (Ling, 1978). Using the student's substitution and the correct production of the target phoneme, which is a same/different word discrimination task, an auditory cue system is developed upon which the student can base an auditory feedback system. It is through this system that speech is developed and refined (Fry, 1978). If an auditory distinction of these differences is not possible, then the contrast items should be presented using the auditory and visual modes (Ross & Giolas, 1978). If the distinction is still not possible using auditory-visual modeling, production training should continue.

Training Principle 3: *Speech training should provide sufficient practice of a target to facilitate transfer to spontaneous speech.*

Transfer of a sound to conversation is related to the level of articulatory proficiency achieved in isolated words and sentences. According to Ling (1976), accuracy of production alone is not an adequate criterion of success. The new skill must be accurately performed without conscious attention to articulation, which would interfere with higher level activities required for spoken language. The SAT program provides opportunities for repeated performance so that the sound can be produced with ease, in various phonetic contexts at a rate required in normal speech.

Training Principle 4: *Learning new articulatory behaviors should occur in a sequential hierarchy of difficulty in perception and production with each step building upon success at the previous step (Winitz, 1969, 1975).*

The speech component of the SAT program consists of 14 steps divided into a hierarchy of six phases. In Phase I, the target is trained in syllables. This is followed in Phase II by practice of the target in CVC words. Phase III incorporates these words into determiner-noun phrases. In Phase IV, the target is trained in simple sentences which include commonly used expressions of high pragmatic value. Sentences involving tense conversions or answers to yes-no questions comprise Phase V. Finally, in Phase VI, sentences are formulated in response to Wh-questions. Progression is controlled by establishing a 90 percent criterion level at each step. Auditory training activities, utilizing the same stimuli, accompany each step in the speech training materials. In addition to program materials, training involves practice of the target at the conversational level. A student does not complete the program for a particular target until 90 percent accuracy is demonstrated in a spontaneous speech sample.

Auditory Training Sequence: Training should begin with discrimination activities that involve large phonetic differences to enable success (thus increasing motivation) and to build an acoustic cue system of features and "non-features" of the target phoneme. Using the same principle, activities should proceed from identification tasks to binary comparisons (same/different activities) to closed set word discriminations and, finally, to discrimination of sounds in running speech. In the SAT program, tasks proceed from identification of the target in syllables (Ling, 1978) to words and finally to words embedded in sentences. The tasks in auditory discrimination of distinctive features are ordered from simple to complex. In this sequence, training to discriminate differences in manner precedes training to discriminate differences in voicing and place of production (Ling & Ling, 1978; Ross & Giolas, 1978).

Speech Training Sequence—Syllables: Consonants should be taught initially in syllables, in the context of the vowels which precede and follow them (Ling, 1976). There are several reasons for beginning with syllable training. First of all, consonants generally do not exist in isolation, but serve to release or arrest syllables with a vowel nucleus (McDonald, 1964). Second, teaching consonants in isolation may impair acquisition and transfer because coarticulatory facilitation is absent. Third, teaching a sound in syllable context avoids the concept of the phoneme as a static neuromuscular event. Finally, words may contain semantic, lexical, and morphemic associations that elicit the error sound, whereas nonsense syllables are less likely to contain these cues (Winitz, 1975). The first step of the SAT program, therefore, involves teaching correct production of the target with the vowels /i,a,u/. These are combined in VC and CV contexts, at a rate of three per second. These three vowels were chosen because they require the extremes of tongue movement, thus avoiding centralization of vowels while teaching variations of the target sound imposed by phonetic context. This syllable training is aimed at automaticity of the target at the phonetic level.

Speech Training Sequence—Words: The newly acquired articulatory skill must be transferred to a variety of phonetic contexts to ensure appropriate coarticulation both within and between words. Transfer requires practice of the numerous variations of the target which result from phonetic environment or the influence of neighboring vowels and consonants. Training for this type of within-word coarticulation is introduced in SAT Phase II, which contains varied CVC words. Between-word coarticulation is trained when targets appear in phrase and sentence contexts. Such contexts provide practice in producing abutting consonants and in developing appropriate coarticulation for all elements in the larger phonetic string.

Training Principle 5: *Transfer of the target from the phonetic level to the phonologic level is facilitated by training production from an auditory-visual model followed by print.*

Hypothetically, an auditory-visual stimulus should provide maximal cues for production of the response. In the SAT program, the student attempts initially to produce words, phrases, and sentences following an auditory-visual model. When this presentation mode is not sufficient, simultaneous exposure to print may provide additional cues based on previously developed sound-letter associations. Later in the program, the student is required to read from print alone. This stimulus provides linguistic and orthographic cues, but requires retrieval of correct target production from memory.

Training Principle 6: *Transfer of the target from the phonetic to the phonologic level is facilitated by requiring the student to self-generate an increasing proportion of the response.*

Beginning with Phase V of the SAT program, the student is provided with an auditory-visual model of a sentence, but must self-generate all or part of the response. Thus, the student's attention is diverted from the act of articulation to the formulation of grammatically correct and meaningful sentences. Correct production of the modeled target word might reflect learning on the phonetic level, yet one might assume that other spontaneous words containing the target or its cognate reflect transfer of the sound to the phonologic level.

Training Principle 7: *Immediate feedback and consistent reinforcement of correct responses enhances learning of the target sound.*

Immediate reinforcement, if specific and consistent, should increase the frequency of correct target productions (Mowrer, 1973). Throughout the materials, every response is monitored. The therapist gives immediate feedback regarding correctness of the target by marking the response sheet. In a less formal manner, the cognate is monitored for accuracy of production, as are other phonemes in the student's phonetic repertoire.

Training Principle 8: *Self-monitoring is necessary for establishing carry-over of the target sound to spontaneous speech.*

Self-cuing is advocated by Winitz (1975) to assist not only in the transfer process from structured to conversational speech but also in maintenance of the acquired level of achievement. Within each step of the program, the student must self-monitor, judging productions as correct or incorrect. The therapist then provides feedback as to the appropriateness of the self-evaluation.

Training Principle 9: *Reinforcement of suprasegmental aspects of speech production, such as rate and blending, must be included in training.*

A characteristic exhibited by hearing-impaired speakers is abnormal or slowed rate of articulation. Therefore, it becomes imperative to establish acceptable rate early in target training. Ling (1976) purports requiring repetition of syllables at a rate of three items per second. The SAT program incorporates this rate of syllable repetition in the initial step of training to facilitate a normal rate of production when the target is transferred to words.

Other prosodic problems include a lack of natural syllable concatenations within phrasal units and inappropriate pause (Stevens, 1978). When these problems are encountered, blending may become a specific target for correction, depending upon student capabilities.

Training Principle 10: *Transfer of learning should be tested since training on a target may generalize to other error sounds* (Winitz, 1975).

Previous research (Hudgins & Numbers, 1942) has shown that production errors are frequently substitutions from within the same manner, place, or voicing categories. When this occurs, the target and its substitution error contain common acoustic and articulatory features which may facilitate generalization of target training.

Studies with normally hearing populations have shown that generalization occurs from trained to untrained phonemes when these errors seem related to inappropriate feature usage rules (McReynolds & Bennett, 1972; Costello & Onstine, 1976). At present, feature usage rules in hearing-impaired speakers seem poorly defined, and research to study generalization has been inconclusive (Metz et al., 1978).

Auditory discrimination training may facilitate generalization if the features of the error phoneme are present in the student's discrimination repertoire as determined by testing. Auditory training may then be designed with contrast activities. By developing a set of auditory cues for a particular phoneme and by contrasting that phoneme with others in the same manner class, the student may develop a cue system for that class which, in turn, can be used in production training. The auditory cues can be used in generalizing information about the class and its members. With hearing-impaired students, better identification of phonemes within a particular category is associated with fewer articulation errors within that category (Ling, 1976).

In the SAT program, probe production tests are used at three points in training to evaluate transfer of target training to other error sounds within the same manner category. The degree of generalization determined by probes serves to guide further training.

Training Principle 11: *Learning is enhanced by listening and speaking practice outside of the structured therapy situation.*

If the student can demonstrate 90 percent accuracy in self-monitoring productions, independent practice can be undertaken to reinforce both production and discrimination training. All discrimination activities are prerecorded. The student listens and writes responses to the stimuli on answer sheets provided. The student then checks responses and listens again to identify errors. By using an additional practice tape, the student can record production of the items he/she has listened to, rewind the tape, and identify errors. Thus, self-monitoring skills are further developed.

Strategies

It should be evident from an understanding of the principles above that the SAT program was designed mainly to achieve improved production of a selected target phoneme and its cognate as a means of increasing intelligibility of spontaneous speech. It is emphasized, however, that simple use of the materials does not assure the goal will be met. The program was not designed as an all-inclusive package accommodating every training need. It serves only as a tool in the hands of a skilled therapist. Application of the principles and the success of training are governed by the student's consonant/vowel discrimination, spoken error pattern, and other training needs. The therapist must employ clinical judgment and intervention strategies when anticipated progress is not achieved in perception and/or production training. Special strategies will be discussed as they relate to each training principle.

Training Strategy 1

The student receives complete articulation and auditory discrimination testing before production training begins. The therapist identifies the error patterns in perception and production by manner category. By comparing perception and production scores, the therapist can choose the target phoneme for correction in which the auditory mode can be utilized to the greatest advantage. The therapist can also identify consistencies in error pattern, and phonemes correctly identified that share features with the target phoneme. These phonemes will be used in the contrast activities to aid in building an auditory cue system for the target phoneme.

Training Strategy 2

The therapist should contrast the target phoneme and the student's error substitution for the phoneme if that substitution is consistent. The items for contrast should be presented in word context. First, the therapist should try an auditory stimulus alone. Correct identification of the word pair as same or different should be reinforced with an auditory-visual model. If the student misses three stimulus items in a row, the stimulus should be presented in both the auditory and visual modes. Thus, in either event the student is developing a total concept of the target phoneme. This is a general sequence followed in all auditory discrimination activities.

Training Strategy 3

Although the training materials provide numerous opportunities to practice a target, it is sometimes necessary to provide additional practice of a selected response. For example, when a target word is wrong on the initial trial, but the student self-corrects or is guided to correction, many repetitions are needed to bring that response to an automatic level. It is also possible to provide practice of an established correct target while shaping production of phonemes across that manner category in a sentence context.

Training Strategy 4

Achieving the 90 percent criterion for correct production at each sequential stage and in conversation does not always occur on the initial trial. Therefore, clinical judgment must serve as a guide. Sometimes only additional trials are needed to meet criterion. If success still is not achieved, intervention strategies are indicated. If such intervention fails, it is possible that the target was not firmly established at an earlier step, thus requiring repetition of that step.

To ensure carry-over of the correct target into spontaneous speech by the termination of the program, 5 to 10 minutes of conversational practice are needed in each therapy session. Percentage of correct productions should be calculated and words containing the target noted for further practice. In the initial phase, the therapist should provide feedback as to phoneme accuracy but, gradually, the responsibility for monitoring should be shifted to the student.

Auditory Training Strategy: Specific items used in auditory contrast activities should be chosen to complement those presented in production training. Auditory discrimination activities are sequenced from same-different contrasts in syllables and words, to discrimination of words within sentences. All auditory contrasts of the target within the same manner category differ first by voicing, then by place.

Speech Training Strategy—Syllables: Since an auditory-visual model is not always sufficient in initial syllable training of a target, numerous strategies can be employed to teach the desired production. Only a few of those more commonly used will be addressed.

In a few instances, only the instruction to use a lighter articulatory contact is needed to enhance air flow on fricatives or to reduce exaggerated plosion on stops. If this is ineffective, then direct training on a feature, or features, might be necessary. For example, training continuancy might be the only strategy necessary to establish an acceptable /s/. The cognate /z/ might then be trained by adding voicing concurrently produced with frication. Similarly, shaping of sounds across manner categories can be enhanced by utilizing correctly established features of sounds in other classes. For example, the place and voicing features of /g/ can be used for shaping /ŋ/.

One problem commonly encountered in training at the syllable level is that students attempt the same articulatory contact point for a phoneme regardless of the adjacent vowel. This lack of proper coarticulation results in either distortion of the vowel or incorrect production of the phoneme. Thus, a student may have to be taught several variations of a phoneme. For example, it might be necessary to explain or visually illustrate the place difference between the /k/ in the syllables /ik/ and /ak/.

Although the target can be produced accurately in single syllables, some students experience difficulty with rapid syllable repetitions. Again, use of a lighter articulatory contact might be employed. Another strategy would be to gradually increase the syllabic units, such as building from "as" to "asa" to "asas," etc., until an acceptable rate is achieved.

Speech Training Strategy—Words: Strategies are sometimes necessary to facilitate transfer from production of the target in repetitive syllables to use of that sound in words and sentences with varied phonetic contexts. For example, a student may be able to produce the syllable /ɪk/ easily and rapidly alone or in the word "kick." However, it may be necessary to teach him to anticipate the more forward tongue placement for /k/ dictated by the initial /θ/ in the word "thick."

Another area of concern deals with production of stops in the final position. For example, the student may be able to produce both an aspirated and unreleased /t/ in the word "cat," but does not know which to use at the sentence level. The therapist might need to specify the phonetic environments which predict the allophonic variations. This can be illustrated by contrasting aspirated /t/ in the sentence "The cat had fleas," and unreleased /t/ "The cat came home."

Between-word coarticulation is sometimes difficult for students who have limited consonant discrimination and/or tend to approach sentences on a word-to-word basis. Therefore, training the production of abutting consonants that share the same manner category, for example, "hot dog," "half full," and "this ship" is one area of focus.

It might also be necessary on the sentence level to train coarticulation of abutting consonants across manner categories. Here it is sometimes helpful to practice on an embedded nonsense word alone, and then within a sentence context, such as /swil/ from "The bus will leave," or /gwəz/ from "The dog was barking." In the above strategies the student is required to produce the sentence at an increasingly more natural rate to ensure proper coarticulation.

Students also tend to have difficulty producing the target correctly in blends and clusters within words. To facilitate production of blends, it is sometimes sufficient to bring to their awareness the fact that both phonemes must be articulated, but with a rapid transition. Other times, it is necessary to provide syllable practice with that blend before expecting production in words.

Training Strategy 5

Students are not always able to imitate an auditory-visual model. However, certain strategies may facilitate comprehension of the stimulus. After presentation of an auditory-visual model, the student should be required to repeat as much of that stimulus as possible. The therapist should then model the sentence again for added exposure on words not comprehended or phonemes misarticulated. If the student still does not identify all the words, the therapist may allow him to read the stimulus. Alternatively, the therapist may choose to isolate the missing word or words. For example, in the sentence, "The *rug* covered the floor," the student may not speechread the stimulus word "rug" because of limited lingual visability or due to its coarticulation with the word "covered." Therefore, the therapist may present the word in isolation, or use it in another context such as "Yesterday, we bought a new *rug*," where the stimulus appears at the end of the sentence. If the student continues to fail, then it is always possible to identify the first or last letter in the word or to write the word.

Another factor influencing some students' repetition of the stimulus is their limited knowledge of the English language. They may receive the sentence correctly, but repeat it incorrectly because of grammatical errors inherent in their expressive language. Alternatively, they may not even comprehend the initial stimulus. Therefore, reading from print provides reinforcement for correct grammatical structures.

A third area of concern is that the student may experience difficulty with pronunciation of unfamiliar vocabulary words. Reading from print may provide sufficient cues to elicit the correct response. On the other hand, the therapist may need to rely on a phonetic symbol system for further clarification of pronunciation.

Training Strategy 6

The therapist's task becomes threefold when a student begins to self-generate responses. First, the student must be given feedback as to the correctness of the trained phoneme in the target word. Second, the therapist must monitor use of the target and its cognate in other words. Third, it is essential to provide feedback regarding the appropriateness of linguistic structures. An example may help to illustrate the above three areas. In step 12 of the /t/ materials appears the sentence, "What did you write?" A hypothetical response might be, "I write a note my Dad," /aɪ raɪt ə not maɪ dæt/. The target word, "write," is scored as correct. However, the cognate appearing in the final position in the word "Dad" is in error, and should be stimulated. Finally, the sentence contains omission of the preposition "to" and inappropriate tense. Clinical judgment must serve as a guide in determining the amount of time spent in language training. All that might be necessary to facilitate the correct response is modeling the linguistic structures, and asking the student to repeat the sentence. Reading from print can also serve to reinforce appropriate English.

Training Strategy 7

In order to provide immediate, consistent reinforcement of correct productions of a target phoneme it is imperative that both the therapist and the student know the criteria for acceptance of the response. This criteria may change during the course of therapy as shaping of the target sound occurs. It might be necessary, for example, to accept a prolonged production of a fricative, such as /z/, in the initial stages of training. This allows the student time to achieve and monitor correct articulation. Once the target is established, the therapist must alter the criteria to accept only those productions at a more natural rate. The student must understand why responses previously reinforced are no longer acceptable.

Similar consistency is necessary when reinforcing the cognate. Monitoring should begin at the word level with verbal reinforcement for correct productions and auditory-visual models if the phoneme is incorrect. This should continue until the target is well established at a phrase level. Then some therapy time might be devoted to direct training on the cognate.

When the student has progressed to training on the sentence level, the three reinforcement principles previously described are employed simultaneously. Most importantly, the student is given immediate feedback regarding every production of the target and its cognate. Second, auditory-visual models are provided for other misarticulated phonemes within that manner category. Finally, correct production of sounds within the student's phonetic repertoire is required.

Training Strategy 8

Most students must be guided in developing self-monitoring skills. Some students are able to readily self-monitor target productions in the practice materials, but must be encouraged to carry over this skill into spontaneous speech. Other students experience difficulty even within the controlled self-monitoring activities. Often the therapist must cue the student to focus on auditory and/or tactile feedback, then make an immediate decision regarding correctness. Feedback on the appropriateness of self-evaluation should follow. Self-monitoring skill is developed through this process of pairing student and therapist judgments. This skill can be expanded to include the following: monitoring multiple occurrences of the target within a sentence; judging production of the cognate; and spontaneous self-correction.

Training Strategy 9

Ideally, in the later phases of training, a phoneme is not scored as correct until it is appropriately blended at an acceptable rate. However, this is not realistic for all students. Appropriate prosodic goals should be apparent from success achieved in target training at the levels discussed under strategies 3 and 4. Generally, no special strategies are required, except perhaps to remind students to produce an entire phrase or sentence on one exhalation.

Training Strategy 10

Student performance on probes should be evaluated to guide further training. An analysis of target and cognate error patterns may dictate a need for additional auditory training. On the other hand, further intervention strategies for production may be warranted. Analysis of the final probe, which assesses production of other sounds within that manner category, should indicate subsequent targets for training.

Summary

In summary, the ultimate goal of speech training with postsecondary students with impaired hearing is to improve functional aural/oral communication skills. Differential approaches in training are dictated by marked variation in student needs and background.

The Speech and Auditory Training (SAT) program was described as one approach used in training students who have semi-intelligible or intelligible speech, reasonable proficiency in voice production, and some auditory discrimination for speech. The need for coupling perception and production training was discussed, with objectives stated for both auditory and speech components. Principles underlying the program were discussed and supported by strategies.

REFERENCES

Asp, C. W. Measurement of aural speech perception and oral speech production of the hearing-impaired. In S. Singh (Ed.), *Measurement procedures in speech-hearing-language.* Baltimore, Md.: University Park Press, 1975.

Black, J. W. Speech pathology for the deaf. In L. E. Connor (Ed.), *Speech for the deaf child: Knowledge and use.* Washington, D.C.: A. G. Bell Association for the Deaf, 1971.

Costello, J., & Onstine, J. The modification of multiple articulation errors based on distinctive feature theory. *J. Speech Hear. Dis.*, 1976, *41*, 199–215.

Ewing, A., & Ewing, E. C. *Hearing aids, lipreading, and clear speech.* Washington, D.C.: A. G. Bell Association for the Deaf, 1967.

Fry, D. B. The role and primacy of the auditory channel in speech and language development. In M. Ross & T. Giolas (Eds.), *Auditory management of hearing-impaired children.* Baltimore, Md.: University Park Press, 1978.

Hudgins, C. V., & Numbers, F. C. An investigation of the intelligibility of the speech of the deaf. *Gen. Psych. Mono.*, 1942, *25*, 289–392.

Humphrey, B., Subtelny, J., & Whitehead, R. Evaluation of structured speaking and listening activities for hearing-impaired adults. *J. Comm. Dis.*, 1979, *12*, 253–262.

Johnson, D. Communication characteristics of a young deaf adult population: Techniques for evaluating their communication skills. *Am. Ann. Deaf*, 1976, *121*, 409–423.

Lieberth, A., & Subtelny, J. The effect of speech training on auditory phoneme identification. *Volta Rev.*, 1978, *80*, 410–417.

Ling, D. *Speech and the hearing-impaired child: Theory and practice.* Washington, D.C.: A. G. Bell Association for the Deaf, 1976.

Ling, D. Auditory coding and recoding: An analysis of auditory training procedures for hearing-impaired children. In M. Ross & T. Giolas (Eds.), *Auditory management of hearing-impaired children.* Baltimore, Md.: University Park Press, 1978.

Ling, D., & Ling, A. *Aural habilitation: The foundations of verbal learning in hearing-impaired children.* Washington, D.C.: A. G. Bell Association for the Deaf, 1978.

Magner, M. E. Techniques of teaching. In L. E. Connor (Ed.), *Speech for the deaf child: Knowledge and use.* Washington, D.C.: A. G. Bell Association for the Deaf, 1971.

Maki, J., & Streff, M. M. *Clinical evaluation of the speech spectrographic display with hearing-impaired adults.* Paper presented at the American Speech and Hearing Association convention, San Francisco, 1978.

Markides, A. The speech of deaf and partially hearing children with special references to factors affecting intelligibility. *Brit. J. Dis. Comm.*, 1970, 5, 126–140.

McDonald, E. *Articulation testing and treatment: A sensory-motor approach.* Pittsburgh: Stanwix House, Inc., 1964.

McMahon, M., & Subtelny, J. *Evaluation of simultaneous listening, reading, and speaking as a technique for improving the conversational speech of the hearing-impaired.* Paper presented at the American Speech and Hearing Association convention, Houston, 1976.

McReynolds, L., & Bennett, S. Distinctive feature generalization in articulation training. *J. Speech Hear. Dis.*, 1972, *37*, 462–470.

Metz, D., Card, S., & Spector, P. *A distinctive features approach to the remediation of voicing errors produced by hearing-impaired adults.* Paper presented at the American Speech and Hearing Association convention, San Francisco, 1978.

Mowrer, D. A behavior approach to modification of articulation. In W. Wolf & D. Goulding (Eds.), *Articulation and learning.* Springfield, Ill.: Charles C Thomas, 1973.

Nutter, M. Development of pronunciation skills. *J. Acad. Rehab. Aud.*, 1975, *8*, 122–125.

Orlando, N. Evidence of success in speech and voice training. *J. Acad. Rehab. Aud.*, 1975, *8*, 51–63.

Oyer, H. J. *Auditory communication for the hard-of-hearing.* Englewood Cliffs, N.J.: Prentice-Hall, 1966.

Ross, M., & Giolas, T. (Eds.). *Auditory management of hearing-impaired children.* Baltimore, Md.: University Park Press, 1978.

Smith, C. R. Residual hearing and speech production in deaf children. *J. Speech Hear. Res.*, 1975, *18*, 795–811.

Smith, J. Speech and voice therapy at NTID. *J. Acad. Rehab. Aud.*, 1975, *8*, 117–121.

Spector, P., Subtelny, J., Whitehead, R., & Wirz, S. Description and evaluation of a training program to reduce vocal tension in adult deaf speakers. *Volta Rev.*, 1979, *81*, 81–90.

Stevens, K. *Word and syllable concatenation in the speech of the deaf.* Paper presented at the A. G. Bell Association for the Deaf convention, St. Louis, 1978.

Subtelny, J. D. Assessment of speech with implications for training. In F. H. Bess (Ed.), *Childhood deafness: Causation, assessment and management.* New York: Grune & Stratton, 1977.

Winitz, H. *Articulatory acquisition and behavior.* New York, N.Y.: Appleton-Century-Crofts, 1969.

Winitz, H. *From syllable to conversation.* Baltimore, Md.: University Park Press, 1975.

13
Summary Comment: Principles, Objectives, and Strategies for Speech Training

Helen R. Golf

"THE MORE ONE LEARNS, the more one finds out how much one does not know!" The current state of the art regarding the speech of hearing-impaired persons exemplifies this old saying well. Information presented at this Institute confirms the fact that more knowledge and research are needed on all aspects of speech training.

It is discouraging to review the literature and see that recent studies suggest that overall levels of speech intelligibility have improved very little over the past 40 years, but we must be realistic and stop ignoring such findings. Advanced hearing aid technology combined with research and emerging knowledge in acoustic phonetics and speech science should have had an influence on the speech of the hearing impaired. Equally discouraging is the study by Jensema, Karchmer, and Trybus (1978), which indicates that particularly above the age of 7, there is no overall improvement in speech intelligibility with age.

Factors Contributing to Attainment of Intelligible Speech

Those characteristics which contribute to the attainment of intelligible speech must be investigated if we are to alter this negative data in succeeding years. There are educational programs which succeed in improving the intelligibility of students' speech during the course of their school years. There are also programs in which high levels of intelligibility are achieved for most students, including those with severe and profound losses. What are the most important factors which seem to account for the differences?

Positive Attitude Toward the Value of Oral Communication

High levels of expectancy for the development of verbal skills, the recognition of the importance of speech communication skills to the hearing-impaired person who seeks to function independently as a member of society at large, and the knowledge and belief that hearing-impaired individuals can develop intelligible speech seem to encourage success. A self-fulfilling prophecy that poor or unintelligible speech is a natural consequence of hearing impairment, prevails in numerous programs.

Effective and Skillful Teachers

The greater the child's hearing loss, the more skilled the person teaching speech must be. Unfortunately, the majority of teachers in this country have received inadequate training and practicum experience and therefore lack the necessary knowledge and skills for effective speech teaching. Inadequate speech programs and/or lack of alternative educational opportunities are forcing many students into manualism, and *not only* those with severe and profound losses.

A Systematic Speech Program

Ling (1976) proposed a model for a systematic program of speech development and evaluation procedures which correlate with the model. It has gained widespread popularity and adoption during the past three years. This certainly has been a very significant contribution and one that was desperately needed, but one needs more than a model to work effectively. One needs the skill to evaluate performance and the ability to select and implement appropriate teaching strategies to develop intelligible speech. Knowledge of alternative techniques is also essential. Individual speech teaching must occur every day and ideally must be scheduled several times a day.

Appropriate Amplification and Maximal Development of Residual Hearing

The optimal use of residual hearing is difficult to achieve. Appropriate, well-functioning hearing aids are the exception rather than the rule in spite of advanced hearing aid technology and the greater availability of audiological services in school programs. If we hope to maximize the use of residual hearing, appropriate amplification is absolutely essential. The quantity and quality of the auditory-verbal experience which is provided for hearing-impaired children will significantly influence their ability to use whatever residual hearing they may possess (Ling & Ling, 1978).

Although a hearing loss undoubtedly distorts the input of speech and reduces the amount of information available, acoustic cues are still available to operate the phonemic system, and each individual brain has the freedom and capability of developing its own cue system. The vital factor is exposure to speech sounds. If a hearing-impaired person hears speech loudly enough and frequently enough, he is capable of developing nearly normal speech and language skills (Fry, 1978).

Adequate Experience Using Speech

In addition to hearing adequate amounts of speech and receiving daily, individualized, systematic speech teaching, students also need ample opportunities to practice speaking, both in and out of school. A large majority of students in this country are lacking this opportunity.

Trybus, Rawlings, and Johnson (1978) report that 69 percent of the total number of hearing-impaired children in Texas (range 55 to 82 percent) use sign language. The students' school programs incorporate signs 73 percent of the time with a range from 56 to 91 percent. The better ear average of the same students indicates the following average hearing threshold levels: 91 dB and above, 37 percent; 71–90 dB, 21 percent; 56–70 dB, 13 percent; 41–55 dB, 8 percent; 27–40 dB, 7 percent; under 27 dB, 8 percent; not reported, 5 percent.

One would assume from these statistics that many children with moderate hearing losses and with losses of less than 91 dB are using sign language. Are these students having adequate opportunities to use and practice speech when the data gathered by Jensema and Trybus (1978) reveal that speech use is always negatively correlated with the use of signs and/or fingerspelling? Data gathered by Jensema, Karchmer, and Trybus (1978) indicate that children with high speech intelligibility ratings use speech frequently and as their use of signs-with-fingerspelling decreases, their speech is more intelligible.

There is no reason to believe that the situation in Texas is unique. I feel that these results are probably representative of most other states.

Development of Effective Auditory Kinesthetic Feedback Systems

In order to develop independence and to continue to improve speech, the hearing-impaired person must have strategies to self-monitor automatic speech patterns. Although some hearing-impaired students have insufficient residual hearing to self-monitor their speech auditorily, a large percentage do have that capability. Many students will reach their potential to use the auditory modality as the primary channel for speech development if teacher/clinicians use a consistent auditory approach whenever feasible. In order to do this, teacher/clinicians must be convinced that students are capable of achieving this goal.

Transfer of Automatic Phonetic Skills to the Phonologic Level

There has been a steady increase over the past few years in the number of programs developing children's phonetic level skills, mainly influenced by the Ling model. These skills are essential, but insufficient prerequisites for intelligible spoken language. Some children, especially those with substantial residual hearing, have little difficulty transferring phonetic level patterns into their spontaneous language. However, the majority of students have difficulty doing it independently.

Discrimination and production practice on the phonologic level seems necessary for the majority of hearing-impaired students in order to enhance phonetic to phonologic transfer. Activities to improve reception and production of speech cannot be considered independent functions. Lieberth and Subtelny (1978) demonstrated significant gains in auditory phoneme recognition as a result of a systematic speech teaching program and also speculated that the improvement in auditory identification contributed to the gains in speech production.

Teachers of the hearing impaired are generally "tuned in" to *what* the student is expressing and making corrections when necessary, but few teachers have the skills to also monitor *how* it is being said and to reinforce correct production. The majority of teachers have difficulty monitoring the phonologic incorporation of mastered phonetic level speech skills. Systematic programs of phonologic reinforcement seem necessary for a large majority of students. Ling, in Chapter 20, suggests relating morphemes to particular semantic notions as a simple and effective method of ensuring the transfer. Production influencers such as those suggested by Fleming (1971) might be considered when developing strategies to ensure the phonetic to phonologic transfer which is so essential for intelligible speech production.

Supportive, Informed, and Cooperative Parents

Behind each hearing-impaired student who develops effective oral communication skills, especially those with severe and profound losses, is at least one if not two somewhat aggressive, knowledgeable parents who provide reinforcement at home. Except in residential programs, the school has accessibility to students for a maximum of seven hours. Cooperation between the school and the parent(s) is vital because consistency of expectation levels is essential for the achievement of maximum potential.

Summary

The prevailing standards for speech communication skills are generally extremely low. If we are committed to developing intelligible speech and consider it an important goal, we must examine the principles and strategies which prevail in programs where high standards of speech production are being achieved. We must then be willing and prepared to provide equal opportunities for all students. I believe all hearing-impaired individuals, even those with severe and profound losses, should be given the opportunity to develop intelligible speech if so desired. When will we be able to optimally prepare the hearing impaired to function independently as members of our highly verbal society?

REFERENCES

Fleming, K. J. Guidelines for choosing appropriate phonetic contexts for speech-sound recognition and production practice. *J. Speech Hear. Dis.*, 1971, *36*, 356–367.

Fry, D. B. The role and primacy of the auditory channel in speech and language development. In M. Ross & T. G. Giolas (Eds.), *Auditory management of hearing-impaired children.* Baltimore: University Park Press, 1978.

Jensema, C. J., Karchmer, M. A., & Trybus, R. J. *The rated speech intelligibility of hearing impaired children: Basic relationships and a detailed analysis.* Washington, D.C.: Office of Demographic Studies, Gallaudet College, 1978.

Jensema, C. J., & Trybus, R. J. *Communication patterns and educational achievement of hearing impaired students.* Washington, D.C.: Office of Demographic Studies, Gallaudet College, 1978.

Lieberth, A., & Subtelny, J. D. The effect of speech training on auditory phoneme identification. *Volta Rev.*, 1978, *80*, 410–417.

Ling, D. *Speech and the hearing-impaired child: Theory and practice.* Washington, D.C.: A.G. Bell Association, 1976.

Ling, D., & Ling, A. H. *Aural habilitation: The foundations of verbal learning in hearing-impaired children.* Washington, D.C.: A.G. Bell Association, 1978.

Trybus, R. J., Rawlings, B. W., & Johnson, R. *Texas state survey of hearing impaired children and youth: A new approach to statewide planning, monitoring, and evaluation of special education planning.* Washington, D.C.: Office of Demographic Studies, Gallaudet College, 1978.

PART III

Evaluation of Speech Training

14
Evaluation of Independent Drill With Visual Aids for Speech Training

Robert A. Houde

SPEECH TRAINING FOR THE DEAF is generally unsuccessful, with the majority of profoundly deaf children finishing their education without attaining intelligible speech. The reason for this failure has been the subject of debate for at least a century. One viewpoint holds that the failure to develop speech is the result of insufficient commitment to the goal of developing oral skills and an insufficient quantity of oral training (Simmons-Martin, 1972). The other viewpoint holds that the amount and intensity of training required is excessively large for many children. The total commitment needed to maintain this training along with the communication deprivation which results from exclusive dependence on inadequate oral skills leads to severe psychological damage to the child (Vernon, 1972).

Although reasons for failure differ, there is general agreement that the quantity of highly skilled teaching required is extremely large, larger than can currently be provided for the majority of deaf students, and that the prospects for speech would be greatly improved if a more efficient means of speech training could be devised.

For the past few decades, considerable effort has been devoted to the development of electronic speech training aids with the hope that they might provide a significant improvement in the efficiency of training. These developments have ranged from simple single-feature displays such as the "S" meter (Risberg, 1968) to very complex systems which present a selection of phonetic characteristics (Nickerson & Stevens, 1973; Stewart, Houde, & Larkin, 1973) and systems which display the speech signal in a relatively unprocessed form as a spectrographic display (Potter, 1945; Stark, 1971; Stewart, Larkin, & Houde, 1976). An excellent review of early instrument development was presented by Pronovost (1967), and a comprehensive up-to-date survey is found in Strong (1975).

Results of these technological developments have been generally disappointing. The few formal evaluations of the effectiveness of instrumental aids in speech teaching have indicated that training with an aid results in only slight improvement over training without an aid (Kopp & Kopp, 1963; Stratton, 1974; Boothroyd, 1973). None of the many aids which were evaluated has come into widespread clinical use. It must be concluded that any benefit provided by the aids was not great enough to justify the added cost and effort involved in their use. These results suggest a reexamination of the speech training process and the role which might be played by electronic aids.

The Speech Training Process

During the early stages of speech development in the profoundly deaf child, the training method usually employed is principally the "natural" technique, in which training is focused on the use of language and vocalization (Simmons, 1968). Little attention is given to the analytic correction of specific sound production problems, and the teacher reinforces the broad general aspects of spontaneous speech. This natural approach is most often used with the preschool age. In this approach, the child achieves some basic ability to use speech. Later, methods may be employed to correct specific speech problems. Unlike the natural methods, the analytical methods may be formal and explicit. In general, analytical methods involve:

1. An analysis of each utterance;
2. Feedback to the student, e.g., the correctness of the utterance; and
3. Directions for modifying the next attempt.

As the student's skill improves, the nature of the teacher's activity changes from instructions for modifying the next trial, to drill activities. In drill activities simple indications of degree of correctness are provided by the teacher, but no specific directions are given to modify the next trial. This drill phase is characterized by a great deal of repetition.

Existing educational facilities do not provide every deaf child with a sufficient amount of individualized speech training. One approach to this problem—to simply increase teaching facilities—is not likely because it would require increased financial support. As an alternative solution, increased efficiency in teaching may be sought, i.e., more training provided at no great increase in costs.

Speech training aids have two potential advantages in improving teaching efficiency. The first may be related to an improvement in teaching skill. Speech displays which provide a phonetic analysis and feedback of the utterance can assist the teacher in the instructional phase of analytical speech training and can be quite well handled by the good teacher. While it is not likely that the aid can significantly change the efficiency of a good teacher, the visual feedback may, however, improve the phonetic analysis and communication capabilities of an average teacher. The second advantage of the aid is to facilitate the drill component of analytical speech training through independent work.

The objectives of this study were to develop a system for providing independent drill by speech displays and to evaluate its effectiveness in training the speech of deaf children.

Independent Drill Procedure

As a primary objective, this procedure must fit into the existing program of speech training at a school for the deaf; i.e., the independent drill procedure should serve as an extension of the speech teacher by providing drill which the teacher would carry out if adequate time were available. The procedure must, therefore, accommodate a very wide range of articulation problems.

The speech display instrument which best serves this need is the Speech Spectrographic Display or SSD (Stewart et al., 1976). This instrument displays speech as an instantaneous sound spectrogram on a television screen. The spectrographic representation of speech preserves most of the phonetic features which must be considered in distinguishing correct from incorrect production of speech sounds. Figure 14.1 shows the SSD and a typical display.

Independent drill is assigned by the speech teacher to stabilize a sound which has been developed to the stimulable level, i.e., the sound can be produced with stimulation, but it is not consistently produced correctly without stimulation. The drill is carried out in daily sessions of 20 minutes under the supervision of a drill monitor. The teacher periodically reviews the student's program in drill and changes the assignment as necessary to fit the student's needs.

The basic drill procedure consists of exercises in producing the assigned target sound in varied phonetic contexts and in words which are ordered into five levels of increasing difficulty. The five levels of

FIGURE 14.1
The Speech Spectrographic Display (SSD): Spectrogram of /s eɪ z u/.

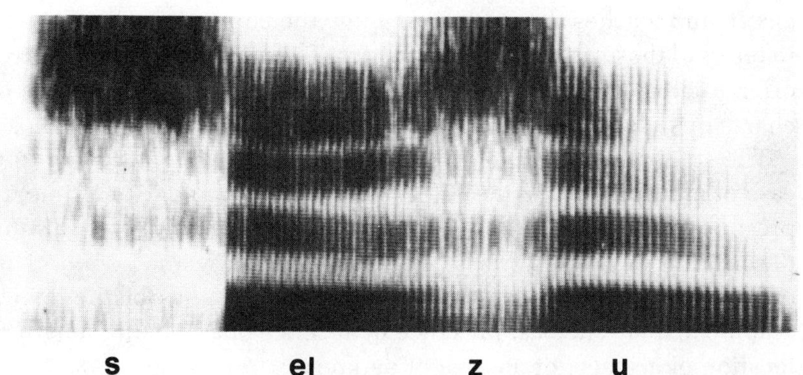

difficulty for consonants in initial positon are shown in Table 14.A. A parallel set of tasks exists for the consonants in final position.

TABLE 14.A
Levels of difficulty for phonetic drill.
(Target /t/)

Level	Phonetic Context	Examples
1	[C] V	ta
2	[C] V C	tam
3	[C] V C V	tapa
4	V [C] V C	atav
5	V C [C] V	anta

The speech teacher assigns the target sound, specifies the levels of difficulty, and selects phonetic materials and words for use in drill. Phonetic tasks are constructed by the teacher to include: a front vowel, a mid vowel, a back vowel, and other consonants which the student can produce consistently. Table 14.B shows the phonetic tasks and words for two levels of difficulty for a student assigned the target /t/, CV words, and who has consistently good production of consonants /n/, /p/, /f/, /b/, and /m/.

Description of Independent Drill: Equipment and Materials

The drill monitor instructs the student in the basic operation of the SSD and in the use of the drill workbook, which contains the student's individual drill program. Before the student begins independent drill, the monitor identifies the critical acoustic (spectrographic) characteristics which distinguish the errors from the correct production of the target, and teaches the student to judge the correctness of production in terms of these critical characteristics. This diagnosis is guided by an error catalog, a listing of the acoustic, articulatory, and perceptual characteristics of each phoneme and its principal errors.

The student is taught to distinguish only one error at a time. In the case of multiple errors, the errors are extinguished one at a time, in a prescribed order. The error catalog provides the monitor with a simple description of the criteria to be used in judging the sound. These criteria are limited to clearly visible characteristics of the spectrographic display such as: presence or absence of a line, the length and location of a space, or an area of darkness.

TABLE 14.B
Drill materials for Levels 1 and 2.
Level 1— [C] V

Phonetic Drill	Words
tee	tea
	toe
	tow
ta	too
	to
	two
too	tie
	toy

Level 2— [C] V C

Phonetic Drill	Words	
teen	tub	time
	tube	teen
	tip	ten
tap	top	turn
	type	ton
	tough	tune
toof	team	town
	Tim	
	Tom	

Figure 14.2 shows the spectrogram of /ma/ and of its error /mba/. The simple error criterion in this case is the absence of energy—the white region—in the upper resonances just before the bilabial release. The student is not taught to read spectrograms, but merely to focus attention on the relevant features and make a simple judgment: *present* vs. *absent, too long* vs. *too short,* etc.

Drill

Worksheets listing the phonetic tasks and words assigned by the teacher are assembled in the student's individual drill program book, along with appropriate spectrographic models and error criterion.

FIGURE 14.2
Spectrogram of /m a/, /m b a/.

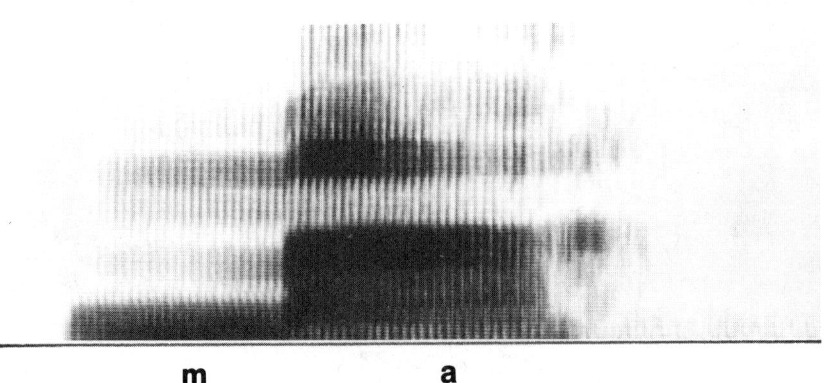

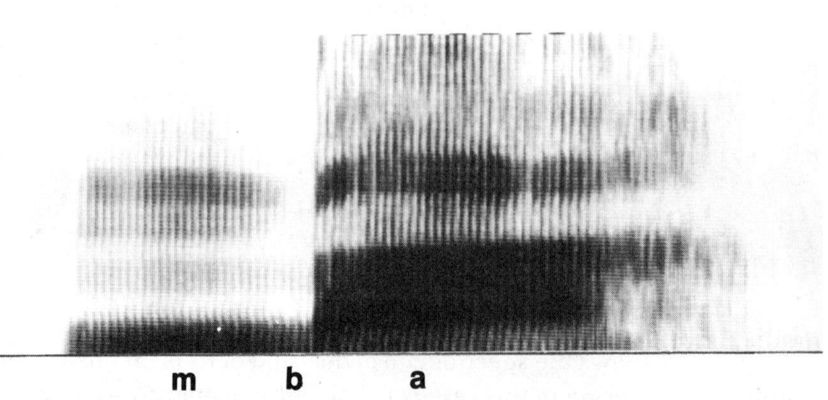

Figure 14.3 shows a student using the individual drill program book, and the detail of the "worksheet" is shown in Figure 14.4.

Using a worksheet, the student independently judges each utterance and marks the next box on the sheet if it is considered correct. Groups of syllables are alternated with groups of words to interrupt any possible motor perseveration. On completing a worksheet (31 correct phonetic tasks, 13 correct words) the student proceeds to the next worksheet. After each set of three worksheets, a test of the student's production is administered by the monitor. The outcome of this "set" test is the basis for deciding if the student should continue at the same level, terminate work on that sound, or be tested for assignment to the next level. A "Level Test" is given at the start of a day's work, before any drill, to assess the student's spontaneous production of the target.

The monitor supervises the independent work of three students simultaneously, as shown in Figure 14.5. In this supervision the monitor 1) listens for the introduction of new errors and provides correction when needed; 2) directs the pronunciation of assigned words and explains the meanings of words; 3) monitors for incorrect judgments and scoring; and 4) administers performance tests as needed.

FIGURE 14.3
Student drill.

FIGURE 14.4
Drill worksheet.

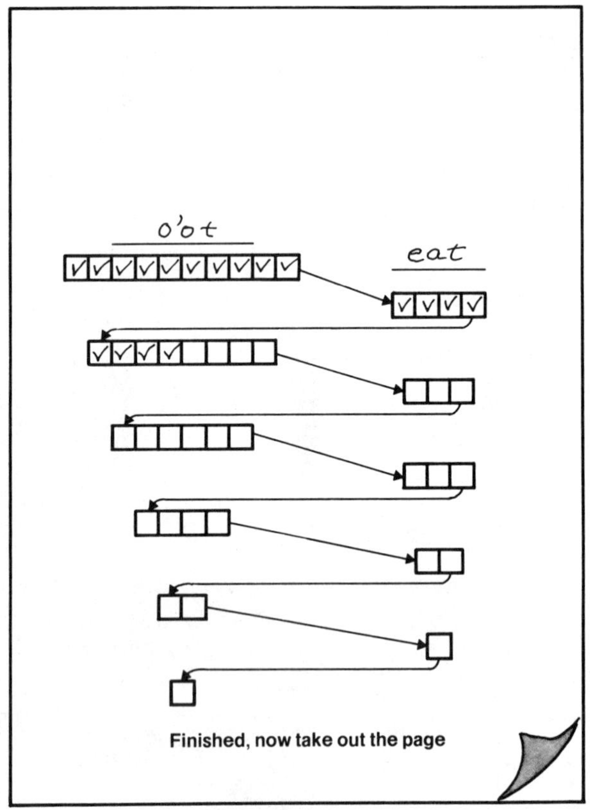

Evaluation of the Independent Drill Procedure

This program involving independent drill was evaluated at the Rochester School for the Deaf. Subjects included 51 children in the first nine classes (6–13 years of age) who were assigned to two experimental groups: the Independent Drill Group and the Drilled-by-Teacher Group. The two groups were defined by dividing each class into two on a random basis. Both groups received 20 minutes of drill per day, four days per week in addition to their regular speech training within the school's program. In the Independent Drill Group, each student drilled independently using a spectrographic display in the procedure outlined above. In the Drilled-by-Teacher Group, each student received equal individual drill from a teacher and with the same general procedure as was provided in the Independent Drill

FIGURE 14.5
Drill carrels.

Group. In the Drilled-by-Teacher Group the teacher substituted for the spectrographic display in providing the student with feedback.

Results

Independent Work

Can young deaf children work independently and effectively with visual displays? Of the 27 students assigned to drill independently, all but one learned to operate the SSD and to judge the spectrographic characteristics of their utterances independently. The number of sessions required to learn to operate the SSD ranged from 1 to 4, with an average of 2.1. The number of sessions required to learn to discriminate errors from correct productions ranged from 1 to 5 with an average of 1.1.

Learning Rate

Learning rate was measured as the number of phoneme levels (levels of difficulty as shown in Table 14.A) mastered per training session. Table 14.C shows the individual average learning rates of both groups. The average rates at which phoneme skills were acquired by individual students drilled with the SSD are shown in Figure 14.6, and the average learning rates for individual students drilled by teachers are shown in Figure 14.7. As reported in Table 14.C, the mean learning rates of the two groups are very similar, both being approximately equal to 0.1 phoneme levels per day. The ranges of

TABLE 14.C
Average learning rates of individual students.

Rank	Drilled by Instrument	Drilled by Teacher
1	.252	.182
2	.204	.173
3	.201	.168
4	.185	.168
5	.183	.163
6	.182	.134
7	.167	.130
8	.154	.126
9	.144	.121
10	.107	.114
11	.097	.112
12	.097	.103
13	.088	.102
14	.076	.097
15	.062	.096
16	.058	.087
17	.053	.084
18	.049	.082
19	.047	.069
20	.047	.067
21	.046	.067
22	.036	.059
23	.035	.058
24	.02	.052
25	.016	
26	.012	
27	.000	
	mean .101	mean .109

FIGURE 14.6
Average learning rates of students drilled by instruments.

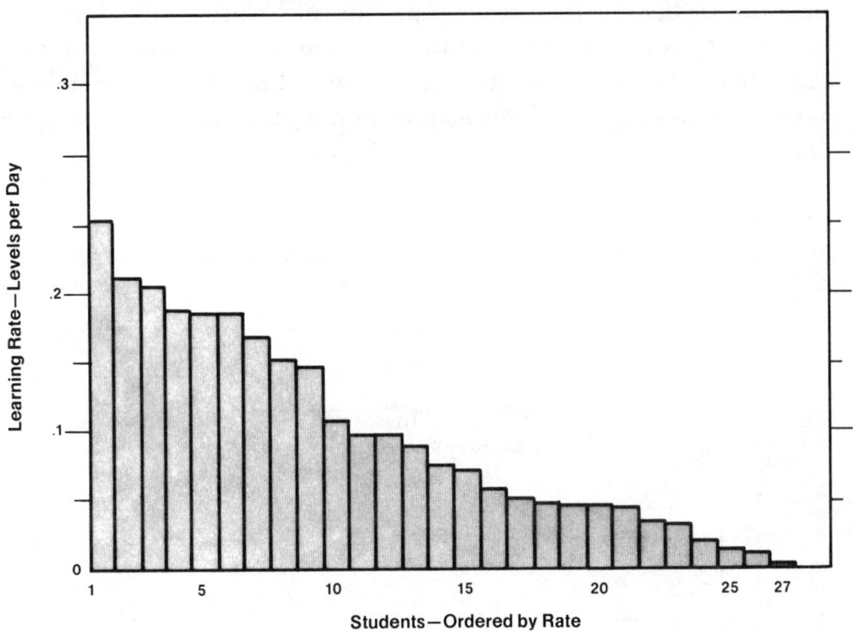

FIGURE 14.7
Average learning rates of students drilled by teachers.

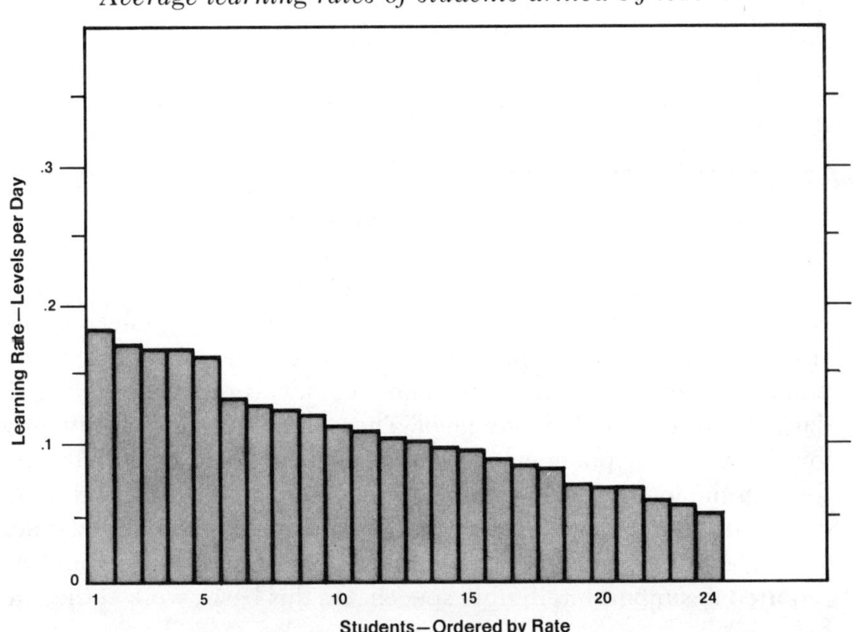

learning rates of the two groups, however, are significantly different. The drilled-by-SSD group exhibited a wider range of learning rates than the Drilled-by-Teacher Group. This difference is shown in Figure 14.8. Above-average SSD-drilled students are seen to have higher rates than above-average teacher-drilled students, while below-average SSD-drilled students had lower rates than the below-average teacher-drilled students.

FIGURE 14.8
Average learning rates of students drilled by instruments and by teachers.

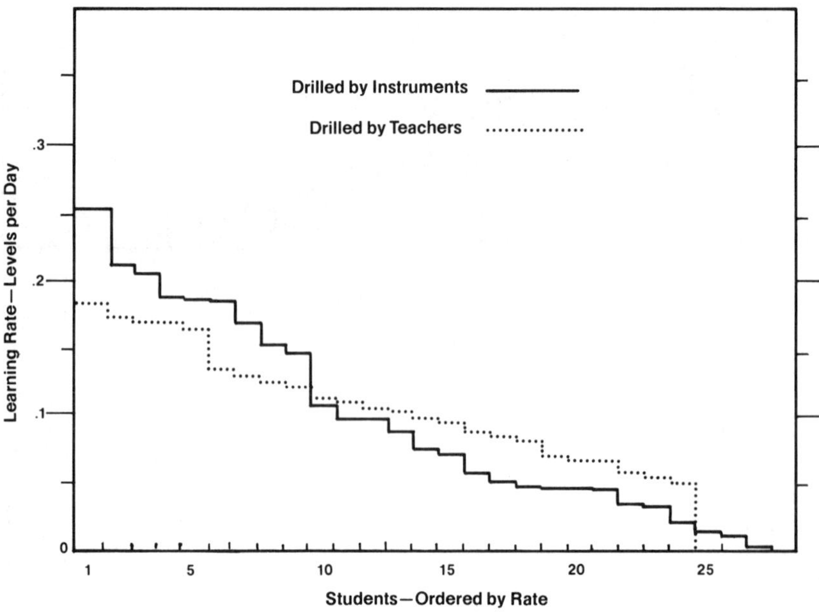

As reported, the mean learning rate of both experimental groups was approximately 0.1 phoneme levels per day. This rate may be converted to a more meaningful unit of phonemes per day and phonemes per year: A rate of 0.1 phoneme levels per day requires 10 days of drill to complete one level. There are five levels of difficulty for training each phoneme. Assuming the phoneme is drilled only through the fourth level, then one phoneme may be stabilized in 40 days of drill, and approximately four phonemes may be stabilized per year. The writer suggests that a minimum of 24 phonemes would be required to support intelligible speech. On this basis, work at the rate of 0.1 levels per day would require six years to achieve minimal intelligibility. In this study population of 27 students drilled with the SSD, 37 percent had average learning rates of less than .05 levels per day (more than 12 years to achieve a minimal set of skills), 59 percent had average learning rates of less than 0.1 levels per day (more than six years to achieve a minimal set of skills), and 15 percent had average learning rates of more than .2 levels per day (less than three years to achieve a minimal set of skills).

Discussion

The observation that a therapist can be more effective than independent work for below-average students is hardly startling. It is surprising, however, to find that the therapist was not as effective as independent drill for the above-average student.

For the purpose of optimizing the design of speech training, these data might be interpreted on the basis of costs or on the basis of time. On a cost basis, because machine drill is approximately half the cost of therapist drill, independent machine drill is found to be more cost effective for approximately 75 percent of the test population. On the basis of training time, the independent machine drill is seen to be more effective than therapist drill for approximately 50 percent of the population.

Figure 14.9 shows the average learning rate of each student grouped by academic classes. The classes are listed in order of academic level, which in general also corresponds to an ordering by class average age. As illustrated, the range of learning rates in each class is quite large

TABLE 14.D

Correlation of learning rate with hearing level, age, and diligence.

Parameter	Independent Drill SSD Group	Therapist Group
Hearing Loss (500, 1000, and 2000 Hz)	−0.21	−0.15
Age (months)	0.42	0.50
Diligence (Number of worksheets completed per day)	0.69	

but, in general, learning rates are below average for the first five classes and above average for the last four. This suggests that learning rates might be related to overall articulation skill and age, and that the ability to carry out independent work is strongly correlated with age.

Correlations of learning rate with hearing level, age, and diligence are summarized in Table 14.D. Learning rate was moderately well correlated with age for both groups, i.e., $r = 0.42$ for independent drill, and 0.50 for therapist drill. Hearing loss was essentially uncorrelated with learning rate. The strongest correlation ($r = 0.69$) is found with diligence—the amount of work completed per day.

Summary and Conclusions

1. In a random sample of 27 students evenly distributed over the first nine classes of a school for the deaf (51 students aged 6–13), all except one were able to use a spectrographic display to judge the correctness of their utterances and to carry out articulation drill independently.

2. Learning rates were fairly evenly distributed from a high of about 0.3 phoneme levels per day (12 phonemes per year) to the above-mentioned low of zero.

3. The average learning rate of students who used independent drill was very similar to that of students drilled individually by teachers for the same amount of time (0.101 and 0.109 phoneme levels per day respectively, which corresponds to about four phonemes per year).

4. The above-average students who drilled independently with displays made significantly faster progress than the above-average students drilled by therapists, while below-average machine-drilled students had significantly lower learning rates than the below-average therapist-drilled students.

5. Learning rate in independent drill was correlated with hearing level ($r = -0.20$), with age ($r = 0.42$), and with diligence (amount of work finished per day) $r = 0.69$.

6. Caution is advised in interpreting the data showing higher learning rates with machine drill. The measure of effectiveness of independent drill is carry-over and not learning rate. Carry-over is currently in the process of being determined for both the independent drill and the teacher-drilled groups.

FIGURE 14.9

Average learning rate with students grouped by classes.

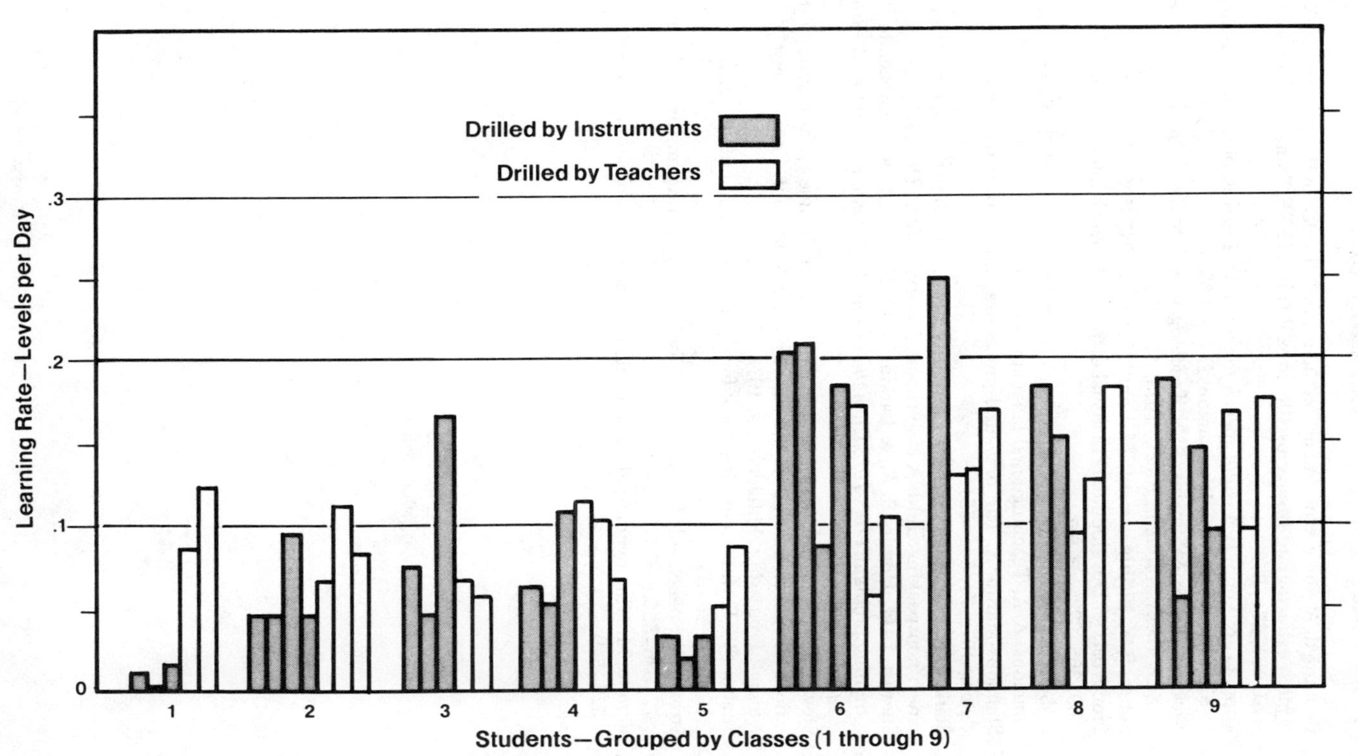

REFERENCES

Boothroyd, A. Some experiments on the control of voice in the profoundly deaf using a pitch extractor and storage oscilloscope display. *IEEE Trans. Aud. and Elect.*, 1973, AU–21, 274–278.

Kopp, G., & Kopp, H. *Visible speech for the deaf,* Final Report, Vocat. Rehab. Agency (SRS) Grant RD–526, Washington, D.C., 1963.

Nickerson, R. S., & Stevens, K. N. Teaching speech to the deaf: Can a computer help? *IEEE Trans. Aud. and Elect.*, 1973, 445–455.

Potter, R. K. Visible patterns of sounds. *Science,* 1945, *102,* 463–470.

Pronovost, W. Developments in visual displays of speech information. *Volta Rev.*, 1967, *69,* 365–373.

Risberg, A. Visual aids for speech correction. *Am. Ann. Deaf,* 1968, *113,* 178–194.

Simmons, A. A. Teaching aural language. *Volta Rev.*, 1968, *70,* 26–30.

Simmons-Martin, A. The oral/aural procedure: Theoretical basis and rationale. *Volta Rev.*, 1972, *74,* 541–551.

Stark, R. E. The use of real time visual displays of speech in the training of a profoundly deaf nonspeaking child: A case report. *J. Speech Hear. Dis.*, 1971, *36,* 397–409.

Stewart, L. C., Houde, R. A., & Larkin, W. D. The VSTA: An approach to the speech training problem. *Proc. 1973 Carnahan Conf. Electronic Prosthetics,* Lexington, Ky., 1973, 10–14.

Stewart, L. C., Larkin, W. D., & Houde, R. A. A real time spectrograph with implications for speech training for the deaf. *Proc. 1976 Internat. Conf. Acoust., Speech, and Signal Processing.* Philadelphia, 1976, 590–593.

Stratton, W. D. Intonation feedback for the deaf through a tactile display. *Volta Rev.*, 1974, *76,* 26–35.

Strong, W. Speech aids for the profoundly/severely hearing impaired. *Volta Rev.*, 1975, *77,* 536–556.

Vernon, M. Mind over mouth, a rationale for total communicatiòn. *Volta Rev.*, 1972, *74,* 529–540.

15
Visual Feedback as an Aid to Speech Therapy

Jean E. Maki

A REVIEW OF LEARNING PRINCIPLES as they relate to a theory of instruction (Hilgard & Bower, 1975) provides supportive rationale for using visual feedback in teaching speech production to the hearing impaired. For the present discussion, several principles taken from two theories of learning were selected because they were considered to be particularly applicable when discussing the potential benefit of using visual feedback in teaching speech production.

Theoretical Basis for Using Visual Feedback in Speech Therapy

One of the concepts critical to stimulus-response learning is that the learner be actively involved in the learning situation. Through the use of appropriate visual feedback, the student can evaluate his own speech, requiring little or no input from the instructor. Within this framework, active involvement of the student is ensured since he alone is making judgments concerning accuracy of production. This eliminates the relatively passive role of simply accepting the instructor's evaluation. Although it is critical for the student to develop awareness of internal sensory feedback, this may not be possible when students have poor hearing discrimination skills or are just beginning to develop auditory, tactile, and/or kinesthetic awareness. Thus, where students initially cannot make accurate judgments using only internal feedback, visual feedback provides information which students can consistently use in evaluating their own productions. This ensures a high level of active involvement and, theoretically, enhances learning.

Closely related to the concept of active involvement is a principle associated with cognitive learning which stresses learning with understanding. Especially useful when the verbal explanation of an articulatory concept is abstract, certain instruments present visual displays which clearly distinguish appropriate and inappropriate production features. Thus, such devices have the potential for increasing the student's understanding of articulation. Secondarily, visual displays provide opportunity for the instructor to assess the student's concepts of speech production by questioning the student concerning interpretation of visual patterns.

Another important component in the learning process relates to providing accurate and consistent feedback concerning accuracy of production. It is conceivable that the combined feedback from both instructor and instrument increases the probability of providing consistent feedback to the student. For example, judging accuracy in producing correct voice onset time may become difficult when the student's production is on the borderline between a clearly perceived /t/ and /d/. In such cases, the student can depend solely on a timing criterion displayed in the visual patterns. This would serve to eliminate the sometimes nebulous feedback which can result from attempting to auditorily evaluate a perceptually indistinct signal.

A final consideration relates to frequency of repetition, i.e., to the amount of time given to practice of motor skills. Speech training aids have the potential for being used independently by students to increase the amount of practice. With a distinctive visual pattern for a target and a means by which instructors can monitor student performance, instrumentation may be used to provide necessary feedback during repetitive practice.

To summarize, theoretical support for use of visual feedback in speech training is based on (1) encouraging active involvement of the learner, (2) increasing understanding of speech production, (3) ensuring consistency of feedback concerning accuracy of production, and (4) providing opportunity for sufficient practice of motor skills. These principles, however, can be applied to the use of visual feedback only if an instrument provides distinctive visual patterns which permit accurate assessment of speech production.

Description of the Speech Spectrographic Display (SSD)

One of the instruments currently available for use in speech therapy is the Speech Spectrographic Display (Stewart, Larkin, & Houde, 1976). This instrument presents a visual display of the acoustic signal in a form similar to a standard spectrogram (Koenig, Dunn, & Lacy, 1946). Frequency is displayed on the vertical axis, time on the horizontal axis, and intensity is reflected in the darkness of the trace. The frequency range analyzed is from 100 to 5000 Hz, and information is displayed using trace durations of either .75 or 1.5 seconds. The shorter duration allows for greater time resolution and the other permits analysis of longer utterances. For display of relative intensity, the instrument has a dynamic range of 30 dB. As the speaker talks, the display appears instantaneously, tracing from left to right on a standard video monitor. The spectrogram is stored and displayed on the monitor, allowing five minutes' maximum viewing time.

If the previously stated rationale for use of visual feedback are to apply to the Speech Spectrographic Display, the visual patterns for the various speech sounds must be distinctive from each other, and hearing-impaired subjects must be able to interpret them correctly. The following research was conducted to begin evaluation of the SSD by (1) assessing distinctiveness of the display features, (2) evaluating display interpretation skills of hearing-impaired adults, and (3) evaluating use of the SSD in teaching specific articulatory skills.

Distinctiveness of Speech Sound Patterns

In a study designed to assess visual pattern distinctiveness (Maki, 1977), two tasks were administered to separate groups of hearing-impaired adults. On a visual discrimination task, 20 hearing-impaired adults were required to discriminate whether the SSD patterns from vowel, fricative, and plosive pairs were the same or different. An average discrimination score of 75 percent correct was achieved. This was significantly above chance performance and was considered high since both members of each test pair had the same manner of production, i.e., vowels were never paired with consonants, and plosives were never paired with fricatives.

An error analysis was performed on the discrimination data for the pairs that were different and incorrectly identified as the same. Results of this analysis showed that visual patterns for the test sounds were not equally distinctive. Based on the data collected, the eight test vowels could be divided into three subgroups according to relative distinctiveness. The commonalities and differences among the three subgroups indicated that subjects probably used formant structure, formant transitions, and vowel duration to discriminate the vowel patterns. When discriminating visual patterns of fricative pairs, most errors occurred for pairs that differed in place of production. Relatively few confusions occurred for those test pairs which differed in the voicing feature. A similar trend occurred for plosive pairs, i.e., most errors resulted when test pairs had the same voicing feature and differed in place of production. For consonant production, then, visual features related to voicing were fairly distinctive, whereas cues to indicate place of production were more difficult to discriminate.

The second task in this study was designed to test the subjects' ability to isolate and remember display characteristics associated with consonant production. During individual testing, hearing-impaired subjects were shown 10 different SSD patterns. Each test pattern was presented once within each of 10 learning trials. For each presentation, the test syllable was displayed twice in succession. On the first presentation, the subject attempted to identify the pattern, and on the second presentation the subject's identification was either verified or corrected. Identification results showed an improvement in scores from 14 percent correct on the first trial to 72 percent correct on the eighth trial. For the remaining two trials, a plateau was maintained at approximately 70 percent correct. Thus, it was found that subjects could associate SSD patterns with appropriate speech sounds in a relatively short time (30 minutes) and without specific instruction concerning display interpretation. The fact that a plateau was maintained after the seventh trial indicated that certain visual features were difficult to identify and additional learning was not evident.

Error analysis for this task supported data obtained from the discrimination task. On the final three trials, an analysis of errors showed that incorrect identification of place of production was involved in 72 percent of the total errors. Of those errors, 41 percent resulted solely from misidentifying place of production. Apparently, subjects had less difficulty identifying voicing and manner of production and comparatively greater difficulty identifying visual features related to place of production.

Interpretation of SSD Patterns From Severely Hearing-Impaired Speakers

Since previous results indicated that the SSD provides distinctive patterns for various types of articulatory features, it was important to determine if hearing-impaired subjects could accurately interpret distorted speech patterns. Using SSD patterns from severely to profoundly hearing-impaired speakers, a study was conducted to assess whether hearing-impaired adults could interpret SSD displays correctly in order to evaluate speech production (Streff et al., 1978).

Ten hearing-impaired subjects who had used the SSD for 30 hours in speech therapy were given the display interpretation task. Photographs of the SSD patterns from pre- and post-therapy productions were shown to each subject. The subjects were told the intended utterance for each test set, and asked to choose the better production for each pair and give reasons for their choice. To illustrate, when asked to choose the better /s/ production in the utterance "I see," four subjects noted the SSD visual characteristics indicating frication (high-frequency random energy) and five subjects noted the absence of visual cues related to voicing (low-frequency periodic energy). These responses were tallied as nine observations and counted as correct. In contrast, two subjects noted the overall vowel duration as a visual cue for accurate production of /aɪ/. These responses were tallied as two incorrect observations.

Overall, subjects identified the improved production with 90 percent accuracy and made a total of 118 observations. Of these observations, 88.1 percent were accurate with respect to speech production. In general, these findings show that hearing-impaired adults can accurately interpret SSD patterns to evaluate speech production. This suggests that hearing-impaired adults would also be able to use the visual feedback from the SSD in evaluating their own speech attempts while acquiring new motor skills.

The types of errors which subjects made while completing this task suggested an additional application of the SSD. There appeared to be two general error types, both of which related to misconceptions which subjects had concerning speech production. One error type involved the relationship between speech sound production and the orthographic representation. For example, on one display, four subjects interpreted the display to include the final "e" on the word *tease*. On another display, one subject indicated that the /m/ in the word *hammer* has a long duration because the letter "m" occurs twice. Both of these observations reflect erroneous conceptions concerning pronunciation. The second error type which occurred related to misconceptions about speech production. For example, one subject believed that speech was produced as separate, unconnected words. As in the previously stated example, other subjects used overall vowel duration inappropriately to judge vowel accuracy.

These errors suggest a possible application of the SSD in assessing and correcting conceptual errors related to pronunciation and speech production. The lack of a one-to-one correspondence between the acoustic signal and the orthographic representation could be a relatively abstract concept for hearing-impaired speakers to master. Application of the SSD in this area would allow presentation of abstract articulatory concepts using a more concrete visual representation of the acoustic signal.

Results of these perceptual studies provide support for use of the SSD in speech therapy with hearing-impaired adults. In addition, the results have provided general guidelines for use of the SSD. These guidelines relate to type of instruction, i.e., motor vs. conceptual learning, and to the specific types of articulatory behavior that present distinctive patterns and to which the SSD might best be applied in remediation.

Evaluation of the SSD in Speech Therapy

In an investigation designed to study the effect of using the SSD in speech therapy (Maki & Streff, 1978), 30 severely to profoundly hearing-impaired speakers were randomly assigned to one of three groups. All subjects received 40 hours of individual speech therapy. Those assigned to Groups A and B received a structured therapy program aimed at teaching production of /i/ and /aɪ/ within varied phonetic contexts. Group A used the SSD during therapy and Group B used no instrumentation. Those subjects assigned to Group C received speech therapy with no instrumentation and no restrictions on therapy objectives or procedures.

Evaluation of pre- and post-therapy speech samples showed that the SSD Group improved significantly for production of vowels within CVC words. Group B showed slight improvement, which was not statistically significant, and Group C showed no improvement. Thus, in comparing the experimental group with the two control groups, it was found that the SSD did serve to enhance learning of vowel production. In speculating as to why this occurred, the rationale for use of visual feedback discussed above provide several possibilities.

Another finding relevant to use of the SSD involved performance of the groups on a test of speech intelligibility when producing sentences. For this measure, the greatest improvement was shown by Group C, who received conventional therapy. It is speculated that subjects in Group C received instruction and practice within a greater variety of speaking situations than did those subjects using the structured program in Groups A and B. This finding emphasizes the importance of providing instruction which reflects the ultimate goal of therapy. It also serves as a caution when using visual feedback. The ultimate goal is that the student be able to judge accuracy of production using internal feedback mechanisms. Care should be taken to ensure that the student has opportunity to develop appropriate use of internal feedback, and that the visual aid is used only to facilitate learning.

Given results from past research, it is concluded that the SSD can be used effectively in speech therapy with hearing-impaired adults since (1) the SSD provides distinctive patterns for many aspects of speech production, (2) hearing-impaired adults can accurately assess speech production using SSD patterns, and (3) there is evidence that learning of specific articulatory dynamics is enhanced through use of visual feedback from the SSD. It should be remembered that these conclusions are based on research conducted with subjects having specific speech and hearing characteristics. In addition, the visual stimuli used in the investigations do not include the full range of visual patterns representing the English language. Thus, although the findings were positive, results must be placed in perspective, acknowledging the fact that the subjects and test stimuli used in the studies do not provide the total picture concerning use of the SSD in speech therapy.

In order to continue work with the SSD and obtain maximum use of the instrument, a hardware system was designed to automate use of the SSD. The following section describes the recording system which was developed and, in addition, presents software needs which would permit use of the SSD for self-instruction.

Independent Use of the SSD: Hardware and Software Support

The hardware system which was developed to permit independent use of the Speech Spectrographic Display has six major components, including: an SSD; a Warren Amplifier (Model D-1 s/s); a Wollensak cassette tape recorder (Model 2590); number encoder and decoder units (Silver, 1979b); and a control unit (Silver, 1979a). The SSD analyzes the acoustic signal and provides the visual display. The Warren Unit allows the option for amplification of the speech signal. Using the Wollensak tape recorder, the student's speech is recorded on one track, and synchronization signals necessary for automatic operation of the SSD are recorded on the sync control track. The number encoder produces a signal which numbers each utterance and, on playback, is digitally displayed by the number decoder. This permits accurate identification of each speech sample. Finally, the control unit coordinates the entire system so that the following sequence occurs:

1. Student presses record button on the SSD:
   a. the previous display is erased and an erase pulse is recorded onto the sync control track of the Wollensak:
   b. the number of the utterance is digitally encoded onto the sync control track;
   c. after a 1-second delay, SSD record function begins.
2. Student speaks while SSD analyzes and visually displays the signal:
   a. speech sample is recorded onto tape;
   b. student sees display instantaneously as he speaks.
3. Using visual pattern for feedback, the student assesses accuracy of production:
   a. if judged incorrect, student repeats process;
   b. if judged correct, the student presses a response button to record "stop" signal onto the sync control track (during playback, this signal stops the tape recorder which indicates to the instructor that those productions were judged as correct by the student);
   c. student continues, repeating the above procedure.

At the conclusion of the practice session, the cassette tape contains the numbered speech samples, the synchronization signals needed to automatically control the SSD, and the "stop" signals after those utterances judged as correct. Using this tape, the instructor can (1) auditorily monitor the student's productions, (2) evaluate the student's judgments of accuracy, and (3) view the associated SSD visual patterns. Thus, the instructor can monitor the student's progress to ensure improvement and to evaluate the student's judgments of accuracy. With this system, the instructor can detect and intervene in those cases where students are practicing incorrect motor patterns because of inaccurate interpretations of the SSD displays.

Using written text and prerecorded tapes, this system can also be used to present self-instruction programs. A tape, recorded by the instructor, can be used to display specific aspects of speech production. With the digital readout to identify the displays, a text can be prepared to describe the important visual features for each display as well as the related articulatory features. The student can listen to the instructor's production from the tape, view the SSD pattern that accompanies each production, and read the information considered important for learning the specific production. Thus, given the necessary hardware and software, the SSD has the potential for providing independent practice and instruction concerning speech production.

Future Considerations

Given an adult hearing-impaired population, there is a need for considerable individualized instruction which incorporates learning principles such as those discussed earlier in this presentation. With the combined purpose of conducting additional research on application of the SSD, providing instruction concerning speech production and perception, and evaluating instructional techniques, the most logical direction would appear to be computer-assisted instruction.

Utilizing visual feedback from the SSD with amplification and computer graphics would provide various forms of feedback to the student simultaneously. An audio recording system and hardcopy unit would provide the instructor with auditory and visual records to monitor student performance. With a computer-based system, ongoing data collection and analysis are possible. This would permit data-based decisions relative to content and organization of further instruction and/or practice. Such a system would allow for (1) self-instruction, (2) practice of skills utilizing visual and auditory feedback, and (3) assessment of both student progress and instructional techniques. This would allow students to receive sufficient instruction and practice of motor and perceptual skills in a structured setting, permitting instructors to concentrate on incorporating those skills in less-structured conversational tasks.

Previous research on the use of visual feedback has provided general guidelines for use of the SSD and some major areas of interest concerning application of the instrument. The availability of a computerized system with accompanying software would provide data on a large number of students. With this information, the effects of using visual feedback in specific cases could be stated more definitively. Thus, through use of a computer system, it is hoped that future research will define more clearly the advantages and cautions of using visual feedback in motor skill learning, perceptual development, and conceptual understanding.

REFERENCES

Hilgard, E., & Bower, G. *Theories of learning.* Englewood Cliffs, N.J.: Prentice-Hall, Inc., 1975.

Koenig, W., Dunn, H., & Lacy, L. The sound spectrograph. *J. Acoust. Soc. Am.*, 1946, *17*, 19–49.

Maki, J. *Visual discrimination and identification of spectrographic patterns by hearing-impaired adults.* Paper presented to the Am. Speech Hear. Assoc. Convention, Chicago, 1977.

Maki, J., & Streff, M. *Clinical evaluation of the speech spectrographic display with hearing-impaired adults.* Paper presented to the Am. Speech Hear. Assoc. Convention, San Francisco, 1978.

Silver, G. *Automated control of the Spectrophonics Speech Spectrographic Display using a Wollensak 2590 A-V cassette recorder and logic interface.* Unpublished technical report. Rochester, NewYork: National Technical Institute for the Deaf, 1979a.

Silver, G. *Digital encoding and decoding of stimulus/trial identification numbers using a 2-channel audio tape recorder.* Unpublished report. Rochester, New York: National Technical Institute for the Deaf, 1979b.

Stewart, L., Larkin, W., & Houde, R. *A real-time sound spectrograph with implications for speech training for the deaf.* Paper presented to the IEEE Internat. Conf. Acoust., Speech, and Signal Processing, Philadelphia, 1976.

Streff, M., Conklin, J., Humphrey, B., & Maki, J. *The speech spectrographic display: Interpretation of visual patterns by hearing-impaired adults.* Paper presented to the Am. Speech Hear. Assoc. Convention, San Francisco, 1978.

16
Evaluation of Speech Training at the Postsecondary Level

Joanne D. Subtelny, Nicholas A. Orlando, and Penelope E. Webster

COMMENTS ON THE EFFICACY OF SPEECH TRAINING for individuals with impaired hearing based upon annual or repeated testing indicate that speech training in the past has not been very effective. To illustrate, Babbini and Quigley (1970), after testing 163 students in six residential schools for the deaf each year from 1963 through 1967, concluded that their subjects "... could speak no more intelligibly at the end of the study than they could at the beginning, regardless of the amount of training they received in between, if any." (Jensema et al., 1978, p. 2).

Although deaf students who enter a postsecondary level of training represent a select group with high achievement, NTID data derived from a 5-point judgment rating scale confirm a disappointing status of speech intelligibility. Only 15 percent of the students entering NTID in 1978 (*n* 289) were rated by speech pathologists as completely intelligible. At the lower end, 7 percent of this group were rated completely unintelligible.

Woofter (1979) recently reported a similar speech status as indicated by the intelligibility ratings for students entering Gallaudet College during the 1978–1979 academic year (*n* 346). Twenty percent were rated completely intelligible with 9 percent falling into the completely unintelligible category. If the two lowest rating categories are combined to indicate unintelligible speech, it is apparent that approximately 25 percent of the academic achievers entering Gallaudet and NTID are speech failures. When the two highest rating categories are combined to indicate intelligible speech which is functional, approximately 50 percent of this select segment of the deaf population have achieved considerable success in oral/aural rehabilitation.

The 25 percent incidence of speech failure at the postsecondary level may encourage us to conclude that educators do not know how to teach speech; or that previous environments have not been conducive to the development and use of speech; or that deaf students cannot or are not motivated to learn speech. We think such conclusions are unwarranted until we know more about the quality and quantity of speech training provided and until we look more discretely at the characteristics of the students.

Within the past decade, research has contributed a great deal to provide a better understanding of:

1. Factors which may influence potential to learn speech (Boothroyd, 1970; Erber, 1974; Smith, 1975);
2. Effective instructional procedures (Boothroyd et al., 1974; Calvert & Silverman, 1975; Danhauer & Singh, 1975; Erber, 1972; Ling, 1976; Maki & Streff, 1978; Mowrer, 1976; Osberger et al., 1978);
3. The perceptual and acoustical features in deaf speech which are relevant to intelligibility (Monsen, 1978; Osberger, 1978), and
4. Appropriate procedures to assess speech and related parameters of communication (Asp, 1975; Ling & Ling, 1978; McGarr, 1978).

The extreme difficulty in obtaining objective measures of language and communication in deaf clients partially accounts for the sparcity of reports specifically related to the evaluation of training. Without adequate measures, it is difficult to evaluate effectiveness. Although the task becomes easier within a population of young adults with higher levels of linguistic and communicative competence, the testing instruments to assess varied parameters of communication still are not as effective as desired.

To illustrate, authorities acknowledge the necessity of evaluating auditory perception of speech; however, Turton (1976, p. 200) has commented, "Despite several attempts to develop effective clinical tests, our profession has not been able to agree upon the type or format of auditory discrimination tests." In a similar vein, Oyer (1975) and Calvert (1976) have drawn attention to a persisting need for the development of a valid and reliable test of lipreading.

There also appears to be a need for the development of more effective and efficient tests of speech production. The variables which affect the intelligibility assessment are well documented in the literature (Asp, 1975; Hudgins & Numbers, 1942; Markides, 1970; McGarr, 1978). The limitations of the traditional articulation measures to evaluate speech learning also have been enumerated (Aungst &

McDonald, 1976; Sommers, 1967). In contrast to limitation, Asp (1975) specifically recommends a phonetic count in working with hearing-impaired children since he has found it clinically practical and effective in measuring the entire continuum from the "subintelligible to the intelligible level."

Considering the current status of test instruments and the need to examine multiple parameters of communication in order to evaluate therapy, it is not surprising that there are few reports describing the effectiveness of speech training at the postsecondary level. If evaluations are to be made, it seems investigators have several options. They may utilize standardized tests, modify existing tests, and/or develop new tests. Since the evaluation of communication training has been essential to program development at NTID, all three options have been exercised in efforts to evaluate training.

Long-Term Evaluation of Speech Training

One long-term evaluation of speech training by Conklin et al. (1976) seems particularly germane to our topic. Seventy-eight students attending NTID from Summer 1972 to Spring 1974 participated in the study. In this group, the mean 3-frequency pure-tone average was 92 dB HTL in the better ear. Within the group, 15 percent (12 students) were completely intelligible and therefore received no individualized speech training. All others received at least 20 hours of individualized instruction, with 93 percent of the poor speakers (rated 1, 2, and 3) receiving 40 or more hours of training over the two-year interval of study. Therapy was scheduled on the basis of two one-half-hour sessions per week, or two one-hour sessions per week for 10-week blocks of time.

Speech measures were accumulated at the time of entry and after two years of residency. Procedures involved a speech intelligibility rating and a measure of intelligibility for words produced within the context of a sentence. Each subject read six sentences which were recorded and played back for three listeners. Percentage scores for word intelligibility were calculated by averaging the responses of the auditors, who wrote the sentences as understood. After the two-year interval of residence these procedures were repeated. Data also were collected to define hearing aid usage and the amount of speech instruction received during the two-year interval of residency.

A statistical analysis of speech status at the beginning and termination of residency showed that there was no significant change as indicated by measures of word intelligibility in sentence context. However, significant improvement in speech ($p > .05$) was indicated by intelligibility ratings. Further study of the distribution of students falling into respective intelligibility rating categories at the time of entry and termination of residence showed the incidence of intelligible speech (rated 4 or 5) increased from 45 to 54 percent over the two-year interval (Figure 16.1). Notice also, there was a slight reduction of semi-intelligible speakers (rated 3). A shift toward an increased incidence of intelligible speech is indicated; but the 12 percent incidence of completely unintelligible speech (rated 1) did not change. The sobering fact is that most subjects with very poor entry-level speech skills and less hearing, received training and yet failed to achieve improvement.

Marked individual variation was observed. The logical question is, "What differentiates the subjects who improved in speech from those who did not?" To pursue this question, subjects were subdivided to include 17 students who made large gains in word intelligibility and nine students who not only did not improve, but regressed in speech.

Since continuation in therapy was determined by student motivation and progress, the number of hours in therapy varied. Comparative study revealed that the subjects with markedly improved speech received more instruction in speech, and also increased their use of hearing aids during residency.

In overview, these results are more positive than other reports for younger age groups. An average approximating 39 hours of individualized speech instruction provided over a two-year interval is considerable; however, it can scarcely be considered adequate for young adults with seriously impaired hearing and speech. Despite this fact, over the long term *some* but not all students improved. Very gross grouping of the entire population obscures this finding.

Since 1974, the principles, procedures, and strategies of training have been modified as a consequence of continued evaluations of therapy over the short term. In these evaluations, therapy has been more adequately described and some of the obstacles in assessment have been partially overcome.

Short-term Evaluations of Therapy at the Postsecondary Level

Speech instruction at NTID has been based upon concepts of speech, voice, and auditory training expressed by many leading authorities in respective areas (Boone, 1971; Calvert & Silverman, 1975; Erber, 1972; Ling, 1976; McDonald, 1964; Milisen, 1976; Moore, 1971; Sanders, 1971, 1977; Winitz, 1969, 1975). In developing materials for training, an early decision was made to design different courses of therapy for postsecondary students who have and have not mastered respiratory and phonatory control to serve speech needs. Developmental or "voice" therapy is offered to students who have deviant voice quality, pitch, or problems in controlling pitch. Such training is considered a prerequisite to gain the aerodynamic control required to correct deviant articulation and prosody.

With respect to articulation and prosody, training has been directed

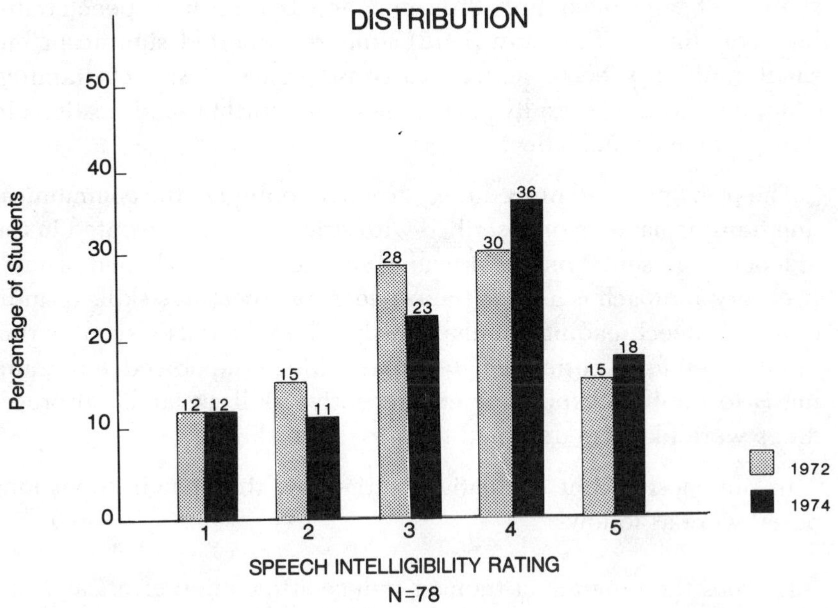

FIGURE 16.1

Distribution of intelligibility ratings for students at the time of entry and termination of residence at the National Technical Institute for the Deaf. Descriptors for the Intelligibility Rating Scale are as follows: 5, speech is completely intelligible; 4, speech is intelligible with the exception of a few words or phrases; 3, with difficulty, the listener can understand about half the content of the message (intelligibility may improve after a listening period); 2, speech is very difficult to understand–only isolated words or phrases are intelligible; 1, speech is completely unintelligible.

by the principle that objectives, materials, and strategies should be based upon the individual's competence in the functional use of English. Although the NTID population is heterogeneous relative to auditory, speech, and linguistic competence, these competencies are considered interdependent for purposes of remediation. Hence, it was hypothesized that broader gains in communication would be achieved if speech, speechreading, and auditory training were integrated to reinforce correct English usage. In this way, each area of instruction should serve to reinforce and supplement other areas of learning (Subtelny & Walter, 1975).

In 1975 and 1976, evaluation of therapy offered some limited support for this concept. Lieberth and Subtelny (1978) reported small but significant gains in auditory discrimination as a result of speech training. Conklin and Subtelny (1978) similarly reported significant but small gains in speechreading as a consequence of speech training. Compositely, these results encouraged some further modifications in therapy to maximize effectiveness.

The principles and procedures currently applied in the communication training have been described with strategies demonstrated in the videotape presentations of previous speakers. As explained, a multisensory approach is used to train speech and receptive skills of audition and speechreading simultaneously. The materials also are structured to reinforce correct English usage. Since the objective of training is to improve expressive and receptive skills, evaluation procedures were likewise designed to assess both skills.

In our most recent evaluation of therapy, the specific questions posed were as follows:

1. Does the program of training reduce articulation errors and improve speech intelligibility?
2. Is auditory perception of speech significantly affected by the training program?
3. Are any changes in visual reception of speech demonstrated?
4. Can any factors be identified which predispose gains in speech production and/or reception?

To pursue these questions, rather extensive tests were administered before and after training to evaluate auditory and visual reception of speech and production of speech.

Tests were selected to provide:

1. Multiple samples of speech ranging in complexity from syllable to conversation, and
2. Measures of auditory discrimination and speechreading which would permit study of changes in performance as a result of training and also facilitate the comparative study of reception and production.

Sample: The 79 NTID students who participated in the study received an average of 28.3 hours of therapy (sd 1.85) scheduled on a two-hour-per-week basis. Fifteen experienced speech pathologists received in-service training in use of materials and then directed the therapy in accordance with the objectives and principles described.

A rather broad range of speech and hearing skills was represented in the sample. Pure-tone averages in the better ear ranged from 65 to 120 dB with a mean of 94 dB (sd 14.84). Within the total group, over half (57 percent) had no discrimination for speech as assessed by key word recognition in the CID Everyday Sentences. Discrimination scores ranged from zero to 64 percent with a mean of 11.05 percent (sd 16.22). Ninety percent of the students were using hearing aids all or most of the time during the interval of this study.

Ratings of speech intelligibility during oral reading indicated the students as a group were semi-intelligible (m. 3.43; sd .62). However, individual ratings ranged from completely unintelligible to intelligible with the exception of a few words. Articulation measures averaged 58 percent correct phoneme production (sd 12.41).

Procedures

Auditory Perception of Speech

Speech perception was evaluated by testing consonant discrimination in CV syllable context and by two additional tests to assess consonant and vowel discrimination within word context. All auditory tests were administered binaurally under earphones.

The first test administered was the Phoneme Identification Test Series (Jones et al., 1976; Sims & Montgomery, 1977), which consists of 64 consonant-vowel items. These syllables include four repetitions of 16 consonants paired with the vowel /*a*/. In response to each syllable, the student identifies the stimulus consonant from a set of 16 possible responses presented on an opscan sheet. Computer scoring yields the total percentage of correct consonant identifications and a breakdown of identification by distinctive features of manner, voicing, and place of production.

To test auditory discrimination of consonants in word context, the Modified Rhyme Test (House et al., 1965) was administered. This test consists of six lists of 50 monosyllabic words. These lists form 50 related sets with six words in each. All six words in each set have the same vocalic nucleus and an identical consonantal element in either the initial or final position. Examples are:

map	mat	math	man	mass	mad
led	shed	red	bed	fed	wed

On this list, the listener identifies the word from a closed set of six responses.

The forms prepared for student responses present all 50 response sets in the appropriate order of recording. Instructions are simply to listen, then circle the word heard within each set of six.

The Vowel Test developed by Horii (1969) was administered to evaluate vowel discrimination using the same principle of closed-set response. This test is comprised of 24 sets with six words in each set. Each set uses 12 different vowels which occur twice. All six words in each set have identical initial and final consonants, i.e.,

lock	lick	lake	look	leak	luck
mass	moose	muss	miss	mess	moss

The Modified Rhyme and Vowel Tests were scored manually to yield percentage scores of auditory discrimination for words, and for consonants and vowels within words.

Speechreading

To evaluate visual recognition of consonants, a speechreading version of the Phoneme Identification Test Series was projected on video cassette without sound. As in the auditory version, each CV syllable appears four times for a total of 64 test items. In responding, subjects watch the speaker, then circle the consonant identified from the closed response set appearing on the opscan scoring sheet. Responses are scored by computer to yield total percentage scores and percentage scores for consonants grouped by manner and place of production.

Speech reception in sentence context using both vision and audition was evaluated by projecting one of the NTID speechreading films described by Johnson (1976). The test, consisting of 10 sentences, was administered individually under headphones. Students responded to sentences by writing the words as understood. Responses were manually scored to determine the number and percentage of words correctly identified.

Speech Production

In order to compare speech production with auditory discrimination and visual reception of speech, subjects produced in speech many of the same items they were asked to identify by audition and/or speechreading. These materials included the CV syllables from the Phoneme Identification Test and the appropriate list of words from the Modified Rhyme and Vowel Tests.

Intelligibility measures and ratings. In administering the Phoneme Identification Test to evaluate intelligible consonant production, the therapist records the client's responses on the opscan sheet. In testing, an explanation of purpose and procedure is given, the therapist models a few productions, and a trial for the student is provided. The client then begins producing syllables as the stimulus is presented in print. No visual or auditory modeling is provided during testing. The therapist scores responses auditorily *without* visual cues. Tests are scored by computer to yield the total percentage of consonants intelligibly produced.

To evaluate the validity of this test for consonant intelligibility assessment, percentages of inter-judge agreement for 16 speech pathologists were calculated after each had received instructions in scoring and had responded to recordings of 10 NTID students producing the test items. Analysis revealed the percentage of agreement was $>$ 81 percent.

To evaluate reliability, the 10 recordings were scored a second time one week later. The correlation coefficient between first and second scoring was $r = +.79$. These statistical results are considered adequate for purposes of comparing consonant production and consonant perception within the constraints of the consonant-vowel /a/ unit (Whitehead, 1978).

The appropriate list of words used to test auditory discrimination was reviewed by each subject to reduce reading difficulties. The words from the Modified Rhyme and Vowel Tests were then presented in print one at a time for recording at five-second intervals. For analysis, tape recordings were played back to five experienced listeners who wrote each word as understood. Each auditor's response to the Modified Rhyme test words was scored to yield the percentage of words and the percentage of consonants accurately identified.[1] The responses of the five auditors were than averaged to yield a single score for isolated word intelligibility and for consonant intelligibility.

Similar procedures were followed in responding to the words produced on the Vowel Test. In analysis, only vowels were scored for intelligibility. The results of the five auditors again were averaged to determine a percentage for vowel intelligibility.

In addition to measures of intelligibility for syllables and for words in isolation, 10 sentences selected from the Speech Intelligibility Test (Magner, 1972) were recorded for each speaker. Forty-one different sets with 10 sentences in each were constructed to minimize practice effect in listening and to modify context to improve equivalence in phonetic composition and in number of words per set. Auditing and scoring for five listeners were undertaken to determine the averaged percentage of intelligible words produced in sentence context.

To complete data collection for intelligibility assessment, recordings were made of students reading the Rainbow Passage and speaking spontaneously in response to sequential picture stimuli. For analysis, the tape recordings were played back to a panel of five experienced auditors who independently rated the intelligibility of each sample on a 5-point scale, ranging from 1, completely unintelligible, to 5, completely intelligible. Since ratings were made at half intervals between integers, the scale actually involves 9 points. The ratings of the five auditors were then averaged to establish a single rating of intelligibility for contextual speech.

Articulation. Because the training program was focused relative to targets for correction, some measures of articulation defined by articulation testing were considered essential to evaluation. To meet these needs, one traditional measure, the Fisher-Logemann Test of Articulation Competence (Fisher & Logemann, 1971), was recorded for each student before and after training. Each recording was phonetically analyzed by two experienced speech pathologists with results averaged and categorized according to features.

The second measure of articulation focused on the accuracy of the sounds targeted for correction and production within conversational context. To implement this measure, the therapist, after identifying the target and cognate for correction, tape-recorded a sample of spon-

[1]When consonant blends were encountered in some of the monosyllabic words, an arbitrary decision was made to score the blend incorrect unless both sounds were intelligible.

FIGURE 16.2
Means for measures of CV syllable, isolated word, and sentence intelligibility secured before and after therapy.

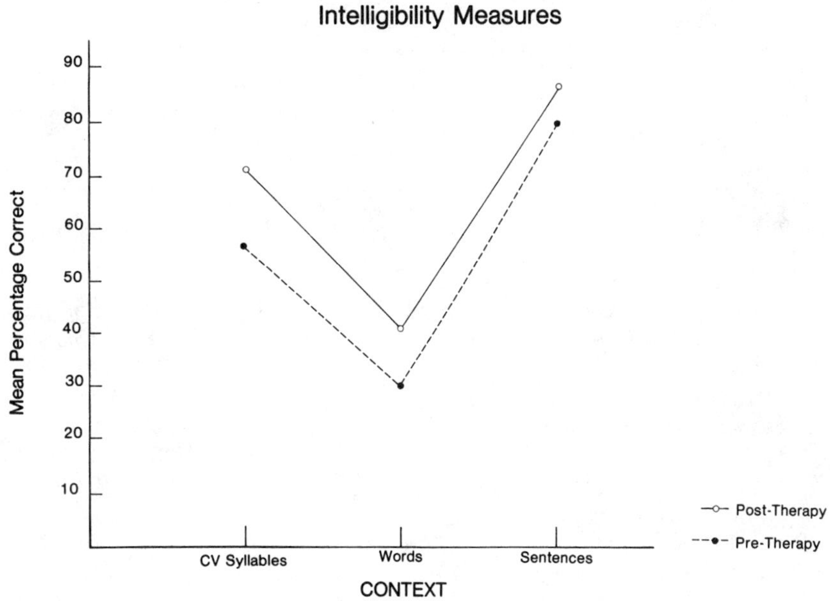

taneous speech. Recordings were then analyzed to determine the number of trials on target and cognate and to determine the percentage of accuracy for each.

Results

Pre- and post-therapy means for intelligibility measures of syllable, word, and sentence production (Figure 16.2; Table 16.A) indicate that significant improvement was achieved on all three measures as a result of training ($p > .01$). Improvement for syllable and word intelligibility averaged 14 percent and 12 percent respectively. The smaller gain for words produced in sentences (approximating 6.5 percent) may be partially explained by a much higher level of intelligibility for words in sentences before therapy was undertaken. In the pre-therapy status, sentence intelligibility averaged 79.20 percent, whereas isolated word intelligibility averaged 29.50 percent. The lower intelligibility for isolated words without sentence context and redundancy is consistent with the literature (Miller et al., 1951; O'Neill, 1957).

TABLE 16.A

*Means and standard deviations for ratings and measures of speech secured before and after therapy. All differences between means are significant at the .01 level.**
(n = 79 NTID Students)

Parameter		Pre	Post
Intelligibility Ratings			
Oral Reading	m	3.41	3.78
(Scale 1–5)	sd	.64	.64
Spontaneous Speech	m	3.17	3.52
(Scale 1–5)	sd	.97	.76
Intelligibility Measurements			
Words—Sentence Context	m	79.20%	85.67%
(Clark Speech Intel. Test)	sd	20.40	15.36
Words—Isolation	m	29.50%	41.36%
(Mod. Rhyme Test)	sd	15.98	18.95
Consonants—Word Context	m	58.75%	68.66%
(Mod. Rhyme Test)	sd	13.73	12.06
Consonants—CV Syllables	m	56.64%	71.05%
(Phon. Id. Test Series)	sd	23.49	23.96
Vowels—Word Context	m	52.92%	57.33%
(Vowel Test)	sd	19.41	19.52
Articulation Measurements			
Fisher-Logemann Test of Articulation	m	58.08%	69.79%
Competence	sd	12.41	12.45
Target in Spontaneous Speech	m	18.39%	71.08%
	sd	22.42	24.73
Cognate in Spontaneous Speech	m	34.24%	59.97%
	sd	34.95	34.70

*Mann-Whitney U tests were applied to evaluate pre/post differences between mean ratings of speech intelligibility. Student t tests were applied for all other measures of intelligibility and articulation.

The syllable test required producing one of 16 consonants always in initial position and always paired with the same vowel /a/. This task is much easier than producing intelligible words which require initial and final consonants embedding varied vowel elements. When this difference is considered, higher levels of performance would be expected for syllable production.

Intelligibility Ratings

Intelligibility ratings for oral reading and spontaneous speech also showed significant improvement. As noted previously (Subtelny,

1977), intelligibility tended to be slightly lower in spontaneous speech than in oral reading. The difficulty in formulating spontaneous speech (without print) may contribute to this difference; however, some of the difference also may be a reflection of the listener's familiarity with the oral reading passage.

The degree of improvement as indicated by scaled rating was highly significant from a statistical viewpoint. The actual degree of improvement is not as great as desired; however, improvement was comparable in spontaneous speech and in oral reading. This finding seems particularly positive since it suggests that without printed stimulus for production, improvement in intelligibility continued to be expressed. Thus, some benefit from articulation training seems to have been effectively carried over into conversation. Further support for this suggestion is indicated by articulation measures.

Articulation

As shown in Figure 16.3, the overall gain in articulation approximated 12 percent. However, the gains in articulatory accuracy for the target and cognate stressed in therapy were much higher, approaching 53 percent and 26 percent, respectively. Since these sounds were targeted, higher gains would be expected; however, the conversa-

FIGURE 16.3

Pre- and post-therapy means for measures of articulation defined by traditional testing, and by evaluating the target and cognate in recorded samples of spontaneous speech.

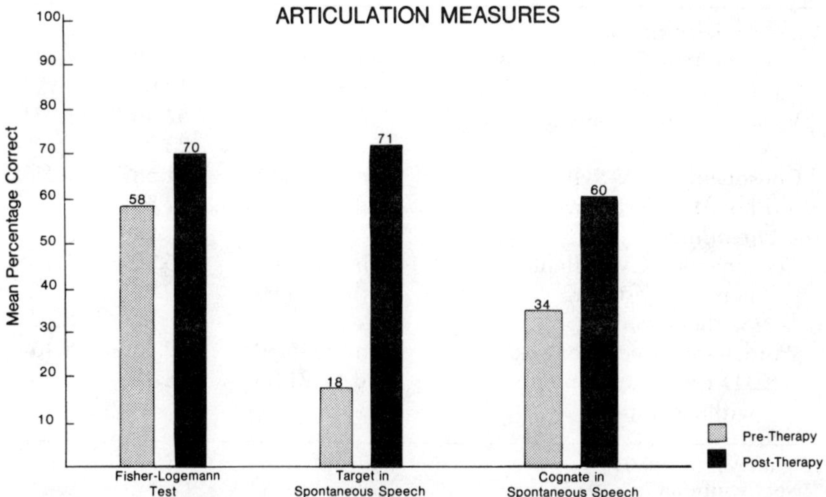

tional context in which they were produced does provide some evidence of effective carry-over, at least for sounds stressed in therapy.

Speechreading With Sound

The tests administered with sound to evaluate speechreading indicate that significant improvement was achieved for combined auditory and visual reception of speech in sentence context. When auditory and visual cues to perception were provided, the mean percentage of words correctly identified increased from 45.80 percent to 57.43 percent as a result of training (Table 16.B). Thus, both overall or global ratings of production and measures of reception as indicated by speechreading with sound revealed significant gains.

Phoneme Identification Test Series

Speechreading tests administered without sound and without sentence context yielded quite different results. The test for visual identification of consonants in syllables, without linguistic context and without auditory input, showed much lower levels of speechreading performance.

TABLE 16.B

Means, standard deviations, and t values for measures of auditory discrimination and speechreading secured before and after therapy.
(*n* = 79 NTID Students)

Measurement		Pre	Post	t
Auditory Discrimination				
Consonents—Word Context	m	37.17%	41.98%	4.71*
(Mod. Rhyme Test)	sd	17.39	18.65	
Vowels—Word Context	m	49.92%	52.49%	1.93**
(Vowel Test)	sd	22.80	23.24	
Consonants—CV Syllables	m	20.15%	21.58%	1.21**
(Phon. Id. Test Ser.)	sd	14.20	17.53	
Speechreading				
Consonants—CV Syllables	m	44.00%	45.96%	1.55**
(Phon. Id. Test Ser. without sound)	sd	10.60	9.27	
Words—Sentence Context	m	45.80%	57.43%	8.46*
(CID Everyday Sentences without sound)	sd	21.33	24.43	

*Significant ($p > 0.01$)
**Not Significant ($p < 0.05$)

FIGURE 16.4
Pre- and post-therapy means for auditory discrimination, visual discrimination (without sound), and production of consonants in consonant-vowel /a/ syllables.

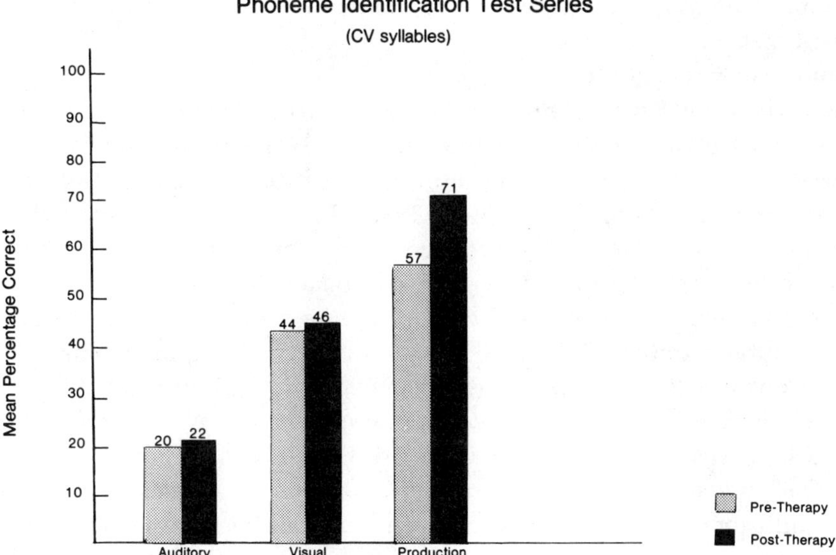

The three different modes of administration for the Phoneme Identification Test Series permit comparative study of an individual's auditory discrimination, visual identification, and intelligible production of consonants. As a first look at these relationships within the total sample, pre- and post-therapy means on all three tests are presented in Figure 16.4. The means for auditory discrimination of consonants before training (m. 20.15 percent) and after training (m. 21.58 percent) are very low, falling within the level of chance. The pre/post comparison of means also indicates no improvement in consonant discrimination within syllable context.

The means for visual discrimination of consonants without sound indicate performance higher than the level of chance. However, again no significant improvement is indicated when the pre-therapy mean of 44 percent is compared with the post-therapy 45.96 percent.

Means established for intelligible consonants produced within CV syllable context indicate that production performance was considerably higher than reception by auditory or visual modes. Furthermore, a comparison of the pre-therapy mean of 56.64 percent with the post-therapy mean of 71.05 percent indicates that significant improvement in intelligible consonant production did result from training. This finding seems particularly positive since it provides some evidence within the constraints of the syllable that significant gains can be achieved in consonant production even though comparable improvement in auditory discrimination and visual perception is not realized.

Relationships Between Production and Discrimination

Consonant and vowel discrimination may be more effectively compared with consonant and vowel production by studying the results of the Modified Rhyme and Vowel Tests. In both of these tests, the stimulus to discriminate or produce is the word, rather than the CV syllable. As shown in Figure 16.5, consonant discrimination within word context averaged 37.17 percent before training and 41.98 percent after training. This small but significant gain, approximately 5 percent in discrimination, was associated with a significant gain of 9.91 percent in intelligible consonant production in word context.

Comparison of means for vowel discrimination before therapy (49.92 percent) and after therapy (52.49 percent) indicates that no significant improvement was achieved from training. The 4.41 percent gain in vowel production was far less than the improvement realized

FIGURE 16.5

Pre- and post-therapy means for discrimination and production of consonants and vowels within word context.

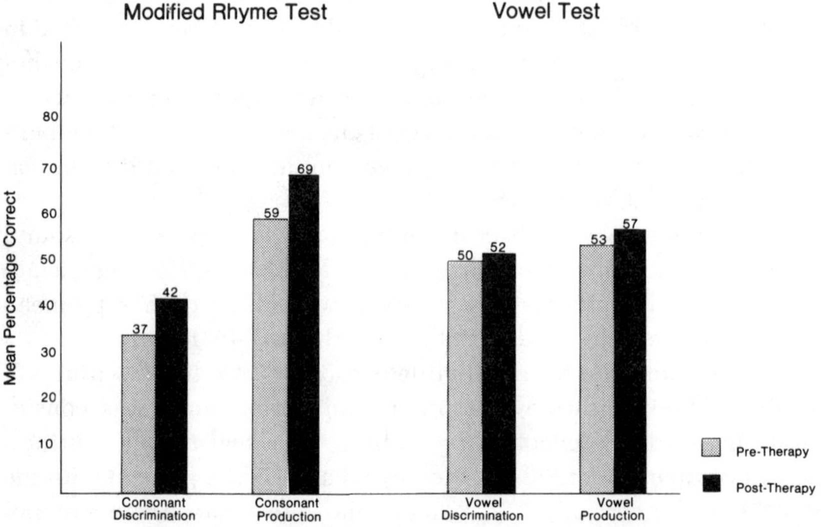

for intelligible consonant production in word context (9.91 percent). The lesser gain in vowel production as opposed to consonant production may be attributed to the fact that consonant discrimination improved in therapy whereas vowel discrimination did not improve.

The proportional greater gain in consonant production also may be attributed to a greater emphasis upon consonant discrimination and consonant production in training. The heavy emphasis in therapy placed upon visual and tactile cues may have had a greater impact upon consonant rather than vowel production. This interpretation seems supported by the fact that consonants provide stronger visual, tactile, and kinesthetic cues for reception and production than those associated with vowels (Calvert & Silverman, 1975).

Other interesting observations may be drawn from the data graphed in Figure 16.5. Although vowel discrimination before and after therapy was superior to consonant discrimination, the reverse of this observation is indicated by the production data. Vowel production before and after therapy was inferior to consonant production.

This observation raises some pertinent clinical questions. If the skill in producing intelligible consonants exceeds that demonstrated in discriminating consonants, why is it that skill in producing vowels does not exceed that demonstrated in discriminating vowels? Since vowels provide stronger acoustical features for auditory discrimination than those provided by consonants, the potential for improving vowels would appear to be present. Why is it then that vowel discrimination did not improve in training? Are current strategies appropriate to achieve gain in vowel discrimination and to improve the small gains realized for vowel production? Should visual feedback, such as the speech spectrographic display, be utilized to improve vowel discrimination and production? Or does the training program which utilizes a combined auditory, visual, tactile, and kinesthetic approach minimize gains which might be achieved exclusively in auditory discrimination? Although no answers to these questions are offered, the lack of improvement in vowel discrimination must be seriously considered in future revision of the training program.

Gain Related to Auditory Discrimination

In a broad general description of communication status before and after training, significant findings may be obscured by the coarse lumping of data for the entire sample. It may be hypothesized that auditory discrimination for speech is the most significant variable in determining response to therapy. To pursue this concept, the entire

TABLE 16.C

Means and standard deviations for pre/post therapy gains in measures of speechreading, auditory discrimination, and speech production for two groups of students. Group I was differentiated from Group II by greater than 0% discrimination for key words in CID Everyday Sentences

Measurement		Group I > 0% Discrim. *n* = 34	Group II 0% Discrim. *n* = 45
Speechreading			
CID Everyday Sentences	m	12.66%	10.86%
(with sound)	sd	12.46	11.95
Auditory Discrimination			
Consonants—Syllable Context	m	5.06%	−1.31%
(Phon. Id. Test Series)	sd	13.46	6.28
Consonants—Word Context	m	5.14%	4.55%
(Mod. Rhyme Test)	sd	9.85	8.52
Vowels—Word Context	m	4.64%	1.93%
(Vowel Test)	sd	11.36	11.91
Speech Production			
Consonants—Syllable Context	m	15.78%	13.75%
(Phon. Id. Test Series)	sd	20.84	16.43
Words—Isolation	m	15.90%	8.59%
(Mod. Rhyme Test)	sd	7.98	7.42
Words—Sentence Context	m	2.54%	9.40%
(Clark Speech Intel. Test)	sd	4.33	10.39
Intelligibility Rating			
Oral Reading	m	.35	.37
	sd	.18	.46
Spontaneous Speech	m	.18	.46
	sd	.39	.53
Articulation	m	11.58%	11.53%
(Fisher-Logemann Test)	sd	7.37	6.98

sample was divided to create two groups: Group I, consisting of 34 students who had greater than 0 percent auditory discrimination for words in sentences, and Group II, consisting of 45 students who had no discrimination. The associated means for pure-tone average at 500, 1000, and 2000 Hz in the better ear were 88.20 dB (sd 10.36) in Group I and 98.11 dB (sd 8.43) in Group II (Table 16.C).

To determine if these two groups differed in response to therapy, averaged gains for respective measures were compared. These data are graphed in Figure 16.6. In general, the students with some discrimination showed slightly better gains in speechreading with sound, in discriminating vowels, and in producing intelligible consonants within syllable context; however, they showed much better gains (means 5.06 percent and 1.31 percent) in discriminating consonants in CV syllable context and in producing intelligible words in isolation (means 15.90 percent and 8.59 percent). The two groups showed equal gains approximating 5 percent in auditory discrimination of consonants as measured by the Modified Rhyme Test, and in articulation as measured by the Fisher-Logemann Test.

Gain in intelligibility for words produced in sentences was much greater (m. 9.40 percent) for students with no discrimination than for students with discrimination (m. 2.54 percent). Some of this indicated difference between groups may be explained by the fact that students who had some discrimination showed much higher levels of performance on this measure before therapy was initiated.

FIGURE 16.6

Gains in performance as indicated by the difference between pre- and post-therapy means for students grouped on the basis of auditory discrimination for speech. Respective means for Groups I and II are graphed for the following measures: speechreading with sound, phoneme identification (auditory), phoneme identification (production), modified rhyme (auditory), modified rhyme (production), sentence intelligibility, articulation, and vowel discrimination (auditory).

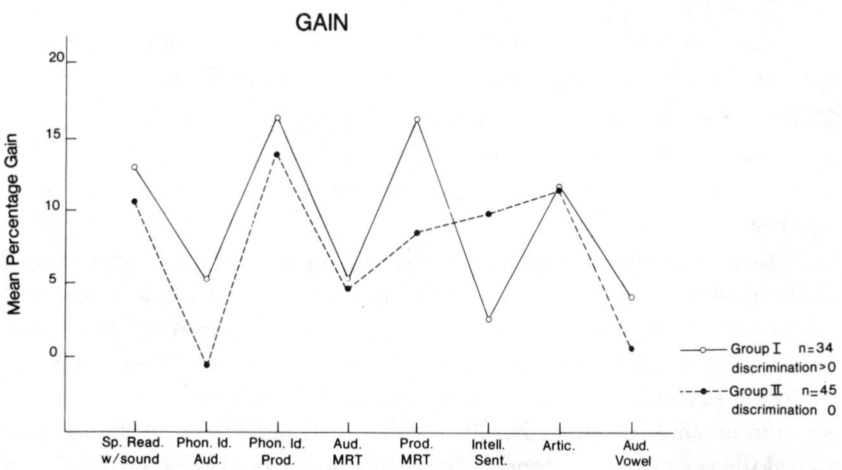

Conclusions

This study was undertaken to evaluate a program of training to improve communication of postsecondary students with severe impairments of hearing. The analysis of data secured is incomplete at the present time; however, on the basis of information presented in this writing, some conclusions can be drawn.

1. The program of training is successful. The improvements in articulation, averaging about 12 percent, were associated with equal gains in isolated word intelligibility and with about a 7 percent increase in intelligibility of words produced in sentence context. All measures and ratings of speech performance at phoneme, syllable, word, sentence, and conversational levels revealed significant improvement.
2. Smaller but significant gains of 5 percent in auditory discrimination, as defined by the Modified Rhyme Test, were associated with the improvements in speech. However, no improvement in vowel discrimination was demonstrated.
3. Speechreading tests of sentence material administered with sound showed significant gains in speech reception; however, speechreading tests administered without sound to evaluate visual identification of consonants in CV syllable context revealed no improvement in speechreading.
4. When the sample was subdivided on the basis of auditory discrimination, greater gains for most speech measures and for auditory discrimination were identified with students who had better hearing.
5. When measures of auditory discrimination for consonants were compared with measures of production for consonants, performance in production consistently exceeded performance in discrimination.

This finding suggests that auditory discrimination for some consonants may not be a realistic goal in training; however, failure in discrimination does not indicate that intelligible consonants cannot be produced.

In this investigation, gains in both auditory discrimination and production of consonants were achieved. At this juncture, a cause and effect cannot be determined. Did the gain in discrimination improve production or did the gain in production improve discrimination? Without resolution to this question, one implication pertinent to aural/oral rehabilitation of young deaf adults may be formulated: The two skills seem interdependent and thus might best be developed and refined simultaneously. In training, the relative emphasis placed on auditory or motoric skill might best be determined by comparing measures of perception with measures of production.

As stated previously, further analysis of data is indicated to study relationships between perception and production as a function of distinctive features, and to relate measures of production and perception to features of the audiogram which define degree and configuration of hearing loss.

The postsecondary population at NTID seems ideally suited to provide valid and reliable measures of perception and production for syllables as well as larger units of speech. Intensive study to better understand relationships between perception and production and their combined relationship to conventional audiologic measures is justified as a means of improving predictions of aural/oral success in younger age groups. With very young children the difficulties in testing are accentuated. Too many times audiometric information is the only objective data available for a child. If this unfortunate situation does exist, valid and reliable interpretation of that data definitely is needed.

REFERENCES

Asp, C. W. Measurement of aural speech perception and oral speech production of the hearing-impaired. In S. Singh (Ed.), *Measurement procedures in speech-hearing-language.* Baltimore: University Park Press, 1975.

Aungst, L. F., & McDonald, E. T. Evaluating articulation therapy. In W. D. Wolfe & D. J. Goulding (Eds.), *Articulation and learning.* Springfield, Ill.: Charles C Thomas, 1976.

Babbini, B. E., & Quigley, S. P. *A study of the growth patterns in language, communication and educational achievement in six residential schools for deaf students.* Illinois University, Urbana: Institute for Research on Exceptional Children, 1970.

Boone, D. R. *The voice and voice therapy.* Englewood Cliffs, N.J.: Prentice-Hall, 1971.

Boothroyd, A. *Distribution of hearing levels in the student population of the Clarke School for the Deaf.* (SARP Report #3), Northampton, Mass.: Clarke School for the Deaf, 1970.

Boothroyd, A., Nickerson, R., & Stevens, K. *Temporal patterns in the speech of the deaf–a study in remedial training.* C. V. Hudgins Diagnostic and Research Center, Northampton, Mass.: Clarke School for the Deaf, 1974.

Calvert, D. R. Communication practices: Aural/oral and visual/oral. *Volta Rev.,* 1976, *78,* 76–81.

Calvert, D. R., & Silverman, S.R. *Speech and deafness.* Washington, D.C.: A.G. Bell Association for the Deaf, 1975.

Conklin, J. M., & Subtelny, J. D. *The effect of articulation training upon speech reading.* Paper presented at the Am. Speech Hear. Assoc. Convention, San Francisco, 1978.

Conklin, J. M., Subtelny, J. D., & Walter, G. G. *Analysis of the communication skills of young deaf adults over a two year interval of technical training.* Paper presented at the Am. Speech Hear. Assoc. Convention, Houston, 1976.

Danhauer, J. L., & Singh, S. *Multidimensional speech perception by the hearing impaired: A treatise on distinctive features.* Baltimore: University Park Press, 1975.

Erber, N. P. Auditory, visual and auditory-visual recognition of consonants by children with normal and impaired hearing. *J. Speech Hear. Res.*, 1972, *15*, 423–38.

Erber, N. P. Pure-tone thresholds and word-recognition abilities of hearing-impaired children. *J. Speech Hear. Res.*, 1974, *17*, 194–202.

Fisher, H. B., & Logemann, J. A. *The Fisher-Logemann test of articulation competence.* Boston, Mass.: Houghton Mifflin, 1971.

Horii, Y. *Specifying the speech-to-noise ratio: Development and evaluation of a noise with speech-envelope characteristics.* Doctoral dissertation, Purdue University, 1969.

House, A. S., Williams, C. E., Hecker, M. H. L., & Kryter, K. D. Articulation testing methods: Consonantal differentiation with a closed-response set. *J. Acoust. Soc. Am.*, 1965, *37*, 158–166.

Hudgins, C. V., & Numbers, F. C. An investigation of the intelligibility of the speech of the deaf. *Genet. Psych. Mono.*, 1942, *25*, 289–392.

Jensema, C. J., Karchmer, M. A., & Trybus, R. J. *The rated speech intelligibility of hearing impaired children: Basic relationships and a detailed analysis.* Washington, D.C.: Office of Demographic Studies, Gallaudet College, 1978.

Johnson, D. D. Communication characteristics of a young deaf adult population: Techniques for evaluating their communication skills. *Am. Ann. Deaf*, 1976, *121*, 409–423.

Jones, K., Whitehead, R., Bancroft, J., & Sims, D. *The performance of students at the National Technical Institute for the Deaf on an auditory speech perception test.* Paper presented at the Am. Speech Hear. Assoc. Convention, Houston, 1976.

Lieberth, A., & Subtelny, J. D. The effect of speech training on auditory phoneme identification. *Volta Rev.*, 1978, *80*, 410–417.

Ling, D. *Speech and the hearing-impaired child: Theory and practice.* Washington, D.C.: A.G. Bell Association for the Deaf, 1976.

Ling, D., & Ling, A. *Aural habilitation: The foundations of verbal learning in hearing-impaired children.* Washington, D.C.: A.G. Bell Association for the Deaf, 1978.

Magner, M. E. *A speech intelligibility test for deaf children.* Northampton, Mass.: Clarke School for the Deaf, 1972.

Maki, J. E., & Streff, M. M. *Clinical evaluation of speech spectrographic display with hearing-impaired adults.* Paper presented at the Am. Speech Hear. Assoc. Convention, San Francisco, 1978.

Markides, A. The speech of deaf and partially hearing children with special reference to factors affecting intelligibility. *Brit. J. Dis. Comm.*, 1970, *5*, 126–140.

McDonald, E. I. *Articulation testing and treatment–a sensory-motor approach.* Pittsburgh: Stanwix House, 1964.

McGarr, N. S. *The difference between experienced and inexperienced listeners in understanding the speech of the deaf.* Doctoral dissertation, City University of New York, 1978.

Milisen, R. An eclectic approach to the management of articulation disorders. In W. D. Wolfe & D. J. Goulding (Eds.), *Articulation and learning.* Springfield, Ill.: Charles C Thomas, 1976.

Miller, G. A., Heise, G. A., & Lichten, W. The intelligibility of speech as a function of the context of test material. *J. Exp. Psych.*, 1951, *41*, 329–335.

Monsen, R. B. Toward measuring how well deaf children speak. *J. Speech Hear. Res.*, 1978, *21*, 197–219.

Moore, G. P. *Organic voice disorders.* Englewood Cliffs, N.J.: Prentice-Hall, 1971.

Mowrer, D. A behavioristic approach to modification of articulation. In W. D. Wolfe & D. J. Goulding (Eds.), *Articulation and learning.* Springfield, Ill.: Charles C Thomas, 1976.

O'Neill, J. J. Recognition of intelligibility test materials. *J. Speech Hear. Dis.*, 1957, *22*, 87–90.

Osberger, M. J. *The effect of timing errors on the intelligibility of deaf children's speech.* Doctoral dissertation, City University of New York, 1978.

Osberger, M. J., Johnstone, A., Swarts, E., & Levitt, H. The evaluation of a model speech training program for deaf children. *J. Comm. Dis.*, 1978, *11*, 293–313.

Oyer, H. J. The measurement of the dimensions of visual communications. In S. Singh, (Ed.), *Measurement procedures in speech, hearing, and language.* Baltimore: University Park Press, 1975.

Sanders, D. A. *Aural rehabilitation.* Englewood Cliffs, N.J.: Prentice-Hall, 1971.

Sanders, D. A. *Auditory perception of speech.* Englewood Cliffs, N.J.: Prentice-Hall, 1977.

Sims, D. G., & Montgomery, A. A. *Multidimensional analysis of auditory and visual perception among the profoundly hearing-impaired.* Paper presented at Acoust. Soc. of Am. Convention, Miami, 1977.

Smith, C. R. Residual hearing and speech production in deaf children. *J. Speech Hear. Res.*, 1975, *18*, 795–811.

Sommers, R. K. Problems in articulatory research: Methodology and error. *Am. Speech Hear. Assoc.*, 1967, *9*, 406–408.

Subtelny, J. D. Assessment of speech with implications for training. In F. H. Bess (Ed.), *Childhood deafness: Causation, assessment and management.* New York: Grune & Stratton, 1977.

Subtelny, J. D., & Walter, G. G. An overview of the communication skills of NTID students with implications for planning of rehabilitation. *J. Acad. Rehab. Aud.*, 1975, *8*, 33–50.

Turton, L. J. Diagnostic implications of articulation testing. In. W. D. Wolfe & D. J. Goulding, (Eds.), *Articulation and learning.* Springfield, Ill.: Charles C Thomas, 1976.

Whitehead, R. *Validity and reliability of phoneme identification test material to assess consonant production.* National Technical Institute for the Deaf, internal report, Rochester, New York, 1978.

Winitz, H. *Articulatory acquisition and behavior.* New York: Appleton-Century-Crofts, 1969.

Winitz, H. *From syllable to conversation.* Baltimore: University Park Press, 1975.

Woofter, H. Personal communication. June 14, 1979.

Acknowledgments

This study was conducted at the National Technical Institute for the Deaf in the course of an agreement with the U.S. Department of Health, Education and Welfare. The authors especially wish to acknowledge Allen Austin and Ann Lieberth for their assistance in analysis of tapes; Dale Metz for statistical analysis of judgment ratings, and Jorge Samper, audiovisual specialist in the Media Production Department, for preparation of illustrations. Obviously, the study would not have been possible as originally designed without the cooperation and understanding of the highly skilled speech pathologists working at the National Technical Institute for the Deaf. The authors are most respectful and appreciative of the many extra hours which were required to document progress and to follow a tightly structured program of speech and auditory instruction. In this regard, we express sincere thanks to Allen Austin, Sidney Barefoot, Sylvia Card, John Conklin, Karen Dobkowski, Marianne Streff Gustafson, Brenda Humphrey, Jacqueline Kelly, Ann Lieberth, Michael McMahon, Lawrence Pschirrer, Jean Smith, Paula Spector, and Beth Ann Vom Eigen.

17
Summary Comment: Current Status of Success in Speech Training

Mary E. Campbell

IT IS OBVIOUS FROM THE PAPERS presented at this conference that a great deal of information is known about speech and speech production. The characteristics have been carefully analyzed and reported.

Some institutions offer excellent training for teachers. Students have learned to analyze and skillfully teach speech to hearing-impaired children with great success. Consistency is maintained for students both in expectations and in methods used in developing speech and language. The utilization of residual hearing is carefully monitored and every advantage is provided to the student by the employment of modern technology.

After over 20 years of experience in teaching, supervising, and consulting with programs for the hearing impaired, I am convinced that most hearing-impaired children can learn to speak—and speak intelligibly. I've seen it happen time and time again. Yet the Office of Demographic Studies report on speech intelligibility indicates little or no measurable gain in speech intelligibility of students who have losses of 90 dB or greater. How can this be? What are the variables? Why isn't it happening with profoundly deaf students on a more consistent basis? I would like to hazard a few guesses.

The Use of Auditory Equipment

It has been demonstrated that with training in the use of properly fitted and operating hearing aids, most hearing-impaired individuals gain considerable information about speech production, both of their own and that of others. However, the analysis and use of such information require specific training and practice with hearing aids which are maintained in excellent working condition. I would wager that 70 to 80 percent of the deaf children in this country have hearing aids which are not fitted correctly, not operating properly, or are not even being used. Thus, these children are deprived of the most normal method of gaining valuable information about what others say, how they say it, and about their own speech production as well. It is an electronic age, but many hearing-impaired children are still back in the dark ages because the technological "know how" of today is not properly employed on their behalf. Could one view this as "neglect" under the Child Abuse and Neglect Code? It depends upon the value placed on the use of residual hearing by the person making the judgment. The neglect may be the fault of the parents, educators, or both. Regardless of blame, such neglect deprives hearing-impaired children of valuable input which could be utilized in the development of speech and language.

Selection of Teachers

Undoubtedly, there are some excellent teachers of speech; but, judging from the results, their numbers must be few. What is there—a secret society? Maybe it requires "special" teachers. No, I believe good teachers can and should be taught to teach speech. I have some serious doubts, however, that education can make anyone who wants to be a teacher a good one. Basic qualities must be present in the individual to make a good teacher. Education only makes them better. Often people who do not have the potential to be teachers go through the process of getting degrees and "get a license" to educationally injure a child's learning experience. That issue needs to be examined. We have all seen it happen. We must investigate ways to predict and avoid such tragedies.

Training at the University Level

Are future teachers obtaining the skills necessary for analyzing and teaching speech, or are they presented with a hodgepodge of information and given little structure or opportunity for developing skills in teaching? Future teachers must acquire specific skills to analyze speech errors and to apply effective procedures and strategies to correct them. When teaching speech and language to the children, the teacher cannot randomly select the next objective. A sequence of skills, considered prerequisites, must be mastered before success at others can be expected. Having specific objectives identified in reasonable sequence is essential for effective training.

Often an eclectic approach to teaching speech is presented by the college or university instructor. Not wanting to bias the future teacher in favor of one method or technique, a little exposure to many different approaches is given. The teacher is then left to choose which approach he/she will use. Unfortunately, many times the future teacher is not proficient and comfortable at using any approach. Inconsistent speech instruction will surely be the end result.

Without program direction and coordination, various individually determined approaches and expectations may be operational within any one school or level. As a consequence, the instruction lacks continuity and children are expected to adjust to marked differences. No wonder they don't learn speech more efficiently!

Another essential aspect of teacher preparation is that of providing practical experience under good supervision. Obtaining enough quality sites and teachers to supervise the practicum is a critical problem, but one which must be solved. Future teachers need both good models and experience under master teachers in order that their skills can be developed to their maximum potential.

Student Motivation and Environment

One of the critical determinants in the achievement of intelligible speech is the child's desire to learn. For many children it is exacting work. The child must view speech as an important skill to develop. If in the student's world, signing and fingerspelling do equally well or better than speech at conveying ideas, the child may well choose to rely on manual communication entirely.

Another important factor in the development of speech skills is the expectations of those significant people who make up the child's world. Children emulate the values and behaviors of others they admire. If parents, friends, and teachers don't use speech themselves and don't value the development of it in their communication with the child, the child's desire to talk and improve speech skills will be adversely influenced.

When parents and teachers do not expect oral/aural communication, functional levels of reception and oral expression are not likely to emerge, and adequate opportunities for practice and development of speech will not be provided.

Summary

1. Properly fitted amplification should be considered basic standard equipment for every hearing-impaired child.
2. Teacher-preparation programs should be improved so that future teachers will acquire the skills necessary to analyze speech critically and to effectively develop and correct it.
3. Environmental factors which will encourage use and improvement of speech must be studied to increase a child's motivation and opportunity to achieve intelligible speech.
4. Further research is needed to identify variables which predispose success in the development of intelligible speech.

PART IV

Contemporary Concepts: Speech and Language Training for the Hearing Impaired

18

Auditory Knowledge and Articulation Disorders of the Hearing Impaired

Harris Winitz

IT IS THE COMPLEXITY OF THE COMMUNICATIVE PROCESS that arouses our interest, but it is service to those who fail to learn or only half-learn to communicate that is our purpose. In recent years, some light has intruded and washed a few shadows away. Perhaps a good place to start is to remember that for the learner who learns speech and language there is a learning process, and for the teacher who teaches speech and language there is a methodology. Having said what is obvious, let us first ask what we mean by a learning process, and second, how we might go about constructing a methodology.

One approach is to compare two intuitively devised methodologies by utilizing control and experimental groups. This writer knows of no circumstance under which this approach has furthered our understanding of the learning process or provided a basis for selecting one teaching methodology in preference to another.

Another, more substantial way, is to study the learning process itself. If we are successful in our understanding of the learning process, our next step is to devise a teaching methodology that encourages those cognitive operations we believe are involved in the learning process.

What form does a teaching methodology take? This is a question without a simple answer. In its most general form a teaching methodology in speech and language would simply provide input which is in accord with the general cognitive processing strategies of the mind. We can illustrate our point by considering an issue that has often been debated, but never resolved: the size of the production segment which should be used to teach articulatory responses. This issue is not a trivial one in view of our knowledge about speech production.

One of the important contributions of the Haskins Laboratory is the finding that a phonetic percept, such as /s/ or /p/, is represented in the acoustic stream by considerable variability. Furthermore, the acoustic cues for a particular sound are often spread over several segments about the size of a syllable or larger. These acoustic variations reflect the fact that speech production consists of a sequence of overlapping and coarticulated segments. Now, it is also well known that a commonly accepted clinical practice is to teach sounds as isolated and exaggerated entities. According to Van Riper, the speech clinician is to locate the sound, isolate it and intensify it, so that it has stimulus value. He recommends using isolated and exaggerated speech as segments of instruction because in this way a sound is not "hidden in the fast torrent of speech" (Van Riper, 1978, p. 210).

To the author's knowledge, there is only one experimental report which provides counterevidence to the proposal that isolated speech production units should be used in training. The effectiveness of using syllable contexts was demonstrated in a study by McReynolds (1972). Children with /s/ errors were taught over several sessions to produce /s/ correctly in isolation or in the syllable /sa/. Following criterion training (90 percent correct when tested on several occasions), transfer to 12 words was assessed. No transfer was observed following isolated /s/ training, but following /sa/ training there was 50 percent transfer. The writer's interpretation of the findings of this study by McReynolds is that the unit of instruction is in accord with a linguistic processing strategy. In brief, learning to produce sounds in words requires that sounds be learned as coarticulated segments.

The author would now like to suggest that there are general as well as specific processing strategies that subjects use to acquire speech and language. In this paper two general principles will be emphasized: (a) implicit processing, and (b) comprehension learning.

The principles proposed are not well accepted as clinical operating procedures at this time. Yet evidence from a variety of sources suggests that they should at least be considered.

In psycholinguistic circles it is generally believed that linguistic knowledge is tacit knowledge. Language users do not have explicit knowledge of the routines they use to generate sentences or to produce sound sequences. The task of the scientist is to make this internalized knowledge explicit. However, it does not follow that the training routines which we develop for our students should involve explicit instruction. Elsewhere the author has used the term "implicit instruction" to characterize this type of teaching strategy (Winitz, in press, a). Although it is a common clinical practice to explain articulatory placement and manner to the learner, this procedure may have little value. Verbal instructions are too simple in content to convey the complexities of speech articulation. How, for example, can transition slope, voice onset time, and forward coarticulation be explained by verbal instruction? Similarly the author does not believe that language can be acquired by teaching grammatical rules. Transformational rules are too complex and difficult to teach to believe that explicit instruction is a reasonable teaching strategy. Rather, it is recommended that articulatory productions (as well as grammatical rules) be taught as an implicit learning experience. As much as possible, the process of sound production should be explicitly available to the instructor so that appropriate units of instruction can be developed.

A second general clinical operating procedure pertains to the often heavy emphasis placed on sound production training. It seems almost axiomatic that articulation learning should involve massive doses of production practice. But what is production practice? It generally involves nothing more than imitation practice with feedback often coupled with some verbal instruction. Even if an electronic signal is used to monitor production, the usual procedure is (a) listen to a stimulus; (b) try to produce it; and (c) receive feedback and verbal instruction.

This model is somewhat simplistic in view of our current understanding of the processes involved in making an articulatory production. Learning to articulate means that we must know: (1) speech motor programming rules; (2) phonological rules; and (3) higher order linguistic rules of syntax and semantics. We apply all of this knowledge when we produce the sentences of a language. It is not entirely unreasonable to assume, then, that before instruction in articulation production is begun we make every effort to teach a considerable amount of this knowledge.

In the study of articulation disorders two investigative areas which have received attention are auditory discrimination and phonological knowledge.

Auditory Discrimination

Comparative studies summarized by Winitz (1969) generally show that children with articulation errors evidence poorer scores on tests of speech sound discrimination. Not all investigations show differences between articulatory defective children and normal-speaking

TABLE 18.A

The correct scores in percentages for three features produced by children with defective and normal articulation.

	Continuancy		Voicing		Stridency	
	Production	Discrimination	Production	Discrimination	Production	Discrimination
Defective	17	83	41	79	6	84
Normal	98	94	98	88	95	94

children. There are a number of reasons which may account for negative results. In some experiments the subjects had relatively few articulation errors, and in other studies the composition of discrimination tests did not always reflect the articulation errors. It has been demonstrated that articulation errors and discrimination errors are related functions when the discrimination tests assess those sounds which are misarticulated (Aungst & Frick, 1964; Prins, 1962; Spriestersbach & Curtis, 1951).

Recently two studies conducted by McReynolds and her colleagues (McReynolds, Kohn, & Williams, 1975; Williams & McReynolds, 1975) have been cited as counterevidence to the belief that discrimination is importantly related to the acquisition of articulatory responses. In the first investigation (McReynolds et al., 1975) it was concluded that children with articulation errors evidence little difficulty in speech sound discrimination. The auditory discrimination and articulation of a small number of articulatory defective and normal-speaking children were studied in a rather interesting way. The auditory discrimination test was developed to assess six Chomsky-Halle features: continuancy, nasality, voicing, stridency, anterior, and coronal (Chomsky & Halle, 1968). The correct scores in percentages for three of the six features are presented in Table 18.A.

The production scores for the articulatory defective children are low. As indicated above, for example, the continuant feature is produced correctly by the defective-speaking children in only 17 percent of the instances tested, and by the normal-speaking children in 98 percent of the instances tested. The differences for the discrimination scores are not as great as one might expect.

The contrasts used in the minimal pair test by McReynolds, Kohn, and Williams can explain why the differences on the discrimination dimension are slight. In particular, the 80 minimal pair test contained only 20 types of same-different pairs (e.g., for /l/ and /r/ the test pairs would be /l/ - /r/, /r/ - /l/, /l/ - /l/, and /r/-/r/). Many of the contrasts were not those which have been found to be common substitution errors; e.g., /w/-/r/, /b/-/v/, /w/-/l/, lateral lisp and /s/ (Snow, 1964). Additionally the test contained contrasts which reflect rare occurrences of substitutions found in the speech of young children, e.g., (/l/-/r/, /d/-/n/, /z/-/v/) (Snow, 1964).

It is concluded that the discrimination test was not necessarily appropriate for each child because each child had a different set of articulation errors. For example, the first child tested had 10 articulation errors. Of the 20 discrimination pairs used, seven of these 20 did not contain sounds which were involved in the misarticulations. That is, only 65 percent of the discrimination pairs were relevant. Of these 65 percent, there is no way to tell from the study whether the contrasting pairs reflected the particular substitutions made by each child. For example, if a child substitutes /t/ for /s/, then the discrimination pair /s/ - /θ/ would not be relevant.

These investigators also report considerable variability in the correctness of each test sound for each child. Each test sound had been examined in a number of contexts using the McDonald Deep Test of Articulation (McDonald, 1968). The observation that the errors were inconsistent in production is in agreement with past findings (Winitz, 1969). It further points to the need to consider phonetic context. Much of the inconsistency in misarticulations can be traced to phonetic context (Spriestersbach & Curtis, 1951). Discrimination assessment should consider context if a valid relationship is to be drawn between production and discrimination.

In a second investigation, Williams and McReynolds (1975) considered the issue of discrimination and production again. This design involved the training of these two functions rather than an assessment of current skills. Unfortunately, this investigation was inappropriately designed to inquire about the relationship between discrimination and articulatory production. Both production and discrimination were individually tailored for four children who misarticulated four or more phonemes. The design provided for two children in each group:

Group I	**Group II**
Production Training	Discrimination Training
Discrimination Probe	Production Probe

TABLE 18.B
Picture-sound association task for production training and discrimination training.

Production Training		**Discrimination Training**	
Picture A	/ʃa/	/va/	Picture A
Picture B	/ʃa/	/ga/	Picture B
Picture C	/dʒa/	/θa/	Picture C
Picture D	/θa/	/θa/	Picture D
Assessment of Discrimination		Assessment of Production	

The subjects in Group I were trained to articulate several sounds correctly, followed by a test of discrimination. The subjects in Group II were trained to discriminate between several sounds, and production was subsequently tested. This design might appear to be straightforward if production and discrimination can be regarded as independent training functions. However, production training involved auditory input as part of the training routine. Additionally, an unusual design was employed to teach the sounds.

In both production and discrimination training a picture association task was used. The picture-sound association task for one subject in production training and one subject in discrimination training is presented in Table 18.B. After the children learned to acquire the production task (naming the pictures correctly) or the discrimination task (selecting the correct picture[s]), discrimination and production were respectively assessed.

In the discrimination probe or assessment the instructions were to listen to the taped presentation of each of the three syllables and select the appropriate picture(s). The two subjects performed well on the discrimination test, a result which indicates that discrimination was a factor contributing to or related to successful articulatory production, although this interpretation was not offered by the authors.

The production probes following discrimination training revealed that articulatory performance did not change at all. The authors drew the conclusion that "... discrimination training had no direct influence on production" (Williams & McReynolds, 1975, p. 411), realizing that this finding could be interpreted to imply that discrimination practice should be omitted in clinical training.

Discrimination pretraining cannot be easily dismissed as an unimportant clinical routine. Most importantly, discrimination practice provides experience in learning to make phonetic discriminations as well as experience in learning to know about the phonological system.

One reason for rejecting the findings and interpretations of the Williams and McReynolds (1975) investigation is that the authors did not correctly program the discrimination contrasts.

An evaluation of the discrimination contrasts can be illustrated best by considering subject 1, who had errors of /ʃ/, /dʒ/ and /θ/. The training, as mentioned above, involved discrimination among these three sounds. Not considered here is the well-accepted fact that for discrimination training to be effective it should involve training between the target sound and the error sound (Winitz & Bellerose, 1975). In this case the child might easily have learned to discriminate between the three target sounds /ʃ/, /dʒ/ and (θ/ without being able to discriminate between each target sound and its respective error. In summary, this investigation by Williams and McReynolds (1975) provides no substantive support for the conclusion that discrimination performance and articulation errors are unrelated.

When the relevant features are not present, a certain degree of production practice is probably important. This latter conclusion receives support from several studies (Guess, 1969; Ruder, Smith, & Hermann, 1974; Ruder, Smith, & Hermann, 1977) in which a small number of imitation trials following auditory training was sufficient to develop correct production responses.

In summary, there is no reason to reject the value of discrimination training. It seems most plausible that a degree of articulatory practice is essential before articulatory control is established, but the role of auditory discrimination cannot be discounted.

Finally, there is another significant reason why discrimination and production may not always be found to correlate highly. Both discrimination and articulation can be regarded as related growth functions which are not necessarily age-correlated. Some time back, Menyuk and Anderson (1969) presented three growth stages of development with regard to perception (or discrimination) and production as follows:

$$\begin{bmatrix} -\text{ discrimination} \\ -\text{ production} \end{bmatrix} \qquad (1)$$

$$\begin{bmatrix} +\text{ discrimination} \\ -\text{ production} \end{bmatrix} \qquad (2)$$

$$\begin{bmatrix} +\text{ discrimination} \\ +\text{ production} \end{bmatrix} \qquad (3)$$

The above schematic representation of the stages simply means that at stage 1, neither discrimination nor production is acquired. At stage 2, discrimination singularly develops. The acquisition of production represents the final stage, or stage 3, of development.

A fourth possibility is:

$$\begin{bmatrix} -\text{ discrimination} \\ +\text{ production} \end{bmatrix}.$$

However, this category is theoretically untenable if the position is taken that auditory skills precede the acquisition of articulation. Eilers and Oller (1976) tested a group of young children less than two and one-half years of age on a variety of phonetic contrasts. Discrimination of contrastive pairs, as well as production of both members of a pair, was assessed. An analysis of the individual responses of children revealed that responses falling within the category $\begin{bmatrix} +\text{ discrimination} \\ -\text{ production} \end{bmatrix}$ were rare, no doubt reflecting inherent subject variability. The bulk of the responses, as expected, fell in categories 1, 2, or 3.

The group marked $\begin{bmatrix} +\text{ discrimination} \\ -\text{ production} \end{bmatrix}$ is of theoretical interest because two contradictory hypotheses can be entertained. First, this group can be considered to be at that point in development at which discrimination has been acquired. Production has not developed prior to this time, presumably because discrimination (or some level of discrimination) must precede production. Possibly, the capacity to produce articulatory responses has developed, but memory constraints impair the recall of correct productions (Winitz & Bellerose, 1975). The absence of production in this group reflects developmental constraints, but it does not deny a relationship between discrimination and production. Second, this group can be used erroneously to deny a relationship between discrimination and production.

The remaining two groups, $\begin{bmatrix} -\text{ discrimination} \\ -\text{ production} \end{bmatrix}$ and $\begin{bmatrix} +\text{ discrimination} \\ +\text{ production} \end{bmatrix}$, indicate early and late developmental stages. At the early stage neither speech discrimination nor articulation has developed. At the final stage both of these skills have developed.

Phonological Knowledge

Beginning with Haas' (1963) paper on the application of phonologic analysis to the disorder of articulation, and heightened by Compton's (1970) subsequent case histories, interest in using phonologic theory to describe articulation errors continues to grow. Stated simply, a phonologic analysis is used to gain insight about the organization of a child's articulation errors. Rules are used to describe the underlying patterns of organization.

It cannot be said with certainty that phonologic rules are a valid representation of the underlying psychologic organization of sound errors. However, it is the most useful tool currently available. We also need to remind ourselves that phonologic descriptions are not statements of cause. We cannot tell the origin of a deviant phonologic pattern. Its causes could be many, including auditory discrimination, articulatory control, and conceptual organization. On the other hand, we should be aware of the fact that a phonologic disorder does not also imply that there is a disability in the areas of auditory discrimination, conceptual organization, or articulatory control. A child may be able to perform correctly in each of these areas, but for some reason does not. All of these considerations must be taken into account when planning a program of treatment (Winitz, in press, b).

A phonologic analysis, then, can be used to infer underlying mental arrangements. The underlying mental arrangements, patterns, or rules are regarded as psychological knowledge. How can this knowledge be taught to deaf or hard-of-hearing children? This author's proposal is to suggest that formalized instruction in articulation practice be delayed until we are confident that we have adequately trained auditory knowledge of all of the many processes involved in articulation acquisition. Essentially I am proposing that articulation production practice not be provided to *hard-of-hearing children.* Instead, it is advocated that intensive experience in auditory comprehension be given. Stated another way, it is recommended that speech production not be taught in the *formal sense.* Rather, attention should be given to the teaching of the understanding of language. The writer believes that only in this way will students have the opportunity to acquire all of the necessary components of the articulation process. In the case of the deaf child, the author recommends, in a second presentation, that reading instruction be used to teach language comprehension and that articulation practice be delayed until a reasonable amount of language has been acquired.

With specific reference to articulation instruction, the importance of auditory comprehension training has largely been ignored. Furthermore, *auditory comprehension has often been incorrectly equated with auditory discrimination.* It is now recognized that children's articulation errors often represent an underlying sound system that is different from that of the community language (Ingram, 1976; Oller, Jensen, & Lafayette, 1978). Phonologic rules have often been used to describe these differences. Auditory discrimination is important, but it is not the same as the comprehension of the sound system of a language.

How does one go about teaching auditory comprehension? It is unlikely that underlying rules can be explicitly taught. Our best approach seems to be to provide the kinds of experiences that a young child receives when he or she is first learning language. A young child is not taught to articulate sounds; rather, he or she is taught to listen to language within the context of communicative interchanges. Now this may all seem obvious, but it really is not. Clinical procedures, as this author has observed them, minimize the role of listening training as part of the communicative act. Exercises in comprehension training are given, but usually they are brief and quickly followed by demands on production. Additionally, children are asked to memorize descriptions of articulatory productions because it is presumed that these explicit instructions can be used by them to perform an articulatory movement. To the author's knowledge, there is no evidence to support this position.

Often comprehension training is regarded as a passive process, and speaking as an active process. This belief cannot be taken seriously. It is a reasonable supposition that the grammar for speaking and for listening is the same (Chomsky, 1965). No doubt the same grammatical principles are applied when one listens as when one speaks. Furthermore, comprehension can be acquired without the ability to speak. There are examples of individuals who comprehended language well despite the fact that they had not learned to articulate (Lenneberg, 1962). Today, speech perception and language comprehension are regarded as active processes. Analysis by synthesis is one example of an active perceptual model which has been applied to the study of speech recognition. Reception, therefore, should not be equated with passivity.

Comprehension learning is largely the responsibility of the student. All we can do as clinicians and teachers is program the input effectively. An effectively programmed input will enable the student to acquire the essential auditory knowledge which, it is believed, should be acquired prior to the introduction of a formalized instructional program in articulation production.

At this point, the principle of comprehension training as we have applied it to the teaching of foreign languages will be illustrated. Foreign language learning is particularly difficult for a large number of American students. It is difficult, the author believes, because the methodology is not in accord with the basic processes individuals use to acquire the grammar of a language: Speaking is demanded before a sufficient quantity of the grammar has been learned.

Our proposed method of instruction is entitled The Comprehension Approach. No speaking is expected of students, and there is no memorization of surface grammatical rules. The learner is asked only to look at pictures and to listen to sentences. Initially, single words are taught; then short sentences are introduced through careful sequencing of sentence patterns. Each sentence corresponds to a picture as illustrated in Figures 18.1 through 18.6.

The figures are taken from our language program entitled *The Learnables* (Winitz, 1978).[1] Figure 18.1 presents the first four items of Lesson 1. In Figure 18.2 Noun-Verb-Object sequences are indicated. Both the subject and object nouns were initially introduced as single items.

Figure 18.3 illustrates a sequence in which the relative clause is introduced (Lesson 24). Right-embedded rather than center-embedded clauses were used to reduce the initial complexity of these structures. In Figure 18.4 the lexical item "forgot" is taught in the context of a story sequence (Lesson 28). The nonreversible passive is introduced in picture form in Figure 18.5 (Lesson 34). In our illustration, "meat" could not be identified as the grammatical subject, because the sentence "the meat ate the dog" is semantically anomalous. The conditional is introduced through a story context (Lesson 37) and is illustrated in Figure 18.6.

With hard-of-hearing children it is recommended that picture programs be coordinated with Asher's (1976) total physical response approach. Asher's procedures are described well in his 1976 teacher's handbook, so they will not be detailed here. Essentially, Asher's

[1]The pictures and sentences are representative of lessons taken from *The Learnables*, published by International Linguistics. Each picture corresponds to a word, phrase, or sentence. The subject listens to an utterance and looks at the appropriately designated picture. The words and sentences which are in parentheses in Figures 18.1–18.6 are not shown to the subject; they are presented here for illustrative purposes only.

FIGURE 18.1
The first four items in Lesson 1.

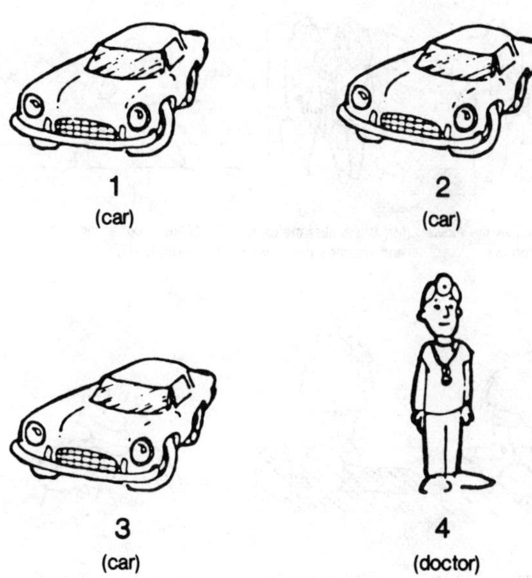

FIGURE 18.2
Noun-Verb-Object sequences in Lesson 1.

FIGURE 18.3

Sequence introducing the relative clause in Lesson 24.

1 (Mrs. Smith watches the movie and eats the candy.)

2 (Mr. Smith eats the candy and watches the movie.)

3 (They see a lady who is fat.)

4 (They see a man who is fat.)

5 (They see a boy who is fat.)

6 (They see a girl who is fat.)

7 (The boy who is fat is eating candy.)

8 (The fat man is the father.)

FIGURE 18.4

Story sequence to teach the lexical item "forgot" in Lesson 28.

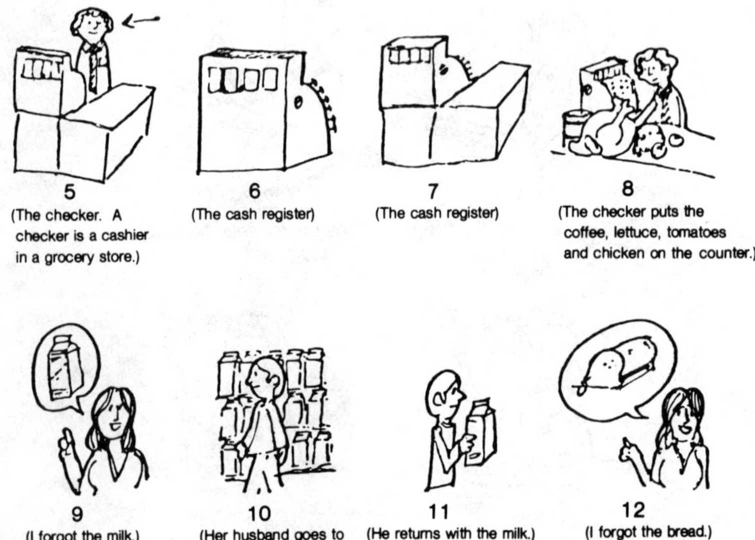

5 (The checker. A checker is a cashier in a grocery store.)

6 (The cash register)

7 (The cash register)

8 (The checker puts the coffee, lettuce, tomatoes and chicken on the counter.)

9 (I forgot the milk.)

10 (Her husband goes to get some milk.)

11 (He returns with the milk.)

12 (I forgot the bread.)

FIGURE 18.5

Nonreversible passive introduced in picture form in Lesson 34.

FIGURE 18.6

The conditional introduced in story context in Lesson 37.

method stresses the comprehension of commands and descriptions of real-life communicative acts. The classroom is an ideal place to conduct this kind of training. This approach is difficult for teachers to accept. They would have to inhibit their urge to teach production. Oral repetition and imitation would not be demanded of the students, and practice in making isolated speech movements would no longer be insisted upon.

The results of Asher's (1976) and others reviewed in Winitz (in press, a) indicate that foreign languages can be acquired relatively easily when students are given extensive experience in listening comprehension. In this regard, the comprehension approach is viewed as a methodology which is in accord with the general processing strategies the learner uses to acquire language. Forced practice in production and the learning of grammatical rules are guarded as having a deleterious effect on language learning, perhaps far greater than is generally realized.

This writer believes that extensive experience in listening should be the fundamental teaching methodology. Only after we are convinced that additional comprehension experience is no longer of value should we implement a formal program of articulation practice. But we must give comprehension practice a chance. In the case of foreign language learning, a full year of comprehension experience in the classroom is required. Thus, for hard-of-hearing children, several years of comprehension practice should be taught before we consider alternatives. If these suggestions are taken seriously, it would mean that structured comprehension experiences should be the primary instructional methodology. (Reading instruction, as will be suggested in my second paper, is an important channel for teaching comprehension.) Articulation instruction would be used to improve or refine the pronunciation of sounds, but it would not be used as the primary teaching methodology.

REFERENCES

Asher, J. J. *Learning another language through actions: The complete guidebook.* Los Gatos, Califiornia: Sky Oaks Productions, 1976.

Aungst, L. F., & Frick, J. V. Auditory discrimination ability and consistency of articulation of /r/. *J. Speech Hear. Dis.*, 1964, *29*, 76–85.

Chomsky, N. *Aspects of the theory of syntax.* Cambridge, Mass: MIT Press, 1965.

Chomsky, N., & Halle, M. *The sound pattern of English.* New York: Harper and Row, 1968.

Compton, A. J. Generative studies of children's phonological disorders. *J. Speech Hear. Dis.*, 1970, *35*, 313–339.

Eilers, R. E., & Oller, D. K. The role of speech discrimination in developmental sound substitutions. *J. Child Lang.*, 1976, *3*, 319–329.

Guess, D. A functional analysis of receptive language and productive speech: Acquisition of the plural morpheme. *J. App. Behav. Anal.*, 1969, 2, 55–64.

Haas, W. Phonological analysis of a case of dyslalia. *J. Speech Hear. Dis.*, 1963, 28, 239–246.

Ingram, D. *Phonological disability in children.* New York: Elsevier, 1976.

Lenneberg, E. H. Understanding language without ability to speak: A case report. *J. Ab. Soc. Psych.*, 1962, 65, 419–425.

McDonald, E. *A screening deep test of articulation.* Pittsburgh: Stanwix House, 1968.

McReynolds, L. V. Articulation generalization during articulation training. *Lang. Speech*, 1972, *15*, 149–155.

McReynolds, L. V., Kohn, J., & Williams, G. Articulatory-defective children's discrimination of their production errors. *J. Speech Hear. Dis.*, 1975, *40*, 327–338.

Menyuk, P., & Anderson, S. Children's identification and reproduction of /w/, /r/, and /l/. *J. Speech Hear. Res.*, 1969, 5, 39–52.

Oller, D. K., Jensen, H. T., & Lafayette, R. H. The relatedness of phonological processes of a hearing-impaired child. *J. Comm. Dis.*, 1978, *11*, 97–106.

Prins, T. D. Analysis of correlations among various articulatory deviations. *J. Speech Hear. Res.*, 1962, 5, 152–160.

Ruder, K. F., Smith, M., & Hermann, P. Effects of verbal imitation and comprehension on verbal production of lexical items in developing systematic procedures for training children's language. In L. V. McReynolds (Ed.), *Am. Speech Hear. Assoc. Mono.*, 1974, *18*, 15–29.

Ruder, K. F., Smith, M., & Hermann, P. Effects of verbal imitation and comprehension training on verbal production. *J. Psycholing. Res.*, 1977, *61*, 59–72.

Snow, K. A comparative study of sound substitutions used by "normal" first grade children. *Speech Mono.*, 1964, *31*, 135–141.

Spriesterbach, D. C., & Curtis, J. F. Misarticulation and discrimination of speech sounds. *Quart. J. Speech*, 1951, *37*, 483–491.

Van Riper, C. *Speech correction: Principles and methods.* Englewood Cliffs, N.J: Prentice-Hall, 1978.

Williams, G. S., & McReynolds, L. V. The relationship between discrimination and articulation training in children with misarticulations. *J. Speech Hear. Res.*, 1975, *40*, 401–412.

Winitz, H. *Articulatory acquisition and behavior.* New York: Appleton-Century-Crofts, 1969.

Winitz, H., & Bellerose, B. Self-retrieval and articulatory retention. *J. Speech and Hear. Res.*, 1975, *18*, 466–477.

Winitz, H. *The Learnables*, Vol. 1–20, Kansas City, Mo.: International Linguistics, 1978.

Winitz, H. (Ed.) *The comprehension approach to foreign language instruction.* Newbury House, in press, a.

Winitz, H. Considerations in the treatment of articulation disorders. In R. W. Reiber (Ed.), *Communication disorders*, Plenum Press, in press, b.

19
Speech Correction Through the Use of Acoustic Models

Norman P. Erber

THE PURPOSE OF THIS PAPER is to describe a method of speech development and correction that is based on *acoustic* stimulation of the impaired ear. In this approach, most of the instructor's speech models are presented with mouth covered, or at least out of the pupil's field of vision. The child compares the perceptual qualities of his own speech with those of the model as he attempts to imitate it. Numerous authors have claimed that residual hearing should play an integral role in multisensory instruction as a child learns both to perceive and produce speech (e.g., Ewing, 1957; Huizing, 1960; Ling, 1976; Simmons-Martin, 1972), and many have described successful attempts to educate children through auditory techniques (Asp, 1973; Beebe, 1953; Goldstein, 1939; Hoxter, 1938; Pollack, 1970; Wedenberg, 1951, 1954). But, unfortunately, none of these clinicians has described in a detailed manner how, and under which conditions, one may teach hearing-impaired children to maximally use their auditory capacity for speech monitoring and control. And so, the techniques that they have developed are not widely applied.

Recently, a long-term observational study was completed at CID by Edson (1978), who attempted to develop self-correction of speech in four severely hearing-impaired children aged 10–15 years through the acoustic method. She found that all of the children were able to learn to accurately imitate her speech (and language) models as she covered her mouth, but that they did not maintain the same precision of production during their daily conversation. Edson concluded that these older students were too dependent on vision and kinesthesia for speech monitoring and control for them to be converted to using residual hearing for feedback. She also felt that it would be difficult to achieve success in acoustic speech training in an educational environment that does not strongly stress audition (to the exclusion of vision) during other instructional periods. Similar views have been expresssed by other practitioners of the method (Asp, 1973; Beebe, 1953; Pollack, 1970). Nevertheless, this project and other clinical experiences have demonstrated that acoustic speech correction can be a potentially effective method for many hearing-impaired children.

If a child learns to use only vision and kinesthesia for speech monitoring and control, accurate production may be limited primarily to those articulations which can be seen or felt clearly. In addition to this apparent limitation, it is impractical for a child to constantly self-evaluate speech by observation in a mirror or by reference to the instructor's facial cues. In recent years, researchers have developed numerous electronic tactile and visual feedback devices to help a child monitor and control various components of speech (Boothroyd, 1973; Nickerson, Kalikow, & Stevens, 1976; Willemain & Lee, 1971), but most of the investigators have reported limited success in carry-over outside the laboratory, where the special apparatus is not present. Many clinicians believe that equally vigorous efforts should be made to teach hearing-impaired children to maximally use the common feedback devices that are available to them at all times—their hearing aids and impaired ears.

An oral hearing-impaired child who does not, or cannot, exploit the acoustic output of the hearing aid(s) for communication probably will perceive only the visible aspects of the speech of others and thus will develop a visual code for receptive language. The same child is likely to self-monitor speech tactually and/or kinesthetically (by feeling articulatory positions and movements). It is not at all clear how this child would establish a framework for speech communication, whether in terms of optical or kinesthetic units. We speculate that, for speech reception, the child might transform the speech that is seen into articulatory analogs, i.e., articulate covertly while lipreading, and for speech production, the child might refer to stored images or oral/facial articulation, i.e., speak as though intending to be lipread by others (Conrad, 1972; Jenson, 1971; Ling, 1976). In either case, it is likely that only surface, i.e., visible, articulatory gestures would play a prominent role in the encoding/decoding scheme. People with normal hearing, in contrast, communicate mainly through the sounds of speech. The surface cues are merely byproducts of their articulation. If the hearing-impaired child were to practice using audition or even vibrotactual perception as a common speech-processing mode, he/she may learn to acquire basic acoustic components of both receptive and expressive oral language. The result would be a better understanding of the nature of speech communication and more successful interaction with hearing people.

Previous work has suggested methods by which the auditory systems of hearing-impaired children may be specifically stimulated to improve multisensory perception (Erber, 1976, 1978, 1979). This paper will briefly review our knowledge about the auditory speech-perception capacities of severely and profoundly hearing-impaired children and explore ways in which a clinician can use this information to attempt acoustic speech correction.

The Imperfect Auditory Systems of Hearing-Impaired Children

It generally is presumed that acoustic modeling can be used effectively for speech correction only with a child who can perceive the distinction between a normal speech model and his/her abnormal speech imitation through a suitable amplification system. The following section will briefly review some general aspects of auditory speech perception by hearing-impaired children.

Voice Pitch

Previous research (DiCarlo, 1964; Gengel, 1969, 1973; Risberg, 1977) has shown that the frequency-discrimination ability of hearing-impaired children often is considerably poorer than that of people with normal auditory sensitivity. Work by Risberg, Agelfors, and Boberg (1975) has provided an understanding of the range of pitch-perception abilities in the hearing impaired (Figure 19.1). In general, for children with hearing levels ranging from about 30–60 dB ("mild-moderate" loss), the difference limen for low frequencies (.125-1 kHz) is essentially normal, i.e., only about 1–2 percent difference is required for discrimination of two neighboring tones. For children with audiograms in the 70–90 dB range ("severe" loss) there are large individual differences in frequency discrimination, ranging from about 2–30 percent, that is, from nearly normal to moderately poor discrimination ability. For children with thresholds poorer than about 100 dB ("profound" loss), the difference limen for frequency tends to be poor, i.e., these children require 5–40 percent difference in frequency to distinguish two tones. This range of poor performance is comparable to that obtained vibrotactually from the hand. A child's tone-discrimination performance has been found to relate closely to his/her

FIGURE 19.1
Summary of results from frequency-discrimination measurements. A large range of DL's was obtained for children whose pure-tone thresholds were in the "severe" range (from Risberg et al., 1975).

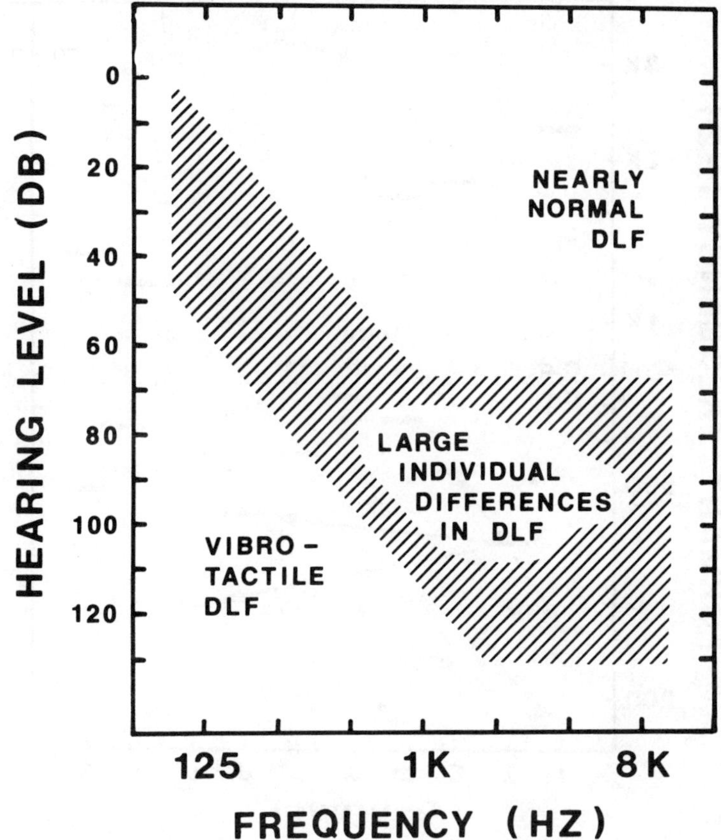

ability to recognize common spondee words (Risberg et al., 1975), and it is speculated that frequency discrimination is an auditory skill that is basic to speech perception, especially identification of voice pitch and formant spectra of voiced phonemes.

Vowels

Many hearing-impaired children with moderate/severe hearing impairments seem unable to accurately perceive the frequency location of vowel formants and so perceptually confuse vowels produced in neighboring articulatory positions. Research data show, for example, that these children tend to identify the vowel /ɪ/ as /i/ or /ɛ/ and thus

FIGURE 19.2

Formant frequencies of 10 English vowels. Arrows indicate common identification errors made by some severely hearing-impaired children (after Peterson & Barney, 1952).

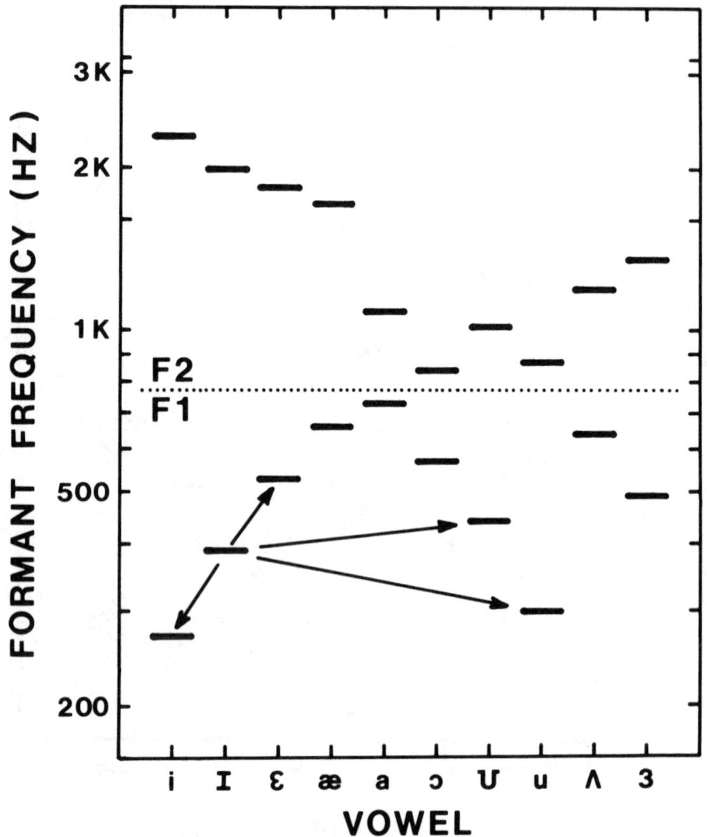

may confuse the words *pin, team,* and *ten* for that reason (Figure 19.2). Other moderately/severely hearing-impaired children seem to have difficulty perceiving the presence of the second formant in vowels (Miller, 1956), and so they perceptually confuse front and back vowels with similar first formants, for example, /i/ and /u/, as in the words *three* and *two* (Figure 19.2). When confronted with this perceptual ambiguity, some children will choose randomly between the two vowels (or words), while others will exhibit definite biases toward the front or back member of the pair. Some severely hearing-impaired children exhibit both kinds of difficulty. That is, they confuse vowels produced with similar articulation and also confuse back/front pairs. A child with this type of auditory deficiency, when presented with the vowel /ɪ/, may identify it as /i/ or /ɛ/, or may label it as /ʊ/ and thus identify the work *pick* as *peek, pet,* or *put* (Hack & Erber, 1979; Pickett et al., 1972, Smith, 1975).

Test results indicate that children with profound hearing impairments (those whose responses suggest that they perceive only intensity cues vibrotactually), can learn to distinguish between "strong" vowels /æ/, /a/, /ɔ/, /ʌ/ and those vowels that are weaker in acoustic energy /i/, /ɪ/, /ɛ/, /ʊ/, /u/. Similar findings were reported by Gault (1926 a,b). Vowel classification simply on the basis of intensity/duration cues is less precise in word or sentence context, where syllable stress can distort the relative durations and intensities.

Consonants

Many of the consonant confusions experienced by moderately and severely hearing-impaired children are similar to those reported previously by Miller and Nicely (1955). In that study, normally hearing adults listened to consonants in syllabic context through filters or in noise backgrounds. Many researchers subsequently have used a filter analogy to describe or simulate hearing loss (Boothroyd, 1967; Ross et al., 1973; Sher & Owens, 1974).

Listeners with moderate-to-severe hearing impairments typically have little difficulty distinguishing categorically between nasals, voiced stops, voiced fricatives, voiceless stops, and voiceless fricatives (Byers, 1973; Owens et al., 1972). That is, they tend to perceive these articulatory classes as separate from one another but confuse the consonants within each group. Our experience indicates that many children with more severe impairments often confuse voiced stops and fricatives with one another and similarly confuse their voiceless counterparts. But it appears that hearing-impaired children even with minimal hearing usually can distinguish nasal from non-nasal consonants, although precise spectral labeling within the nasal group may be very poor (Erber, 1972). When nasal consonants are misclassified, they are most frequently confused with the liquids and semivowels /r/, /l/, /w/, /y/ (Walden & Montgomery, 1975) which in turn may be confused with vowels with similar low-frequency spectra. Words containing several consonants in the group /m/, /n/, /r/, /l/, /w/, /y/ tend to be very difficult for severely hearing-impaired children to identify acoustically (e.g., *money, always, really, woman*).

Although the frequency-discrimination abilities of most profoundly hearing-impaired children are poor, they usually can perceive changes in speech intensity as a function of time. Thus, for example, they are able to distinguish stop from voiced continuant consonants in a medial position, as one class is characterized by distinct breaks in the sound pattern and the other is not (Figure 19.3). Initial or final stop consonants in words, however, may not be labeled correctly. For example, in the word /pæt/, the energy bursts in /p/ and /t/ are weak, of relatively high frequency, and so produce little intensity disturbance before or after the vowel. Thus, a profoundly deaf child might not be able to distinguish between /pæt/ and /æ/ alone, because of a lack of high-frequency sensitivity.

Nasals and liquids/semivowels may be recognized as a distinct category (depending on speech context) on the basis of the slow rise and decay of the syllable envelope. And, so, many profoundly deaf children can learn to classify the envelope pattern for /mæn/ as different

FIGURE 19.3

Envelope patterns of six consonants spoken in the context /a/–C/a/, as displayed on the screen of a storage oscilloscope. The amplitude and duration of intervocalic energy can provide information regarding the category of consonant that was presented (from Erber, 1978).

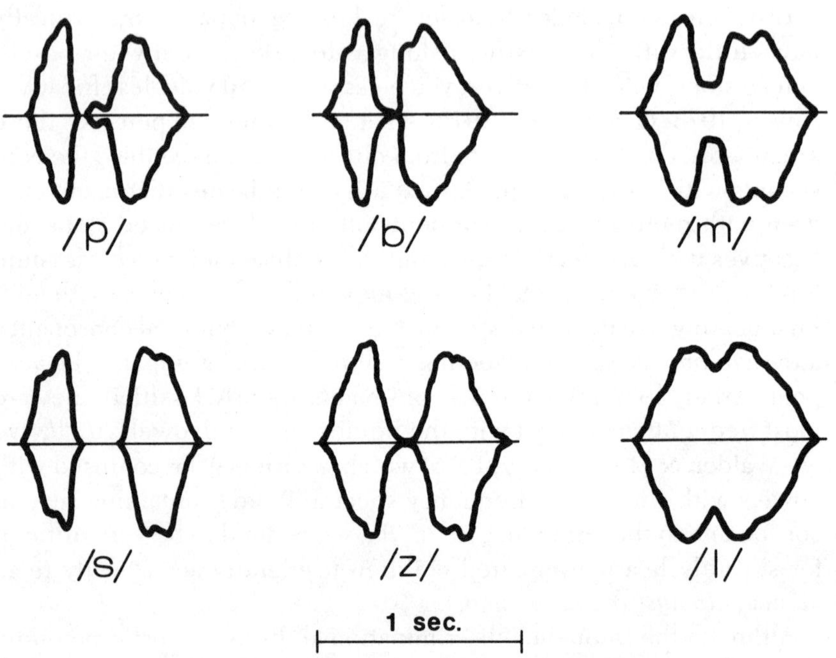

FIGURE 19.4

Envelope patterns of two sample sentences: (a) one contains mainly stop consonants; (b) the other contains mainly continuant consonants. A profoundly hearing-impaired child can easily learn to distinguish contrastive patterns of this sort.

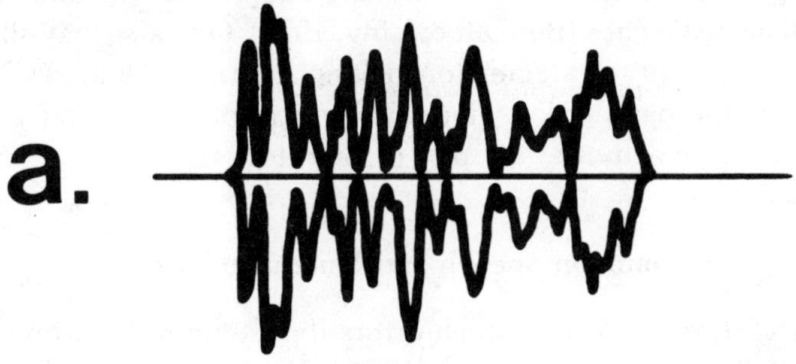

"THE BABY TOOK THE BROKEN TOY TRAIN TO DADDY."

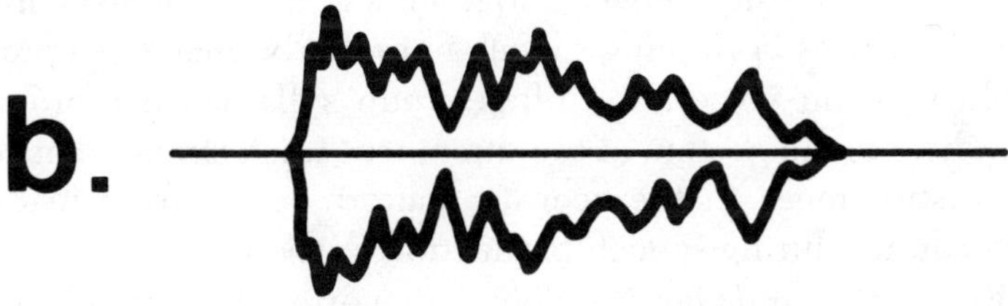

"THE LAMB ALWAYS RUNS AWAY WHEN I MOVE MY HAND."

from /bæt/, or, as another example, the name *Bobby* from *Mommy*. To illustrate the effect of the many intensity and duration cues that occur in connected speech, contrast the envelope pattern of the two sentences: "The baby took the broken toy train to daddy." and, "The lamb always runs away when I move my hand." The first contains numerous stop consonants and thus brief silent intervals; the second does not (Figure 19.4).

The auditory capabilities and limitations of the students outlined above summarize the results of many research studies and clinical observations. These findings do not define a specific child's potential for perceptual learning. Often, a clinician may help a child improve speech-perception performance by giving practice in attending to minimal acoustic cues (Bennett & Ling, 1977). One also may show the child how to apply strategies for making informed "guesses" (when unsure) on the basis of knowledge of typical phoneme and word sequences. These activities are part of "auditory training."

Common Speech and Language Errors

Many children exhibit speech errors that seem to be a function of their impaired perception (Smith, 1975). Often, the sounds that a child omits or misarticulates are those that are not detected or perceived clearly, either through audition or lipreading.

1. *Intensity Patterns.* Errors are likely to occur in rhythm, stress pattern, syllable rate, or overall duration of a sentence (Hudgins & Numbers, 1942). These aspects of an utterance are characterized by intensity changes in speech, somewhat independent of pitch, articulation, and the message content. Typically, hearing-impaired children utter syllables in speech too slowly, do not differentiate sufficiently in duration and intensity between stressed and unstressed syllables, insert or fill pauses in running speech improperly (may even produce a syllable with no voice), and often group syllables inappropriately, which distorts the rhythm of the utterance. It is claimed that some of these disturbances in the acoustic pattern result from inadequate breath control during speech production (Nickerson, 1975).

2. *Voice Pitch and Quality.* Voice pitch errors tend to fall into main categories: The child may exhibit an inappropriate average pitch, and/or may change pitch improperly. Many children produce a voice pitch that is abnormally high. Monotone voice and abrupt pitch breaks also are common problems; the intonation contour of a sentence may not be appropriate to its content (e.g., a lack of pitch change in the sentence, "Do you want a red pen or a blue pen?"). Many of these voice pitch errors are thought to be the result of improper muscle use or control (Mártony, 1968; Nickerson, 1975).

The voice quality of hearing-impaired children has often been described as "breathy" or "tense" (Calvert, 1962). This has been attributed to inappropriate positioning of the vocal folds during speech.

3. *Articulation.* Poor control of the raising or lowering of the velum (or soft palate) is a source of difficulty in the speech of many deaf children. Inappropriate velar control can contribute to confusion for the listener as he attempts to distinguish voiced stops /b/, /d/, /g/ from their nasal counterparts /m/, /n/, /ŋ/. Often it is difficult for the deaf child to produce intelligible consonant clusters containing nasals, e.g., /nt/, /nd/, /mp/.

Inability to produce appropriate vowel sounds also is a problem common to many hearing-impaired children. The child may produce a sound heard as a neighboring vowel or as a vowel of changing quality (diphthong). Investigators have reported a reduced range of both F_1 and F_2 in vowels for hearing-impaired talkers (Angelocci, Kopp, & Holbrook, 1964), indicative of a limited range of tongue movement which is inadequate to clearly differentiate the vowels. The limited range of vowel articulation also may impair the intelligibility of adjacent consonants, whose correct identification depends on appropriate formant transitions (Monsen, 1978).

Typical consonant articulation problems exhibited by hearing-impaired children include: failure to distinguish voiced/voiceless consonants, particularly the stops; misarticulation of certain speech sounds, particularly those with high-frequency components (e.g., /s/, /ʃ/); and difficulty in producing smooth transitions in CV or VC syllables, in consonant blends, or in abutting consonants. Several authors have commented on the role of visibility of articulation on the face of a teacher/model as a determiner of ease with which hearing-impaired children learn correct production (Levitt, 1974; Monsen, 1976; Nober, 1967); but this finding may simply reflect the current state of the art in auditory training and acoustic speech modeling techniques.

4. *Linguistic Errors.* Omissions of an unstressed syllable or verb ending are relatively common in the spontaneous speech of many hearing-impaired children. Although these errors commonly are labeled as errors in expressive "language," they are probably derived from auditory or lipreading deficiencies. For example, verb endings (e.g., *-s*, *-ing*) and many other unstressed syllables typically are hard to hear or see when produced. Numerous children also misperceive unstressed prefixes and suffixes, plurals, pronouns, and prepositions and thus use them improperly or not at all in running speech production.

Clinical experience suggests that many of these speech errors can be minimized through careful and systematic instruction (Ling & Ling, 1978). This teaching may include the use of acoustic imitation techniques as well as reliance on visual and tactual modeling.

General Principles of Acoustic Speech Instruction

Rationale

The preceding sections have surveyed the auditory capacities and limitations of severely and profoundly hearing-impaired children, as well as common expressive errors that occur. How can these two sources of information be interrelated in teaching hearing-impaired children to use acoustic feedback for speech monitoring and control?

We assume that acoustic correction is desirable and should be attempted whenever possible (Beebe, 1953; Ling, 1976; Pollack, 1970). For communication to occur through spoken language, a correct series of acoustic events must be transmitted from a talker to a receiver. Thus, a hearing-impaired child who can learn to encode language in terms of acoustic cues should more easily express ideas meaningfully to others through speech.

Speech training with continued reference to *acoustic* similarities between the teacher's model and the child's imitation may help convey to the child the degree to which hearing people depend on sound for speech perception and thus may motivate more careful attention to the acoustic component of his speech. Visual, tactual, and manual methods cannot achieve this effectively. Also, audition may be superior to vision for encoding, storage, and retrieval of speech and language. If so, a hearing-impaired child who can learn to encode acoustic aspects of language should have less difficulty developing an efficient processing system.

Typical Sequence

In general, the following steps are followed during acoustic speech instruction. The clinician develops an inventory of the child's speech production errors during conversation, as well as in a structured test situation. The clinician also identifies the child's capacity for auditory perception to anticipate whether the child will be capable of perceiving certain distinctions between his own speech and that of his instructor or whether further practice in perceiving speech qualities will be required. To correct an error when a child produces improper voice, speech, or language, the acoustically oriented clinician covers the mouth and attempts to use sound as a stimulus before providing visual cues, exaggerating articulation, employing phonetic signs, or writing. Various useful acoustic strategies are available: repetition, exaggeration, intentional distortion, verbal instruction, and gestural prompts (Erber & Greer, 1973). One repeatedly encourages the child

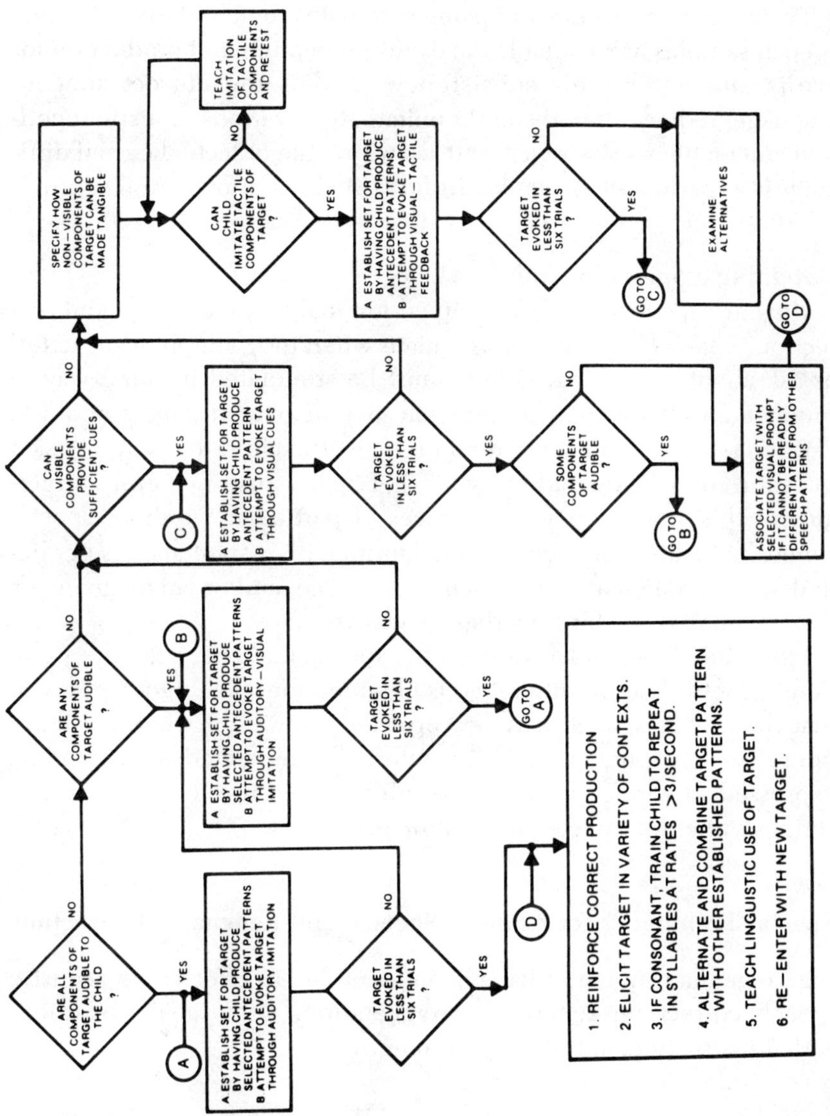

FIGURE 19.5

Suggested sequence through which a clinician may employ the child's various sense modalities to teach speech production (Ling & Ling, 1978).

to imitate the clinician's acoustic speech model, and thus learn to monitor and correct himself through auditory feedback.

To summarize (Figure 19.5), one stimulates the child to talk so that speech samples are available, analyzes perception and production for errors and notes their consistency, models the correct speech/language, requests that the child imitate, tries various acoustic repetition and emphasis strategies, and allows visible or tactual cues if difficulty is experienced (Ling & Ling, 1978).

Obtaining a Speech Sample

How are speech samples obtained for analysis, modeling, and correction? Many children will articulate when they simply want to tell or ask about something. Others must be stimulated in some way to produce an utterance. The clinician may display an object and ask, "What is this?," write a word and request the child to say it, or ask a question (e.g., "How old are you?"). Teachers use numerous strategies of this sort to obtain utterances of particular words or speech sounds for analysis and correction. During either spontaneous or elicited speech, one may note articulation, voice, and/or language errors that are candidates for remedial acoustic therapy.

When the clinician has elicited the speech and language, the situation is controlled; the utterance is obtained for teaching purposes so that the child's speech may be corrected. However, when the child utters speech spontaneously, an internally generated idea is being expressed. If correction is not carefully applied in such cases, it may seriously disrupt the communication act.

Special Techniques for Acoustic Speech (and Language) Instruction

Five general strategies have been identified as effective in acoustic speech correction: repetition, exaggeration, intentional distortion, verbal instruction, and gestural prompting.

Repetition

Situational factors may affect the child's perception of his/her own speech or that of the model, e.g., lapse of attention, misperception due to reduced signal intensity, or environmental noise. Simple repetition of the child's utterance or the model may be sufficient to elicit an accurate imitation in these instances.

Exaggeration

Often, a speech element or word will not produce a prominent perceptual image for the child because of auditory limitations or because of distortion by the hearing aid. For example, the child may not differentiate stress in the two syllables of the word *bottle.* The clinician may attempt correction by exaggerating differences in syllable intensity or duration (*bot*tle). An omitted pause between clauses may be cued by modeling an exaggerated silence in the appropriate place to increase its perceptual prominence. If the child produces an utterance with monotone pitch, it may be modeled by exaggerating the magnitude of the correct intonational contour.

Exaggeration also may be used effectively in correcting articulation, as in substitution of one consonant for another in the child's repertoire. For example, if a child produces /raɪd/ for the word *right,* one may attempt to correct this error by covering the mouth first and then exaggerating the intensity and duration of the final plosive burst. In the case of vowel substitution or error in precision, correction often can be accomplished by prolonging articulation of the vowel while it is at target position. Segments of diphthongs also may be exaggerated in like manner.

Whenever a child substitutes or omits a word (zoo—*the* zoo) or morpheme (farmer—farm), exaggeration may be used in modeling by producing the element with greater intensity and/or by isolating it between brief pauses. For example, the phrase *in car* can be modeled for the child as in . . . a . . . car to achieve correct production.

Intentional Distortion

A generally accepted rule is that one should apply an acoustic technique to correct a speech error only if the child seems capable of distinguishing acoustically between his/her incorrect production and the clinician's correct modeling of the sound. This is a reasonable minimal requirement for attempting acoustic correction. In some instances, however, the application of intentional distortion to the model can make the desired acoustic quality perceptually available to the child, although the sound could not be detected before. For example, omission or gross misarticulation of a stop or fricative (especially unvoiced elements, such as /t/ or /s/), frequently can be corrected by moving the microphone very close to the mouth to create low-frequency turbulance in the breath stream (Schulte, 1978). The resulting noise usually can be detected by the child and marks that point in the utterance where the particular speech sound should be present.

Later, although the child receives no auditory feedback at all when producing the sound (e.g., /s/) correctly, he/she may substitute the acoustic image of the instructor's (distorted) production as the appropriate speech element is articulated. In this way, the child may be constantly reminded of the importance of each speech *sound* for correct perception by a normal-hearing listener.

Omission of an /s/ sometimes can be corrected by cuing the child with an intentionally misarticulated /s/ which is more like /ʃ/ in quality. This lower frequency sound often is audible. Various frequency transposition techniques accomplish this effect to an extent by electronic means (Ling, 1968).

The distortion technique is used mainly to elicit omitted phonemes; the object is not so much to model correct acoustic patterns but to convince the child that it is the *sounds* of speech that are important for perception by a normal-hearing person, not the appearance of visible articulation. Once the child seems to appreciate this concept, then the correct production may be modeled and imitated along with its minimal feedback.

Verbal Instruction

Clinicians often provide a variety of suggestions, hints, and rules to help children develop self-reliance in correcting their speech when they fail to communicate (Calvert & Silverman, 1975). Some common verbal strategies are conveyed by the following: "I don't understand your speech." (general); "You forgot a sound in the last word." (more specific); or "You left out the /l/ sound in the word *please*." (very specific). These instructions may even be presented acoustically, and can prepare children for the type of feedback typically given by listeners who have little experience in communicating with hearing-impaired persons.

Gestural Prompting

Gestures, although not acoustic in nature, may be used to cue the child's attention to acoustic events such as pitch change, pause, stress, or to important speech features such as voice, nasal, stop, or fricative. These gestures may be formalized in the nature of a phonetic sign system (Jenson, 1971; Schulte, 1978; Zaliouk, 1954) or may be more spontaneous, as in body movements intended to convey rhythm and emphasis in speech (Guberina, 1964).

Caution

When a clinician employs any of the special acoustic cues and prompts described in the sections above, the activity should be completed by withdrawing the supplementary information and returning to a normal acoustic model before continuing. That is, the intent is to transfer the child's speech monitoring and imagery to the acoustic domain, not to increase the child's dependence on substitute feedback provided by the clinician.

Additional Strategies

There are a variety of additional strategies that have been found useful in acoustic speech instruction in the clinic and classroom.

For example, if the child is successful in matching an acoustic model, one should acknowledge this success to give confidence in hearing aids and ears as speech monitoring mechanisms. If the child continues to produce the error, however, apparently due to auditory limitations, the clinician must choose an alternate, more appropriate instructional strategy. Sometimes an auditory-visual compromise is effective, without resorting to obvious visual cuing or prompting. For example, if the child persists in producing /toʊk/ for the word *Coke*, the clinician may simply uncover his/her mouth briefly to show the initial velar place of articulation, and then re-cover the mouth and model the entire word acoustically. That is, provide a relevant visual cue, but ultimately present the entire model utterance acoustically and require the child to listen.

A profoundly hearing-impaired child can be taught to use the output of a vibrator to compare the speech qualities of the instructor's model and his/her imitation. This technique is most effective for correcting those gross aspects of speech that are apparent in the intensity pattern, such as rate of syllable production (Erber, 1978). But sometimes even minimal distinctions can be demonstrated in this way. For example, some profoundly deaf children can be taught to distinguish harsh (rough) or loud voice from a normal (smooth) or soft voice. It can be useful for the clinician to produce the incorrect voice quality and contrast this with a correct vocal pattern. This, of course, would be done with the mouth covered. The child may be asked to imitate both tactual qualities and describe the differences between them.

During a speech therapy session, it can be very helpful to discuss topics of interest to the child to motivate communication through speech. Nonvisual communication practice (e.g., by telephone) is especially useful for convincing a child of the importance of acoustically correct speech. A child who is aware of the value of speech communication will allow a clinician to disrupt a conversation repeatedly to model segments that were judged to be incorrect, and the child will be willing to try repeatedly to match the acoustic quality of the model. Still, an alert clinician will continually assess the situation to determine at what point to terminate acoustic speech instruction and resume auditory-visual conversation. Decisions of this sort depend on experience with individual children.

Summary and Conclusion

Both clinical experiences and research findings have helped to quantify some of the perceptual errors that hearing-impaired children commonly experience and to relate these findings to errors observed in their speech and language production. In this paper, the author has explored some ways that clinicians apply this knowledge in correction of speech through acoustic modeling. It is a clinical method that deserves further application and study. We must define the scientific foundations of this procedure; we must understand the instructional decision process more completely; and we must specify the conditions under which acoustic speech correction techniques have proven to be effective.

Acknowledgment

Preparation of this paper was supported by Program Project Grant NS 03856 from NINCDS to CID. Appreciation is expressed to Carol L. DeFilippo, Ellen L. Estes, and Randall B. Monsen, who provided valuable assistance.

REFERENCES

Angelocci, A. A., Kopp, G. G., & Holbrook, A. The vowel formants of deaf and normal-hearing eleven- to fourteen-year-old boys. *J. Speech Hear. Dis.*, 1964, *29*, 156-170.

Asp, C. W. The verbo-tonal method as an alternative to present auditory training techniques. In J. Wingo & G. Holloway (Eds.), *An appraisal of speech pathology and audiology*. Springfield, Ill.: Thomas, 1973.

Beebe, H. *A guide to help the severely hard of hearing child.* Basel, Switzerland: Karger, 1953.

Bennett, C. W., & Ling, D. Effects of voiced-voiceless discrimination training upon articulation of hearing-impaired children. *Lang. Speech*, 1977, *20*, 287–293.

Boothroyd, A. The discrimination by partially hearing children of frequency distorted speech. *Internat. Audiol.*, 1967, *6*, 136–145.

Boothroyd, A. Some experiments on the control of voice in the profoundly deaf using a pitch extractor and storage oscilloscope display. *IEEE Trans. Audio Electroacoustics, AU-21*, 1973, 274–278.

Byers, V. W. Initial consonant intelligibility by hearing-impaired children. *J. Speech Hear. Res.*, 1973, *16*, 48–55.

Calvert, D. R. Deaf voice quality: A preliminary investigation. *Volta Rev.*, 1962, *64*, 402–403.

Calvert, D. R., & Silverman, S. R. *Speech and deafness.* Washington: A.G. Bell Association for the Deaf, 1975.

Conrad, R. Profound deafness as a psycholinguistic problem. In G. Fant (Ed.), *Speech communication ability and profound deafness.* Washington: A.G. Bell Association for the Deaf, 1972.

DiCarlo, L. M. *The Deaf.* Englewood Cliffs, N.J.: Prentice-Hall, Inc., 1964.

Edson, S. *The acoustic approach to speech correction.* independent study, St. Louis: Washington University, 1978.

Erber, N. P. Auditory, visual, and auditory-visual recognition of consonants by children with normal and impaired hearing. *J. Speech Hear. Res.*, 1972, *15*, 413–422.

Erber, N. P. Auditory-visual perception of speech with reduced optical clarity. *J. Speech Hear. Res.*, in press, 1979.

Erber, N. P. The use of audio tape-cards in auditory training for hearing-impaired children. *Volta Rev.*, 1976, *78*, 209–218.

Erber, N. P. Vibratory perception by deaf children. *Internat. J. Rehab. Res.*, 1978, *1*, 27–37.

Erber, N. P., & Greer, C. W. Communication strategies used by teachers at an oral school for the deaf. *Volta Rev.*, 1973, *75*, 480–485.

Ewing, A. W. G., (Ed.), *Educational guidance and the deaf child.* Washington: Volta Bureau, 1957.

Gault, R. H. On the interpretation of speech sounds by means of their tactual correlates. *Ann. Otology*, 1926a, *35*, 1050–1063.

Gault, R. H. Touch as a substitute for hearing in the interpretation and control of speech. *Arch. Otolaryngol.*, 1926b, *3*, 121–135.

Gengel, R. W. Practice effects in frequency discrimination by hearing impaired children. *J. Speech Hear. Res.*, 1969, *12*, 847–856.

Gengel, R. W. Temporal effects in frequency discrimination by hearing-impaired listeners, *J. Acoust. Soc. Am.*, 1973, *54*, 11–15.

Goldstein, M. A. *The acoustic method for the training of the deaf and hard of hearing child.* St. Louis: Laryngoscope Press, 1939.

Guberina, P. Verbotonal method and its application to the rehabilitation of the deaf. *Proceed. Internat. Cong. Educ. Deaf and 41st Meeting Convention Amer. Instruct. Deaf*, Washington: U.S. Government Printing Office, 1964.

Hack, Z. C., & Erber, N. P. Auditory, visual and auditory-visual recognition of vowels by hearing-impaired children. *Res. Dept. Periodic Prog. Rep. 22,* St. Louis: Central Institute for the Deaf, in press, 1979.

Höxter, R. The Barczi method and its application in the school for the deaf of the Alliance Israelite Universelle. *Am. Ann. Deaf,* 1938, *83,* 386–403.

Hudgins, C. V., & Numbers, F. C. An investigation of the intelligibility of the speech of the deaf. *Genet. Psych. Mono.,* 1942, *25,* 289–392.

Huizing, H. Potential hearing in deaf children: Its early development and use for auditory communication. In A. Ewing (Ed.), *The modern educational treatment of deafness.* Manchester: The University Press, 1960.

Jenson, P. M. The relationship of speechreading and speech. In L. E. Connor (Ed.), *Speech for the deaf child: Knowledge and use.* Washington: A.G. Bell Association for the Deaf, 1971.

Levitt, H. Comment. In R. E. Stark (Ed.), *Sensory capabilities of hearing-impaired children.* Baltimore: University Park Press, 1974.

Ling, D. *Speech and the hearing-impaired child: Theory and practice.* Washington: A.G. Bell Association for the Deaf, 1976.

Ling, D. Three experiments in frequency transposition. *Am. Ann. Deaf,* 1968, *113,* 283–294.

Ling, D., & Ling, A. *Aural habilitation.* Washington: A.G. Bell Association for the Deaf, 1978.

Mártony, J. On the correction of the voice pitch level for severely hard of hearing subjects. *Am. Ann. Deaf,* 1968, *113,* 195–202.

Miller, G. A. The perception of speech. In M. Halle (Ed.), *For Roman Jakobson.* The Hague: Mouton & Co., 1956.

Miller, G. A., & Nicely, P. An analysis of perceptual confusions among some English consonants. *J. Acoust, Soc. Am.,* 1955, *27,* 338–352.

Monsen, R. B. Normal and reduced phonological space: The production of English vowels by deaf adolescents. *J. Phonetics,* 1976, *4,* 189–198.

Monsen, R. B. Toward measuring how well hearing-impaired children speak. *J. Speech Hear. Res.,* 1978, *21,* 197–219.

Nickerson, R. S. Characteristics of the speech of deaf persons. *Volta Rev.,* 1975, *77,* 342–362.

Nickerson, R. S., Kalikow, D. N., & Stevens, K. N. Computer aided speech training for the deaf. *J. Speech Hear. Dis.,* 1976, *41,* 120–132.

Nober, E. H. Articulation of the deaf. *Except. Child.,* 1967, *33,* 611–621.

Owens, E., Benedict, M., & Schubert, E. Consonant phonemic errors associated with pure-tone configurations and certain kinds of hearing impairment. *J. Speech Hear. Res.,* 1972, *15,* 308–322.

Peterson, G., & Barney, H. Control methods used in a study of the vowels. *J. Acoust. Soc. Am.,* 1952, *24,* 175–184.

Pickett, J. M., Martin, E. S., Johnson, D., Brand Smith, S., Daniel, Z., Willis, D., & Otis, W. On patterns of speech feature reception by deaf listeners. In G. Fant (Ed.), *Speech communication ability and profound deafness.* Washington: A.G. Bell Association for the Deaf, 1972.

Pollack, D. *Educational audiology for the limited hearing infant.* Springfield, Ill.: Thomas, 1970.

Risberg, A. *Hearing loss and auditory capacity.* Paper presented at the Res. Conf. on Speech Processing Aids for the Deaf, Gallaudet College, 1977.

Risberg, A., Agelfors, E., & Boberg, G. Measurements of frequency-discrimination ability of severely and profoundly hearing-impaired children. *Speech Transmission Laboratory QPSR* 2–3. Stockholm: Royal Institute of Technology, 1975.

Ross, M., Duffy, R. J., Cooker, H., & Sargeant, R. L. Contribution of the lower audible frequencies to the recognition of emotions. *Am. Ann. Deaf,* 1973, *118,* 37–42.

Schulte, K. The use of supplementary speech information in verbal communication. *Volta Rev.,* 1978, *80,* 12–20.

Sher, A., & Owens, E. Consonant confusions associated with hearing loss above 2000 Hz. *J. Speech Hear. Res.,* 1974, *17,* 669–681.

Simmons-Martin, A. A. The oral-aural procedure: Theoretical basis and rationale. *Volta Rev.,* 1972, *74,* 541–551.

Smith, C. R. Residual hearing and speech production in deaf children. *J. Speech Hear. Res.,* 1975, *18,* 795–811.

Walden, B., & Montgomery, A. A. Dimensions of consonant perception in normal and hearing-impaired listeners. *J. Speech Hear. Res.,* 1975, *18,* 444–455.

Wedenberg, E. Auditory training of deaf and hard of hearing children. *Acta-Otolaryngol.,* 1951, Suppl. 94.

Wedenberg, E. Auditory training of severely hard of hearing pre-school children. *Acta-Otolaryngol.,* 1954, Suppl. 110.

Willemain, T. R., & Lee, F. F. Tactile pitch feedback for deaf speakers. *Volta Rev.,* 1971, *73,* 541–553.

Zaliouk, A. A visual-tactile system of phonetical symbolization. *J. Speech Hear. Dis.,* 1954, *19,* 190–207.

20

Integration of Diagnostic Information: Implications for Speech Training in School-Aged Children

Daniel Ling

"THEORY IS NEVER OF ANY DIRECT INTEREST to the person who trains children or patients," according to Lepschy (1975, p. 35). That theory will, nevertheless, dominate the present paper is inevitable, since most of the research reported on speech production among hearing-impaired children has simply described its generally impoverished nature. Our present guidelines for integrating diagnostic information into effective programs of speech development for individual children are largely derived from theory supplemented by clinical teaching experience. Exceptions are those studies in which the relative efficiency of training strategies has been investigated and the validity of theories relating to speech development has been measured.

In its truest sense, speech is not the production of unrelated sound patterns but the meaningful use of spoken language, primarily in acts of communication. Speech training, if it is to result in a hearing-impaired child's effective use of verbal skills for social and personal purposes, must, therefore, embrace diagnostic information and therapeutic concern with:

1. The child's expressive skills at phonetic and phonologic levels and in discourse
2. The child's speech reception capacities;
3. The child's linguistic competence; and
4. The environmental influences that govern the quantity and quality of the child's exposure to spoken language (Figure 20.1).

To be successful, the speech specialist cannot be concerned with any of these areas to the exclusion of others. In short, an effective program should, as Miller and Yoder (1972) suggest, ensure that the child has something to say, a way to say it, and a reason for saying it (and, one might add, someone to say it to).

The purpose of this paper is to examine current knowledge in each of the four areas specified above, to pinpoint various aspects of work that require further research, and to indicate how our present knowledge can be integrated into the training of specialists able to work effectively in helping hearing-impaired children to talk.

Speech Production

General Comments

Numerous hearing-impaired children and adults have intelligible speech and use it as their primary means of communication. Some of them are totally deaf and have been so from birth. Their ability to talk demonstrates that deafness, in itself, is not an insuperable barrier to the acquisition of speech. Nevertheless, the majority of children in special educational programs for the deaf do not learn to speak well, and some do not learn to talk at all. In the programs surveyed by

FIGURE 20.1
Areas involved in spoken language development.

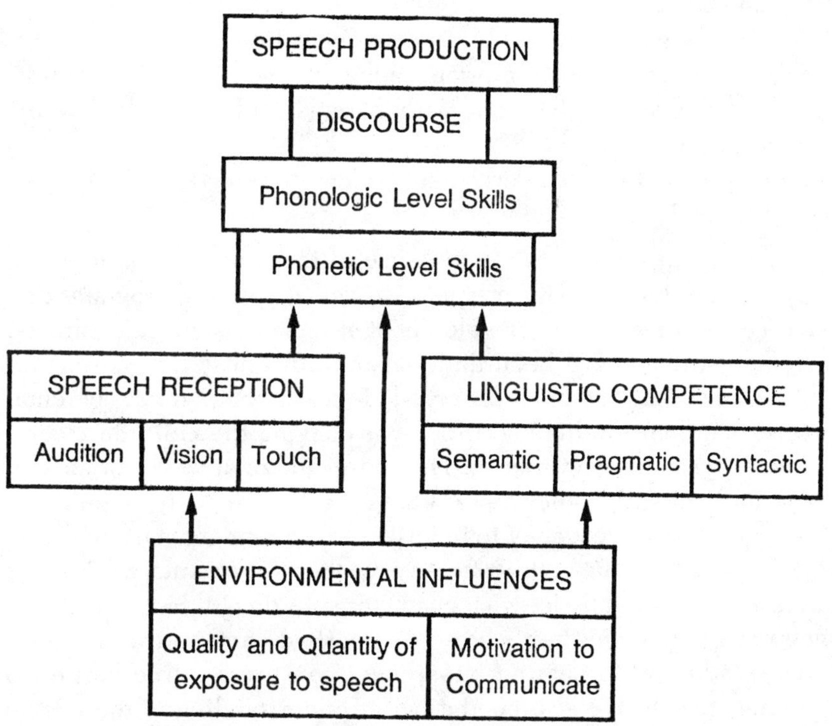

Jensema, Karchmer, and Trybus (1978) there was no overall trend for children to improve their speech with age. Speech ability among children in secondary schools was no better than among children in the early primary grades.

Diagnostic procedures can be applied to programs as well as to people. To determine why some programs produce children who can talk and other programs fail to do so, the most obvious diagnostic step is to compare the characteristics of each, not only in relation to speech attainments but according to the type, quality, and philosophy of the education provided by them. This has not been formally attempted. However, indirect evidence from various surveys and informal observation indicates that programs which produce hearing-impaired children who speak have many of the following characteristics, and those which fail to do so have few if any of them:

1. Commitment to teaching speech;
2. Skillful speech and language teachers;
3. Systematic speech and language programs;
4. High levels of expectation in relation to the development of verbal skills;
5. Primary emphasis on speech communication;
6. Consistent use of appropriate and well-maintained hearing aids;
7. Continuing involvement with parents and normally hearing peers; and
8. Provision from an early age for one-to-one teacher/child or parent/child interaction.

No ranking in order of the importance of these features is implied.

Speech production skills may also vary greatly within programs that have a commitment to the development of spoken language. Again, no adequate studies have been undertaken to diagnose the reasons for the variance that has been observed. Teacher competence, parental involvement, and individual differences among the children clearly account for some such variance. The nature and relative importance of these and possibly other variables that interfere with or enhance speech acquisition have yet to be explored. One might start by investigating what it is that highly effective teachers (or parents) do that less successful ones fail to do; what characteristics do children who speak well possess that children who speak poorly do not; and what conditions in addition to hearing impairment constitute a true barrier to learning speech. We also need a better understanding of the effects that the interactions of more than one such condition may produce.

In the absence of research-based data, teacher/clinicians are currently using many teaching strategies that have yet to be substantiated or refuted by controlled studies. They have no alternative. They are faced day by day with children whom they must attempt to teach as best they can. Most teacher/clinicians have received inadequate training in teaching speech to hearing-impaired children and are unfamiliar with research methods. Accordingly, their work is often inefficient and results in less than optimal speech skill development. Surveys of the speech of children currently being taught in various programs must, therefore, reflect the strengths or deficits of the programs, the skills or weaknesses of the teacher/clinician, and the outcome of the strategies they use (Geffner et al., 1978; Levitt, 1976).

There is a danger in studies of "deaf speech" that originate from a single program. Studies of this type invite unwarranted generalizations. They tend not only to designate but to preserve the *status quo* in that they are often interpreted both by the researchers (who are not teacher/clinicians) and the teacher/clinicians (who do not understand research) as specifying reasonable expectation levels. In short, description of the speech that hearing-impaired children generally achieve in no way indicates what such children could achieve if they were taught more effectively (Bernstein, Rollins, & Stevens, 1978).

Descriptive studies typically list common errors of speech production as including poor breath control; poor voice quality; neutralization, nasalization and prolongation of vowels; intrusive voicing, unclear voiced-voiceless distinctions, and omission or distortion of various consonants (Ling, 1976; Nickerson, 1975). Work undertaken by the writer and his colleagues (Ling, 1976) has shown that none of these characteristics is the inevitable outcome of deafness *per se* since simple strategies applied within a carefully sequenced program can be shown to prevent the development of or effect the remediation of such errors. We require far more studies involving the training of children by competent teacher/clinicians within programs that recognize the relative importance of the four aspects of the task specified on page 242. Only when the results of such studies are disseminated can we anticipate that effective spoken language skills will be generally expected of hearing-impaired children.

Phonetic Level Skills

Phonetic level skills may be defined as the range of abilities required to control intensity, duration, and voice frequency during vocalization and to produce, repeat, and alternate segmental patterns within syllables. Phonetic level skills are necessary but insufficient prerequisites for spoken language. They relate to discourse in much the same way that tuning an instrument relates to musical performance. Just as one must be able to tune a stringed instrument in order to play it, so must one call upon phonetic level skills in order to talk.

The diagnostic information available from the phonetic level speech evaluation described by Ling (1976) has been demonstrated to be a useful tool both as a means of identifying the sequence in which speech patterns can most efficiently be developed (the first items failed are the first items to be taught) and as a guide to the level of speech intelligibility that a child can achieve (Nicholls, 1979; Novelli-Olmstead, 1979; Young, 1978). In Nicholls' study of 18 profoundly or totally deaf children, phonetic level skills correlated closely with phonologic use of speech patterns ($r = .71, p < .001$) and with intelligibility ratings ($rho = .71$, $p < .001$). Phonologic scores and intelligibility ratings were even more closely correlated ($rho = .95$, $p < .001$).

Novelli-Olmstead's work demonstrated rapid acquisition of phonetic-level speech target behaviors by seven profoundly hearing-impaired children over the course of 30 training sessions of 15 minutes' duration. Comparison of the group's pre- and post-training test scores showed a mean gain of 50 points on phonetic level training. (1 point was awarded for inconsistently produced targets, and 2 points for those consistently produced.) These gains were significant beyond the .01 level of confidence ($F = 34.8$; $df = 1, 6$). Young, in her two-year study of 106 children, found the sequential ordering of steps in the evaluation to be both valid and reliable. Further, she found that the results of the evaluation correlated with intelligibility as assessed by either teachers or naive listeners beyond the .01 level of significance.

In the three studies quoted above, phonetic level evaluations were used in programs that also employed phonetic level training, i.e., training in which the purpose was to develop production of speech patterns first in nonmeaningful units. A strong case can be made for this procedure. It was reported by Shaffer (1942) as yielding progress superior to that obtained through teaching exclusively in meaningful verbal contexts. Clinical experience with the procedure indicates that young children, particularly those with substantial residual hearing, have relatively little difficulty in generalizing patterns learned to a high level of automaticity at a phonetic level into their meaningful speech. Apparently, their experience with alternated vowels ensures natural sounding formant transitions; skill in repetition of syllables ensures that consonants are learned in various vowel contexts in initial, medial, and final positions, and with appropriate breath and voice control; and skill in alternation of syllables provides them with the flexibility required to produce words and series of words. Older children who habitually use faulty approximations in meaningful patterns seem to have far more difficulty in transferring newly developed phonetic level skills into phonology. An interference effect such as that described by Winitz and Bellerose (1978) evidently operates. Possible ways of overcoming such interference are discussed in more detail below.

Several different types of research on phonetic level evaluation and training are needed. We need to know what levels and types of skills are required in order to administer the evaluation reliably; whether diadochokinetic rates of three per second are adequate for all syllables; how far oral-peripheral anomalies relate to performance on the evaluation; how many speech targets should be tested beyond the level at which the child begins to fail; whether as Ling (1976) suggests, six is the optimal number of target behaviors to be taught concurrently, and what factors should be considered in deciding how many of these behaviors should be taught at a phonetic level; whether one can specify the optimal duration and frequency of phonetic level training sessions relative to particular types of children; how teachers can accommodate their schedules to meet the need for frequent rehearsal of skills; what strategies are most likely to be successful in evoking and rehearsing the various target behaviors in children relative to their age, hearing levels, and other characteristics; and how far are different types of visual or tactile speech training devices necessary, sufficient, or advantageous relative to noninstrumental techniques, in evoking and/or rehearsing phonetic level skills. The list could be much more extensive.

Phonologic Level Skills

Phonologic level skills may be defined as the range of abilities required to use the various suprasegmental and segmental patterns of speech in meaningful verbal contexts. Formal evaluation of such skills provides the teacher/clinician with the diagnostic information required to ensure systematic development of intelligible spoken language. Strategies for the evaluation of these skills have been discussed in detail by Ling (1976) and by Ling and Ling (1978). It is at the phonologic level of speech production that phonetic level skills interface with language. Spoken language samples can therefore be used both for linguistic and phonologic analyses.

The primary interest in phonologic analysis is to determine which speech patterns are consistently present, inconsistently used, or absent. Patterns that are present in the child's phonetic level repertoire may be inconsistently used or absent in a phonologic sample for a variety of reasons. Given that children have sufficient language, they may be unaware of the pronunciation of particular words, and hence do not attempt to use certain patterns in their approximations to them; attention to the semantic or syntactic content of the utterance or its complexity may detract from accuracy; practice at a phonetic level may have been inadequate to establish the accuracy, speed, economy of effort, and flexibility required to produce the pattern in more complex utterances; previously used approximations may have become habitual and thus interfere with the production of the desired pattern; or the pattern may not be represented in a sample of the length obtained. Even in samples of a hundred utterances involving complex language, particular blends may not appear. Once a phonologic analysis has been made, there is, therefore, need to identify the reasons for inconsistent use or absence of a pattern within a phonologic sample. Such further diagnosis is required if effective developmental or remedial procedures are to be initiated. It would, for example, be futile to concentrate on phonetic level drills if the problem were simply due to the child's lack of knowledge relating to pronunciation.

The development of speech patterns at the phonologic level requires considerably more research. Of primary interest is the process of generalization from a phonetic to a phonologic level of production, which has not yet been studied among hearing-impaired children. Work with normally hearing children (Garnica, 1973; Shvachkin, 1973) suggests that sounds that can be differentiated phonetically may have to be "learned again" in phonologic environments. The same may be true of speech production. Guess, Baer, and Sailor (1978), writing within the framework of teaching language-delayed children, considered the issue of generalization to be the most current and pressing of all aspects of teaching communication skills. They proposed several tactics by which generalization of training might be enhanced. Expressed in the writer's words, these tactics included:

1. Training several targets rather than one at a time;
2. Not allowing reinforcement to be context dependent;

3. Teaching sufficient examples of a certain type so that a set is provided to help the child generalize to untaught items of the same type;
4. Ensuring that characteristics of the training have something in common with those of the situations the child will meet outside therapy;
5. Treating generalization as a response in itself; and
6. Selecting target behaviors that are highly functional in real life.

As implied by Guess, Baer, and Sailor (1978), there is support for the current practice of teaching the child to produce words, phrases, and sentences that contain patterns previously evoked and rehearsed at a phonetic level. However, if such production is limited to the therapy session, it may have little effect on the development of phonologic skill. It would seem necessary to demand and reinforce speech patterns learned in individual therapy in a variety of verbal and situational contexts: for example, in different words; to express different semantic notions; in different syntactic structures; at different times outside the therapy sessions; in lessons other than speech lessons; in locations other than the therapy room; in conversation with people other than the speech teacher, particularly parents and peers; and in play and other activities unrelated to school. Research is required to determine which of these contexts are the most conducive to phonologic growth and what strategies can best be employed to exploit them. Research is also required to determine the extent of experience needed by different children, trained under different conditions, to produce significant gains in their phonology. Research by Dodd (1976), Dodd and Hermelin (1977), and by Oller, Jensen, and Lafayette (1978) indicates that phonologic development may be substantially influenced by the sense modality principally employed in training the child.

Discourse

Discourse may be defined as the organization of sentences in larger units of expression (Chafe, 1972). Recent interest in discourse has been largely focused upon linguistic content and semantic structure (Ervin-Tripp & Mitchell-Kernan, 1977; Frederiksen, 1975), rather than on the characteristics of speech within discourse. However, the mechanics of talking within the framework of discourse are important to the refinement of speech production skills. In discourse the rate of production of a given sentence will differ according to the length of the message. One sentence will require more stress than another in order that the overall intent of the message is made clear. Intonation contours will change to reflect the meaning of the message and also to signal when the speaker expects the listener to take his turn in a conversation or when a pause signals emphasis rather than the conclusion of a statement. It is in discourse, then, that flexibility of production is required so that the macrotime units (breath, suprasegmentals) and the microtime units (segments, features) can enmesh.

When prevailing standards of achievement at phonetic and phonologic levels of speech production have been generally improved, more attention will no doubt be given to speech in discourse. Some hearing-impaired speakers are capable of discourse. Research on their performance to date has related to their intelligibility rather than to discourse skills as such. Studies of their speech in discourse would probably lead to the diagnosis of certain problems that would have implications for training at simpler levels of speech production. Such research is, therefore, strongly recommended.

Speech Reception

Speech can be received by the ear, the eye, and/or the skin. Diagnostic information relative to speech reception must therefore include information on the acuity of hearing, vision, and touch and, so far as can be clinically determined, the ability of the child to process speech stimuli through these senses, either separately or in combination. Speech reception is also a part of speech production in that the speaker, particularly in the learning stages, must be aware of the patterns that he or she produces. Awareness should be fostered, not only through the ear, the eye and/or the skin, but also through the sensory-motor information generated by tactile and kinesthetic sensation from the speech organs (Ling, 1976).

The only type of diagnostic information that remains relatively stable over the prolonged period of training and experience required for the acquisition of speech is that related to sensory acuity. Acuity reflects the relative integrity of the sensory system which in turn reflects the amount of information on speech that can be detected. A child's abilities to discriminate, identify, and comprehend speech do not relate directly to sensory acuity. Indeed, such abilities are usually the dependent variables chosen to measure the results of training. This being so, they can not be used in initial evaluations to predict a child's performance or to specify potential for acquiring spoken language.

Defective hearing and imperfect vision can usually be helped by means of hearing aids and eyeglasses. Such devices can serve to optimize speech detection. Diagnostic information showing the extent to which sensitivity can be improved by their use is essential to the teacher/clinician responsible for a child's speech skill development.

Although eyeglasses can usually correct defective vision, hearing aids can rarely, if ever, compensate fully for severe or profound hearing impairment. Sensitivity to sound usually remains reduced relative to normal even when the most appropriate hearing aids are used (Ling & Ling, 1978). This fact has important implications for the teacher/clinician since detection of speech sounds is a prerequisite for their discrimination, identification, and comprehension.

Audition

The frequency range of audition available to hearing-impaired children is at least as important as their average hearing levels (Moore, 1975; Strizver, 1958). Many hearing-impaired children with average hearing levels greater than 90 dB who nevertheless have audition for high-frequency sounds (2000 to 4000 Hz) are usually able to process most speech patterns through hearing alone when suitably aided and trained to do so. In comparison, those with hearing levels averaging 90 dB or more with no measurable hearing beyond 1000 Hz can be expected to detect, discriminate, and identify fewer speech patterns through hearing alone but to understand some spoken language primarily through audition (Ling, 1975, 1976; Wedenberg, 1951). Speech patterns available to such children include most suprasegmental features of speech (variations in duration, intensity, and voice frequency); one or more formants of all vowels (Baldwin & Houchins, 1976; Doehring & Ling, 1971), several manner distinctions among consonants (Aston, 1972) and the voiced-voiceless distinction (Bennett & Ling, 1973). Children with measurable hearing up to only 500 Hz can make several such distinctions, and some may be able to utilize spectral information within their auditory range. Others, including totally deaf children, may feel rather than hear sounds presented at high-intensity levels (Erber, 1972; Nober, 1967).

Children who hear, and those who only feel, high-intensity sounds cannot be easily distinguished. Those who hear are generally able to utilize spectral (frequency) cues and discriminate certain words more readily than those who feel (Risberg & Agelfors, 1978). Yet, since frequency discrimination can be improved through auditory training (Gengel, 1969) as can speech discrimination (Ling & Maretic, 1971), definitive separation of the two groups is a formidable task. This is particularly true for all young children and for those who have not had abundant and/or effective auditory training and experience. Current data (Erber, 1974a; Nicholls, 1979; Stoker, 1977) indicate that pupils within, and products of, different training programs may, in spite of equivalent hearing levels, develop quite different auditory discrimination abilities.

Although detection measures (thresholds) are, in general, relatively stable over a given period of training, they are subject to either permanent change (e.g., due to additional sensorineural loss) or temporary fluctuation (e.g., due to middle ear disease or problems with the hearing aid). The alert teacher/clinician should be aware of the child's optimal detection capacity. By administering the five-sound test (Ling, 1978a) prior to each teaching session, the teacher/clinician will notice any deterioration in response. Upon observation of a decreased capacity for detection, the hearing aids should be checked and, if they are not at fault, the cause of the problem should be immediately diagnosed and, if possible, treated. Factors external to the child such as degraded listening conditions (Downs & Crum, 1978; Ross & Giolas, 1971) should not be ignored.

During training, careful records of the child's ability to discriminate, identify, and comprehend speech should be kept. Problems with the development of auditory memory should also be identified through regular tests of memory span. Discrimination skills in children may often appear worse than in fact they are because the discrimination task overloads the child's memory capacity. It is not uncommon to find hearing-impaired children who have developed only brief (about 3-second) and restricted (2-3 item) capacity for stimuli of the type normally used in discrimination tests (A.H. Ling, 1975, 1976; Novelli-Olmstead, 1979). Such a finding is less common among hearing-impaired children who can produce the stimuli used in speech tests of hearing, since their spoken language skills permit them to recall and rehearse more readily. The extensive influence of speech production on speech perception, predicted by Denes (1967) and Liberman et al. (1967), has also been demonstrated by Lieberth and Subtelny (1978) and Novelli-Olmstead (1979).

Diagnostic information relative to cause of hearing loss has not yet been shown to correlate either with ability to use residual hearing or with capacity to develop speech skills. Research is certainly required in this area, but is presently not feasible. Its validity would clearly depend not only upon the reliability of the diagnosis but upon whether it would be reasonable to assume that training and experience in the use of hearing and in the acquisition of speech had provided the children with optimal opportunities for learning. The present state of the art would not permit such assumptions, for we cannot yet claim to have developed adequate auditory and speech training procedures.

Most of the burden of obtaining diagnostic material relevant to the role of speech reception in speech skill acquisition must rest with the teacher/clinician, for it has to be obtained in the course of ongoing treatment. It is the teacher/clinician who must decide, not on the basis of an audiogram, but on the basis of the child's responses during training, how far the child's hearing and hearing aids permit him to learn to discriminate between speech patterns, to identify and comprehend them, and to monitor his own speech production. That this burden is not widely acknowledged is evidenced by the trend toward the separation, rather than the integration, of diagnosis and therapy. If rapid progress in spoken language skills is, as the writer believes, a reasonable goal for most hearing-impaired children, then evaluation must be an integral part of every teaching task.

Unfortunately, teacher/clinicians generally lack the tools for ongoing evaluation of progress or the systematic development of auditory skills. Thus criterion-referenced training (Glaser, 1963) is beyond their reach. Auditory training programs such as those advocated by Grammatico (1975), A.H. Ling (1977), and Hoversten (1979) provide some guidelines but do not satisfy current needs. Training in discrimination associated with speech training (Ling, 1976) also does not satisfy current needs. Research aimed at providing teacher/clinicians with the tools to evaluate and structure auditory training and experience to meet individual children's speech reception and speech production needs should, therefore, receive high priority.

Vision

Ability to receive speech through vision has gained considerable attention. The bulk of research on speechreading has been reviewed by Berger (1972) and by Erber (1974b), and more recent work has added relatively little to our knowledge of the process. In brief, about 30 to 40 percent of nonsense syllables can be correctly identified by speechreaders under everyday viewing conditions. The visual reception of meaningful materials (sentences) is influenced by linguistic and situational context. Under conditions in which context cues can be effectively used, scores for words in sentences can be substantially better than for nonsense materials. Very little study of discourse level reception has been undertaken. Available data are not reassuring to the teacher/clinician seeking to instruct through speechreading alone. For example, Binnie (1974) found scores for discourse to average only 6.8 percent, a level much lower than that for other materials.

There is no convincing evidence that current tests can identify children who will be able to receive speech sufficiently well through speechreading to acquire normal speech or spoken language skills. Because efficiency in speechreading is so closely linked with language competence—which hopefully will increase with training—the teacher/clinician must periodically obtain diagnostic information on a child's progress in speechreading. They should therefore utilize both standard tests and make pragmatic assessments of the child in the course of teaching.

The main implication of research on speechreading to date is that its inherent difficulty severely limits its usefulness as an educational tool except when it either supplements, or is complemented by, parallel information. Thus, for example, speechreading can supplement the use of residual hearing (or vice versa) so that the two modalities together lead to performance that is superior to that achieved with either vision or audition alone (Erber, 1972; Ewing, 1944; Risberg & Agelfors, 1978).

Not all children have useful hearing. It is, therefore, important to find other avenues to supplement speechreading. Two main approaches are being made to this problem: the use of tactile aids (Pickett, 1977) and the use of Cued Speech (Cornett, 1967). The development of tactile aids is still in its infancy and so far results of work on such aids, though encouraging, have been limited (Sparks et al., 1979). Results of work with Cued Speech have shown that it far surpasses any other system as an efficient speechreading aid for profoundly or totally deaf children. Cued Speech is, essentially, an oral system. Ling and Clarke (1975) and Clarke and Ling (1976) showed that it was effective in increasing the speech reception skills of children who had failed to progress through traditional oral teaching. Nicholls (1979) has shown that over 80 percent of nonsense syllables and over 95 percent of key words in sentences can be accurately received by profoundly hearing-impaired children who use Cued Speech.

The diagnostic information required relative to Cued Speech has yet to be defined. Failure to make adequate progress on an auditory-oral system should certainly be regarded as one criterion for considering its use. The criteria for specifying "adequate progress" and for predicting whether a child could benefit from Cued Speech have yet to be specified. Research is required to determine the range of characteristics common to children with whom Cued Speech can be successfully used. Preliminary work (Ling, 1978b) has shown that it can be an aid in speech teaching, since it can unambiguously specify for a profoundly or totally deaf child the exact nature of the segmental patterns that the teacher wishes him to produce, repeat, or alternate.

Touch and Kinesthesis

Direct touch is a very powerful tool in speech teaching. There are numerous ways in which it can be used by skilled teacher/clinicians either to help evoke or to prompt any given sound pattern (Calvert & Silverman, 1975; Ling, 1976). Diagnostic information on the child's ability to utilize cues provided by touch is probably unnecessary, since such cues are relatively gross. Of more basic interest is the ability of a speaker to learn and to maintain speech patterns that he or she cannot hear through reference to the tactile and kinesthetic (orosensory-motor) patterns generated by the speech act itself. Certain adventitiously hearing-impaired persons maintain very clear, if not normal, speech patterns, while others lose their speech following deafness of late onset. A better understanding of the role played by orosensory-motor information in speech maintenance would be helpful in formulating more effective speech teaching strategies. Until more work has been carried out in this area, the creation of diagnostic tests relating to orosensory-motor control is not feasible.

Linguistic Competence

What patterns a child can perceive in speech reception and differentiate in speech production will both influence and be influenced by his or her linguistic competence (Ling, 1978a). Diagnostic information relative to the child's mastery of the semantic, pragmatic, and syntactic components of language is therefore essential in formulating an individualized speech acquisition program.

Semantic Aspects

Meaningful use of speech requires that a child develop not only a vocabulary that provides a set of referents common to his or her community, but ways of relating words within an utterance so that they specify relationships that are semantically significant to the child and to the listener (Bruner, 1974). The semantic notions expressed by young, normally hearing children in the early stages of language acquisition, such as nomination, agent, possession, object, location, etc. (Bloom, 1970; Dale, 1972; Leonard, 1976) tend closely to follow and reflect their cognitive development (McLean & Snyder-McLean, 1978). This is not the case with most hearing-impaired children. Learning speech and language at a later stage, their cognitive development usually far outstrips their ability to express themselves verbally. Nevertheless, if spoken language is to be learned, it must be related to a child's needs, cognitive skills, and the people, objects, and events in his or her life. Thus generalization of speech patterns acquired at a phonetic level can, and should, be taught and demanded in all of the semantic-linguistic contexts that can be observed in the spoken language of normal-hearing infants.

Relating speech to semantic categories serves a reciprocal purpose: It enhances the retention of speech skills through making them meaningful within specific contexts, and enhances language skills by demanding the inclusion and differentiation of morphemes. For example, possession is signified by the morphemes /s/, /z/. Initially to demand their consistent use only in the possessive case (e.g., Bob's ball, Pete's bike), helps to focus attention on the production of /s/, /z/ in limited but meaningful context, provides opportunity for the sounds to be practiced (specifying possession is a very frequent speech event), and ensures that possession is not confused with some other semantic category. Clinical experience suggests that relating specific sounds (morphemes) to particular semantic notions is a simpler and more effective way to ensure phonetic to phonologic transfer than random correction or general exercises in word pronunciation.

To relate speech skill and semantic-linguistic development in the manner described above clearly requires the phonetic, phonologic, and semantic analyses of a sample of each child's speech. Such analysis is a useful diagnostic tool, in that it readily yields clearly definable teaching targets. Regular analyses of these types can also provide useful measures of the effectiveness of training. In our current research these measures are also helping us to specify and develop improved procedures for ensuring generalization of phonetic level skills into a child's phonology.

Pragmatic Aspects

Language is a means to an end. Its primary purpose is to permit various personal-social communicative acts. Pragmatic analysis is concerned with the specification and classification of the purposes or functions language can be made to serve. Dore (1975) and Halliday

(1977) have each studied the functions served by language as it has emerged. Dore's work was with two children at a single-word stage and Halliday's with one child (his son Nigel) from a pre-speech to a discourse level of development.

Dore (1975) designated the various pragmatic categories he observed as "Primitive Speech Acts." These included labeling, repeating, answering, requesting action, requesting answer, calling, greeting, protesting, and practicing. The list is given here in order to demonstrate the variety of uses to which single words, when overlaid with intonation, can be put, even by a young child.

Halliday (1977, p. 37) postulated, and later found, that earliest phases of language could serve seven functions: instrumental (I want), regulatory (let's play), interactional (hello), personal (here I come), heuristic (tell me), imaginative (let's pretend), and informative (I want to tell you). He suggested (p. 56) that in adult language these functions could be classified as serving either ideational or interpersonal purposes. In our work with hearing-impaired children we have found it helpful to use finer (i.e., more specific) pragmatic categories than those proposed by Halliday. To state that a child can employ language informatively is inadequate for teaching purposes. One needs to know if he can use it to admit, announce, argue, chat, confess, contradict, convince, defend, deplore, describe, exclaim, express, exaggerate, gabble, gossip, inform, lie, mention, protest, preach, pun, rant, recite, recount, state, suggest, and tell tales or a story. This list, which is not exhaustive, indicates how each of Halliday's categories can be expanded and how items can then be used as specific pragmatic targets in developing spoken language. Considerable work needs to be done before a developmental order for the teaching of such targets could be specified.

Even without adequate research on these pragmatic aspects of language, it is possible for the teacher/clinician to relate specific speech targets to pragmatic functions. For example, the use of /n/ in "No way," "Not now," "No more," "Not me," and other such phrases ensures that the child has an effective means of protesting and that there is recurrent opportunity for the child to use this phoneme. (All children frequently protest, with or without cause.)

Diagnostic tests of pragmatic function need to be developed, and ways in which speech can be more fully integrated into the various pragmatic categories specified. It is likely that the range and proportion of pragmatic categories developed and used by hearing-impaired children will be found to vary according to the type of program in which they are enrolled. Certain language functions would be more difficult to develop in the classroom than in the home, in group situations than in individual interaction and, of course, vice versa. Work in this area with normally hearing children (Miller, 1978) and hearing-impaired children (Prutting, 1979) is beginning to indicate how diagnostic information can be obtained and used.

Syntactic Aspects

Syntax may be considered as the system of rules that governs how words may be combined to form sentences. Each word may be considered as having a form (e.g., noun, verb, etc.), a function (e.g., subject, object) and position in a sentence. Children's syntax is not an impoverished form of the adult model but a system with its own rules and regularities which change over time (Bloom, 1970; Brown, 1973). Approaches to teaching spoken language to hearing-impaired children through reference to a system based on adult syntax are therefore suspect. While the ultimate goal is the development of adult forms, their achievement is most likely to be fostered through reference to data on normal child language development (Ling & Ling, 1978).

Various diagnostic tools for the assessment of syntax exist. Of the many available, those involving spoken language sampling and analysis (Tyack & Gottsleben, 1974; Crystal, Fletcher, & Garman, 1976) are the most germane in relation to the teaching of speech. Such tools permit one to specify what syntactic structures are present, what structures are emerging, and what speech sounds are essential for the effective development of a given syntactic form. For example, the unreleased /d/, /t/ are essential for the adequate production of the regular past, and /ŋ/ for the present progressive tense; and the /n/ is required for the negative and most prepositions. A teacher/clinician who gathers diagnostic information on her children's syntactic development can readily employ the speech patterns they are learning at a phonetic level in meaningful linguistic structures.

Syntax in spoken language can not develop without fairly advanced skills in the reception and production of speech. Such skills are needed for the development of a basic vocabulary, but more so for understanding and using words that define the precise meaning of a sentence. Thus it is not surprising that many hearing-impaired children who cannot differentiate alveolar consonants use telegraphic forms of speech in which the meaning of the utterance is unclear. The normally hearing child at a two-word level of production will use situational and other nonverbal cues as well as suprasegmental patterns (particularly intonation) to define the semantic intention of a phrase such as "Mummy car" (which may be pronounced /ta/). If a hearing-impaired child has acquired voice patterns, vowels, and some consonants differentiated by manner of production, he will be in a similar position. However, the alveolar sounds that any child requires to convey meaning through syntax will be missing. These sounds occur in most of the words that serve a structural/relational purpose: that is, words that have no meaning in their own right. A few sentences using the words *mummy* and *car* illustrate this point:

Syntactic Structure	Consonants required for this syntactic structure
Mummy is in the car.	s/z, n, ð
That's Mummy's car.	ð, t, s
Is that Mummy's car?	s/z, ð, t
Where's Mummy's car?	w, s/z
Mummy has a car.	h, s/z
Is Mummy in the car?	s/z, n, ð
Mummy has no car.	s/z, n
That's not Mummy's car.	s/z, n, t, ð

The above examples demonstrate that spoken language as a rule-governed system involving syntax demands the development of alveolar consonants. The reverse is also true: Consistent phonologic use of alveolar consonants demands the concurrent development of basic syntactic structures. Since there are relatively few structural words in English and fewer alveolar consonants, the task may not appear to be enormous. However, these structural words are the most frequently used in English, and the difficulties that exist in teaching them plague all teacher/clinicians. Examined within an adequate diagnostic framework, these difficulties can be seen to reflect not only inadequate teaching strategies, but problems intrinsic to the child's hearing deficit. Receptively, the alveolar consonants are among the most difficult for profoundly deaf children to differentiate through either residual audition and/or speechreading (Asp, 1975). This does not, however, render them or the syntactic role they play impossible to develop.

Environmental Influences

There has been relatively little objective study of the effects of environment on speech acquisition by hearing-impaired children. It is, however, clear that a number of environmental factors will influence their speech and spoken language development.

Quantity and Quality of Exposure to Speech

Environmental factors include the extent of exposure to normal speech patterns, peer group influences, and whether alternative forms of communication are employed (Ling, Ling, & Pflaster, 1977). Children in programs that permit them to live at home usually have more exposure to normal speech patterns than do children in residential programs and they tend to develop more effective speech skills (Jensema & Trybus, 1978; Quigley & Frisina, 1961). Classroom teachers' expectations of the child also influence the extent to which speech skills are developed. Many do not consider speech and spoken language an integral part of every lesson and hence fail to encourage or reinforce the correct use of patterns that a child can actually produce (Markides, 1970).

The quantity of exposure required in order to learn speech and language may be expected to vary from one child to another. Most hearing-impaired children have limited experience of spoken language. Their deafness prevents them from hearing speech except over short distances, and the need for severely and profoundly deaf children to use vision as a supplement or alternative to audition usually restricts the amount of spoken language that they can receive incidentally. Current work on auditory, visual, and auditory-visual speech reception shows that even the spoken language that is intentionally directed to them may be received, under good acoustic and lighting conditions, in such a degraded form that its semantic and syntactic structure cannot be discerned (Ivimey, 1977).

In the absence of adequate research on environmental influences, the teacher/clinician must rely upon common-sense intervention in helping to optimize the conditions under which the hearing-impaired child has to function and learn. Parents and teachers can be encouraged to speak and teach within the child's auditory range, provide optimal acoustic and lighting conditions, encourage and reinforce acceptable spoken language patterns, ensure interaction with normal peers, as well as create and exploit situations and activities that demand verbal interaction. The effective teacher/clinician will also ar-range to monitor such environmental influences and thus diagnose, and seek to prevent or remediate, problems that may stem from environmental inadequacies.

Motivation To Communicate Through Speech

A motive may be considered as a goal; and motivation as the drive required to expend the effort to attain it. Unlike a reason, a motive is not necessarily spawned by conscious consideration. For reason to create sufficient drive to reach a goal, the end result must be considered as worth the effort required to achieve it. To maintain reason-based drive, one must continue to think it probable that the end result will be achieved through such effort (Woodworth, 1921, p. 85).

Only older children can be given, or find, reasons to communicate effectively through speech. They can be expected to understand that speech and spoken language can help them in many ways. It can bring them into closer contact with members of their family who can communicate only through speech, open up a greater variety of social and employment opportunities, provide more personal freedom and independence, and lead to better socioeconomic standing than would otherwise be the case (Lunde & Bigman, 1959; Schein & Delk, 1974).

Children of all ages can be motivated unconsciously by what Maslow (1951) has termed "instinctoid" needs. These include curiosity, freedom from restraint, food, sleep, safety, love, self esteem, and self actualization. Their satisfaction leads to advantages, approval, and acceptance. McNeil (1966, p. 65) considers that a further need—to reduce "cognitive clutter" by finding some means to differentiate and disambiguate the spoken message—also operates in the child's acquisition of communication skills.

To relate motivation for speech communication to the general needs mentioned above is not enough. How the teacher/clinician is to help meet these needs has also to be specified. Sloane and MacAuley (1968, p. 20) suggest that it is necessary, in training sessions, for the teacher/clinician to provide: interesting and stimulating materials; a structured program and strategies that lead to a high probability of success; specific indications of success such as grades; various forms of social reinforcement that indicate approval, such as smiles, pats, and verbal encouragement; primary reinforcers, such as food; token reinforcers that can be exchanged for candy, trinkets, etc.; and paired social and primary reinforcement. They also suggest that nonproductive, or disruptive, behaviors should be systematically extinguished by eliminating any form of reinforcement when they occur. They point out (p. 9) that motivation can be increased when the child's needs have not been met for a period of time. Thus food becomes a stronger need and a more powerful reinforcer when the child is hungry, and the drive toward conversation is greatest following a period of little verbal interaction. They warn (p. 10) of the need for generalized reinforcers such as a mother's voice, which is paired not only with food, but with warmth and care. This point is strongly supported by Ferster (1972), who states that unless there is a viable plan for natural reinforcers to take over and maintain new response patterns, behaviors developed in training will not be generalized. The exclusive use of primary reinforcers as a training strategy is doomed to failure.

In order to motivate children to talk, parents and teacher/clinicians must, in Woodworth's terms, first be convinced that speech production skills and intelligible spoken language are feasible goals for hearing-impaired children to achieve; and, second, that his or her efforts in helping them to achieve these goals will meet with both short-term and long-term success. Unless teacher/clinicians are highly motivated they have little chance of encouraging parents and teachers to be so.

Preparing Personnel To Teach Speech to Hearing-Impaired Children

In order to teach speech effectively, personnel must be prepared who have in-depth training leading to competence in each of the four areas discussed above: namely, speech production, speech reception, language development, and manipulation of environmental influences. These areas involve the disciplines of Education of the Hearing Impaired, Audiology, and Speech/Language Pathology. The Preparation of such personnel at various levels of training has been discussed in detail by Ling, Ling, and Pflaster (1977) and by Ling and Ling (1978).

A teacher-preparation program designed specifically to train personnel who are able to develop high-level spoken language skills in hearing-impaired children has been created at McGill University. It has been operating for only four years, an insufficient time for more than tentative evaluation of its function and potential. This program is part of a graduate school which also prepares audiologists and speech-language pathologists. Teacher/clinicians participating in this program share many common-core courses with students in these related fields. Three types of training are available to those specializing in work with hearing-impaired children:

1. Basic and advanced training over two years and two summers (80 graduate credits) leading to the Master of Science (M.Sc. Applied) degree. Prerequisites for admission include a first-rate undergraduate degree and qualification as a regular teacher.

2. A three-semester program of advanced study and research leading to the Master of Science (M.Sc. Research) degree. Prerequisites for admission include high standing at an undergraduate level and basic certification as a teacher of the hearing impaired.

3. Advanced research training leading to the Ph.D. degree. Prerequisites are professional qualification in any area of speech and hearing, including Education of the Hearing Impaired, and previous research experience such as that provided by the M.Sc. research degree or demonstrated through publications.

For both options 2 and 3, above, a program of course work and research is designed that permits each student to overcome perceived weakness in prior training and to extend knowledge through individually guided study. Experience with the first type of preparation has led us to estimate that, for a student to learn effective skills in teaching speech to profoundly hearing-impaired or totally deaf children at a phonetic level (skills that permit measurable progress in the children's speech production), requires a minimum of eight semester hours of course work and 240 clock hours of supervised practicum following a full semester of training in the speech and hearing sciences. We also estimate that the skills required to develop effective spoken language among profoundly hearing-impaired children cannot be learned without at least as much further course work and practical experience. We have found that at least six semester hours need to be allocated for seminars and practicum specifically for students to discuss and demonstrate ways of integrating information from other courses, particularly their diagnostic skills, with the teaching of speech and the development of spoken language communication.

The content of course work and practicum leading to a student's acquisition of effective skills in teaching speech to profoundly and totally deaf children can, at best, be only approximately defined. At present, each teacher/clinician preparation program would be likely to define it differently, have different methods of presenting the content considered essential, and place different emphases on various facets of the task. Hopefully, this conference will lead to more general agreement on content, form, and function within programs designed to train specialist teacher/clinicians in speech work with hearing-impaired children.

Acknowledgments

The writer is grateful to Agnes Ling Phillips, Doris Leckie, Gaye Nicholls, and Tina Novelli-Olmstead for their comments on the draft of this paper.

REFERENCES

Asp, C. W. Measurement of aural speech perception and oral speech production of the hearing impaired. In S. Singh (Ed.), *Measurement procedures in speech, hearing, and language.* Baltimore: University Park Press, 1975.

Aston, C. H. Hearing-impaired children's discrimination of filtered speech. *J. Aud. Res.*, 1972, *12*, 162–167.

Baldwin, R. L., & Houchins, R. R. Generalization with the vowel discrimination learning of hearing-impaired children. *J. Aud. Res.*, 1976, *16*, 71–77.

Bennett, C. W., & Ling, D. Discrimination of the voiced-voiceless distinction by severely hearing-impaired children. *J. Aud. Res.*, 1973, *13*, 271–279.

Berger, K. W. *Speechreading: Principles and methods.* Baltimore: National Educational Press, 1972.

Bernstein, J., Rollins, A. M., & Stevens, K. N. *Word and syllable concatenation in the speech of the deaf.* Presented at the A.G. Bell Association for the Deaf Convention, St. Louis: 1978.

Binnie, C. A. Auditory-visual intelligibility of various speech materials presented in three noise background. *Scand. Audiol.*, 1974, Suppl. 4, 255–280.

Bloom, L. *Language development: Form and function in emerging grammars.* Cambridge: MIT Press, 1970.

Brown, R. *A first language: The early stages.* Cambridge: Harvard University Press, 1973.

Bruner, J. From communication to language: A psychological perspective. *Cognition*, 1974, *3*, 255–287.

Calvert, D. R., & Silverman, S. R. *Speech and deafness.* Washington, D.C.: A.G. Bell Association for the Deaf, 1975.

Chafe, W. Discourse structure and human knowledge. In R. Freedle and J. Carroll (Eds.), *Language comprehension and the acquisition of knowledge.* New York: V.H. Halstead, 1972.

Clarke, B. R., & Ling, D. The effects of cued speech: A follow-up study. *Volta Rev.*, 1976, *78*, 23–34.

Cornett, R. O. Cued speech. *Am. Ann. Deaf,* 1967, *112*, 3–13.

Crystal, D., Fletcher, P., & Garman, M. *The grammatical analysis of language disability: A procedure for assessment and remediation.* London, England: Arnold, 1976.

Dale, P. S. *Language development: Structure and function.* Hinsdale, Ill.: Dryden Press, 1972.

Denes, P. B. On the motor theory of speech perception. In W. Wathen-Dunn (Ed.), *Models for the perception of speech and visual form: Proceedings of a symposium.* Cambridge: MIT Press, 1967.

Dodd, B. The phonological systems of deaf children. *J. Speech Hear. Dis.*, 1976, *41*, 185–198.

Dodd, B. & Hermelin, B. Phonological coding by the prelinguistically deaf. *Perception and Psychophysics*, 1977, *21*, 413–417.

Doehring, D. G., & Ling, D. Programmed instruction of hearing-impaired children in the auditory discrimination of vowels. *J. Speech Hear. Res.*, 1971, *14*, 746–754.

Dore, J. Holophrases, speech acts and language universals. *J. Child Lang.*, 1975, *2*, 21–40.

Downs, D. W., & Crum, M. A. Processing demands during auditory learning under degraded listening conditions. *J. Speech Hear. Res.*, 1978, *21*, 702–714.

Erber, N. P. Speech-envelope cues as an acoustic aid to lipreading for profoundly hearing-impaired children. *J. Acoust. Soc. Amer.*, 1972, *51*, 1224–1227.

Erber, N. P. Pure-tone threshold and word-recognition abilities of hearing-impaired children. *J. Speech Hear. Res.*, 1974a, *17*, 194–202.

Erber, N. P. Visual perception of speech by deaf children: recent developments and continuing needs. *J. Speech Hear. Dis.*, 1974b, *39*, 178–185.

Ervin-Tripp, S., & Mitchell-Kernan, C. (Eds.) *Child discourse.* New York: Academic Press, 1977.

Ewing, I. R. *Lipreading and hearing aids.* Manchester: Manchester University Press, 1944.

Ferster, C. B. Clinical reinforcement. *Seminars Psychiat.*, 1972, *4*, 101–111.

Frederiksen, C. H. Representing logical and semantic structure of knowledge acquired from discourse. *Cognitive Psychol.*, 1975, *7*, 371–458.

Garnica, O. The development of phonemic speech perception. In T. Moore (Ed.), *Cognitive development and the acquisition of language.* New York: Academic Press, 1973.

Geffner, D. S., Levitt, H., Rothman Freeman, L., & Gaffney, R. Speech and language assessment scales of deaf children. *J. Comm. Dis.*, 1978, *11*, 215–226.

Gengel, R. W. Practice effects in frequency discrimination. *J. Speech Hear. Res.*, 1969, *12*, 847–856.

Glaser, R. Instructional technology and the measurement of learning outcomes: Some questions. *Am Psychol.*, 1963, *18*, 519–521.

Grammatico, L. F. The development of listening skills. *Volta Rev.*, 1975, *77*, 303–308.

Guess, D., Baer, D., & Sailor, W. A remedial approach to teaching speech deficient children. *Human Comm.*, 1978, *3*, 55–69.

Halliday, M. A. K. *Learning how to mean: Explorations in the development of language.* New York: Elsevier, 1977.

Hoversten, G., et al. *Auditory skills instructional planning systems.* N. Hollywood: Forewords, 1979.

Ivimey, G. P. The perception of speech: an information processing approach. Part 3—Lipreading and the deaf. *Teacher Deaf,* 1977, *1*, 90–100.

Jensema, C. J., Karchmer, M. A., & Trybus, R. J. *The rated speech intelligibility of hearing impaired children: Basic relationships and a detailed analysis.* Washington, D.C.: Office of Demographic Studies, Gallaudet College, 1978.

Jensema, C. J., & Trybus, R. J. *Communication patterns and educational achievement of hearing impaired students.* Washington, D.C.: Office of Demographic Studies, Gallaudet College, 1978.

Leonard, L. B. *Meaning in child language.* New York: Grune & Stratton, 1976.

Lepschy, G. Some problems in linguistic theory. In E. Lenneberg and E. Lenneberg (Eds.), *Foundations of language development. (Vol. 1.)* New York: Academic Press, 1975.

Levitt, H. *Language communication skills of deaf children, 1973-75.* Proceedings of Language Assessment for the Hearing Impaired—A Work Study Institute, May, 1976.

Liberman, A. M., Cooper, F. S., Schankweiler, D. P., & Studdert- Kennedy, M. Perception of the speech code. *Psych. Rev.*, 1967, *74*, 431–461.

Lieberth, A., & Subtelny, J. D. The effect of speech training on auditory phoneme identification. *Volta Rev.*, 1978, *80*, 410–417.

Ling, A. H. Memory for verbal and nonverbal auditory sequences in hearing-impaired and normal-hearing children. *J. Am. Audiol. Soc.*, 1975, *1*, 37–45.

Ling, A. H. The training of auditory memory in hearing impaired children: some problems of generalization. *J. Am. Audiol. Soc.*, 1976, *1*, 150–157.
Ling, A. H. *Schedules of development in audition, speech, language and communication for hearing-impaired infants and their parents.* Washington, D.C.: A.G. Bell Association, 1977.
Ling, D. Amplification for speech. In D. R. Calvert and S. R. Silverman (Eds.), *Speech and deafness.* Washington, D.C.: A.G. Bell Association, 1975.
Ling, D. *Speech and the hearing-impaired child: Theory and practice.* Washington, D.C.: A.G. Bell Association, 1976.
Ling, D. Auditory coding and recoding: An analysis of auditory training procedures for hearing impaired children. In M. Ross and T. Giolas (Eds.), *Auditory management of hearing-impaired children.* Baltimore: University Park Press, 1978a.
Ling, D. Research in progress. *Cued speech news*, 1978b, *11*, 7–8.
Ling, D., & Clarke, B. R. Cued speech: An evaluative study. *Am. Ann. Deaf,* 1975, *120*, 480–488.
Ling, D., & Ling, A. H. *Aural habilitation: The foundations of verbal learning in hearing-impaired children.* Washington, D.C.: A.G. Bell Association, 1978.
Ling, D., Ling, A. H., & Pflaster, G. Individualized educational programming for hearing-impaired children. *Volta Rev.*, 1977, *79*, 204–230.
Ling, D., & Maretic, H. Frequency transposition in the teaching of speech to the deaf child. *J. Speech Hear. Res.*, 1971, *14*, 37–46.
Lunde, A. S., & Bigman, S. K. *Occupational conditions among the deaf.* Washington, D.C.: Gallaudet College, 1959.
Markides, A. The speech of deaf and partially-hearing children with special reference to factors affecting intelligibility. *Brit. J. Dis. Commun.*, 1970, *5*, 126–140.
Maslow, A. H. Higher needs and personality. *Dialectica*, 1951, *5*, 257–264.
McLean, J. E., & Snyder-McLean, L. K. *A transactional approach to early language training.* Columbus, Ohio: Charles Merrill Publishing Co., 1978.
McNeil, D. Developmental linguistics. In F. Smith and G. A. Miller (Eds.), *The genesis of language.* Cambridge: MIT Press, 1966.
Miller, L. Pragmatics and early childhood language disorders: Communicative interactions in a half hour sample. *J. Speech. Hear. Dis.*, 1978, *43*, 419–436.
Miller, J., & Yoder, D. A syntax teaching program. In J. McLean, D. Yoder and R. Schiefelbusch (Eds.), *Language intervention with the retarded: Developing strategies.* Baltimore: University Park Press, 1972.
Moore, E. M. Hearing characteristics: Implications for auditory training and hearing aid use. *J. Acad. Rehab. Audiol.*, 1975, *8*, 80–89.
Nicholls, G. H. *Cued speech and the reception of spoken language.* M.Sc. thesis, McGill University, Montreal, 1979.
Nickerson, R. S. Characteristics of the speech of deaf persons. *Volta Rev.*, 1975, *77*, 342–362.
Nober, E. H. Vibrotactile sensitivity of deaf children to high intensity sound. *Laryngoscope,* 1967, *77*, 2128–2146.
Novelli-Olmstead, T. *Production and reception of speech by hearing-impaired children.* M.Sc. thesis, McGill University, 1979.
Oller, D. K., Jensen, H. T., & Lafayette, R. H. The relatedness of phonological processes of a hearing-impaired child. *J. Comm. Dis.*, 1978, *11*, 97–105.
Pickett, J. M. *Speech processing aids for the deaf.* Proceedings of a conference held at Gallaudet College, Washington, D.C., May, 1977.
Prutting, C. Process \ prä|, ses \ n: The action of moving forward progressively from one point to another on the way to completion. *J. Speech Hear. Dis.*, 1979, *44*, 3–30.
Quigley, S. P., & Frisina, D. R. *Institutionalization and psycho-educational develop-*

ment of deaf children. Washington, D.C.: Coun. Excep. Child., Res. Mono. Ser. A, No. 3, 1961.

Risberg, A. & Agelfors, E. On the identification of intonation contours by hearing-impaired listeners. *Speech Trans. Lab.–Quart. Prog. Status Rep.*, Royal Inst. Tech. Stockholm, 1978, *2*, 51–61.

Ross, M., & Giolas, T. G. Effects of three classroom listening conditions on speech intelligibility. *Am. Ann. Deaf,* 1971, *116,* 580–584.

Schein, J. D., & Delk, M. T. *The deaf population of the United States.* Silver Spring, Md.: National Association of the Deaf, 1974.

Shaffer, C. M. The kinesthetic method of speech development and speechreading. *Am. Ann. Deaf,* 1942, *87,* 421–422.

Shvachkin, N. K. The development of phonemic speech in early childhood. In C. Ferguson and D. Slobin (Eds.), *Studies of child language development.* New York: Holt, Rinehart and Winston, 1973.

Sloane, H. N., & MacAuley, B. D. *Operant procedures in remedial speech and language training.* Boston: Houghton Mifflin, 1968.

Sparks, D. N., Ardell, L. A., Bourgeois, M., Wiedmer, B., & Kuhl, P. K. Investigating the MESA (Multipoint Electrotactile Speech Aid): The transmission of connected discourse. *J. Acoust. Soc. Am.,* 1979, *65,* 810–815.

Stoker, R. *Auditory abilities of the profoundly deaf and their relationship to speech understandability.* M.Sc. thesis, University of Salford, England, 1977.

Strizver, G. L. Frequency discrimination of deaf children and its relationship to their achievement in auditory training. *Volta Rev.,* 1958, *60,* 304–306.

Tyack, D., & Gottsleben, R. *Language sampling, analysis and training.* Palo Alto, Ca.: Consulting Psychologists Press, 1974.

Wedenberg, E. Auditory training of deaf and hard of hearing children. *Acta Otolaryngol.,* 1951, Suppl. 94, 1–129.

Winitz, H., & Bellerose, B. Interference and the persistence of articulatory responses. *J. Speech Hear. Res.,* 1978, *21,* 715–721.

Woodworth, R. S. *Psychology, a study of mental life.* New York: Holt, 1921.

Young, B. *A two year study of speech skills.* Presented at the Convention of the A.G. Bell Association for the Deaf, St. Louis, 1978.

21
Pragmatics: Development in Normal-Hearing and Hearing-Impaired Children

Richard R. Kretschmer and Laura W. Kretschmer

WITHIN THE PAST TWO DECADES, much has been written in linguistics on the semantic/syntactic component of language. We have witnessed the age of Chomsky (1957, 1965) and the syntactic models of linguistic description and then the era of case grammars as suggested by Chafe (1970) and Fillmore (1968) along with generative semantics (Antinucci & Parisi, 1976), as a possible explanation of how meaning interfaces with syntactic performance. These theories have all tended to examine language outside of its normal context, namely, conversations or discourse. We are now entering another era of great research activity, namely, the age of pragmatic considerations. Pragmatics are the rules that explain how language (syntax/semantics) functions in the larger context of interpersonal communication (Clark & Clark, 1977). Pragmatic research is particularly valuable in work with hearing-impaired persons. Too often, hearing-impaired children/adults master syntactic principles through isolated language exercises, but do not know how to use this knowledge in conversation. This may be due to the fact that hearing-impaired children are not given opportunity to learn the mechanics or constraints of conversations, or to derive the organization of spoken or written discourse.

It is now clear that conversations have organization in their own right, organization that children normally master at early ages. A review of some of these organizational principles will be of value in order to understand how pragmatic issues apply to instruction of hearing-impaired children/adults. This paper also will summarize some of what is known about how conversations develop in young children, followed by consideration of instructional issues.

Theoretical Model

Although pragmatics have been of interest for some years, contemporary definitions of some features are helpful. We will consider presupposition and its related concepts of topicalization and informativeness; speech acts; conversational devices; and, finally, conversational strategies, which encompass the notions of clarification and repair strategies.

Presupposition

When two individuals begin a conversation, one ordinarily assumes the speaker's role and the other, the listener's role. If a conversation is to emerge, however, the potential for role reversal must exist, so that the speaker and listener can contribute actively to building the conversation. Speakers and listeners begin conversations by making certain presuppositions about each other with regard to general competence, amount of information available, linguistic sophistication, and social/power status (Clark & Clark, 1977). Other presuppositions are also important, but these four appear to determine the level of conversation. As the conversation proceeds, these assessments can be adjusted depending on the reaction of the other conversational partner.

One of the most important presuppositions concerns the degree of information the listener has about the speaker's topic for discussion (Bates, 1976). The speaker opens conversation by nominating a topic for discussion. This topic nomination depends solely on the speaker's estimate of the listener's previous or shared information about the topic. If the speaker can assume that the listener has maximum shared information, conversation can begin by using a nominalized or verbalized form of the topic, i.e., "Mrs. Reckham" or "swimming." If the listener fails to recognize the topic, then it is the speaker's responsibility to provide more information. In most conversations, if the topic is introduced in nominal form, the employment of qualifiers such as adjectives and relative clauses associated with indefinite pronouns is used. For example, if the speaker says, "I saw the boy today," and the listener says, "What boy?," then a topic has been nominated, but the listener apparently has failed to recognize the topic. Now it is the speaker's responsibility to clarify the topic. This may be accomplished by saying, "The red-headed boy" or "The boy who works at Smith's grocery store." If this fails, he might continue by saying, "You know, the one who goes with Lisa Grant." At this point, if the listener acknowledges understanding of the topic and gives agreement to proceed (by nodding, by saying "uhuh," or by waiting expectantly for the next sentence), the speaker normally provides the intended comment on the nominated topic.

This entire process of establishing a mutually agreed-upon topic is labeled topic negotiation and is a critical aspect of conversational exchange. Importantly, certain linguistic principles, i.e., embedded adjectives and relative clauses, are critical components of this process. Teaching such forms apart from their pragmatic function in conversation seems to lead invariably to unusual language productions by deaf children, i.e., as the written sentence "The boy who is white is standing next to the table." When there is clearly only one child present in the picture, a simple nominalized form would have been sufficient.

As noted previously, nominated topics may be verbal units such as verbs, adverbs, or adjectives. In these cases, statement of the verb, adverb, or adjective should be sufficient to establish the topic. If prolonged topic negotiation is required, again complex forms such as relative adverbial constructions, infinitives, or embedded adverbial forms can be employed to clarify the topic. For example, if the speaker says, "We went shopping." and failed to solicit an appropriate response, the speaker might try, "We went shopping over at Pal's Shopping Center." or, "We went to buy some new summer clothes; we went shopping, right?" Again, complex forms have definite purposes in the process of topic negotiation. This is critical knowledge for hearing-impaired children to acquire if they are to master the use of English syntactic forms.

The listener may nominate a topic if it is decided not to pursue the topic nominated by the speaker. This give and take continues until both speaker and listener agree to pursue a particular subject. This agreement is signaled by each person's willingness to comment on the topic and to maintain the discussion over more than just a few exchanges. Of course, once a mutually agreed-upon topic has been exhausted, each participant in the conversation has the option of introducing a new topic for discussion. When a new topic has been introduced, there must be topic negotiation using procedures similar to those already mentioned.

One purpose of topic negotiation is to establish the amount of information shared by speaker and listener. This ensures that each participant can contribute new information about a topic during the building of a conversation (Keenan & Schieffelin, 1976). For productive conversation, each new contribution should add new information to the discussion while allowing for the other participant to build responses on what has been said (Katz & Langendoen, 1976). It could be said that conversations consist mainly of establishing a base of old or shared information to which new information is added (Clark & Clark, 1977). Stated differently, conversations involve issues of informativeness.

Informativeness can be viewed in two ways: overall conversation (Chafe, 1976) and sentence organization (Clark & Clark, 1977). A topic nominated for discussion becomes old or shared information to which each participant is expected to contribute new information. New information once articulated becomes part of the wellspring of old information that is common knowledge between the two participants and serves for extension to new information. For instance, let us imagine a conversation. Tom says, "I want to go to the movies," to which Jack says, "I do too. I understand The Alien is good." Tom replies, "Is it a sci-fi flick?" In the first exchange, the topic is Tom's desire to go to a movie which Jack confirms as his desire as well and then adds a specific possibility. Tom picks up on the new information, which has become old by its articulation, and asks a question. The focus of the topic has changed from "wanting to go to a movie" to "the movie itself." This conversation is an example of using new information, once articulated, as old information in order to generate additional new information.

Extension to new information can also be made by implication, as well as by explicit statements about the relationship between old and new information (Fillenbaum, 1966). Implicit statements are called implicatures and play an important part in conversational exchanges. Without implicature, conversations may consistently be too lengthy due to the need for highly repetitive or redundant exchanges. To provide an example, Bernie says, "I just saw a body lying on the sidewalk outside," to which Maury replies, "Oh, how terrible!" Bernie says, "The knife was lying in the grass." The last sentence is an example of implicature, that is, Bernie assumes that since Maury seems to understand, he should know that bodies can result from either natural or unnatural causes, one of which is a knife, and that grass lies next to sidewalks in most communities. This should give meaning to the sentence, "The knife was lying in the grass." The additional implication of this last sentence is that the knife and body are probably in close proximity, which would allow Bernie to generate the next sentence, "I saw it immediately." It is this very function of implicature which often proves so difficult for hearing-impaired children. Not infrequently the deaf child in conversation lacks the information that would allow use or understanding of implicature. To allow for this possibility, teachers tend to be explicit in their presentations, which reinforces "concrete" or "literal" language usage by hearing-impaired children while thwarting development of the ability to understand the use of implicatures.

At the sentence level, informational organization also plays an important role, for it is now clear that most syntactic principles are used by the speaker in encoding old and new aspects of knowledge for the listener (Bates, 1976; Katz & Langendoen, 1976; Kempson, 1975). Syntactic principles are used either as tagging devices or as framing devices to highlight new information in favor of old information. English, for example, has developed several devices that can be attached to either nouns or verbs to indicate whether information has been indicated previously in a conversation or is a new contribution. For example, pronouns are employed as old informational tags (Clark & Clark, 1977). If we say, "I went to the movie. It was neat.", "it" indicates that the information has been previously introduced in the conversation, in this case in the preceding sentence.

Other kinds of informational tags can be seen—for example, the determiner system, particularly the use of "a" and "the" (Warden, 1976). In general conversational use, these determiners are used to signal the informational status of the nominalized forms that follow. A new topic in the conversation is usually introduced with "a," particularly if the speaker questions the degree of shared context existing between the speaker and listener about the projected topic. Once introduced into the conversation, we automatically shift to "the" as the old information tag. If the speaker concludes that the context shared with the listener is sufficient to warrant the presupposition of common knowledge, then any new topic can be introduced with "the." If I say, "I saw a boy," then I do not expect you to know which boy; but if I say, "I saw the boy," I clearly expect that you will recognize which boy I am talking about.

Verb tense is another type of informational tag, and is particularly effective when implicature is involved. Checking verb tense is one of the best ways for the listener to check the pursuit of a topic. By tying sentences to each other with the same tense indicator, the speaker provides the listener with the linguistic information that the same topic is being discussed.

Syntax also seems to aid the speaker in framing thoughts in such a way that new information is emphasized and the status of old information reduced. In most simple sentences, the general convention is to locate old information at the beginning of the sentence and the new information at the end. In the sentence, "The boy hit the ball," we can assume that previous discussion centered on the boy hitting something and the new information, highlighted by stress in the spoken form, is either *hitting the ball* or *the ball* itself.

To cue violations of the old-new information contract in sentences, English tends to employ syntactic and/or phonologic strategies (Clark & Clark, 1977). Syntactic devices involve use of constructions such as "There was. . ." or "It was. . .," the so-called "there" transformation or cleft sentence. If a person says, "There's a boy at the door," it can be assumed that previous discussions involved identification of who was at the door, leading one of the conversational participants to produce the above sentence.

Shifts in the suprasegmental patterns cue changes *in loci* of new information, and this device is more favored by speakers of English. Normally, the intonational contours of spoken English favor stressing the ends of sentences to reinforce the syntactic highlighting of new information. If new information is placed at the beginning of a sentence, stress patterns can also be rearranged to cue the location of the new information. In the sentence, "John hit the BALL," we understand that the previous topic was probably John hitting something, whereas in the sentence, "JOHN hit the ball," the previous topic was probably someone hitting the ball. Clearly, the importance of suprasegmental patterns lies not only in identification of phrasing and constituent boundaries, but also in allowing the listener to identify *loci* of new information. Ability to attend to suprasegmental aspects could allow a very young child to follow the conduct of a conversation, if not the meanings conveyed. This alone justifies the early introduction of amplification with hearing-impaired children.

To this point, we have been talking about simple sentence organization, but what about more complex sentences? For example, in some subordinate conjunction constructions, the English sentence is arranged so that the newest information is contained in the main clause. In the sentence, "We didn't go because it was raining," it can be assumed that the fact that it had been raining was shared information, with the new information being the fact that "we didn't go." Certainly, the subordinate conjunction itself could constitute new information. That is, it may be common knowledge that it rained and we did not go, but the fact that rain prevented us from going may not be shared knowledge. The use of the particular subordinate clause indicator helps the listener to relate the two bits of information to understand their relationship. To produce such complex sentences, the child must realize that the sentence should contain old and shared information, along with whatever new informational comment the speaker wishes to make.

Speech Acts

In addition to presupposition and its related concepts of topicalization and informativeness, pragmatic literature has introduced the notion of speech act. Each sentence is now seen to have at least two basic components, a proposition, or the actual message contained in the sentence, and an illocutionary force, or the intention of the speaker with regard to that sentence (Austin, 1962; Dore, Gearhart, & Newman, 1978; Searle, 1969). When a sentence is produced, the speaker has a specific communicative intent for that utterance; the listener is expected to behave in predictable ways with reference to that proposition. Based on the listener's reaction to the statement (the perilocutionary effect), the speaker's illocutionary expectation is either fulfilled or denied. Given that the listener fails to respond appropriately, the speaker has the option of pursuing his illocutionary intent further, dropping it, or modifying his expectation. This illocutionary expectation is called the speech act.

To be specific, if a speaker says, "What's your name?," the normal expectation is that the listener will provide an answer that is within the semantic domain of the requested information. If this expectation is not satisfied, the speaker has the choice of repeating the question, changing the sentence format to make the intention even more explicit—"I asked you what your name is"—or not pursuing the issue.

In English, there are many speech acts, but the most common are: declarative, interrogative, imperative, commissive, and performative (Clark & Clark, 1977). Declarative speech acts intend that the listener listen to, integrate, and believe the truth value of statements made by the speaker. If the listener interrupts, makes subsequent statements off the topic, or challenges the truth value of the statement, the expectations of the declarative speech act have not been met.

Interrogative speech acts expect the listener to supply the information being requested or to confirm the validity of the propositional content of the interrogative. In the sentence, "What is your name?," new information is being solicited, whereas in the sentence, "Is your name Rick?," confirmation of information is being sought. The failure to supply information or to confirm information would be a failure to respond to the speech act intention of the production.

Imperative speech acts require the listener to comply with the propositional content of the sentence. The intention is to motivate action on the part of the listener. The sentence, "Go get your coat," has a specific intention that the listener is to perform some action, in this case walk over to the coat rack and retrieve his coat. Failure to comply with this injunction serves to violate the illocutionary force of the sentence and, obviously, the social force as well.

Commissives are statements in which the speaker pledges future action; in other words, the speaker promises fulfillment of self-imposed obligations. The intent is that the listener agrees with the need for the obligation, agrees to the propositional content of the statement (obligation), and finally believes the validity of the act. For example, in the statement, "I promise to stop smoking," the listener must agree that the speaker does smoke and will/can stop if he/she wishes to. More importantly, both the speaker and listener must believe that the speaker wants to stop and is sincere in this desire.

Performative speech acts involve statements that automatically change the state of the environment. For instance, if we say, "Let's pretend that. . . ," this statement changes the state of affairs for objects or conditions temporarily. "I now pronounce you man and wife" is also a performative speech act through which the marital status of two individuals in profoundly changed.

Speech acts are usually signaled by either the syntactic format of the sentence, or by explicitly including the illocutionary intention as a stated performative at the beginning of the sentence. For instance, questions can be cued by *wh*-words, by auxiliary verb shifts, or by the initiation of sentences with "I asked you why you. . . ."

English, particularly American English, tends to have an imperfect match between syntactic forms and illocutionary intents (Searle, 1975). It is not uncommon in normal conversations to use the same syntactic constructions for different communication purposes. For instance, "It's hot in here" may be a simple statement about the room's temperature, or it may be an imperative to do something about the temperature. Use of a declarative sentence as an imperative is referred to as an indirect speech act, that is, an act in which the illocutionary intent of the sentence does not match the syntactic expectations for that sentence. Indeed, every syntactic pattern can be used for a variety of illocutionary intents. For instance, question forms can be used for imperative intents or for declarative intents. If a nursery school teacher says, "Wouldn't you like to close the door?," this is probably intended not as a question, but as a command to action. Such rhetorical questions are meant to be processed as declarative sentences.

Because of indirect speech acts, many conversations can be quite difficult to follow. The speaker's statements by form may not be what he "really meant," so that either contextual, intonational, or both modes may have to be used for indirect explication of the intent. Not only can different illocutionary intents be associated with one syntactic pattern, but several illocutionary intents may be signaled simultaneously within a single sentence, which results in highly ambiguous sentences. If the teacher says, "Why don't you tell the class about your recent trip?," it may not be entirely clear to the student what is intended. Is it a command to comply with the latter part of the sentence, or an answer to comply with the first part of the sentence, i.e., "Why don't you?" Under most circumstances, we would assume the latter portion of the sentence to be the newest information, and thus indirectly, the real reason for the statement, but this is not always clear.

Conversational Devices

As previously indicated, conversations have rules that govern their own conduct. Important aspects of this internal organization are called conversational devices, or conventions that regulate the initiation, maintenance, and termination of conversations (Sacks, Schegloff, & Jefferson, 1974; Schegloff, 1968; Schegloff & Sacks, 1973). These conversational devices or markers allow the listener to know when conversations are beginning, when they are changing, and when they are ending. In this way, the listener can mobilize his contributions to assist in this process, or to abort premature beginnings, changes, or terminations when he wishes to do so.

An integral component of conversational exchange is the process of turn-taking. For conversations to run smoothly, the speaker and listener must know that each can have a turn. They must know also how to exercise their conversational rights. In other words, the first speaker in a conversation must know how to assume the listener role when the first listener exercises his right to become a speaker. Thus, experience and practice in turn-taking are prerequisite, mandatory components of learning appropriate conversational exchange.

For a conversation to begin, one of the participants must introduce some stereotypical utterance such as "Hi" or "How are you today?" The listener may respond to this opening by making a statement that allows for continuation, or by terminating the exchange with a response such as, "Hi, I can't talk now," or simply walking away. If the partners are strangers, a certain amount of preliminary interaction is necessary for assessment of each other's linguistic competence, information base, and social status. Based on these exchanges, topic negotiation and nomination can proceed.

Topic changes occur with frequency in conversations. Stereotypical devices are often used to cue abrupt topic shifts such as, "Oh, by the way. . . . ," or "Speaking of elephants. . . ," or even more directly, "I know we weren't talking about Jane, but. . . ." It is helpful if both participants are aware of these strategies in order to facilitate conversational development.

Conversations are also terminated in very regular ways. For example, one of the participants may intimate the desire to conclude the conversation with a summary-like statement such as, "Okay, I'll see you tonight at seven, right?" The conversational partner may either agree to conclude the conversation, or decide to nominate a new topic for discussion. If the listener elects the second option, the conversation continues until another summary-like sentence is produced. If the partner elects the former option, then the participants go through a series of confirmative statements until one specifically terminates the conversation with an utterance such as "Good-bye."

Conversational Strategies

The last topic for discussion is the notion of conversational strategies. As participants involve themselves in conversation, the purposes of the interaction will shape the direction and format of the conversation, i.e., a cocktail party as opposed to a job interview. It is also clear that as conversations progress, certain rituals are employed as participants manipulate or control each other's behavior. Finally, it is also clear that when there are breakdowns in conversation, repair or clarification strategies must be employed to get the conversation back on track.

Research suggests that the context itself will shape the types of conversational exchanges that emerge. For example, a dominant conversational format in classroom interactions is examination dialogue. Topic negotiation and confirmation remarks are more characteristic of conversation outside the classroom particularly when more than one participant is involved (Hall & Cole, 1978). The verbal conduct of arguments differs significantly from the verbal conduct of rule-formation in games (Brennis & Lein, 1977; Garvey, 1977). Thus, the child must come to understand that language is relative to the task at hand, the number of conversational partners involved, and the social context in which the conversation occurs.

To provide a more specific example of conversational strategies, consider an exchange among preschool children preparing to color (Garnica, 1979). At the beginning of the task, each child claims a magic marker. As the children begin to work, each begins to lay claim to the magic marker that he/she wants next, by producing utterances such as, "Are you finished with the pink one yet?" or "I want the pink one next, okay?" The child who has completed coloring with "the pink one" then puts the magic marker up for bid with statements such as, "I'm finished." The interested children then make their offers to the child who made the first claim, attempting to exercise their prerogatives. Unfortunately, the final decision is made by the auctioneer who may or may not honor "first to me" claims. Bids are usually made by raising one's hand, yelling louder, or speaking before other claimants. It was observed by Garnica (1979) that there were always certain children whose legitimate claims were usually ignored by the remainder of the group, thus preventing full participation in the conversational exchange. Conversational rituals have also been observed in trick-or-treating sequences at Halloween, in games with flexible rules, and in children's arguments (Berko-Gleason & Weintraub, 1976; Brennis & Lein, 1977; Garvey, 1974). A young child must learn not only the forms of language, but must understand how language works within conversations, as well as the formulas or rituals children use as they negotiate with each other in conversational exchanges. Because each new situation seems to engender its own set of rituals, this type of sociolinguistic development may be difficult to achieve.

Part of conversational organization revolves around presuppositions of power and recognition of the distribution of power among the participants. For instance, telling a younger brother to move over is less risky than telling an older brother to move over (Berko-Gleason, 1973). The latter often involves rituals that require hints, implicit suggestions, or other such techniques, whereas the younger brother may be explicitly ordered and/or threatened—which usually works. This type of conversation involves both organizational changes and code switching, that is, framing sentences in more polite forms when dealing with authority figures and less polite forms when dealing with inferiors. Clearly, what is said on the playground does not parallel what is said in more formal situations, and the one does not seem to be preparation for the other.

It is axiomatic that conversations break down because of a lack of clarity about the topic, the illocutionary intent, the conversational organization, or other aspects. At such times, participants—if they wish to proceed—must engage in repair or clarification strategies to discover the source of the problem, to clarify or repair the presuppositions made (Corsaro, 1977). The repair sequence is often referred to as a side sequence to the conversation. When a conversation breaks down, the listener may say, for example: "What?" or "What did you say?"; the response to this clarification request can then lead to precise pin-pointing of the breakdown with responses such as: "Do I hear you saying. . . ?" or "Am I correct in assuming that. . . ?" Unfortunately, such clarification may mean several things, such as "You said it too softly, so repeat," or "I don't understand you," or "I don't believe what I'm hearing."

In summary, pragmatic theory is providing insight into the development and conduct of conversations, particularly with respect to the issues of presupposition, illocutionary intent, conversational devices, and, finally, the organization of the conversation itself. Let's now turn our attention to a brief discussion of the development of conversational skills or communicative competence in normal-hearing children. This information suggests some interesting and critical issues for instruction of hearing-impaired children.

Development of Communicative Competence

Children must learn language, that is, syntactic/semantic patterns, within the context of conversational exchanges (Bloom, Rocissano, & Hood, 1976; Scollon, 1976). They learn language by engaging in conversations. Therefore, the authors firmly believe that the foundation of language acquisition and growth is the communicative act. Children quickly learn that the utterances they produce have an effect on others within their environment. This knowledge of the effects of communication or the understanding of the functions of language is referred to as pragmatic understanding (Dore, Gearhart, & Newman, 1978).

It is now clear that communication is established the moment a mother is given her child at birth (Condon & Sander, 1974). She and her infant immediately seek an accommodation that is communicative in nature. The mother interacts with her newborn as a communicative partner whose potential is yet to be realized. She engages the infant in conversation by providing the infant's side of the dialogue when the baby is too young to participate fully (Phillips, 1973). With maturity, the infant becomes increasingly skilled in visually attending to the mother (Trevarthen, 1977). These incidental gaze events become cues to mother to engage in "talks" with her child (Bruner, 1977).

In this way, mother and child are establishing the turn-taking, conversational relationship which is central to the establishment of normal pragmatic control. What is also important about this activity is that this turn-taking behavior revolves around topics that are nominated, albeit nonverbally, by the child. As the infant's gaze extends to objects and social interchanges outside the immediate mother-child relationship, mother switches her talk to include discussion of the infant's choice of objects or social exchanges. This must be viewed as training in turn-taking, on topics mutually agreed upon by both participants. As indicated in the earlier theoretical summary, turn-taking behavior is central to development of conversations. One of the first, indeed imperative, tasks in a conversation is the establishment of a mutually nominated topic. Topic establishment or nomination is presumed to develop early, albeit nonverbally, as infants engage in dialogue with their primary caretakers.

At about 4 to 5 months of age, when the infant begins to produce a variety of vocalizations and to respond consistently to mother's communicative efforts by smiling, maternal comments change from statements solely about the child, herself, or the environment, to include imitations of the child utterances (Saporito, in preparation). This play will lead, by the time a child is a year old, to the notion that one takes turns in conversations, that is, when the child talks, mother does not talk, and when mother talks, the child does not talk (Schaffer, Collis, & Parsons, 1977).

Maternal linguistic input also undergoes a significant change in its syntactic/semantic make-up when infants begin to smile consistently (Saporito, in preparation). Mothers tend to begin using single words or short phrases that are elongated so that their time envelopes match those used previously with whole sentences. In other words, prior to the appearance of smiling behavior in her infant, a mother might say, "I see the pretty baby"; but after smiling begins, the mother uses, "Pretty baby," but elongates the vowels so that this phrase lasts as long as the five-word utterance. By this strategy, mothers reduce the complexity of verbal input, but maintain the prosodic characteristics of utterances.

At approximately 9 to 11 months, the child begins meaningful communication of a nonverbal nature. Among the most prominant of these nonverbal communicative attempts are the show-me gesture (proto-declarative), the do-for-me gesture (proto-imperative), and the that's-mine gesture (proto-possessive) (Bates, 1976; Carter, 1978). Such gestures become more prevalent as the child attempts to regulate the actions of others, and by 10 to 13 months, meaningful vocalizations begin to occur as part of these communicative acts (Bates, 1976). The baby begins to combine vocalizations with gestures.

Initially, these vocalizations are not adult modeled and somewhat unstable phonologically, but soon they become conventionalized and stable in form and are often identified as baby's first words. These first "words" are expressions of interest in communication and constitute part of the communicative act itself; they are not acts of reference *per se*. For example, the child often points to objects and says "Mommie" or indicates he/she wants to be picked up by waving a hand and saying "up." Normally, children do not use these words outside the communicative frame. Thus, these vocalizations should not be regarded as real words, but as communicative acts or beginning speech acts usually of declarative or imperative function.

Eventually, the child begins to use words apart from any gestures and it is at this point that the child can be said to have words that communicate for their own purpose, and not as part of a more general communicative framework. Words now appear in a variety of communication situations and for a variety of communicative purposes (Bloom & Lahey, 1978; Dore, Gearhart, & Newman, 1978). The most common communicative intents include: a) requests for action or information, i.e., the child making the request "up" for the command "Pick it up," or making the verbal request "What dat?"; b) responses to requests from others, i.e., the child saying "Harry" when asked "What's your name?"; descriptions or statements about the ongoing world, i.e., the child saying "fly away" while looking at a bird flying toward a tree; d) statements of inner feelings or delineation of social rules governing group activity, i.e., the child saying "pretty" while looking at a new dress, or "hi" to initiate a social exchange; e) performatives or statements of pretense or fantasy, i.e., the child saying "teddy-bear" when taking a toy bottle and pretending to feed this teddy-bear. As can be seen, words are not used in a vacuum; they are said for a purpose; they represent primitive speech acts. Many of these communicative intents given through verbal expression have their foundation in nonverbal performatives (pragmatic acts) of the infant. There does not appear to be any discontinuity in the child's development of communication; the infant's gestures are father to the child's verbalizations.

When young children talk, they intend to communicate, but they are also imparting specific information. Observation of the young child's utterances reveals that he/she is most interested in a limited set of topics, specifically: the existence of objects or actions; the nonexistence or disappearance of objects and actions; the recurrence of objects or actions; the fact that objects can have an effect on other objects in certain places; and, finally, that objects belong to other objects or persons (Bloom, 1973; Brown, 1973). Although children do make statements about their feelings or about the state of objects, these topics do not appear with the same frequency as other categories in children's language. This is not particularly surprising, given what we know about aspects of cognitive development in children. We know, for instance, that children spend the first year of life finding out how objects relate to one another in space and the effects that objects have on each other (Piaget, 1954). These cognitive developments have a striking parallel to the topics eventually chosen by children to talk about in communicative situations. So strong is this relationship that states of linguistic readiness based on corresponding cognitive stages have been postulated by many researchers (Bloom & Lahey, 1978; Cromer, 1974; Morehead & Morehead, 1974; Sinclair, 1973).

Investigation of communicative/language productions in young children indicates that very young children, as young as one year of age, are aware of the informational demands of communication (Greenfield & Zukow, 1978). As previously stated, when communicating with one another, we generally do not talk about what we already know. Instead, we attempt to expand the listener's knowledge to new information, which may include feelings about a topic rather than more factual information about that topic. This use represents another foundation of communication, the exchange of new information. Very young children apparently understand this function too.

Young children tend to say what, from their perspective, is most informative to the listener. For instance, if a child carries a broken toy to the mother, the child will probably name the culprit who broke the toy, rather than saying "broken" or "toy" since the latter are obvious information in this case. In other words, the child understands from a very young age the relative communicative value of selecting one word over another even when the child is only able developmentally to produce one word at a time. The distinction between the relative merit of new and old information is learned early with the situation, or conversational exchange itself, allowed to carry the old information or topic, so that the child needs only to articulate his comment or new information.

As the normal-hearing child approaches 2 years of age, he/she begins to put words together. The bridge between the one- and two-word stages includes at least one transitional phenomenon of communicative importance (Bloom, 1973). The 18-month-old may produce a string of single words such as, "Timmy. Toy. Broken," which appear to represent components of the underlying semantic relationships, but not necessarily forming a cohesive syntactic unit. These words are usually replicas of previous semantic (one-word) utterances, but they are organized informationally, so that the first word is the most informative to the listener, the second less informative, and so forth (Greenfield & Smith, 1976). This string of single words does not adhere to the syntactic conventions of English; instead, the organization seems to be for communicative function. This important step allows the child to recognize that a particular communicative statement can involve more than one word.

Eventually, these single-word sequences yield true two-word combinations such as, "me go," "it pretty," or "no ball." As was true in the single-word stage, the early two-word combinations tend to express: a. nonexistence (no ball); b. existence (that ball); c. recurrence (more ball); d. the actor-action-patient-locative relationship (me hit; hit ball; me ball; or ball window); e. locative relationships (that table); and f. possessive relationships (my ball) (Bloom & Lahey, 1978). These early productions are also organized initially informationally, not syntactically, so it is not uncommon to hear combinations like "window ball" meaning "The ball broke the window" (Greenfield & Smith, 1976). Instead of using conventional word order cues, children often use contrastive stress patterns to signal new information. The most heavily accented form is the new information, and the least heavily accented word is the old information (Wieman, 1976).

Once the child has mastered use of two-word combinations, he/she quickly moves to productions of longer, more complex utterances including sophisticated use of syntax such as coordination, relative clauses, negation, and question-formation (Limber, 1973). Importantly, the child continues to learn these forms and to use them effectively in conversational exchanges (Ervin-Tripp, 1977).

Children first initiate conversations by getting their listener's attention, usually by repeating the listener's name over and over, then putting forth a topic, seeking some acknowledgment of the topic, and adding new information (Corsaro, 1977). As a listener, young children will often repeat the topic nominated by the speaker as an acknowledgment of that topic (Keenan & Schieffelin, 1975). It is not uncommon, for example, to hear conversations of this sort between young children, 2 to 3 years of age: Bea: "See doggy." Art: "Doggy." Bea: "Doggy. Me want doggy."

Topics change quite rapidly among young children, and it is not until much later, about 6 years of age, that sustained exchanges on the same topic over time are consistently possible. As the child matures (3 to 4 years), more conventionalized methods of opening are learned, usually with the introduction of lexical items such as, "You know what" or "what" (Garvey, 1975). Interestingly, however, termination strategies other than merely walking away from the conversation are not learned until much later (Keller-Cohen, 1977). When young children have no further comments about a topic, they usually stop. They do not fill in or tie topics together to minimize the gaps between successive turns. And when they want to end a conversation, they don't bother with elaborate closings; they just leave, or turn their attention to another situation.

As children approach 6 years of age, their illocutionary acts become more formalized and adult-like (Berko-Gleason & Weintraub, 1976; Ervin-Tripp, 1977; Garvey, 1975; Grimm, 1975). They begin to add illocutionary intents such as commissives or promises, and more importantly begin to expand their range of linguistic encodings, particularly of performatives with the addition of polite forms such as, "Please," "Thank you," and "I'm sorry." These latter forms emerge as the child begins to understand the social expectations placed on anyone who interacts with authority. As children approach age 6, they also learn the function of indirect forms, particularly hints. This knowledge is also tied to their growing perception of social roles and functions within society.

The exchange of information is the heart of conversation. It depends on the ability of the speaker and listener to produce consecutive utterances semantically related to prior utterances from their partner. This ability increases substantially over time, particularly from age 2 to 3 years in normally hearing children (Bloom, Rocissano, & Hood, 1976). When contingency is initially mastered, the child produces utterances that refer to the same event in context: this is contextual contingency. An example would be: Daddy: "I need some help." Child: "Me get mommy." As children mature further, they learn linguistic contingency, that is, adopting the previous lexical item(s) and sharing new information about those items such as: Daddy: "I see an elephant." Child: "Me see big, fat elephant." In most situations, children learn to replace *wh*-constituents, add a subject-verb-complement constituent, or modify a subject-verb-complement constituent that was already stated in the prior adult utterance. In this fashion, children are learning the various strategies for contributing to conversations. It has been argued that these exchanges are the mechanisms by which children acquire and use new lexical items and/or grammatical expressions (Bloom & Lahey, 1978; Scollon, 1976).

In addition to learning the formal mechanisms of conducting conversations and to learning how to maintain conversations over a longer period of time, young children also learn the grammatical conventions that relate to topicalization and informational organization, important skills for eventual sophisticated language use (Clark & Clark, 1977). More specifically, the function of articles, shifting deixis, ellipsis, contrastive stress, and syntactic structuring that shifts framing of new information from the end of the sentence to the beginning are learned (deVilliers & deVilliers, 1978). Through mastery of each of these skills, children become more adept at aiding the listener in understanding topic changes, as well as highlighting the significance of their informational contributions to conversation exchanges.

The specific encoding proclivities of children seem to be a function of the linguistic environment provided them. For instance, a recent project examining the growth of negation in young children observed that the way children tend to encode negation is directly related to how adults use the forms in exchanges with these children (deVilliers & deVilliers, 1979). For example, three children in the study tended to encode negation for the same semantic reason, namely, to reject or deny. However, two of the subjects tended to use a negation tagging system, and another child used the standard modal form. Negation tagging consisted of utterances like: "No, me go home." This was found to be a negation of a previous statement given the child, which in this case could have been "You can go to Billy's house." The child negates the proposal and makes his own counterproposal of "me go home." Standard modal negation forms are similar to "I'm not going to Billy's house." This differential use in encoding strategies seemed highly related to the types of linguistic encoding strategies used by the subjects' parents.

As can be seen from this discussion, the heart of language acquisition is communication development along with mastery of the pragmatic function of syntactic patterns. Without mastery of this knowledge, the child will lack the capacity to have sustained, meaningful conversational exchanges.

Implications

Before considering implications, we wish to state two assumptions that we have made about pragmatic issues. First, if what has been said about communication is true of the development of communication competence in normally hearing children, there is no reason to assume that these requirements are different for hearing-impaired children, particularly as they speak or sign the English language. Second, it is reasonable to assume that hearing-impaired children must go through the same developmental stages outlined for normally hearing children, if they plan to become competent communicators in English, especially spoken English.

If the roots of language growth are communication development between mother and child, the implications for early identification and programming of hearing-impaired infants are obvious. However, several points should be stressed. First, it is now clear that the mother's knowledge of a hearing handicap in her child can interfere with natural communicative processes (Moses, 1978). When parents learn that their child is deaf, they lose the dream of a normal child. This loss can be expected to have profound emotional effects on the parents' relationship with the child; the loss of their dream precipitates a mourning period during which they must eventually come to grips with their feelings about the situation. While parents are fighting the grief they feel, they must maintain (or be helped to maintain) normal communication patterns with their hearing-impaired child.

If management at this point involves the introduction of a hearing aid, the child becomes even less normal to the parents. One of the most important aspects of early identification and management programs must be the establishment of communication between parents and child and the eventual focus on the child's assets rather than his liabilities. It is not, for more and more compelling reasons, possible to talk about educational programs for hearing-impaired infants or preschoolers that focus on the child either alone or in groups of other deaf children. Instead, the focal point of educational efforts must be on the parents and on the parent-child communication relationships as the predominant theme.

Since it is obvious that visual cuing is an integral part of communication, it is important that mother-child interactions, when the child is hearing impaired, emphasize both auditory and visual interaction. This is not to say that auditory practice in the form of listening activities is not important to the development of language or self-monitoring; but the natural mother-child relationship is founded on the interplay between the auditory and visual components of language/communicative exchange. It is important for mothers to accept as well as use visual demonstrations of communication, while encouraging the development of oral/auditory performance.

As previously indicated, there is ample evidence that communicative acts begin in the first moments of life. This observation offers sufficient justification for the earliest possible identification and management of hearing loss in infants. For the majority of children, personal amplification must be part of this program. Without systematic listening, without a variety of auditory experiences, the hearing-impaired child may never learn to monitor his vocal apparatus in the communicative act or acquire the full range of language samples from the environment to ensure acquisition of all aspects of the spoken language, particularly the function of contrastive stress.

Investigations into the early utterances or gestures of young hearing-impaired children indicate that they too engage in the same sets of communicative acts as hearing children, and that they tend to concentrate on the same set of semantic categories (Edwards, in preparation; Feldman, 1975; Goldin-Meadow, 1975; Hess, 1972; Juenke, 1971; Kretschmer & Kretschmer, 1978). In view of this observation, we urge that the early educational efforts of hearing-impaired children emphasize the communicative aspects of language development, rather than merely its referential function. Hearing-impaired children should be encouraged to master words for their communication function, not just for their representational function. It is also important that hearing-impaired children be exposed to vocabulary that encodes the basic concepts interesting to all children. Too often emphasis is still given to vocabulary that is not cognitively salient, useful, or interesting to children, i.e., colors; while more crucial aspects of language usage are overlooked.

We urge that the focal point of management programs be pragmatically based, which means a premium should be placed on conversational use of syntactic principles, new vocabulary, and expressions of meaning. Pragmatic functions can be identified nonverbally as well as verbally in hearing-impaired children (Edwards, in preparation; Goldin-Meadow, 1975). If a reasonable amount of communicative interest is not observed in a young hearing-impaired child, there is no reason to expect that child to be ready to produce symbolic behavior. We are beginning to explore ways to evaluate knowledge of conversational constraints in normal-hearing preschool children with language disorders and/or speech motor problems as well as those with significant hearing loss (Rolph, 1979).

It is increasingly clear to us that while the importance of interpersonal communication has been stressed for a long time, too much of what is taught to hearing-impaired children still focuses on communication of the obvious. Drills on object names or repetition of sentences about actions that are developed by others reinforces for the deaf child the idea that English is used only in the classrooms to communicate the obvious, not as a medium of informational exchange, interpersonal communication, and pleasure.

REFERENCES

Antinucci, F., & Parisi, D. *Essentials of grammar.* New York: Academic Press, 1976.

Austin, J. *How to do things with words.* Oxford: Oxford University Press, 1962.

Bates, E. *Language and context: The acquisition of pragmatics.* New York: Academic Press, 1976.

Berko-Gleason, J. Code switching in children's language. In T. Moore (Ed.), *Cognitive development and the acquisition of language.* New York: Academic Press, 1973.

Berko-Gleason, J., & Weintraub, S. The acquisition of routines in child language. *Lang. Soc.,* 1976, *5,* 129–136.

Bloom, L. *One word at a time: The use of single word utterances before syntax.* The Hague: Mouton, 1973.

Bloom, L., & Lahey, M. *Language development and language disorders.* New York: John Wiley and Sons, 1978.

Bloom, L., Rocissano, L., & Hood, L. Adult-child discourse: Developmental interaction between information processing and linguistic knowledge. *Cog. Psych.,* 1976, *8,* 521–552.

Brenneis, D., & Lein, L. "You fruithead": A sociolinguistic approach to children's dispute. In S. Ervin-Tripp & C. Mitchell-Kernan (Eds.), *Child discourse.* New York: Academic Press, 1977.

Brown, R. *A first language: The early stages.* Cambridge: Harvard University Press, 1973.

Bruner, J. Early social interaction and language acquisition. In H. R. Schaffer (Ed.), *Studies in mother-infant interaction.* London: Academic Press, 1977.

Carter, A. The development of systematic vocalizations prior to words: A case study. In N. Waterson & C. Snow (Eds.), *The development of communication.* New York: John Wiley and Sons, 1978.

Chafe, W. *Meaning and the structure of language.* Chicago: University of Chicago Press, 1970.

Chafe, W. Giveness, contrastiveness, definiteness, subjects, topics, and point of view. In C. Li (Ed.), *Subject and topic.* New York: Academic Press, 1976.

Chomsky, N. *Syntactic structures.* The Hague: Mouton, 1957.

Chomsky, N. *Aspects of the theory of syntax.* Cambridge: M.I.T. Press, 1965.

Clark, H., & Clark, E. *Psychology and language.* New York: Harcourt Brace Jovanovich, 1977.

Condon, W., & Sander, L. Neonate movement as synchronized with adult speech: Interactional participation and language acquisition. *Science*, 1974, *183*, 99–101.

Corsaro, W. The clarification request as a feature of adult interactive styles with young children. *Lang. Soc.*, 1977, *6*, 183–207.

Cromer, R. The development of language and cognition: The cognition hypothesis. In B. Foss (Ed.), *New perspectives in child development*. Baltimore: Penguin Books, 1974.

deVilliers, J., & deVilliers, P. *Language acquisition*. Cambridge: Harvard University Press, 1978.

deVilliers, P., & deVilliers, J. *The acquisition of negation and the integration of form and function in language*. Paper presented at the Language Awareness Conference, Rhode Island School for the Deaf, Providence, R.I., 1979.

Dore, J., Gearhart, M., & Newman, D. The structure of nursery school conversation. In K. Nelson (Ed.), *Children's language: Volume 1*. New York: Gardner Press, 1978.

Edwards, B. *Pragmatic functions of interpersonal communications between preschool children in classrooms for the hearing impaired*, University of Cincinnati, in preparation.

Ervin-Tripp, S. Wait for me, roller-skate! In S. Ervin-Tripp & C. Mitchell-Kernan (Eds.), *Child discourse*. New York: Academic Press, 1977.

Feldman, H. *The development of a lexicon by deaf children of hearing parents, or there's more to language than meets the ear*. Doctoral dissertation, University of Pennsylvania, Philadelphia, 1975.

Fillenbaum, S. Memory for gist: Some relevant variables. *Lang. Speech.*, 1966, *9*, 217–227.

Fillmore, C. The case for case. In E. Bach & R. Harms (Eds.), *Universals of linguistic theory*. New York: Holt, Rinehart, and Winston, 1968.

Garnica, O. *Child-child conversational interaction and the socialization process*. Paper presented at the Socialization of Children in a Changing Society Conference, University of Cincinnati, Cincinnati, 1979.

Garvey, C. *Interaction structures in social play*. Paper presented at the Am. Psych. Assoc. Convention, New Orleans, La., 1974.

Garvey, C. Requests and responses in children's speech. *J. Child Lang.*, 1975, *2*, 41–60.

Garvey, C. Play with language and speech. In S. Ervin-Tripp & C. Mitchell-Kernan (Eds.), *Child discourse*. New York: Academic Press, 1977.

Goldin-Meadow, S. *The representation of semantic relations in a manual language created by deaf children of hearing parents: A language you can't dismiss out of hand*. Doctoral dissertation, University of Pennsylvania, Philadelphia, 1975.

Greenfield, P., & Smith, J. *The structure of communication in early language development*. New York: Academic Press, 1976.

Greenfield, P., & Zukow, P. Why do children say what they say when they say it?: An experimental approach to the psychogenesis of presupposition. In K. Nelson (Ed.), *Children's language: Volume 1*. New York: Gardner Press, 1978.

Grimm. H. On the child's acquisition of semantic structure underlying the wordfield of prepositions. *Lang. Speech*, 1975, *18*, 97–119.

Hall, W., & Cole, M. On participants' shaping of discourse through their understanding of the task. In K. Nelson (Ed.), *Children's language: Volume 1*. New York: Gardner Press, 1978.

Hess, L. *The development of transformational structures in a deaf child and a normally hearing child over a period of five months*. Master's thesis, University of Cincinnati, Cincinnati, 1972.

Juenke, D. *An application of a generative-transformational model of linguistic description of hearing impaired subjects in the generation and expansion stages of language development*. Master's thesis, University of Cincinnati, Cincinnati, 1971.

Katz, J., & Langendoen, D. Pragmatics and presupposition. *Lang.*, 1976, *52*, 1917.

Keenan, E., & Schieffelin, B. Topic as a discourse notion: A study of topic in the conversations of children and adults. In C. Li (Ed.), *Subject and topic.* New York: Academic Press, 1976.

Keller-Cohen, D. Repetition in the non-native acquisition of discourse: Its relation to text unification and conversation. In R. Freedle (Ed.), *Discourse processes: Advances in research and theory, volume II.* Norwood: Ablex Publishing, 1977.

Kempson, R. *Presuppositions and the delimitation of semantics.* Cambridge: Cambridge University Press, 1975.

Kretschmer, R., & Kretschmer, L. *Language development and intervention with the hearing impaired.* Baltimore: University Park Press, 1978.

Limber, J. The genesis of complex sentences. In T. Moore (Ed.), *Cognitive development and the acquisition of language.* New York: Academic Press, 1973.

Morehead, D., & Morehead, A. From signal to signal to sign: A Piagetian view of thought and language during the first two years. In R. Schiefelbusch & L. Lloyd (Eds.), *Language perspectives: Acquisition, retardation, and intervention.* Baltimore: University Park Press, 1974.

Moses, K. *Effective parenting for the hearing impaired child.* Paper presented at the A.G. Bell Association for the Deaf Convention, St. Louis, 1978.

Phillips, J. Syntax and vocabulary of mothers' speech to young children: Age and sex comparisons. *Child Dev.*, 1973, *44*, 182–185.

Piaget, J. *The construction of reality in the child.* New York: Basic Books, 1954.

Rolph, T. *Development of a test of pragmatics for children ages 3, 4, and 5.* Master's thesis, University of Cincinnati, Cincinnati, 1979.

Sacks, H., Schegloff, E., & Jefferson, G. A simplest systematics for the organization of turn-taking for conversation. *Lang.*, 1974, *50*, 696–735.

Saporito, D. *Linguistic and paralinguistic dimensions of one mother-child interactional style.* University of Cincinnati, in preparation.

Schaffer, H., Collis, G., & Parsons, G. Vocal interchange and visual regard in verbal and pre-verbal children. In H. R. Schaffer (Ed.), *Studies in mother-infant interaction.* London: Academic Press, 1977.

Schegloff, E. Sequencing in conversational openings. *Am. Anthrop.*, 1968, *70*, 1075–1095.

Schegloff, E., & Sacks, H. Opening up closings. *Semiotica*, 1973, *8*, 289–327.

Scollon, R. *One child's language from one to two: The origins of construction.* Honolulu: University of Hawaii Press, 1976.

Searle, J. *Speech acts.* Cambridge: Cambridge University Press, 1969.

Searle, J. Indirect speech acts. In P. Cole & J. Morgan (Eds.), *Syntax and semantics, volume 3: Speech acts.* New York: Seminar Press, 1975.

Sinclair, H. Language acquisition and cognitive development. In T. Moore (Ed.), *Cognitive development and the acquisition of language.* New York: Academic Press, 1973.

Trevarthen, C. Descriptive analysis of infant communication behavior. In H. R. Schaffer (Ed.), *Studies in mother-infant interaction.* London: Academic Press, 1977.

Warden, D. The influence of context on children's use of identifying expressions and references. *Brit. J. Psych.*, 1976, *67*, 101–112.

Wieman, L. Stress patterns of early child language. *J. Child Lang.*, 1976, *3*, 283–286.

22
Reading and Language Training for the Hearing Impaired

Harris Winitz

A YEAR AGO I FINALLY TOOK THE TIME to read Frank Smith's *Understanding Reading* (1978), a fascinating and compelling account of the reading process. Perhaps one reason I enjoyed this book so much is because Smith thinks about the teaching of reading in very much the same way I think about the teaching of language. Learning to read, as Frank Smith sees it, is an implicit process. I do not believe that Smith's position is largely understood. What he is saying is that the many thousands of reading rules of English orthography cannot be explicitly taught. Rather, these rules are learned by having contact with the sentences of English.

In the past year or so, the writer has examined a number of commercial reading programs. It is a surprising fact that the early readers, the so-called basal readers, reflect little if any of the scientific discoveries made in the past 25 years. Unfortunately most reading programs are developed by staffs of commercial houses. They do consult with reading specialists, but apparently they are little influenced by what they are told. A number of professors of reading, some consultants for large publishing firms, have reported that whatever input is provided is shaped to fit the commercial ideal. Reading publishers publish what they believe reading teachers and school boards want. Why Johnny and Jane can't read, so it seems, is because specialists can exert little influence, if any, on commercial publishers. There are, of course, exceptions, such as the publishing of the Initial Teaching Alphabet.

Let us not dwell on this issue any longer. Rather, let's consider how we might go about constructing a reading program, knowing what we know about cognition, speech recognition, and sentence perception. Let me add here that I read Frank Smith's book after I had decided to invest time and effort in the area of reading instruction. I read it to see if I could find support for what appeared to me to be an obvious set of operating procedures. I discovered, of course, that it was all there in Smith in black and white. What was missing in Smith was the product. And that is what I want to present to you. I would be most pleased to hear of your reaction to my proposal.

Principles of Construction

The following principles guided the construction of the reading program:

1. Learning to read is an implicit process whereby the learner discovers the rules of English orthography. These rules are great in number and are difficult to explain. Although they can be directly placed in the storage cells of a computer, as was done for the Kurzweil Reading Machine for the blind, it does not necessarily follow that we can "place" by explicit instruction these rules into a child's head. It is unrealistic to assume that young children or even adults can be taught the logic of English reading rules as they are learning to read.
2. The content of the reading lessons should be systematically presented. Lack of consistency will only delay the reading process. Consistency can be developed only if the initial goal is not to read sentences. In order to present the material in a systematic way, we must make a fundamental change in the way we now teach reading.
3. Orthographic segments should be taught as units within words and not as isolated entities. Traditional methodologies isolate the letter and attach a sound to it. Often the sound that corresponds to the letter is its alphabetic name, sometimes it is an exaggerated production, and at other times it is a distortion (e.g., telling a child to listen to the [nʌ] in *can't*). These productions depart significantly from the speech the child has heard, and can serve no purpose other than to confuse the child.
4. Central to learning to read is knowing in advance the meaning of the material, yet traditional methodologies ignore this most basic property. Every effort should be made to assure that children understand what they are reading. For this reason Smith (1978) recommends that the first step in learning to read is being read to.

Children are often asked to read blindly through a story. There is no direction to their story reading. Often they do not know what the story is about, and often they do not know important vocabulary items which are used in their stories.

Description of the Reading Program

At this point a beginning reading program which was developed within the framework of the four principles presented will be described. Initially, discrimination of sound-letter correspondence is taught. Second, discrimination of complex graphemic relations is taught, and, finally, sentence reading is introduced. In all instances meaning is provided prior to each of these instructional tasks.

Lesson 1 consists of 20 sentences in picture form in which the words *cat* and *cup* are isolated, as indicated in Figures 22.1–22.5. The

FIGURE 22.1

Lesson 1 of a beginning reading program consisting of 20 sentences in picture form. The words cat *and* cup *are isolated as indicated. The teacher reads the story emphasizing the words* cat and cup *and their referents, as follows: Picture 1. The cat and the cup; Picture 2. The cat sees the cup; Picture 3. The cat moves slowly over to the cup; Picture 4. The cat touches the cup.*

FIGURE 22.2

The story continues as the teacher reads: Picture 5. The cat looks inside the cup; Picture 6. There is nothing in the cup; Picture 7. No water; Picture 8. No milk.

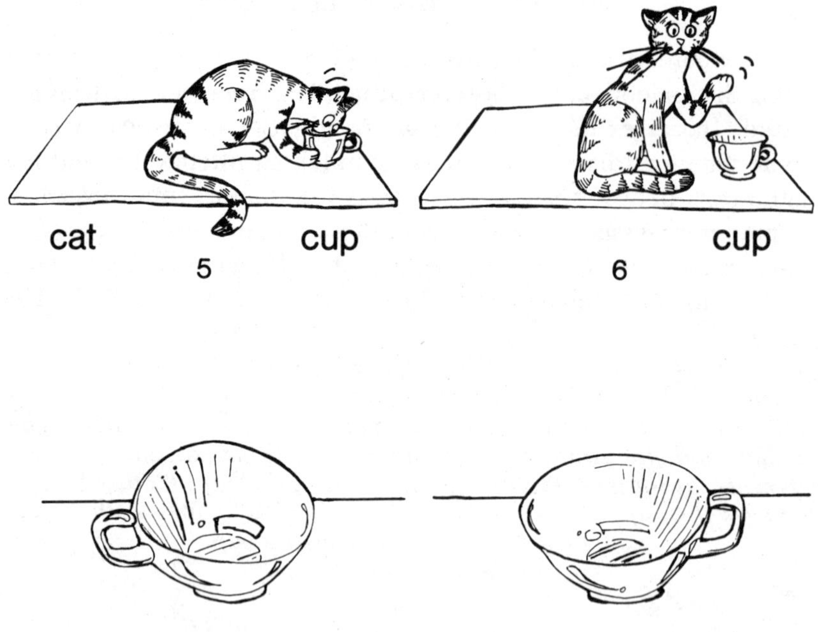

teacher reads the story page by page, emphasizing the words *cat* and *cup*, and their referents. The student is instructed to notice the words which appear below each picture.

Following the reading of the story, each child participates in a word discrimination exercise, as indicated in Table 22.A (page 298). The child is to select from two words, the one said by the teacher.

This general format is employed to teach the basic sound-letter correspondences. Difficulty in letter discrimination and sound-letter associations can be easily determined from a child's performance on the discrimination exercises. Using this procedure, the teacher can easily determine troublesome areas for particular children. Should a child have difficulty discriminating between certain sounds or sound sequences, he or she can receive special attention. Furthermore, this procedure does not force a child to read before there has been adequate preparation in discrimination experience. Reading out loud by the child, then, is not done at this phase of training.

Consistency of symbol and sound is critical at this point. Unlike the Initial Teaching Alphabet (ITA), this instructional format does not demand the introduction of a phonetic alphabet. It is relatively easy to provide a consistent relationship between sound and letter when sentence reading is not taught. Examples of sound-symbol consistency are presented in Table 22.B (page 299).

After a sufficient number of simple letter-sound correspondences are acquired, complex letter-sound correspondences are taught. A complex letter-sound correspondence is one which extends beyond the relationship between a single sound and letter. As an illustration, consider the words *up*, *hat*, *phone*, and *upheaval*. In the first two words the letters *p* and *h* correspond to the individual sounds /p/ and /h/, respectively. In the third word the sequence *ph* is pronounced as /f/, and in the fourth word the letters *p* and *h* correspond again to the

FIGURE 22.3

The story continues as the teacher reads: Picture 9. The cat runs under the table; Picture 10. Someone is filling the cup with milk; Picture 11. The cat goes over to the cup; Picture 12. The cat touches the cup.

FIGURE 22.4

The story continues as the teacher reads: Picture 13. The cup falls over; Picture 14. The milk spills out; Picture 15. The cat runs quickly under the table; Picture 16. Someone is filling up the cup again.

individual sounds /p/ and /h/, respectively. Experience with words of this type will broaden a child's perspective on English spelling. He or she will soon learn that there are instances for which the rule of simple letter-sound correspondence does not apply. Other more complex relationships must be attended to. In the above illustration two rules of reading are applied: (1) two letters can correspond to one sound, and (2) syllable or word boundary can constrict the use of rule (1).

However, in the writer's opinion, one reason that some educators have found that the ITA has not been entirely successful is because it succeeds in teaching simple letter-sound rules, but does not prepare the student for complex letter-sound rules.

Another complex rule applies to the /ʃ/ sound. The following three words are examples of a complex "right-to-left" rule: *tension, trans-*

mission, and *conviction*. A rule[1] which partially describes the sound-letter correspondence for these words and similar words is:

$$\left.\begin{matrix} s \\ ss \\ t \end{matrix}\right. \longrightarrow /\int/ \ \_\_\_\_\text{ion} \quad (1).$$

The students who apply rule (1), or a form of it, implicitly know that the letters and sequences *s*, *ss* and *t* can correspond to the single sound /ʃ/. Furthermore, they implicitly know that the three letters *-ion* comprise a single configuration.

Table 22.B lists the order of introduction for the words in the reading program which is under development. The goal is to maintain phonetic consistency until a large number of vocabulary items (at least 1,000 words) are introduced. Phonetic consistency, however, will not be restricted to simple sound-letter correspondences. Complex

FIGURE 22.5

The story concludes as the teacher reads: Picture 17. The cat goes over to the cup; Picture 18. The cat looks inside the cup; Picture 19. The cat sticks out his tongue; Picture 20. The cat drinks the milk from the cup.

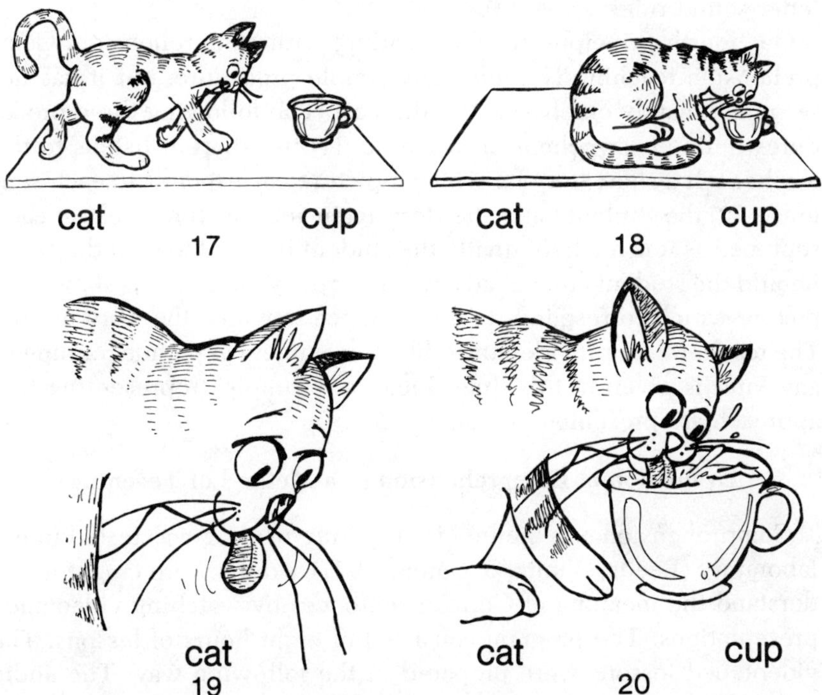

TABLE 22.A
Discrimination exercise for Lesson 1 of the reading program.

1.	cat	___
2.	___	cat
3.	cat	cup
4.	cup	cat
5.	cup	cat
6.	cat	cup
7.	cup	cat
8.	cup	cat
9.	cat	cup
10.	cat	cup

letter-sound rules, such as the rule given in (1), will also be used. As long as the reading of sentences is not a goal, consistency of sound-letter rules can be maintained.

After the student has learned a significant number of simple and complex letter-sound rules, sentence reading would be introduced. A rough guess as to when sentence reading would be introduced is difficult to say. The interval of discrimination training should last at least six months so as to assure learning of a great number of complex letter-sound rules.

Our fourth principle involves reading with comprehension. Comprehension teaching is a relatively simple procedure, but it has not been adequately emphasized in the past. The following three procedures define comprehension teaching: (1) the student listens to the teacher tell a short story for which a picture corresponds to each sentence; (2) the student hears the story again and this time looks at each sentence as it is read; (3) finally the student is asked to read the story. Should the student fail to read a word correctly, he or she is shown the picture which corresponds to the sentence in which the word occurs. The teacher then provides an auditory example. No phonic training of any kind is given at this time. Pictorial examples representing this approach are presented on pages 293–297.

Evaluation of Comprehension as a Method of Teaching

Comprehension as a method for teaching reading was tested in our laboratory (Reeds, Winitz, & Garcia, 1977). Adults were taught to understand the meaning of German sentences by watching videotaped presentations. The program consisted of eight hours of lessons. The videotaped lessons were prepared in the following way: The audio

TABLE 22.B
Examples of sound-letter correspondence introduced in the early phases of discrimination learning.

Sound	Letter	Word
k	c	cup
k	c	cat
r	r	rub
r	r	ran
ʌ	u	cup
ʌ	u	rub
ʌ	u	but
t	t	cat
t	t	but
æ	a	cat
æ	a	ran
æ	a	fat
æ	a	hat
i	e	he
i	e	me
i	e	we
ɪ	i	bit
ɪ	i	sit
ɪ	i	in
u	oo	too
u	oo	boot

channel is used to present a German word, phrase, or sentence as the monitor screen remains blank. Approximately two seconds later several pictures appear on the monitor, each appearing in one of four quadrants. The German audio is repeated at which time the subject selects the picture corresponding to the German utterance. Initially, of course, only one quadrant is filled. Only after several frames of the first lesson are presented are pictures placed in all four quadrants. The eight hours of lessons contain active declarative sentences of the form NVO, NVPrep., etc. The total number of words is 225.

Subsequent to using the tape-presented lessons, the students were asked to translate the several German sentences indicated below:

(1) *Die Frau sieht das lange Brett. Es ist auf der Treppe. Der Affe steht auf dem Brett. Der Mann kocht das Ei und der Affe frisst es. Der Affe ist tot.*

(2) *Der Arzt kauft das Bier. Er trinkt es. Er ist glücklich. Der Arzt isst den Fisch auf dem Tisch. Der Arzt gibt dem Kellner das Geld.*

(3) *Der Mann und die Frau lesen das Buch. In dem Buch sehen sie einen Flieger. Der Flieger ist in dem Flugzeug.*

The above sentences were developed by selecting lexical items from the programmed materials and using them to generate "new" sentences, that is, sentences they had not heard before, although the syntax and vocabulary (with the exception of *frisst* and *einen*) were not new.

Two groups of students served as experimental subjects. Group I was comprised of graduate students enrolled in a course on normal language development. The high school students in Group II were selected from a group enrolled in a German class for which the presentation of videotaped lessons was their first unit of instruction. Both groups of students had no previous exposure to German orthography.

For the college students the average proportion of correct words was .80, and for the high school students was .70. A control group of 16 graduate and undergraduate psychology majors was tested. These students had no knowledge of German. The average proportion of correct words was .24. This proportion establishes the guessing rate for the German passages used in this experiment.

Some may view the practical utility of this investigation with skepticism, especially because it seems to apply only to second language learning. The author feels, however, that the results are generalizable to first language reading. It seems to demonstrate the underlying importance of comprehension in learning to read.

Comprehension Techniques To Teach Orthography

Comprehension techniques can also be used to teach a new orthography. Recently, Winitz, Reeds, and LaRiviere (1979a) authored a programmed instructional manual on the teaching of phonetics entitled *Phonetics: A Manual for Listening*. This manual arose out of the authors' desire to find a solution to the difficulty some students have in learning the International Phonetic Alphabet (IPA). The purpose of this manual is to introduce students to elementary English phonetics by giving them extensive practice in listening.

The rationale behind this work is as follows: (1) Learning to transcribe does not require an explicit understanding of physiological and acoustic phonetics; (2) Receptive skills should precede production skills; (3) Items which produce interference are introduced late; and (4) When possible, easy phonetic distinctions are introduced early. Perhaps all of the above are clear with the exception of (3). One way to minimize interference is to present first those symbols which have a phonetic value similar in most cases to their value within the modern standard English orthographic system. Thus, the following consonants are introduced early: /p/, /r/, /n/, /v/, /d/, /m/, /l/, /t/, /b/, /h/, /f/, /w/, /k/, /z/. Early vowels are: /a/, /u/, /ɪ/. With regard to the consonants, the next symbols to be introduced are /ʃ/, /ð/, /ŋ/, /ʒ/, /θ/ because they have a

FIGURE 22.6

The first 50 frames of Lesson 1 of Phonetics: A manual for listening. *Baltimore: University Park Press, 1979.*

LESSON 1

1	———	pa	26	da	la
2	———	pa	27	ap	a
3	ra	———	28	da	ap
4	ra	pa	29	ra	ap
5	ra	pa	30	av	pa
6	ra	pa	31	ra	lạ
7	———	na	32	av	ap
8	pa	ra	33	av	va
9	ra	nạ	34	ra	ma
10	pa	na	35	ap	av
11	va	———	36	av	al
12	na	pa	37	al	av
13	da	va	38	ma	ap
14	na	ra	39	ap	ạn
15	pa	ra	40	av	an
16	ma	ra	41	al	an
17	mạ	da	42	ap	al
18	pa	da	43	na	va
19	ma	na	44	ar	ap
20	ma	ra	45	an	ar
21	pa	ra	46	al	ar
22	da	na	47	al	ar
23	va	ma	48	da	al
24	la	ra	49	ma	la
25	ra	la	50	ạm	an

4 / Lesson 1

FIGURE 22.7

The last 50 frames of Lesson 16 of Phonetics: A manual for listening. *Baltimore: University Park Press, 1979.*

51	klæʃgaɪd	klæʃɚ	76	hẃɪtʃtʃɝl	hwɪtʃgɝl
52	plizəz	plæzəz	77	stilθs	stɛlθs
53	tækts	tæskt	78	hjudʒiz	hjudʒəz
54	tækts	tæḳst	79	gwɛnzeɪl	gwɛnɪl
55	trʌdʒhoʊm	trɛdzoʊn	80	dɔrfs	dwɔrfs
56	hwɔrfs	wɔrfs	81	twɛlvz	twɛlfθ
57	plịzɪŋ	pleɪsɪŋ	82	pɪnʃt	pɪntʃt
58	hɔrnz	hɑrmz	83	θwɔ̣rtʌs	θwɔrtɛs
59	glɛn͡deɪl	glɛndʒeɪl	84	flɔnts	flænts
60	brɛsts	broʊsts	85	trækʃuz	trækkoʊtʃ
61	flɪntʃt	flɛnst	86	pɪŋks	paɪnts
62	tɔrts	tɑrts	87	fridʒɪn	freɪdʒin
63	krʌnʃt	klɪnʃt	88	plɑnts	plænts
64	θrɛḍɪŋ	θrɛdɪn	89	trɛkʃuz	trækʃuz
65	hjudʒpɑdʒ	hjudʒfʌdʒ	90	skrɑd	skrud̚
66	pænts	peɪnts	91	krɛnʃt	krʌnʃt
67	skrudʒ	skrætʃ	92	skẉɪn	skrɪm
68	djudeɪz	djutiz	93	pænts	pʌnts
69	flɛnst	flɛnʃt	94	trɪmθɛm	trɪmðɛm
70	flɛʃdʒeɪd	flɛdʒd	95	θroʊtʃɪn	θroʊtʃin
71	skjud	skrud	96	kwɛstɚz	kwɛsts
72	swɪtʃgɝl	switkɝl	97	krɪsts	krɛsts
73	skrɑd	skrʌd	98	glɑtpæθ	glʌtpæθ
74	kɔrts	kɑrts	99	pʌntʃt	pɑntʃt
75	tɔrts	tɑrts	100	krɪṃṗs	grɪmps

Lesson 16 / 35

unique form within the IPA consonant inventory in that they are not part of the orthography of modern English. Symbols /g/ and /s/ are in a class by themselves in that they are highly ambiguous within the interfering orthographic system. For example, /s/ is represented orthographically by the letters *c, z, sc, ss, st,* and no doubt by other letters in addition to *s*. A description of the remaining symbols and their presentation order is provided by Winitz, Reeds, and LaRiviere (1979b).

The format for the presentation of the phonetics program is given in Figures 22.6 and 22.7. In Figure 22.6 the first 50 items of the first lesson are presented. Each lesson consists of 100 paired comparisons, and there are a total of 16 discrimination lessons or 1,600 programmed listening frames. Note in Figure 22.6 that the student first hears the item /pa/ in frames 1 and 2, and only /ra/ in frame 3. In frame 4 the students hears (ra/ and is to select the correct answer by underlining either /ra/ or /pa/.

The last 50 items of Lesson 16 are displayed in Figure 22.7, from which you can readily see the level of complexity which can be achieved after 16 lessons (the average lesson length is only about 20 minutes).

No transcription exercise is recommended before all the symbols are receptively taught. Assume you have taught the vowel [ɛ], but not the [e], and only a limited number of other phonetically distinct vowels. Then you ask students to transcribe syllables in which the [ɛ] vowel appears in contexts such as [bɛm]. The following have been typical student responses in our experience: 1. /bem/, 2. /bEm/, 3. /bɛm/, 4. /bΣm/. Errors of the sort described above are not very likely to occur when the student has been taught the entire vowel system in listening lessons.

Utilization of Comprehension-Based Reading Program With the Hearing Impaired

Now that a comprehension-based reading program has been explained, one might ask the question: How might this approach be utilized with the deaf and hard of hearing? My suggestions are the following: Initially all reading instruction would be done with words printed in the symbols of the International Phonetic Alphabet (IPA). The student will not necessarily need to know that each symbol corresponds to a "discrete" articulatory production. After students have achieved considerable experience with language through the reading process, formal speech training would begin.

Some may view with skepticism this aspect of my proposal because they have observed so many students who have had difficulty acquiring basic reading skills. Similarly, foreign language teachers are skeptical of new teaching approaches because of the many years of frustration which they have endured. Yet the current systems for teaching reading differ markedly from the procedures of comprehension training proposed here.

Formal training in articulation practice would involve traditional speech instruction, but with the following modification: The student would be instructed to produce sounds in sequence within a certain *time* framework. For example, if the word to be taught is *dog,* the sounds would be represented visually in IPA on a card, and the instructor would begin the teaching of the segments dɔg. The instructor's production would be displayed as a straight line between two points on an oscilloscope with the amplitude voltage turned down. The student's task would be to imitate the instructor's production and then try to produce the articulatory movements within a specified time interval. The interval would be specified by the instructor, and the oscilloscope would be used for feedback displays. In this way coordinated speech movements might be learned. The ability to learn should be enhanced because students will have a fairly good implicit understanding of English phonology and syntax.

The proposals suggested for reading and articulation instruction involve processes which have been termed implicit learning. Normal-hearing children acquire native competency in articulation and reading through the process of implicit learning. Extensive comprehension training has been advocated as the major educational methodology that fosters implicit learning. Implicit learning has never been strongly emphasized as a basic teaching routine. Possibly, our educational system has stressed "learning-by-doing" for so long that it has failed to recognize that production follows comprehension.

REFERENCES

Smith, F. *Understanding reading.* New York: Holt, Rinehart and Winston, 1978.

Reeds, J. A., Winitz, H., & Garcia, P. A. A test of reading following comprehension training. *Internat. Rev. Appl. Ling.*, 1977, *15*, 307–319.

Winitz, H., Reeds, J. A., & LaRiviere, C. L. *Phonetics: A manual for listening.* Baltimore: University Park Press, 1979a.

Winitz, H., Reeds, J. A., & LaRiviere, C. L. *Teacher's guide to phonetics: A manual for listening.* Baltimore: University Park Press, 1979b.

[1]This rule is not complete. It must take into account the fact that ⟨ss⟩ is uttered /ʒ/ in *fussion*, ⟨t⟩ is /tʃ/ in *question*, and ⟨s⟩ can be /tʃ/ in *pension*, and /ʒ/ in *conversion*.

23
Summary Comment on Contemporary Concepts: Speech and Language Training for the Hearing Impaired

Kathleen E. Crandall

A WIDE ARRAY OF TOPICS have been addressed in Part IV, Contemporary Concepts, ranging from diagnosis to application of communication skills in daily interactions with other human beings. All of these components are necessary to the process of communication. However, the authors differ in the way they approach the teaching and learning of communication skills.

Ling in his paper rightly points out the fundamental need for appropriate diagnostic tools. He refers to the need for measurement beyond the diagnosis of the existence of a hearing loss and the prescription of amplification, areas in which significant progress has been evidenced during the past decade. The tools now needed must give the teacher more specific information on the hearing-impaired individual's capacity to acquire linguistic skills in the areas of phonology, syntax, semantics, and pragmatics. Without these tools, the teacher spends much time in trial-and-error procedures, a high risk to the hearing-impaired individual who is already behind in language acquisition.

Ling also states that "approaches to teaching spoken language to hearing-impaired children through reference to a system based on adult syntax are therefore suspect." This statement should be extended into the area of diagnosis as well. That is, an assessment of an individual's capacity to acquire linguistic knowledge is not a measure of how much of the adult model he or she has mastered nor of the degree of discrepancy between his or her knowledge and the adult model. Nonetheless, many popular assessment tools are based on an adult model of linguistic competence, e.g., The Test of Syntactic Abilities (Quigley et al., 1978) and Developmental Sentence Analysis (Lee, 1974). An assessment of pedagogical significance is one that tells the teacher what kinds of linguistic rules the learner has acquired (not which adult rules the learner uses), the consistency of their application, and the ease with which they are modified and updated to agree with input the individual receives. This type of assessment calls for an ongoing or longitudinal commitment.

The majority of the content in the papers of Part IV deals with specific methodologies for improving hearing-impaired students' language abilities. In two of the papers, the first Winitz paper and Erber's paper, the emphasis is on auditory stimulation—the learning of the language system through audition. The goal for the learner conveyed in both these papers appears to be the mastery of the sound system of the language. However, the similarities go no further; the specific methods to accomplish the goal are radically different.

Winitz argues that expressive spoken language and, specifically, articulatory control are dependent upon the comprehension of the sound system of the language and recommends, therefore, that no articulation instruction be given until the individual has gained some facility in auditory comprehension. Winitz also argues for "implicit" auditory comprehension instruction as opposed to giving the learner explicit language rules for comprehension. The fact that most language rules are either too complex to be understood by the learner or have not yet been fully established by linguists are the premises upon which Winitz bases his argument for not providing any explicit information to the learner. Another reason for implicit teaching is to more closely parallel the processes used by the first language (child) learner. The acquisition versus learning process is well known in the field of second language (Krashen, 1978) and is by no means a settled issue. In fact, adolescents and young adults are usually not satisfied with implicit language teaching procedures exclusively and will either demand language rules from their teacher or consciously formulate and verify self-constructed language rules if they are not provided. Thus, Winitz may eventually need to alter his position for adolescent and adult language learners.

With respect to the delayed oral practice approach, this also is a well-known topic of controversy in second language. Gary (1978) has reviewed the research dealing with this topic and interprets the results to indicate that adult and children foreign language learners who are not required to speak immediately make greater gains in listening comprehension, reading, and writing and often in speaking as well, compared to those in a typical audiolingual approach who are required to speak immediately. With both this and the above implicit acquisition process, we cannot automatically apply principles from the field of second language to that of the hearing impaired without thorough scrutiny through research with a hearing-impaired population.

Winitz suggests that the auditory comprehension approach to speaking may be best suited to the hard-of-hearing population and that for the student with a profound hearing loss speech training should be delayed until a "reasonable amount of language" has been acquired through reading instruction. From Winitz's remarks it is not at all clear what level of comprehension skill in listening or reading he considers a prerequisite for speech training other than the statement that a hard-of-hearing child will probably need several years of comprehension training before other approaches are considered. I wonder if the hearing-impaired child has several years to risk. Winitz also says with respect to comprehension training that if "relevant features" are missing there will probably be a greater need for speech production practice. Here it is not clear if he is referring to relevant acoustic features or what.

The reading program proposed by Winitz in the last paper of this section is also based upon implicit processing and discrimination training—discrimination of sound-letter combinations rather than of speech alone. This program was subjected to evaluation with hearing high school and college students. The experimental group received eight hours of the reading lessons in German while a control group received no German lessons. Even though the experimental group out-performed the control group by learning approximately 50 percent more German words, there was no group in the study who received eight hours of another approach to reading German. Thus, little can be said about the superiority of this approach compared to another.

In adapting the reading program for the hearing impaired, Winitz recommends a comprehension-based reading program initially focusing on instruction using the International Phonetic Alphabet and further recommends that this instruction should precede formal speech training. He claims that with such instruction hearing-impaired students will demonstrate greater ability to learn speech movements because they "will have a fairly good implicit understanding of English phonology and syntax." Here, Winitz appears to assume that one can learn the phonology of a spoken language through a symbolic visual secondary representation. I am not aware of evidence that such learning is possible. Furthermore, the features of stress, timing, and intonational contour are not present in written systems. Research in the field of reading shows an early advantage for children learning to read languages that have close letter-sound relationships, but this advantage disappears by the fourth grade (Gibson & Levine, 1975). Chomsky (1970) presents a case for English orthography being well suited for the English language in that standard orthographic systems are not surface phonemic transcriptions, but represent linguistic structures at a deeper level and contain information not predictable from the surface structure. Thus, semantic similarities of words are conveyed graphically, e.g., sign-signature, courage-courageous, photograph-photography. These clues would not be present in a pure letter-sound system and their absence may detract from the reader's ability to gain meaning from print.

Erber, as does Winitz, stresses the importance of acoustic stimulation for speech development and correction. Erber stresses the need for early auditory stimulation and points out that adolescents who do not produce in their speech what they have learned to discriminate auditorily are too dependent upon previously established visual and kinesthetic speech monitoring habits. Erber's approach differs from Winitz' in that acoustic and production training are offered concurrently. Furthermore, Erber directly states the need for scrutiny of this method—its scientific foundations need definition, and conditions under which it is effective need specification. He does not prescribe this approach for all hearing-impaired individuals.

Ling also addresses techniques for improving the spoken language skills of the hearing impaired. Ling advocates early training in speech production and has categorized this training into two levels—phonetic and phonologic. At the phonetic level, practice on nonmeaningful articulatory patterns is included. Such practice is not advocated by the other authors in this section. In fact, both Winitz and the Kretschmers appear to focus only on training in meaningful contexts. Ling reports that hearing-impaired adolescents typically have difficulty incorporating learned nonmeaningful articulatory patterns into their meaningful spoken utterances. This observed difference in learning between age groups also observed by Erber supports the need for early intervention and the application of different teaching approaches when early intervention is not accomplished. Ling, as Erber, recognizes the need for research evaluating his instructional hypotheses and procedures. He especially calls for research to determine contexts and strategies conducive to achieving phonologic carry-over and generalization.

Ling also discusses the relationships between the syntax of spoken language and speech reception and production. He states that "fairly advanced" speech reception and production skills are probably needed for the development of syntax. Examples of the importance of alveolar sounds in the functor morphemes *in, is,* and *not* are given as examples of this relationship. We are unable to verify this statement without a clearer definition of what is meant by "fairly advanced." By 3 years of age, normal-hearing children typically have correctly incorporated the *is* copula form, *in,* and *on,* as well as some negative forms using *no* and *not* into their spoken syntax (Clark & Clark, 1977); these same children, however, have not achieved accurate production of all of the sounds in these words.

With respect to parents and teachers providing speech input, Ling encourages them "to speak and teach within the child's auditory range." How this can be accomplished for the child with a profound hearing impairment is not evident, nor are alternatives for such a child provided.

In the paper authored by the Kretschmers, we see a move away from a discussion directed at specific speech feature reception and production toward one stressing the importance of conversational pragmatics. An excellent review of presupposition, topicalization, turn-taking and initiation, maintenance, and termination of conversations is included with a review of communicative competence achievements made between birth and early childhood. This knowledge and investigation into the area of pragmatics has led the Kretschmers to hypothesize that hearing-impaired individuals demonstrate poor carry-over and generalization of syntactic principles into their meaningful conversational exchange because they have been taught syntactic principles removed from conversational relevance. They further assert that requirements for developing overall communicative competence probably do not differ if hearing-impaired children are learning to speak or to sign English. One additional point made by the Kretschmers and not by others represented here is the finding that visual cuing is an important feature in conversation for the hearing and therefore most likely for the hearing impaired as well. The work of the Kretschmers is a good example of the need for professionals involved in speech instruction for hearing-impaired children to be familiar with findings in related areas so that appropriate research questions can be formulated.

In summary, all of the approaches suggested in this section merit consideration. Currently most are at the hypothesis stage and in need of extensive experimentation with various hearing-impaired populations to determine their specific utility and efficacy. At the same time, we need to recognize the importance of continued encouragement for the development of creative approaches to reducing the communication problems posed by hearing impairment. All of the authors included in this section are deserving of praise for their innovations.

REFERENCES

Chomsky, N. Phonology and reading. In H. Levine and J. P. Williams (Eds.), *Basic studies on reading.* N.Y.: Basic Books, 1970, 1–18.

Clark, H. H., & Clark, E. V. *Psychology and language.* N.Y.: Harcourt Brace Jovanovich, Inc., 1977.

Gary, J. O. Why speak if you don't need to? The case for a listening approach to beginning foreign language learning. In W. C. Ritchie (Ed.), *Second language acquisition research.* N.Y.: Academic Press, Inc., 1978. 175–183.

Gibson, E. J., & Levine, H. *The psychology of reading.* Cambridge, Mass.: MIT Press, 1975.

Krashen, S. D. Individual variation in the use of the monitor. In W. C. Ritchie (Ed.), *Second language acquisition research.* N.Y.: Academic Press, Inc., 1978, 185–199.

Lee, L. *Developmental sentence analysis.* Evanston, Ill.: Northwestern Univ. Press, 1974.

Quigley, S. P., Steinkamp, M. W., Power, D. J., & Jones, B. W. *The test of syntactic abilities.* Beaverton, Oregon: Dormac, Inc., 1978.

Response to Comments on Contemporary Concepts

Harris Winitz

I wish to respond to several of the points raised by Crandall:

(1) Crandall states that adolescents and young adults are not usually satisfied with implicit language teaching procedures and will demand language rules. Students usually want to know language rules (except when they are too complex, as is the case with most rules) because this method is part of their training. Students have been repeatedly told throughout their educational career that explicit instruction in rules is essential in order to learn a language. However, the research of Postovsky (1976) and Asher (1972) clearly demonstrates that when adults are told that explicit instruction in rules will not be part of the instructional format, they are perfectly satisfied not to ask for a rule. The research on comprehension teaching indicates that students are satisfied to learn the language and not the rules.

(2) Crandall remarks that I did not specify exactly how much auditory comprehension a "hard-of-hearing" student should receive prior to training in speech production. Since this is only a proposal of mine, it is difficult to specify the details she wishes. What I am suggesting is that a child not be forced to produce speech before he or she is ready. The readiness point will vary with individual children.

Considerable understanding of language and speech is viewed as an essential prerequisite to learning to talk. The alternative to this approach is to force speech production before there is sufficient comprehension. Crandall's criticism here is that she is unwilling to recognize that forced speech drills involve auditory comprehension and speech discrimination as major components. I am simply recommending that instruction in speech drills be delayed.

There have been experimental tests of this paradigm in articulation learning (Winitz & Preisler, 1965) and foreign language learning (Asher, 1972). It, therefore, seems to be a reasonable approach to try with hard-of-hearing individuals.

My use of the term "features" refers to articulatory features in the general sense. My comments in this regard mean that if correct articulatory production is not acquired through comprehension practice, speech drills may be necessary. I regard this as a last resort. It should not be attempted too soon in the training program.

(3) Crandall's comments on the German reading experiment are correct in that no reading method other than comprehension was tested. However, the point of the experiment was to test the effect of comprehension training on learning to read when the words and structures were precisely controlled. The very question raised by Crandall was answered by her when she reviewed the research of Gary (1978). Delaying speech instruction, Crandall reports, has repeatedly shown to provide greater gains in reading, writing, and speaking than when speaking is stressed. May I add that this almost automatic transfer of meaning to reading which we observed would not take place if the letter-sound correspondences of German were not similar to English.

(4) Crandall remarks that evidence is lacking which suggests that one can learn the phonology of a spoken language from a visual system. There is also no evidence to the contrary. She regards my argument as defective because the features of stress, timing, and intonation contour are not present in the written system. I explicitly stated that certain aspects of speech would need to be taught subsequent to instruction in reading. One procedure along these lines was, in fact, presented.

I am in agreement with the prevailing opinion held among linguists that English orthography is a useful system and should not be tampered with. However, this argument need not apply to the teaching of reading and speech to deaf children. The normal-hearing child has learned to speak before reading instruction is begun. He can apply his implicit understanding of English phonology and his understanding of words to graphic forms. The circumstances are different for the deaf child. He is often taught to read and speak prior to having an understanding of language. My proposal is to teach meaning through reading and to use a phonetic script to later assist the child to learn to speak. Crandall remarks that using a phonetic script "may detract from the reader's ability to gain meaning from print." Hebrew is a language in which the spelling of stems corresponds closely with pronunciation changes, and yet there seems to be no problem in teaching children who speak Hebrew to learn to read Hebrew. Adults, too, seem to have no difficulty in deriving deeper linguistic structures in Hebrew when seeing words in print for the first time. Crandall is really discussing a different issue, and it pertains to whether or not English spelling should be altered to conform to surface pronunciations. This is not the issue to which my remarks were made. I am concerned with teaching reading so as to assist the young deaf child to learn to speak. For this purpose, I am recommending that a phonetic alphabet be used with the deaf child. We should remember that the deaf child cannot speak and need not be taught to read by recognizing semantic similarities represented in graphic form.

A deaf child may learn to speak more easily by knowing the surface graphic form of words. For example, a deaf child who understands the meaning of the graphic sequences /foto/ and /fotəgræf/ (and additionally *photographer* and *photographic*) may be better prepared to begin speech training than one who does not have this knowledge. He would know that *photo* has *graph* appended to it, that the second vowel of *photo* differs in representation from the second vowel in *photograph*, and that many of the sounds of these two words are similar. The normal-hearing child who can hear and understand the meaning of *photo* and *photograph* knows two pronunciations of *photo*, but these variations pose no problem in establishing an implicit relationship between these two words. Similarly, the deaf child may be able to establish this same implicit relationship through phonetic script and, additionally, derive other relationships as well. It is an interesting research question that should be explored, but not dismissed out of hand.

REFERENCES

Asher, J. J. Children's first language as a model for second language learning. *Modern Lang. J.*, 1972, *56*, 133–138.

Gary, J. O. Why speak if you don't need to? The case for a listening approach to beginning foreign language learning. In W. C. Ritchie (Ed.), *Second language acquisition research*. New York: Academic Press, 1978.

Postovsky, V. The priority of aural comprehension. The language acquisition process. *Proceedings of the Fourth International Congress of Applied Linguistics*, Vol. 3, G. Nickel (Ed.). Stuttgart: HochschulVerlag, 1976.

Winitz, H., and Preisler, L. Discrimination pretraining and sound learning. *Percept. Motor Skills*, 1965, *20*, 905–916.

PART V

Current Research: Implications for Training Speech of the Hearing Impaired

24
Relationships Between Speech Perception and Speech Production in Normal-Hearing and Hearing-Impaired Subjects

Katherine S. Harris and Nancy S. McGarr

THE PURPOSE OF THIS paper is to consider, once again, the problems that a deaf speaker faces in learning to produce intelligible speech. We will argue that while we have made substantial progress in integrating ideas from research on normal perception and production into deaf training programs, we have still not entirely freed ourselves of the conceptual straightjacket of regarding speech production as the serial concatenation of steady-state events. In particular, even though training programs have turned away from a heavy emphasis on static articulator placement, we have focused on some suprasegmental characteristics of deaf speech which can be shown to be deviant, on the assumption that if these characteristics become more normal, the resulting speech will be improved. We will argue that in spite of the gross deviancy of deaf speech rhythms, they do, in many cases, reflect some "facts" about normal speech production. Indeed, the correction of those particular aspects of production which are deviant does not result in enormous improvements in intelligibility. Important as the aspects of production are (usually described as "suprasegmental,") we have not yet fully recognized the importance of deviant interarticulator programming at the segmental level. We will therefore conclude by summarizing some work on perception and production in the deaf and normal, which suggests the importance of this concept.

A Modern View of Speech Training

No account of speech production in the deaf can avoid beginning with the pivotal work of Ling (1976), who has attempted to systematize training, based on a rationale derived from the modern speech science literature. At the center of his contribution lie two great themes. The first of these is that speech production skills should be developed in their natural order—that is, in the order in which they develop in normal children. He suggests that breath and voice control be developed early, with the development of segmental aspects of production coming later, following the order in which sounds develop in the child.

This idea has its basis in a view of speech as overlaid on the normal functions of the articulatory mechanism. The effect of teaching the individual sounds of speech to the deaf after respiratory and phonatory control has been mastered should be that the filter function, the result of movement of the upper articulators, is superimposed on a matrix of adequate source function control. At a linguistic level, speech can be viewed as organized by stress and intonation into suprasegmental units, with the segmental units nested within. The effect of the proposed teaching order might be to promote normal suprasegmental relations in speech, and thus to give the listener help in decoding the message.

The second theme is that we teach "sounds" within a dynamic framework by rooting out, as a basis for training, the "posture and glide" view of speech. Ling says, "The concept has probably taken a long time to die because tongue postures are typically shown in textbooks and because it is simple to think of phonemes as succeeding one another like letters on a printed page. . . . The temptation to regard tongue postures as static rather than dynamic targets must be resisted, as must seduction by analogy with the written form" (1976, p. 109). It is to the relationship between these themes that we wish to address ourselves. We know a little bit, though not very much, about the development of phonatory patterns in normal-hearing and deaf speakers. What is the relationship between suprasegmental and segmental patterns in normal development? Which faults are at the base of the unintelligibility of deaf speech?

The Development of Suprasegmental Strategies in Normal Speech

Some years ago, Lieberman (1967) developed an ingenious theory of the origins of intonation in normal speech production. He pointed out that the intonation contour characteristic of most utterances may develop out of the relationship between respiration and phonation. In respiratory breathing, expiration and inspiration are of approximately equal duration, while in speech breathing, the expiratory limb occupies about 90 percent of the cycle. In phonation, the vocal folds must be brought into the air stream, as air is (typically) expelled from the lungs. The duration over which air can be expelled provides a limit for the length of a phrase. In infants, as in adults, subglottal pressure typically drops at the end of a phonatory phrase (Bosma, Truby, & Lind, 1965). Since fundamental frequency of phonation is affected by subglottal pressure (van den Berg, 1958), one might expect a fall of fundamental frequency to mark the end of utterances. In a slightly different formulation—the "delination line" ('t Hart & Cohen, 1973)—a continuous F_0 of stress peaks as well as unstressed valleys might be generated by falling subglottal pressure.

Objections have been raised to Lieberman's theory on several grounds. His assumption was that the mechanism for the pitch fall was a pressure drop across the glottis, but he substantially overestimated the numerical value of the relationship; the values found by Baer (1979), 2 to 5 Hz/cmH_2O, have been obtained by a number of investigators (Fromkin & Ohala, 1968; Hixon, Klatt, & Mead, 1971). Since an inspection of data by Lieberman (1967), Collier (1975), and Atkinson (1973) suggests a pressure drop of 3 to 5 cm H_2O for sentences without emphatic stress, passive mechanisms would account for only about a 15 Hz of the frequency drop. However, Maeda (1976) found F_0 drops of from 20 to 40 Hz in the productions of a corpus of sentences by an adult male. The discrepancy between F_0 fall and subglottal pressure drop suggests some kind of active use of the fundamental frequency contour to mark syntactic boundaries, since F_0 fall does not become greater, the longer the utterance (Breckenridge, 1977). This result implies that speakers use a pitch look-ahead strategy in production, adjusting the slope of pitch fall to produce the same fall in long utterances as in short. Apparently, then, even if the pitch fall has its origin in respiratory dynamics, normal adult speakers use it in an active way to code syntactic information.

Durational manipulation is used by normal adult speakers in a strategy which is quite similar to that proposed for fundamental frequency—that is, to organize speech with respect to various syntactic considerations (Klatt, 1975). Vowels are longer in terminal positions in an utterance, and before clause boundaries. Vowel lengthening is also used to mark stressed syllables in an utterance. Indeed, a complex organization of interlocking duration rules is evidently used by a speaker to time syllables according to their position in words, clauses, or sentences, or with respect to the pattern of adjacent unstressed and stressed syllables (Fowler, 1977; Lindblom & Rapp, 1973). Tendencies of this sort of organization have been shown for many languages (Lehiste, 1970) although there are language-to-language differences in the way that apparently universal tendencies toward rhythmic performance organizations are applied (Allen, 1975).

Apparently, then, we may hypothesize that the primary aspects of acoustic production which mark the suprasegmentals, fundamental frequency of phonation, and vowel duration are organized by adult speakers over at least utterance lengths, using some kind of look-ahead strategy.

While this strategy has, perhaps, a physiological origin, it is clearly used actively by adult speakers to convey syntactic information about the structure of an utterance. If listeners depend on this information to decode segmental as well as suprasegmental information, then a failure to provide it might be an important source of the characteristic unintelligibility of deaf speech. In what follows, we will try to review what is known about suprasegmental production in deaf speakers.

Development of Pitch and Duration Control in Prelingually Deaf Speakers

We know very little about the development of respiratory and phonatory control in deaf infants—indeed, we know very little about the development of such abilities in normal infants. Lenneberg, Rebelsky, and Nichols (1965) and Mavilya (1969) have suggested that in the first three to six months, the sounds produced by deaf and normal-hearing infants are much the same. Since phonatory output is affected by respiratory control, one might think that normal interaction between phonation and respiration was maintained in these children; however, probably the phonatory output of the children was too incompletely studied for us to be at all confident of its characteristics. Furthermore, audiological assessment of the individual infants studied was inadequate to allow a specification of the degree of hearing loss. However, Stark (1972) has shown that spontaneous vocalizations of a group of severely to profoundly deaf children of ages 16 to 28 months are deviant in many ways. While some characteristics are like those of hearing children of a younger age, some are never seen in a normal population. Older deaf children and deaf adults show deviant control of both respiration and phonation. Modern techniques for the study of speech respiration have been used by Forner and Hixon (1977) and, more recently, by Whitehead (1979), here at the National Technical Institute for the Deaf. We will not comment further on

Whitehead's important work, except to remark that he shows that the deaf do not use respiration in a way that would allow them to produce utterances of normal length, without great effort, due to a tendency to take in inadequate quantities of air, and waste it during phonation. When we turn to phonation, we find that the most unintelligible deaf children show evidence of poor control of phonation, in the form of pitch breaks (McGarr & Osberger, 1978). Interestingly enough, in this last study, judgments of pitch deviancy were not very highly correlated with overall intelligibility.

The best documented aspect of deaf suprasegmental production is the overall deviance in timing. Deaf speakers produce fewer words per minute than normal-hearing speakers, both because they prolong words and syllables, and because they pause for abnormal periods between words. They have, in addition, been reported to equalize the duration of stressed and unstressed syllables in sentence production, but careful studies by Reilly (1979) and Osberger (1978) show that this tendency is less salient than had been believed.

FIGURE 24.1

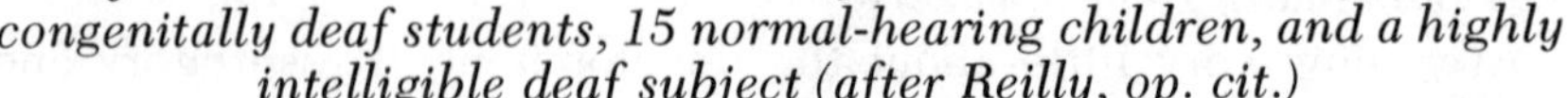

Syllable nucleus durations in disyllables. Mean values for 16 congenitally deaf students, 15 normal-hearing children, and a highly intelligible deaf subject (after Reilly, op. cit.)

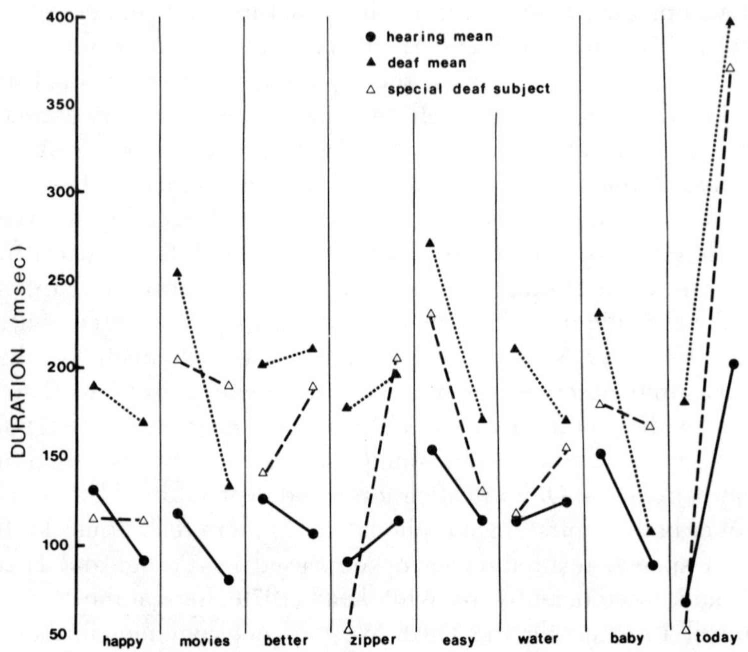

In spite of the deviancy of deaf pitch and duration control, there is some evidence that deaf speakers know some of the rules applied by speakers with normal hearing. In the paper we mentioned previously, Breckenridge asked two deaf speakers to produce sentences of different lengths. She found that the deaf speaker paused between words and that their overall durations were grossly longer than those characteristic of speakers with normal hearing. There was, nonetheless, a tendency for a declination of pitch through the sentence. Reilly (1979) found that deaf speakers use duration to differentiate between stressed and unstressed syllables in disyllables (Figure 24.1), between primary and weak syllables in stress (Figure 24.2) and between prepausal and nonprepausal syllables (Figure 24.3). Thus, deaf speakers give evidence that they have some knowledge of the rules underlying suprasegmental production, even though their overall control of respiration and phonation is deviant. It is interesting to note that deaf speakers from traditional training programs probably were not explicitly taught these rules, since the kind of general theoretical discussions of suprasegmental organization in production are relatively recent in the research literature. Of course, whatever low-frequency residual hearing the deaf possess could be used to recover fundamental frequency and durational information.

Before going on to consider the effects of abnormally long durations on intelligibility, we should note an observation by Osberger (1978) that the prolongation often noted in deaf speech production is due chiefly to prolongation of vowels. Such acoustic events as friction duration tend to be quite short. A somewhat similar observation has been made by Monsen (1976) for the voice onset time of voiceless stops. One might believe that an overall prolongation of syllables would result in long voice onset times for voiceless consonants but, in fact, voice onset times are characteristically short. We believe that these "short" consonants result from a failure of correct programming of the timing of glottal and supraglottal events, that is, failure of interarticulator programming, as we will discuss below.

Returning to the role of deviant suprasegmental production in generating unintelligible speech, there have been no studies, to my knowledge, of the role of pitch, but there have been attempts to assess the effect of training in the correction of timing, on the intelligibility of deaf speech. The results are inconsistent. Heidinger (1972) and John and Howarth (1965) found improvements in the intelligibility of the speech of children who were given training emphasizing timing, while Boothroyd, Nickerson, and Stevens (1974) and Houde (1973) did not. There is some indication that the changes in temporal control were accompanied by changes in other aspects of the children's speech. The other changes, whose patterns differed from one study to another, may have accounted for the intelligibility changes.

However, a better way to test the hypothesis that inappropriate timing is a significant contributor to the unintelligibility of deaf speech is through an analysis-by-synthesis approach; that is, by exam-

FIGURE 24.2
Mean syllable nucleus durations for primary and weak stress syllables; groups as described above (Reilly, op. cit.).

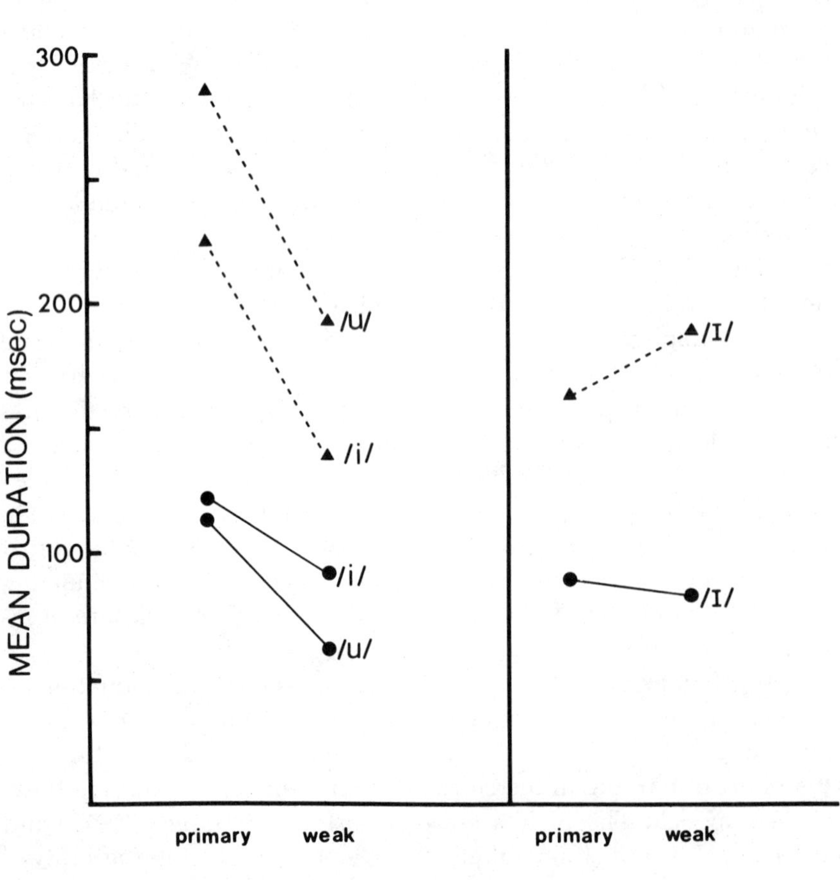

ining the effect of instrumental manipulation of recorded sentences. Following two preliminary studies (Bernstein, 1977; Lang, 1975), this approach was explored in detail by Osberger (1978). She quantified the effect of correcting pauses and vowel segment durations by adjusting the duration of the waveforms of simple sentences produced by deaf children. Her results are shown in Figure 24.4. Intelligibility scores for six children were averaged over six sentences.

The manipulations were correction (removal) of pauses, correction of stressed/unstressed syllable duration ratios, and correction of absolute duration. Corrections of pause and duration were also combined. The results show modest improvement for only one condition, the correction of relative timing. Whatever else may be said of the interpretation of this important experiment, it suggests that gross

FIGURE 24.3
Mean syllable nucleus durations in prepausal and nonprepausal syllables; groups as described above (Reilly, op. cit.).

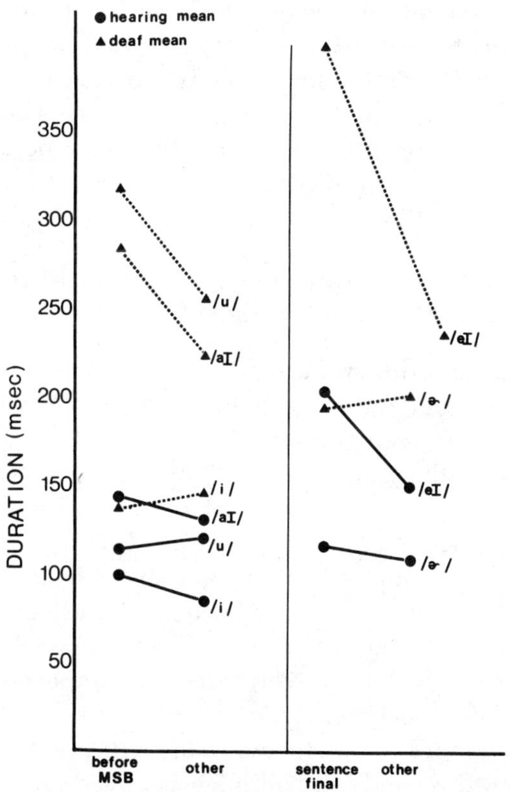

steady-state deviance of syllable duration in deaf speech is not a very large factor in the unintelligibility of the speech. This is not to say that durational information is not used by listeners in decoding speech. In Osberger's study, the sentences with the greatest number of perceived vowel errors showed the greatest improvement when relative duration was corrected, perhaps because segmental duration information about vowels became available. Indeed, studies of vowel duration production and perception in normal-hearing subjects (Nooteboom, 1973) suggest that listeners are extremely sensitive to the duration that a vowel should have in a given context. Rather, the result suggests that for pronunciation that is grossly deviant, improvement of overall timing is insufficient to allow the listener to decode adequately. Neither does the result suggest that teaching children an appropriate suprasegmental strategy is unimportant. It has been shown by Calvert (1961) that experienced listeners to deaf speech cannot identify speech as deaf unless they hear at least syllable-length productions. Even if the sole effect of the characteristic deaf syllable prolongation were to make the deaf conspicuous and tedious to listen to, correction of deaf suprasegmental structure would still be a desirable training objective. But, as we will argue in the remainder of this paper, there are other aspects of speech timing which are preceptually so deficient that they may be an important contribution to the intelligibility of the speech, and hence should be more fully investigated.

Some Effects of Articulatory Timing on Segmental Distinctions in Normal-Hearing Subjects

Some time ago, in addressing an earlier conference on the education of the deaf, our colleagues discussed the question of why speech spectrograms are hard to read (Liberman et al., 1968). They described speech as a code, rather than a cipher. When listeners are attempting to decode speech from an acoustic signal, they use cues which overlap along the time line—that is, they process information about one phoneme while they process information about another. This argument is related to that made by Ling, quoted earlier, that it is the dynamics of speech which have been neglected in deaf training. Recent perceptual experiments reinforce the importance of such dynamic factors in speech perception.

We will not attempt a complete review but will stress vowel perception because, until recently, it had been believed that vowels were

FIGURE 24.4

Intelligibility scores of deaf utterances averaged across six subjects and six sentences for six types of durational manipulation: (1) sentences unaltered; (2) pauses corrected; (3) relative timing corrected; (4) absolute syllable duration corrected; (5) relative syllable duration and pauses corrected; (6) absolute syllable duration and pauses corrected (after Osberger, op. cit.).

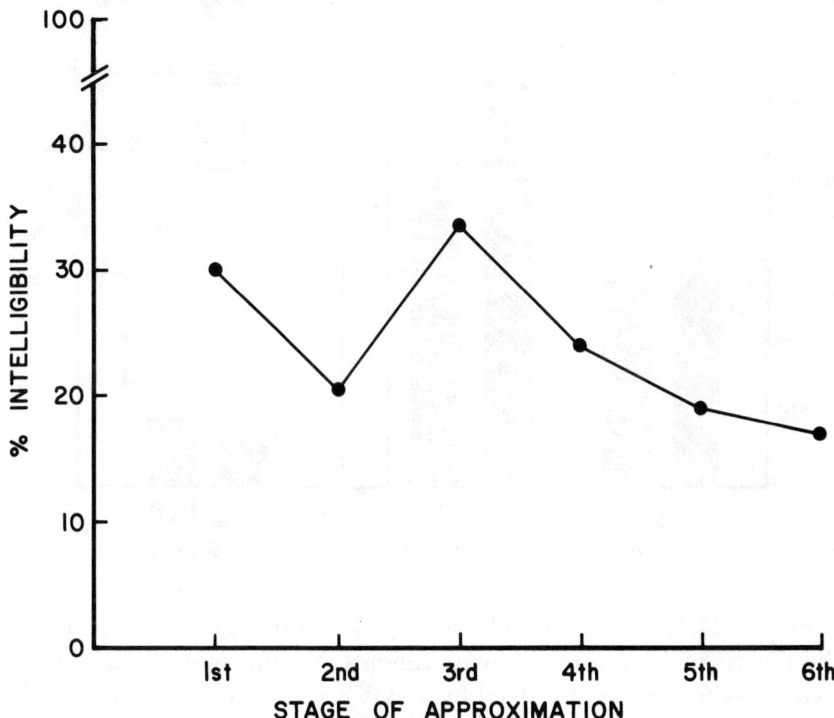

identified largely through their static spectral characteristics. These acoustic measures are associated with the central, quasi-steady-state region of a syllable and correspond to the cavity resonances of a static articulatory configuration. Strange, Verbrugge, Shankweiler, and Edman (1976) compared the identifiability of natural isolated vowels (which approximate sustained targets) and vowels spoken in a /pVp/ consonantal environment (where formant values are sustained minimally or not at all). Listeners identified the vowels with greater accuracy when listening to the /pVp/ syllables, indicating that sustained target information is not a sufficient condition for the highest accuracy to be achieved.

FIGURE 24.5

Percent identification errors for vowels as sampled from the speech of two speakers, and synthesized. "Natural" vowels were produced as isolated vowels. "Steady-state" vowels were produced by iterating two pitch periods. CVC syllables were produced in the context /bVb/.

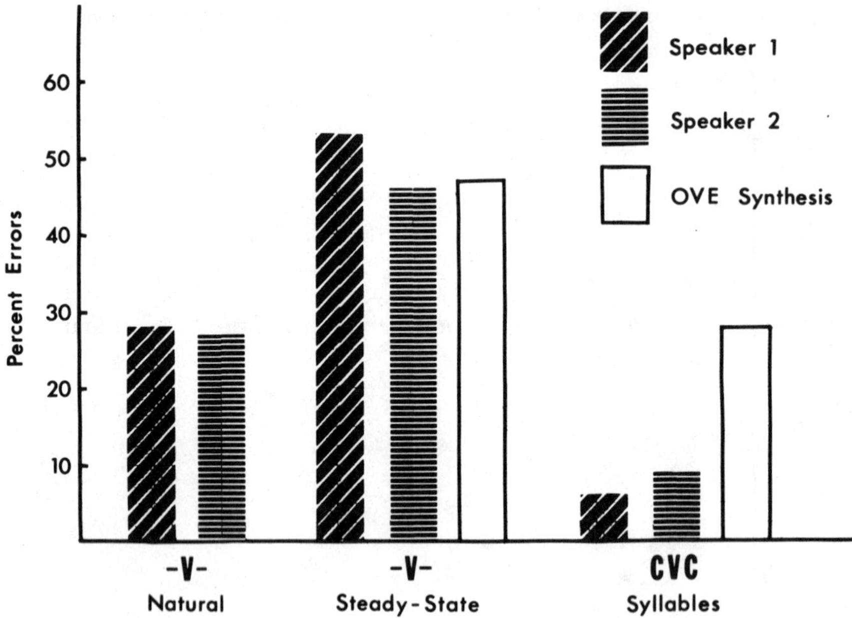

Figure 24.5, from an unpublished paper of this group, summarizes the results of several related experiments. Vowels were produced by two speakers, and synthesized by an OVE synthesizer, in three types of context. Condition "Natural" had sustained natural vowels. In condition "Steady State" a few pitch periods from a sustained vowel were iterated, using computer techniques, to produce a syllable equal in duration to the matching natural vowel, with no formant movement at all. A CVC context /bVb/ was also used. Clearly, CVC syllables are better identified than isolated vowels, but natural isolated vowels are more identifiable than iterated vowels. The relationship between OVE synthesized vowels in steady state and CVC context is the same as for the same two conditions for speakers. Apparently, even the minimal dynamics of a natural isolated vowel carry segmental information, but sustained "target" values are relatively uninformative.

When we turn to the consonants, there is a great deal of information indicating the importance of dynamic parameters in segment identification. For example, Figure 24.6 shows the results of an old experiment on the discrimination of stops, semivowels, and diphthongs (Liberman et al., 1956).

The results show that a synthetic CV syllable with a transition of short duration will be perceived as beginning with a stop. If the transition is made somewhat longer, it will be perceived as beginning with a semivowel, while if it is made longer still, the syllable is perceived as a vowel of changing color. Indeed, it is clear, as Miller (in press) has observed, that "prosodic and segmental information is so intertwined in speech that only by studying both factors will it ultimately be possible to build a model of segmental perception."

In production, dynamic information is generated by the movement of the articulators. Changes in dynamics can be generated by changing the speed of movement of individual articulators, or by changing the relative timing. It is this last type of change in articulator dynamics that is of greatest interest to us.

FIGURE 24.6
Distribution of identification by subjects presented with synthetic stimuli with the transition durations indicated below (after Liberman et al., op. cit.).

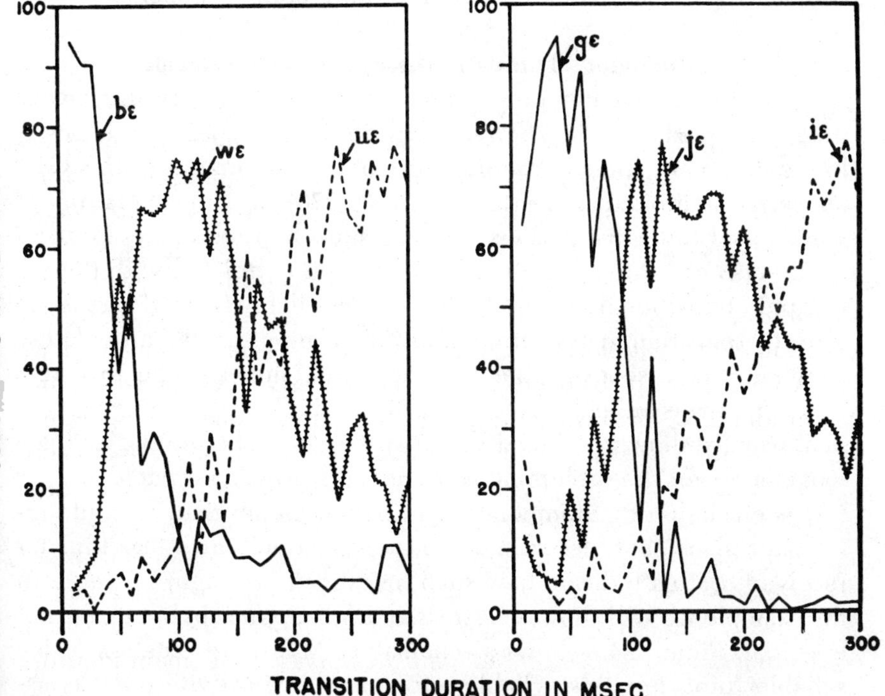

The best-known example of interarticulator programming is voice onset time. Figure 24.7 shows the distribution of voice onset times for stops in English. It is well known that the timing of the release of oral occlusion relative to the onset of glottal pulsing distinguishes the voiced from the voiceless stop (Lisker & Abramson, 1967). It can also be shown that the difference between aspirated stops seems to be one of articulatory timing (Lofqvist, in preparation). While aspects of laryngeal-supralaryngeal timing have been most widely investigated, one can find examples in the literature that suggest that the relative time at which articulators move is crucial in other ways in producing segmental information. For example, Kent and Moll (1975) used cine-fluorography to investigate the articulation of consonant clusters beginning with /sp—/ and found that closure for /p/ and release of the constriction for /s/ occurred almost simultaneously irrespective of linguistic environment. Recent work of our own suggests that when syllables are produced with varying stress or speaking rate, while there are changes in vowel duration and target vocal tract shape, the relative time of onset of movement (as inferred from electromyographic [EMG] measures) for tongue fronting and lip closure varies relatively little. We believe that a failure to control interarticulator programming contributes substantially to the unintelligibility of deaf speech.

Articulatory Timing in the Speech of the Deaf

While interarticulator programming has not been examined very much in considering the aberrant qualities of deaf speech, it is possible to find many hints in the literature of the importance of this variable. We mentioned above that Monsen (1976) has shown a failure of voice-onset-time distinctions in deaf speech production. Monsen (1978) also noted that intelligibility was well correlated with the extent of F_2 transition in the production of the syllable /ais/. Of course, an acoustic transition in a spectrogram is the result of several articulatory events. In the case given, the transition might appear to be abnormal either if vowels are not correctly placed (and it is well known that the deaf usually show a reduced vowel space), or if the tongue and jaw movements for the diphthong were not correctly coordinated.

It is our belief that temporal coordination, rather than absolute articulator placement, deserves more investigation than it has thus far received. Let us indicate how such investigations might proceed. In the example we will show, we stress an EMG approach, but that is not essential. Figure 24.8 shows a schematic EMG representation of the syllable /pip/. For this syllable, orbicularis oris/activity (OO) is as-

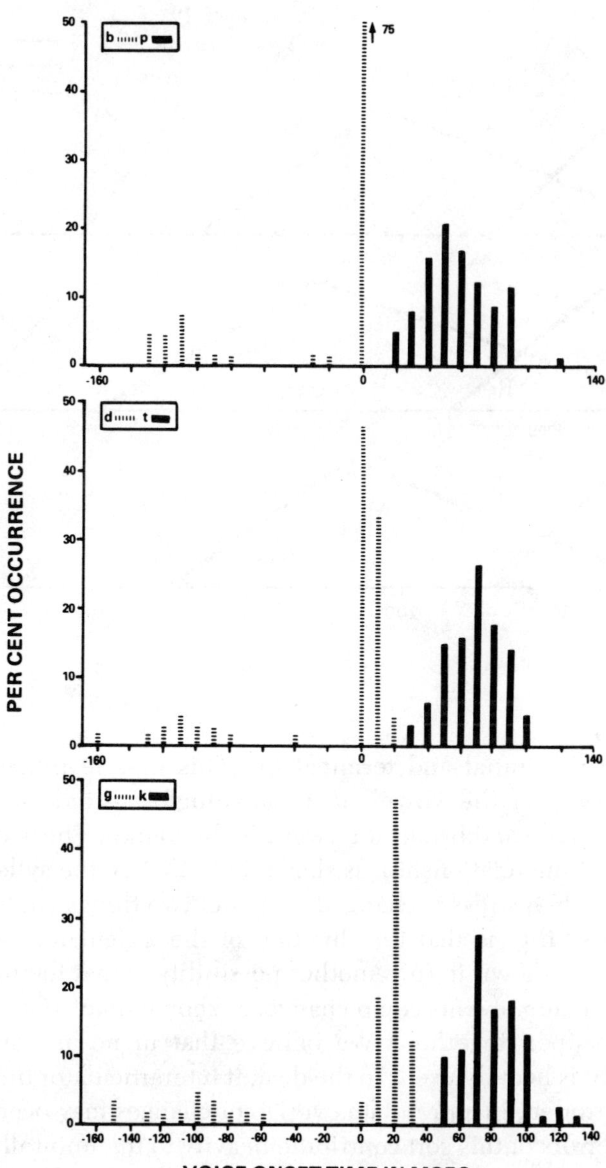

FIGURE 24.7
Distribution of voice onset time for stops in isolated words. (after Lisker & Abramson, op. cit.).

FIGURE 24.8
Hypothetical dynamics of /pip/ production of (a) normal duration and (b) and (c) lengthened duration (after Bell-Berti, in press).

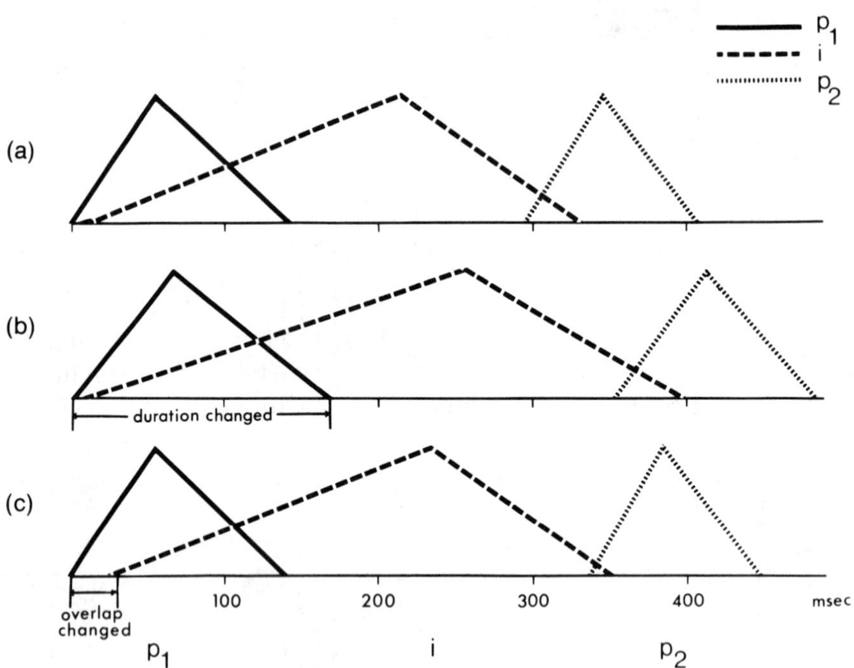

sociated with the initial and terminal /p/. This muscle purses and closes the lips. For the vowel /i/, the genioglossus/muscle (GG) bunches the tongue and brings it forward in the mouth. These events have a normal time relationship, as shown in (a). When the syllable is prolonged, as when stress is changed, either of two things could happen. One possibility is that the duration of the articulatory events could change, as shown in (b). Another possibility is that the overlap between articulatory events could change, as shown in (c). (Of course, both could happen together.) We believe that in normal speech, mechanism (b) is heavily used. In the deaf, if interarticulator timing is less well controlled, inappropriate overlap or changes may occur. We believe that errors of this sort contribute heavily to the unintelligibility of deaf speech.

We have done a pilot experiment which demonstrates such a failure of interarticulator programming. In this study, acoustic and electromyographic measures were made of an adult deaf speaker and a hearing speaker. The prelingually deafened speaker (mean pure-tone average 150 dB+ ISO) is a graduate of an oral school for the deaf and has received remedial speech classes as an adult. The hearing speaker has frequently served as a subject for EMG experiments.

Each subject produced many repetitions of each of several utterance types, including /ə pip*a*p/ with stress on /i/ and or /*a*/. Surface electrodes were used in recording from the orbicularis oris, while conventional hooked wire electrodes were inserted into the genioglossus. Electromyographic data were analyzed by previously described techniques (Kewley-Port, 1973). All the utterances analyzed were intelligible to listeners.

Some rather typical data for the hearing speaker are shown in Figure 24.9 for the utterance type /ə ˈpip*a*p/. At the top of each column—either GG or OO—is the ensemble average, obtained by averaging all the repetitions of the utterance type; four single tokens are seen in the columns below. For each utterance type, the line-up point for EMG and acoustic events is indicated by the dashed line at *θ* msec; the acoustic event at this time is the closure release of the second /p/.

Looking first at the GG column, we find that peak activity is higher for /i/ than /*a*/, as would be expected. Indeed, peak GG activity for the vowel occurs approximately at the time as the acoustic line-up—the /p/ burst release event. Turning to the OO column we find three well-defined peaks corresponding to the lip movement for the /p/ gestures, with the line-up falling between peaks 1 and 2. A striking feature of these data is the similarity of the EMG patterns observed for the individual tokens, for both muscles.

Figure 24.10 shows data for the utterance /əpi ˈp*a*p/, the hearing speaker. The duration of the genioglossus activity is shorter in this utterance type, and the time between the peaks of OO activity is shifted. Both these changes are direct effects of the shortening of /i/ as stress is shifted to /*a*/. Another effect of de-stressing /i/ is the decrease in average peak height. All these characteristics of the effects of stress change have been previously noted (Harris, 1978). Note, however, that the pattern of peak activity for GG still occurs with simultaneous /p/ release.

Figure 24.11 shows the data for the deaf subject's production of /ə ˈpip*a*p/. First, examining average EMG activity for OO, we see that as in data for the hearing subject, there are three well-defined peaks at activity and that duration is greater between peaks 1 and 2 than between peaks 2 and 3. Duration is prolonged overall for the deaf speaker, and /p/ release falls essentially between the peaks 1 and 2 as

FIGURE 24.9
/ə'pipap/ as produced by a normal speaker. Data plots at the top show EMG averaged for about 16 tokens for the genioglossus and orbicularis oris muscles. Four individual tokens for each muscle are shown below. Dotted lines indicates acoustic release of /p/ closure.

/ə'pipap/

FBB

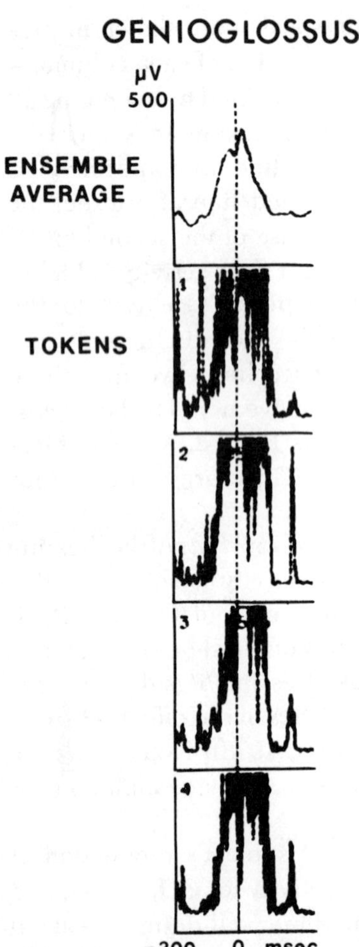

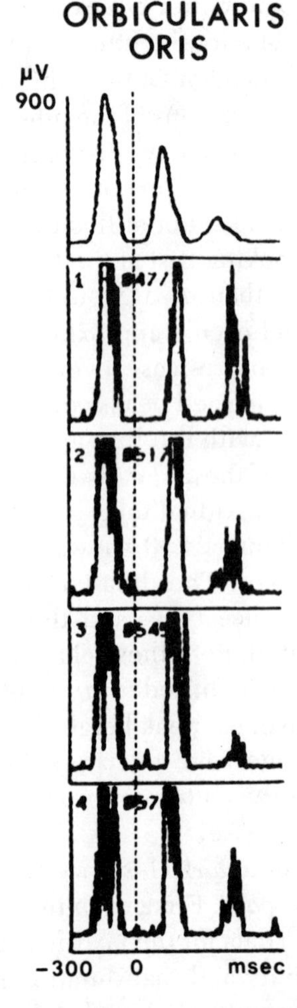

FIGURE 24.10
/əpiˈpap/ *as produced by a normal speaker. Data presented as in Figure 24.9.*

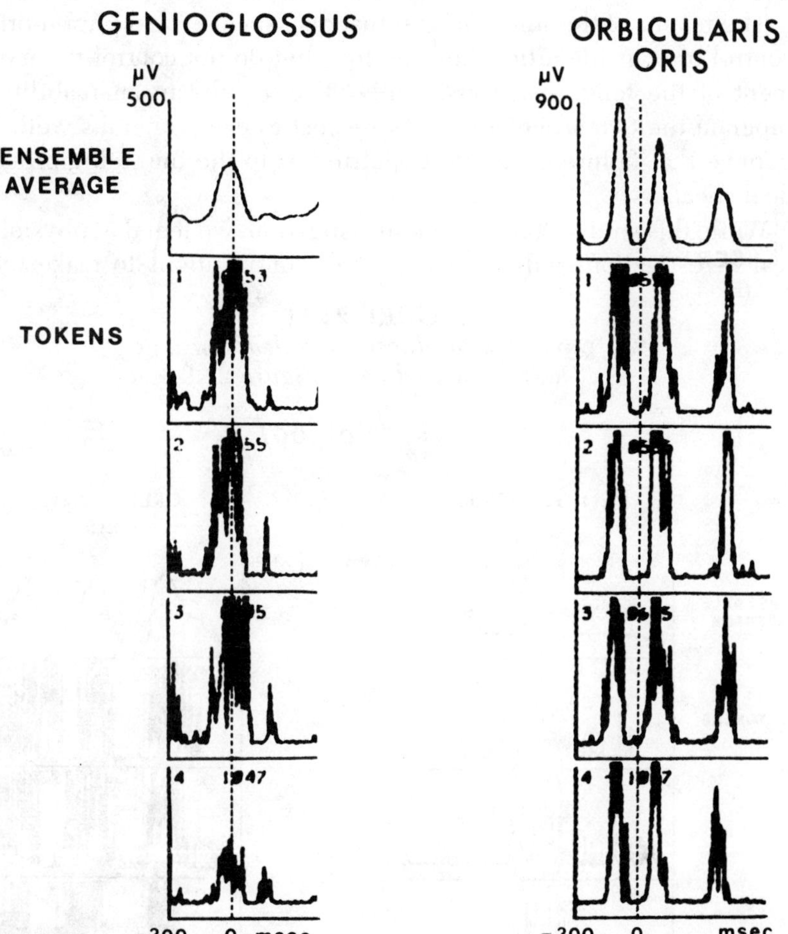

we observed for the hearing speaker. Turning to GG, peak activity is less well defined and appears later relative to burst release, compared to the hearing speaker's pattern. That is, peak activity occurs after the deaf speaker produced the acoustic /p/ release.

In other words, activity for lip closure for the consonant and tongue bunching for the vowel overlap more in the hearing than for the deaf speaker. Further, there is considerable variability in duration of GG activity from token to token. In some instances, this activity starts fairly early (e.g., Token 2) and at other times, later (e.g., Token 1). Token-to-token variability is far more striking for GG than for OO.

Figure 24.12 shows the data for the deaf speaker's production of /əpi ˈp*a*p/. The same comments may be made as for the previous figure.

The results of the study suggest that deaf speakers have appropriate control of a visible articulator, the lips, but do not control the movement of the tongue so consistently. This results in an inability to program the two articulators with respect to each other, as well. We believe that failure of this sort contributes to the unintelligibility of deaf speakers.

While this study is only a pilot investigation, we feel that physiological investigations will have important contributions to make to an

FIGURE 24.11
/əˈpip*a* p/ *as produced by a deaf speaker. Data presented as in Figure 24.9.*

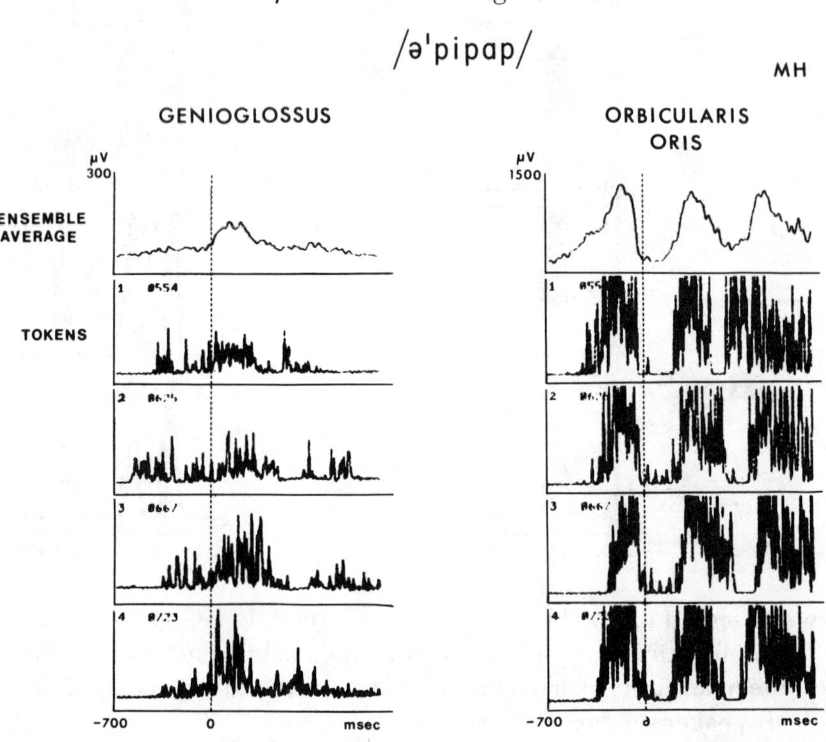

understanding of deaf articulation, and that consideration of interarticulator programming in deaf speakers is an important new direction for conceptualization of their error pattern.

FIGURE 24.12
/əpi ˈpap/ *as produced by a deaf speaker. Data presented as in Figure 24.9.*

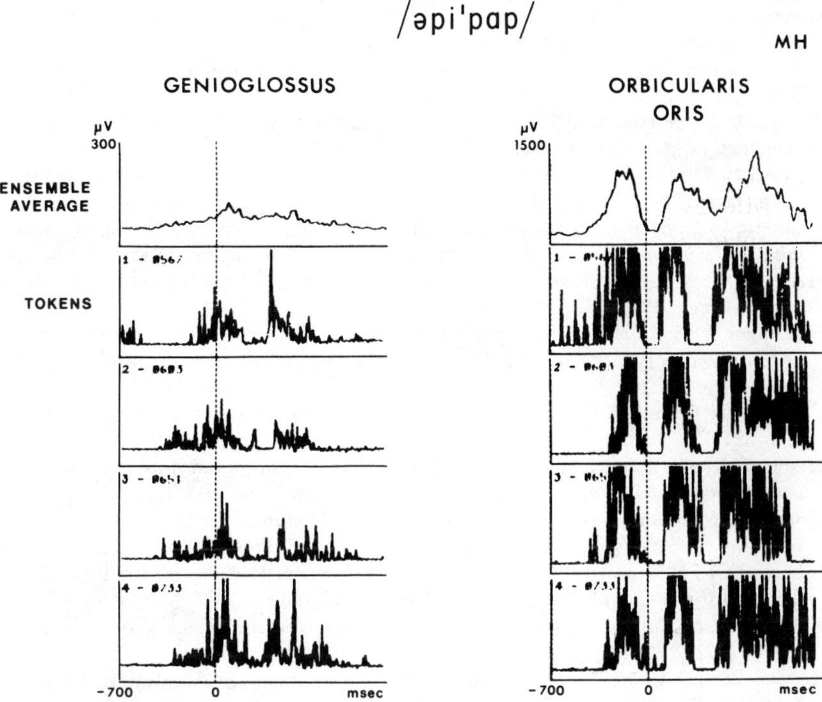

REFERENCES

Allen, G. D. Speech rhythm: Its relation to performance universals and articulatory timing. *J. Phonetics*, 1975, *3*, 75–86.

Atkinson, J. E. *Aspects of intonation in speech: Implications from an experimental study of fundamental frequency.* Doctoral dissertation, University of Connecticut, 1973.

Baer, T. Reflex activation of laryngeal muscles by sudden induced subglottal pressure changes. *J. Acoust. Soc. Am.*, 1979, *65*, 1271–1275.

Bell-Berti, F. Inter-articulator programming and clinical advice to "slow down." *J. Childhood Comm. Dis.*, in press.

van den Berg, J. Myoelastic aerodynamic theory of voice production. *J. Speech Hear. Res.*, 1958, *1*, 227–244.

Bernstein, J. Intelligibility and simulated deaf-like speech. *Conference Record*, IEEE Internat. Conf. Acoustics, Speech and Signal Processing, Hartford, Conn., 1977.

Boothroyd, A., Nickerson, R., & Stevens, K. *Temporal patterns in the speech of the deaf–a study in remedial training.* C. V. Hudgins Diagnostic and Research Center, Clarke School for the Deaf, Northampton, Mass., 1974.

Bosma, J. F., Truby, H. M., & Lind, J. Cry motions of the newborn infant. In J. Lind (Ed.), *Newborn infant cry.* Uppsala: Almqvist & Wiksell, 1965.

Breckenridge, J. *Declination as a phonological process.* Unpublished manuscript. Bell Laboratories, 1977.

Calvert, D. *Some acoustic characteristics of the speech of profoundly deaf individuals.* Doctoral dissertation, Stanford University, 1961.

Collier, R. Physiological correlates of intonation patterns. *J. Acoust. Soc. Am.*, 1975, *58*, 249–255.

Forner, L. L., & Hixon, T. J. Respiratory kinematics in profoundly hearing-impaired speakers. *J. Speech Hear. Res.*, 1977, *20*, 373–497.

Fowler, C. *Timing control in speech production.* Doctoral dissertation, University of Connecticut, 1977.

Fromkin, V. A., & Ohala, J. Laryngeal control and a model of speech production. *Working papers in phonetics, University of California at Los Angeles*, 1968, *10*, 98–110.

Harris, K. S. Vowel duration change and its underlying physiological mechanisms. *Lang. Speech*, 1978, *21*, 354–361.

Heidinger, V. A. *An exploratory study of procedures for improving temporal patterns in the speech of deaf children.* Doctoral dissertation, Teachers College, Columbia University, 1972.

t'Hart, J., & Cohen, A. Intonation by rule; a perceptual quest. *J. Phonetics*, 1973, *1*, 309–327.

Hixon, T. J., Klatt, D., & Mead, J. Influence of forced transglottal pressure change on vocal fundamental frequency. *J. Acoust. Soc. Am.*, 1971, *49*, 105(A).

Houde, R. *Instantaneous visual feedback in speech training for the deaf.* Paper presented at the Am. Speech Hear. Assoc. Convention, Detroit, 1973.

John, J. D. J., & Howarth, N. J. The effect of time distortions on the intelligibility of deaf children's speech. *Lang. Speech*, 1965, *8*, 127–134.

Kent, R. D., & Moll, K. L. Articulatory timing in selected consonant sequences. *Brain Lang.*, 1975, *2*, 304–323.

Kewley-Port, D. Computer processing of EMG signals at Haskins Laboratories. *Haskins Stat. Rep. Speech Res.*, 1973, *(SR-33)*, 173–183.

Klatt, D. Vowel lengthening as syntactically determined in a connected discourse. *J. Phonetics*, 1975, *3*, 129–140.

Lang, H. G. *A computer based analysis of the effects of rhythm modification on the intelligibility of the speech of hearing and deaf subjects.* Master's thesis, Rochester Institute of Technology, 1975.

Lehiste, I. *Suprasegmentals.* Cambridge, Mass.: M.I.T. Press, 1970.

Lenneberg, E. H., Rebelsky, F. G., & Nichols, I. A. The vocalization of infants born to deaf and hearing parents. *Human Develop.*, 1965, *8*, 23–37.

Liberman, A. M., Cooper, F. S., Shankweiler, D., & Studdert-Kennedy, M. Why are speech spectrograms hard to read? *American Ann. Deaf*, 1968, *113*, 127–133.

Liberman, A. M., Delattre, P., Gerstman, L., & Cooper, F. S. Tempo of frequency change as a cue for distinguishing classes of speech sounds. *J. Exper. Psych.*, 1956, 52, 127–137.

Lieberman, P. *Intonation, perception and language.* Cambridge, Mass.: M.I.T. Press, 1967.

Lindblom, B. E. F., & Rapp, K. Some temporal regularities of spoken Swedish. *Papers from the Institute of Linguistics*, University of Stockholm, *21*, 1973.

Ling, D. *Speech and the hearing-impaired child: Theory and practice.* Washington, D.C.: A. G. Bell Association for the Deaf, 1976.

Lisker, L., & Abramson, A. S. Some effects of context on voice onset time in English stops. *Lang. Speech*, 1967, *10*, 1–28.

Lofqvist, A. Interarticulator programming in stop production. *Haskins Labs. Stat. Rep. Speech Res.* In press.

Maeda, S. *A characterization of American English intonation.* Doctoral dissertation, Massachusetts Institute of Technology, 1976.

Mavilya, M. P. *Spontaneous vocalization and babbling in hearing-impaired infants.* Doctoral dissertation, Teachers College, Columbia University, 1969.

McGarr, N., & Osberger, M. J. Pitch deviancy and intelligibility of deaf speech. *J. Comm. Dis.*, 1978, *11*, 237–247.

Miller, J. The effect of speaking rate on segmental distinctions. In P. D. Eimas and J. Miller (Eds.), *Perspectives in the study of speech.* Hillside, N.J.: Lawrence Erlbaum Associates, in press.

Monsen, R. B. The production of English stop consonants in the speech of deaf children. *J. Phonetics*, 1976, *4*, 29–41.

Monsen, R. B. Toward measuring how well deaf children speak. *J. Speech Hear. Res.*, 1978, *21*, 197–219.

Nooteboom, S. C. The perceptual reality of some prosodic durations. *J. Phonetics*, 1973, *1*, 25–45.

Osberger, M. J. *The effect of timing errors on the intelligibility of deaf children's speech.* Doctoral dissertation, City University of New York, 1978.

Reilly, A. P. *Syllable nucleus duration in the speech of hearing and deaf children.* Doctoral dissertation, City University of New York, 1979.

Stark, R. Some features of the vocalizations of young deaf children. In J. F. Bosma (Ed.), *Third symposium of oral sensation and perception.* Springfield, Ill.: Charles C Thomas, 1972, 431–446.

Strange, W., Verbrugge, R. R., Shankweiler, D. P., & Edman, T. R. Consonant environment specifies vowel identity. *J. Acoust. Soc. Am.*, 1976, *60*, 213–224.

Whitehead, R. L. *Some respiratory patterns in deaf speech.* Paper presented at the New York State Speech Hear. Assoc. Convention, 1979.

25

Approaches to the Study of the Relationship Between Intelligibility and Physical Properties of Speech

Raymond S. Nickerson and Kenneth N. Stevens

YOU ARE A TEACHER of speech to deaf children. One of your charges is a 15-year-old boy with no measurable hearing, deaf from birth. His speech is slow and halting; he produces syllables at less than half the normal rate, pausing frequently and often at syntactically inappropriate places. No distinction is apparent between stressed and unstressed syllables, either in terms of duration, pitch, or amplitude. Pitch is monotone except for occasional abrupt jumps into falsetto voice. Consonants are frequently omitted; vowels are not consistently differentiated. The voice is breathy and nasal and not pleasant to the ear. Intelligibility varies between 10 percent and 30 percent depending on who measures it and how.

You know that this boy will never have perfect speech, but you believe it should be possible to make his speech much more functional than it is. The time that you can spend with him is limited; he has other things to learn and other interests to pursue, and your responsibilities include teaching several other children besides him. The question is: How can you spend the limited time you have to best advantage? Where should you put your effort so as to realize the greatest possible increase in the functionality of this boy's speech? Where are the points of leverage?

This illustrates, we believe, a fundamental if not *the* fundamental problem that currently faces speech teachers, and speech scientists who are concerned about remediation of the speech of deaf children. The challenge is to be able to determine what there is, not only about the speech of a particular individual, but about a particular utterance, that makes it unintelligible, and to specify exactly how its physical characteristics would have to be changed in order for its intelligibility to be assured.

To answer this question will require much greater understanding than we now have of how intelligibility relates to—depends upon—the physical properties of the speech signal and how these properties in turn relate to—depend upon—the activity of the speech production system. Ideally, one would like to have a model that would relate intelligibility to the physical properties of speech, and that would, in turn, relate these properties to the movements and activities involved in the speech production process. Given such a model, one should be better able not only to diagnose specific speech deficiencies, but to establish training objectives and prescribe training procedures that would maximize the chances of modifying the speech of individual children so as to realize significant intelligibility gains.

Development of such a model will require an enormous effort, in part because of the complexity and variability of normal speech. Different instantiations of a given utterance may differ considerably with respect to objectively measurable properties while maintaining a high degree of intelligibility; consequently the establishment of criteria of normalcy for specific measures is likely to prove to be very difficult. Moreover, what constitutes normal values of many of the measurements that might be obtained on an utterance is likely to depend to some degree on the linguistic and situational context in which the utterance is made. Finally, we expect that the interpretation of measurements often will be interdependent, such that whether the value of a given measurement is considered to be within the range of normalcy will depend on the values of other measurements that are obtained. Another way of making the last point is to say that intelligibility may prove to be sensitive to the interactions among various objective properties as well as to their combined individual effects.

In spite of these difficulties, we believe the development of a model that relates intelligibility to the objective properties of speech, and those properties to production activities, should be a high-priority goal for speech scientists who are concerned about the problem of teaching speech to deaf children. Our aim in this paper is far less ambitious than this, but is in keeping with such a goal. We discuss briefly four different approaches that have been used in the study of the relationship between the objectively measurable properties of speech and intelligibility in the past: (1) correlational studies; (2) studies of the effects of training on the objective and perceptual properties of speech; (3) studies involving the instrumental modification of natural speech; and (4) studies involving manipulation of the parameters of synthesized speech. We note the possibility of a fifth approach, involving the use of coded speech. We present some data to illustrate a sixth approach, which is one that we are currently taking in an effort to understand better the basis for the low intelligibility of some specific speech samples taken from deaf children with whom we have been working. Finally, we illustrate another approach that has not yet been used but that we think has potential for the future.

Correlational Studies

The most common approach to the study of the relationship between intelligibility and the physical properties of speech is that of correlating intelligibility scores with one or more objective measurements obtained on the speech signal. Figures 25.1 and 25.2

FIGURE 25.1

Scatterplot showing relation between intelligibility and ratio of average durations of stressed to unstressed vowels in phrases and sentences for 20 deaf students. Procedures for evaluating the intelligibility are described in Nickerson, Stevens, & Rollins, 1979.

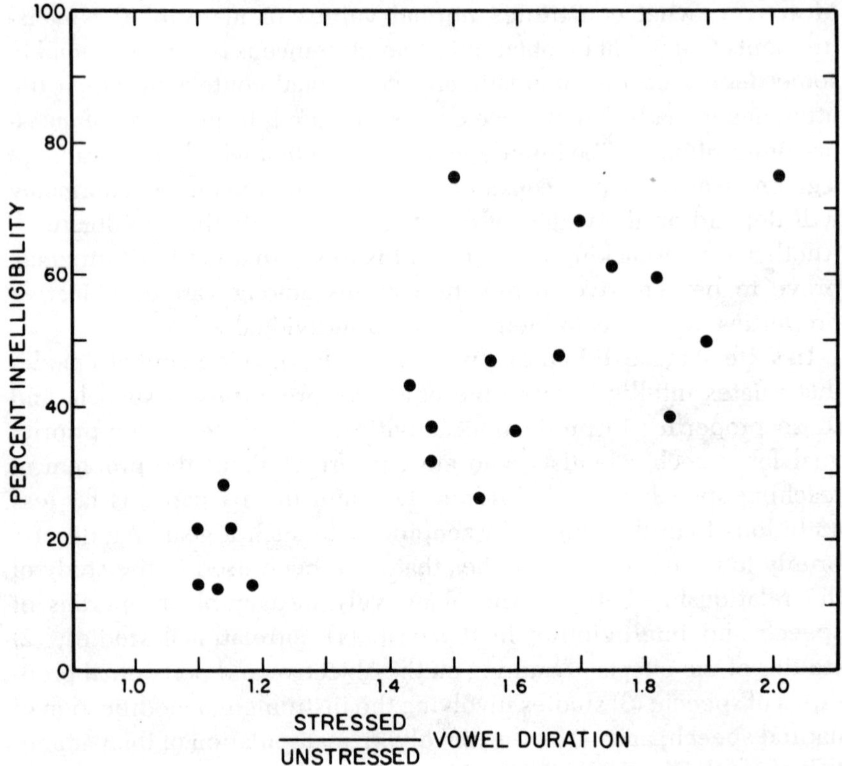

FIGURE 25.2

Scatterplot showing relation between intelligibility and range of fundamental frequency (F_0) in phrases and sentences for 15 deaf students. Procedures for evaluating maxF_0 minF_0, and intelligibility are described in Nickerson, Stevens, & Rollins, 1979.

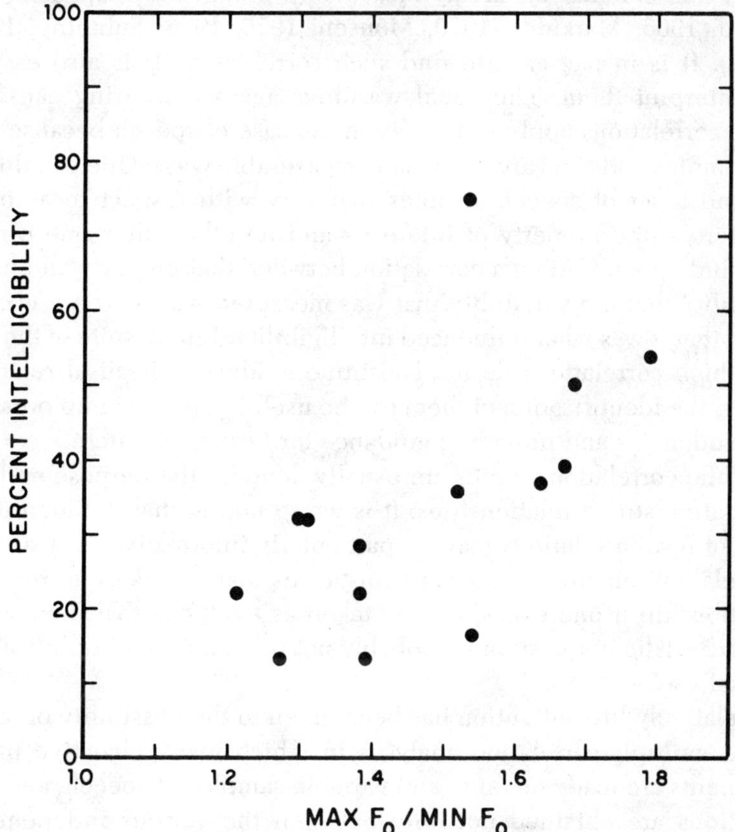

adapted from Nickerson, Stevens, and Rollins (1979) illustrate this approach. Figure 25.1 shows the relationship between intelligibility and the ratio of the durations of stressed and unstressed vowels in speech samples from 20 deaf children. The correlation between intelligibility and the stressed-unstressed vowel ratio in this sample was .79. Figure 25.2 shows, for speech samples from 15 students, the relationship between intelligibility and the range of fundamental frequency (F_0), more specifically the mean of the ratios of the maximum and minimum F_0's used by each child in each utterance. The correlation in this case was .59. We have found similar correlations between intelligibility and other factors, such as the range of second formant frequency and the tendency to glottalize syllable concatenations (Stevens, Nickerson, & Rollins, 1979). In the latter case the correlation was negative.

Other investigators have also noted correlations between intelligibility and certain objectively measurable properties of speech (e.g., Hood, 1966; Markides, 1970; Monsen, 1975, 1976; Subtelny, 1975, 1977). It is in fact easy to find such correlations. It is also easy to misinterpret them. The usual warnings against inferring causality from correlations apply especially in the case of speech because it is so complex and can vary in so many measurable ways. One is unlikely to find a set of speech samples that vary with respect to a single property—the property of interest—and no other; thus one cannot conclude upon finding a correlation between that property and intelligibility that the variability that was measured was all there was, or even that it was what influenced intelligibility. But, in spite of the fact that high correlations do not constitute evidence of causal relationships, the identification of them can be useful in pointing up possible dependencies and providing guidance for further research.

While correlation studies are usually done for the purpose of demonstrating strong relationships, it is worth noting that the identification of low correlations may be particularly informative. A near-zero correlation, obtained under circumstances that are likely to reveal a relationship if one exists, can be taken as evidence that the speech characteristic in question is probably not related to intelligibility in a causal way.

Relatively little attention has been given to the possibility of large-scale multiple-correlation analyses in which many objective measurements are made on large and variable samples of speech, and correlations are obtained not only between the various independent measures and intelligibility but also among the independent measures themselves. One step in this direction has been taken by Monsen (1978), who obtained correlations between intelligibility and nine measurements derived from spectrograms of speech samples from 37 hearing-impaired adolescents. Intelligibility was represented by a score that differentially weighted correctly recognized words according to their frequency of occurrence in the language, greater weight being given to lower-frequency words. A regression analysis showed that three of the nine variables measured bore a multiple correlation with intelligibility of about 0.85, accounting for 73 percent of the variance in the intelligibility scores. These three variables were: (1) the difference between voice-onset times of /t/ and /d/, (2) the difference between the second formant frequencies of /i/ and /o/, and (3) the ability (binary judgment based on spectrographic patterns) to produce liquid and nasal sounds. The first two variables accounted for about 69 percent of the variance in the intelligibility scores.

Monsen cautions that the fact that intelligibility could be predicted reasonably well from only two variables does not mean that these are the only variables that are important as determinants of intelligibility. Other variables that individually correlate with intelligibility are also undoubtedly important; the fact that intelligibility is predictable from a subset of the variables that may affect it is what would be expected if the predictor variables themselves were highly correlated. Monsen makes a similar point with respect to his earlier finding (1975) of a correlation between intelligibility and the temporal differentiation of voiced and voiceless consonants; he notes that the ability to make this distinction correctly may be coupled with an ability to produce many other aspects of speech normally, and, therefore, to produce intelligible speech.

Multiple correlation studies involving speech intelligibility are neither easy to conduct nor trivial to interpret. The selection of predictor variables, speech materials, speakers, and methods of intelligibility measurement requires much thought. Metz, Schiavetti, and Sitler (1979) have noted some of the possible sources of artifacts in such studies. Moreover, obtaining the large number of objective measurements that are required is painstaking and tedious work, at least insofar as those measurements have to be obtained manually. We believe, however, that more studies along the lines of those reported by Monsen could produce information that would considerably increase our understanding of the relationship between the objective properties of speech and intelligibility.

Assessment of Effects of Training

While the primary purpose of training efforts typically is not that of studying the relationship between intelligibility and physical properties of speech, such efforts often do produce data that are relevant to this issue. Usually speech training is undertaken for the purpose of improving speech intelligibility. Consequently, training activities typically include the evaluation of intelligibility before, after, and perhaps at various points during the training program. Insofar as training goals involve the modification of specific aspects of speech in objectively measurable ways, these training programs provide an opportunity to study how intelligibility is affected by whatever modifications of specific aspects of the speech are realized.

The approach is illustrated by a study by John and Howarth (1965) in which an attempt was made to improve certain temporal properties of the speech of 29 deaf children and then to measure the effects of such training on intelligibility. Training consisted of spending a few minutes working on the phrase timing of each of several sentences selected from each child's spontaneous speech. Untrained observers listened to recorded before- and after-training samples. Intelligibility (percent of words recognized) was about 19 percent and 30 percent for the before- and after-training samples, respectively.

It is tempting to conclude that the gains in intelligibility resulted from the improved timing and to take this result as evidence of the dependence of intelligibility on appropriate timing at the suprasegmental level. A problem with this reasoning is that one cannot be sure that timing was the only thing that was affected by the training process. This caution is reinforced by the fact that some investigators have obtained improvement in timing accompanied by no change or even

FIGURE 25.3

Data on vowel nasalization for eight children who were trained in the posture and control of velopharyngeal structures. The boxes show the percent of vowels that were inappropriately nasalized before training began (i) and at the termination of a period of training (f).

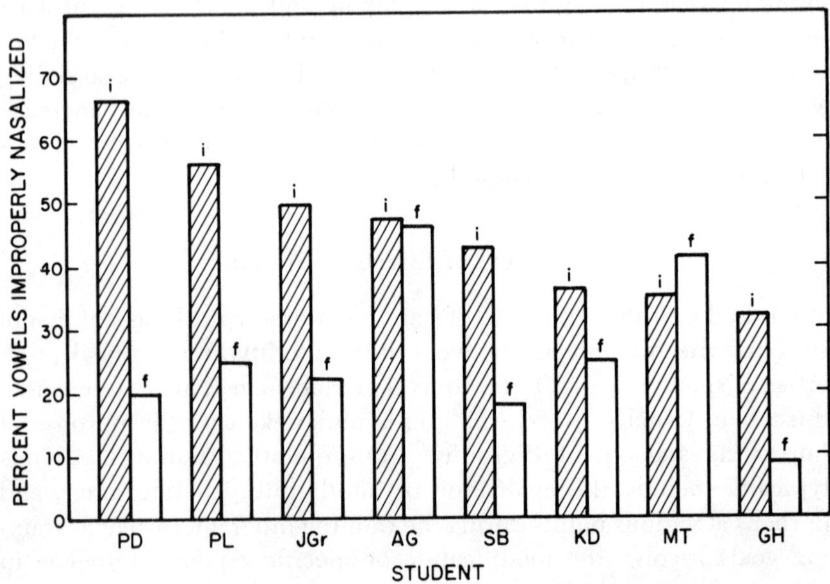

FIGURE 25.4

Number of final vowels (out of a total of 18) for which the final F_0 in the last syllable deviated significantly (by more than 40 Hz) from the minimum F_0 for the speaker. The data indicate, in effect, the degree to which the student failed to place a final F_0 fall on the contour. Data for initial (i) and final (f) recordings are shown.

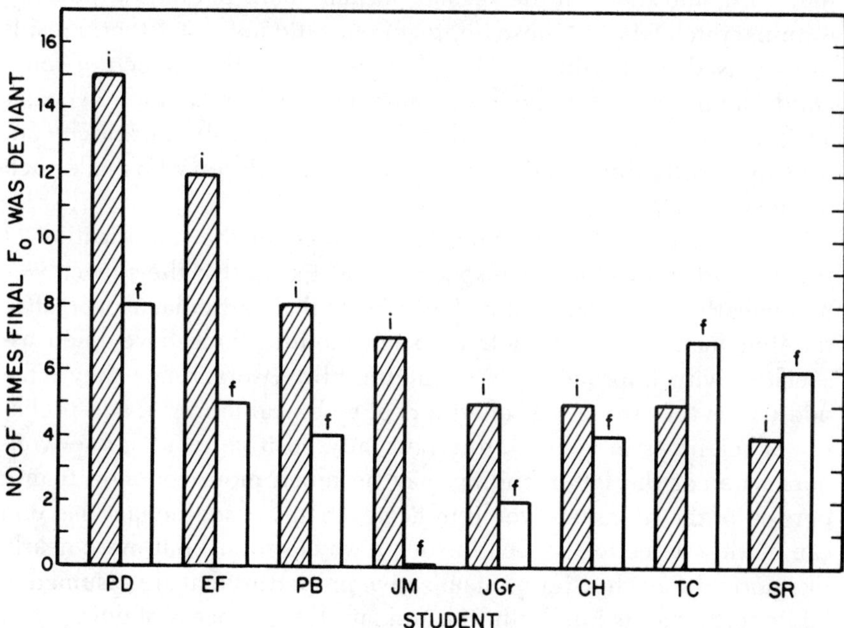

decreases in intelligibility (Houde, 1973; Stratton, 1973). Nor is timing the only speech characteristic of which this is true. Figures 25.3 and 25.4 illustrate some of our own attempts to improve intelligibility by modifying specific objectively measurable properties of speech through training.

Figure 25.3 shows the effect of training on the tendency of eight deaf children to nasalize vowels that should not be nasalized (Nickerson, Stevens, & Rollins, 1979). All these children tended, before training, to nasalize vowels inappropriately and were, therefore, given training in the posture and control of velopharyngeal structures. Nasalization was objectively defined and a procedure was developed for assessing it. (For details, see the report cited above, or Stevens, Nickerson, Boothroyd, and Rollins, 1976.) Figure 25.4 shows the effect of training on the consistency with which a child placed falling pitch contours on the final vowels of declarative sentences. The eight children in this group had been judged to be especially in need of training with respect to several aspects of pitch control, including the production of a terminal fall.

Most of the children in both groups showed improvement over the course of training. Those in the first group reduced the relative frequency with which they nasalized vowels that should not have been nasalized, and those in the second became more likely to produce a terminal pitch fall. But these improvements did not consistently result in increased intelligibility. The intelligibility of the speech of some children improved, but the improvements could not be unequivocally attributed to improvements with respect to nasalization or pitch control; and intelligibility did not increase for all children who made such improvements.

To summarize, often training has resulted in the modification of speech with respect to some specific aspect such that the speech was more nearly normal (at least with respect to that particular aspect) after training than before. Sometimes such modifications have been associated with improvements in intelligibility; sometimes they have not. Given the strong bias of editors of technical journals, and probably of scientists in general, to report only positive results, one wonders whether the latter finding may be much more common than a perusal of the literature would indicate. In any case, the fact that one can modify defective speech in such a way as to make it more nearly like normal speech in terms of objective properties that are assumed to be important to its intelligibility, and fail in the process of doing so to increase its intelligibility, establishes the need for a better understanding of how intelligibility relates to the objective properties of speech. It also points up the frustration of many people working in the field: We know how to change various aspects of speech; we do not know what needs most to be changed. The result also illustrates the need to consider what types of changes may have occurred with respect to speech properties other than those on which training was focused, in assessing how changes in physical properties have affected intelligibility.

From the point of view of increasing our understanding of the relationship between intelligibility and the physical properties of speech, it is not always clear how to interpret either of the possible outcomes of training. If intelligibility is improved, one cannot conclude that the improvement was a direct result of the modification of the property(s) on which training was focused, unless one has good evidence that none of the other properties of the speech was changed as well. If intelligibility is not improved, one cannot conclude that the property in question is therefore not important to intelligibility. It is quite possible that having a certain characteristic may be a necessary but not sufficient condition for intelligibility, in which case improving speech with respect to that condition might or might not lead to improvements in intelligibility. This is not to suggest that efforts should not be made to determine the effects of training on intelligibility; we simply mean to note that such efforts may well yield results that are ambiguous with respect to the question of how intelligibility relates to the physical properties of speech.

Instrumental Modification of Natural Speech

If enough were known about the relationship between intelligibility and the physical properties of speech, one should be able to increase the intelligibility of defective speech by recording it and modifying its physical properties instrumentally in appropriate ways. Levitt (1973) did some early exploratory work along these lines. More recently, Osberger (1978) has reported a study that nicely demonstrates the approach.

Speakers with normal hearing differentiate between stressed and unstressed vowels, in part, by making the former longer in duration than the latter, often by a factor of two or three. Deaf speakers sometimes fail to adequately differentiate stressed and unstressed vowels in this way. The speech of deaf persons also often differs temporally from that of hearing persons with respect to the frequency and placement of pauses: Deaf speakers use more and longer pauses than hearing speakers and are more likely to insert them in syntactically inappropriate places. Osberger recorded the speech of several deaf children and attempted to improve its intelligibility by instrumentally modifying the durations of vowels and pauses so as to make the speech more nearly like that of hearing children with respect to these temporal aspects. The adjustments that were made to the relative durations of stressed and unstressed vowels increased intelligibility by a small amount, whereas the changes in pause duration produced a decrease in intelligibility.

The results with respect to pauses again demonstrate the fact that making speech more nearly normal with respect to some particular feature will not necessarily increase overall intelligibility. And again, it does not follow from such a finding that the feature in question has no relevance for intelligibility; it could be that the effect of that feature interacts with that of others in complicated ways. In the case of suprasegmental timing, for example, it may be that gross deficiencies are sufficient to assure low intelligibility, whereas proper timing is not sufficient to assure high intelligibility if, say, the speech is deficient with respect to its phonetic composition.

The converse of what Osberger has done also represents a possible way of studying how intelligibility relates to the physical properties of speech. One could take recorded speech that is highly intelligible and observe the effects on intelligibility of distorting it instrumentally in different ways.

One of the limitations of the approach of instrumentally manipulating recorded speech is the fact that many of the aspects that one might want to modify are not easily manipulated individually. To change the pitch contour while leaving everything else the same, for example, or to denasalize all the nasal consonants without affecting other aspects, are difficult things to do. A way around some of these difficulties is to use synthesized rather than natural speech, thereby increasing somewhat the feasibility of investigating the effects of changing features one at a time, a point to which we will return.

Manipulation of Synthesized Speech

Speech scientists working on systems or procedures for synthesizing speech are usually interested in designing synthesizers that will produce speech that is highly intelligible and as natural-sounding as possible. The existence of systems that are capable of producing high-quality speech offers an opportunity, however, for systematically exploring the effect on intelligibility of modifying the objective properties of the synthesized speech in specific ways. The possibility also exists of attempting to synthesize speech that resembles the speech produced by particular deaf individuals. A study of how the parameters of the speech synthesis algorithm have to be adjusted to produce the desired effects should be suggestive with respect to how specific characteristics of the speech of a deaf person may be accounted for in terms of the production process.

Little has yet been done along these lines, and synthesis technology has some way to go before it can produce truly natural sounding speech. One study by Huggins (1978), however, illustrates the approach and gives some indication of the possibilities. Using a synthesis program developed by Klatt (1972), Huggins synthesized several sentences from a set used at the Clarke School for the Deaf (Magner, 1972) in the testing of the intelligibility of the speech of deaf children. Four versions of the sentences were synthesized: one in which the durations and pitch levels of segments were appropriate to normal stress patterns; one in which durations were inappropriately assigned; one in which pitch levels were inappropriately assigned; and one in which both durations and pitch levels were inappropriately assigned. The misassignment of durations adversely affected intelligibility (dropping it from 86 percent to 52 percent words correct) as did the misassignment of pitch levels (63 percent correct). Simultaneous misassignment of both durations and pitch levels also decreased intelligibility, but by not much more than did misassignment of durations alone (48 percent correct).

The use of synthetic speech to explore systematically the relationship between intelligibility and the objective properties of speech is, we believe, a very promising approach to the problem because it gives the investigator control over the variables of interest. Moreover, the effectiveness of the approach should increase as speech synthesis algorithms are improved, and especially as better models are developed to relate the parameters of these algorithms to the activity of the natural speech production system. Given adequate models, one should be able to explore the effect on both intelligibility and the objective properties of speech of specific changes in the synthesizer, and to say how the natural speech production system would have to behave in order to produce the same effects.

Manipulation of Coded Speech

A possible approach that would be similar in many respects to that of using synthesized speech is that of using natural speech that has been digitally coded (Nickerson & Stevens, 1977). Several digital coding procedures have been developed for the purpose of decreasing the band-width requirements of voice communication systems (Flanagan, 1972). Coding procedures differ considerably in details, but they all follow the same general approach of analyzing the speech signal in order to produce a representation of it in terms of certain basic parameters such as vocal-tract excitation, fundamental frequency, formant frequencies, and so forth. The values of these parameters, rather than the speech signal itself, are transmitted over the communication channel at a great savings in band-width requirements. At the receiving end of the transmission the parameters are used to drive a speech production system that will, hopefully, yield speech that is similar in sound to that which was originally produced by the speaker at the sending end.

Coded speech could be used in much the same way as could synthesized speech to investigate systematically the effects on intelligibility of distorting the speech signal in specific ways. A possible advantage in the use of coded, as opposed to synthesized, speech is the fact that one starts with a speech signal that is known to be "natural" inasmuch as it was produced by a human speaker.

To our knowledge, coded speech has not been used explicitly to investigate the relationship between intelligibility and the physical properties of speech; however, some work has been done on the problem of evaluating the intelligibility and quality of speech processed by different vocoders and identifying the perceptual dimensions in terms of which listener evaluations of the outputs of different vocoders seem to be made (Nickerson & Huggins, 1977; Viswanathan, Makhoul, & Huggins, 1978).

Detailed Phonetic Analysis

Each of the above-mentioned approaches to the study of the relationship between intelligibility and the physical properties of speech has something to recommend it. The work that has already been done with these approaches has provided most of the knowledge we currently have about this relationship, and further work along all of these lines should increase that knowledge. In what follows, we present some data that illustrate an approach to the study of how intelligibility relates to the objective properties of speech; the approach differs somewhat from each of those described above. It involves detailed inspection of certain aspects of speech samples, representing different degrees of intelligibility, with a view to identifying specific deficiencies that may account for the intelligibility differences.

We do not mean to suggest that the idea of comparing more and less intelligible speech with respect to specific physical properties is new, because it is not. Ando and Canter (1969) made measurements of intensity, duration, and fundamental frequency on words such as *contrast, conflict,* and *contest* when used as a noun and when used as a verb by hearing and deaf speakers. The results indicated that the deaf speakers used intensity, duration, and fundamental frequency less consistently than did the hearing speakers to signal primary stress, and that listeners frequently failed to perceive stress to be on the syllable intended by the deaf speakers. Angelocci, Kopp, and Holbrook (1970) measured frequency and amplitude of the fundamental and three lowest formants in the steady-state portions of several vowels spoken within an h-d context by deaf and hearing adolescent boys. The mean fundamental frequency was higher for the deaf than for the hearing boys for all vowels. The range of mean values of F_1 and F_2 was greater for the hearing than for the deaf boys; but plots of F_2 against F_1 showed the degree of overlap among areas representing different vowels to be much greater for the speech of the deaf, which is to say the deaf speakers showed less distinction between vowels with respect to F_1 and F_2 values.

Other studies could also be cited that have produced data useful in characterizing how speech that is produced by deaf speakers tends to differ physically from that produced by hearing speakers. These data do not, however, provide a firm basis for diagnosing the inadequacies in the speech of a specific child and for specifying objectives and procedures for training to rectify those inadequacies.

The approach on which we wish to focus differs from that represented by these examples primarily in its aim. The intent is not to demonstrate that samples of intelligible speech differ from samples of unintelligible speech, on the average, with respect to some specific physical property or properties, but rather to identify a variety of aspects of an individual speech sample that might account for its lack of intelligibility. We would like ultimately to be able to relate the properties that are identified as being responsible for the lack of intelligibility to the particular aspects of the speech production process that are responsible for those properties. In other words, the ultimate goal is to define an approach that will yield not only a diagnosis of what is wrong with the physical characteristics of the speech, but a prescription that will specify how the speech production process must be modified in order to correct the deficiencies. We seek a set of measurements that will be predictive of intelligibility on the one hand and indicative of what is wrong with the production process on the other. We do not claim to know what measurements should be taken to realize this goal. We report here only the results of an initial effort to explore some possibilities.

Selection of the aspects of speech that are to be inspected is made on the basis of assumptions about where in the acoustic signal the information that is most critical to speech perception lies. What one can hope to accomplish by this approach is to identify specific, and presumably important, ways in which intelligible and unintelligible speech differ. Then, the importance of such differences could be further clarified with some of the procedures mentioned above (in which defective speech is modified systematically by instrumental manipulation, or the parameters of a synthesizer or vocoder are set so as to produce speech with specified defective characteristics).

The choice of the physical properties to which the data we shall report relate is based on currently available information about the acoustic attributes that provide a listener with the necessary cues for speech perception. This information comes from a variety of sources, including studies of the acoustic characteristics of speech sounds, and studies of the perception of speech. (See, for example, Stevens & House, 1972; Studdert-Kennedy, 1975.) In particular, we draw upon the results of recent studies of the ability of observers to read spectrograms—studies that we believe have provided new insights into the variety of acoustic attributes that give information about the role of particular phonetic features in speech perception.

These studies have suggested that the important acoustic information in speech lies in two types of regions: (1) the points in time at which the acoustic parameters are changing rapidly, almost in a discontinuous manner—corresponding to times when the articulatory structures are moving toward or away from a constricted consonantal configuration; and (2) the syllable nuclei where the vocal-tract opening is at its widest during the syllable. These time regions are those at which maximum information is conveyed concerning the various phonetic features related to such important aspects of speech as place of articulation, manner of articulation, and voicing. Portions of the speech signal representing transitions between regions of abrupt change and regions of relatively steady states could also provide information concerning certain phonetic features. It is convenient, however, to think of these transition regions as the acoustic material that provides smooth links or connections between the two regions of primary interest (Cole & Scott, 1974; Stevens & Blumstein, 1978). One goal of a physical analysis of the speech of the deaf, then, might be to obtain quantitative measures of the adequacy of each consonantal event and each syllable nucleus. We expect that a decrease in the adequacy of production of speech as reflected in such measures will be associated with a reduction in intelligibility.

The procedure for carrying out this kind of analysis is illustrated in the spectrogram in Figure 25.5. This spectrogram represents the sentence "Five boys climbed up the hill" spoken by a deaf child. (Figure 25.6 shows a spectrogram of the same sentence spoken by a normal-hearing adult male.) At each of the appropriate points representing consonantal events, three types of assessment are made: (1) whether the consonantal place of articulation is correctly represented in the

FIGURE 25.5
Spectrogram of the sentence "Five boys climbed up the hill" spoken by a deaf child.

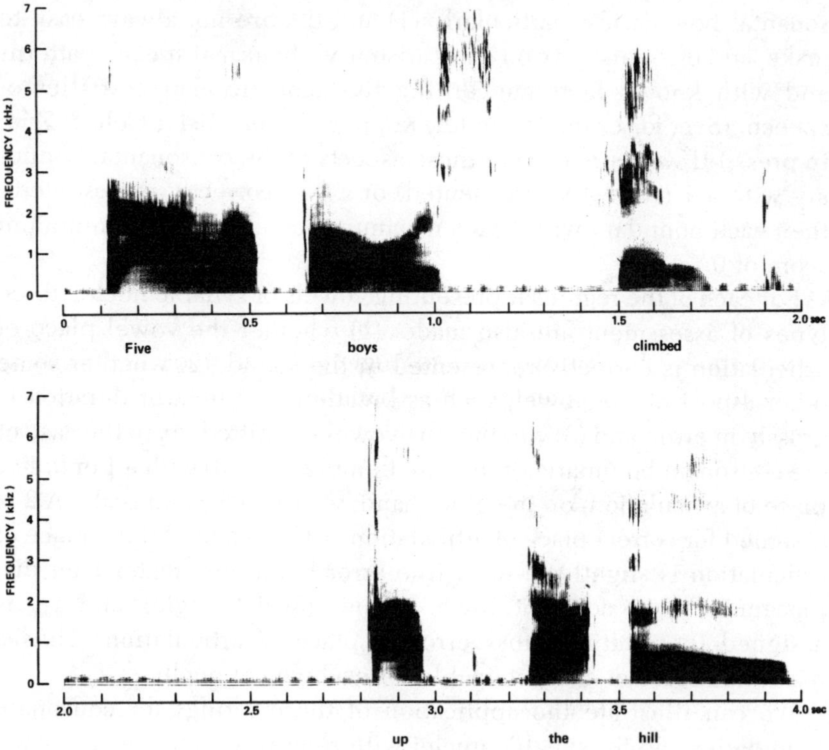

FIGURE 25.6
Spectrogram of the sentence "Five boys climbed up the hill" spoken by a normal-hearing adult male.

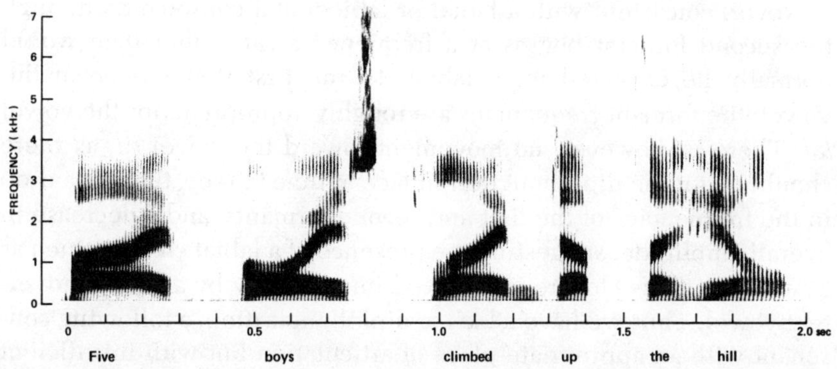

sound, (2) whether the manner of articulation or the voicing characteristic of the consonant segment is correctly represented, and (3) whether an extra boundary is inserted, or the correct boundary is inadvertently omitted. Judgments regarding these aspects of the consonantal boundaries, particularly (1) and (2), are not always easy to make, and one must rely on comparisons with normal speech patterns and with known facts concerning the acoustic characteristics of speech. (See, for example, Potter, Kopp, & Green, 1947; Cole & Zue, in press.) If we score each of these aspects of the consonantal boundary with a 1 (correctly represented) or a 0 (incorrectly represented), then each boundary will have a maximum score of 3, and a minimum score of 0.

For each of the regions representing vowels or syllable nuclei, three types of assessment are also made: (1) whether the vowel place of articulation is correctly represented in the sound, (2) whether some other aspect of the vowel, such as breathiness, pitch, or duration is grossly in error, and (3) whether the vowel is omitted. As in the case of the consonant boundaries, we score items (2) and (3) with a 1 or 0. For place of articulation, on the other hand, we use a 3-point scale. A 2 is assigned for correct place of articulation, a 1 is assigned if the place of articulation is slightly in error (the error being no greater than displacement to an adjacent vowel in the vowel triangle), and a 0 is assigned for a rather gross error in place of articulation. Thus a maximum score of 4 is obtainable for each vowel nucleus.

We can illustrate the application of these ratings for consonant boundaries and for syllabic nuclei with reference to the spectrogram in Figure 25.5. Results of the rating scheme for this example are given in Table 25.A. At the initial boundary /f/, there is an abrupt onset of voicing, and no evidence of frication noise for the /f/ immediately preceding voicing onset. The onsets of the formants in the vowel are, however, consistent with a labial or labiodental consonant, although the second formant begins at a frequency a bit higher than would normally be expected for a labial. In the first 0.2–0.3 sec of the vowel, the formant frequencies are roughly appropriate for the vowel /a/. There is, however, no movement toward the vowel /i/, as there should be for the diphthong/aɪ/. In fact, at time 0.3 sec, there is a drop in the frequencies of the first and second formants, and a decrease in overall amplitude, suggesting the presence of a labial closure, such as a /w/ or /v/. This closure is followed immediately by a brief inadvertent vowel. Thus we have a lack of diphthongization, a following consonant with an appropriate place of articulation but with insufficient

TABLE 25.A

Ratings of consonantal boundaries and vowel nuclei for the utterance "Five boys climbed up the hill" produced by a deaf student (DK, 6/77).

CONSONANTAL BOUNDARIES

	Place	Manner and Voicing	Omission or Insertion	Total	
fa	1	0	1	2	
iv	1	0	1	2	
vb	0	0	0	0	
bo	1	1	1	3	
iz	1	0	1	2	
zk	0	1	1	2	
kl	0	0	0	0	
la	1	0	1	2	
im	1	1	1	3	
md	1	0	1	2	
dʌ	0	0	1	1	
ʌp	1	1	1	3	
pð	1	0	1	2	
ðə	1	0	1	2	
əh	1	0	1	2	
hɪ	1	0	1	2	
ɪl	0	1	1	2	
	12/17	7/17	14	32/51	= 63%

VOWEL NUCLEI

	Place	Vowel Manner	Omission	Total	
ai	0	1	1	2	
oi	1	0	1	2	
ai	0	0	1	1	
ʌ	2	1	1	4	
ə	2	1	1	4	
ɪ	0	0	1	1	
	5/12	3/6	6/6	14/30	= 47%

closure (i.e., inappropriate manner of articulation), and an extra inserted syllable.

At time 0.5 sec, there is a silent interval corresponding to closure for the consonant /b/, followed by release of the consonant, with what appears to be a proper burst and initiation of the vowel spectrum. The vowel in the next .15 sec following the consonantal release has a low first and second formant corresponding to the vowel /ɔ/. However, at time 0.8 sec, there is a lowering of the second formant and a decrease in the amplitude, again corresponding to a labial consonant such as /n/ or /w/. Following this quasi-consonantal interval there is a rise in amplitude again, and an increase in the second formant frequency as the articulators move toward the fricative consonant. This formant movement could be construed as a partial attempt to move toward an /i/-like sound to complete the diphthong /ai/, but it is an inadequate rendition of the diphthong.

Some kind of fricative is produced following the vowel, and it has a high-frequency noise characteristic of /s/. However, this noise is much weaker than would normally be expected for this consonant. Apparently the airstream for the fricative is not being directed against the teeth, and thus insufficient turbulence noise energy is generated. Furthermore, the spectrum of the fricative at the beginning and end differs from the spectrum in the middle. Apparently the position of the tongue blade is not suitably stable throughout the production of the sound.

Following the fricative there seems to be an interval of silence, as there should be preceding the release of the stop consonant /k/ in the next word. However, the release of this consonant is not sufficiently abrupt. The time interval (1.4 to 1.5 sec) is closer to what would be appropriate for some kind of weak fricative, such as an /x/. Thus the manner of articulation for the /k/ is in error, although the place of articulation is roughly correct.

There is no evidence for an /l/ following the release of /k/. Rather, the nucleus for the vowel has a low first formant and a high second formant, and is similar to the vowel /i/. Thus there is an omitted segment /l/ and an inappropriate vowel.

Following the vowel, the nasal /m/ seems to be produced properly, as evidenced by the low-frequency energy for the nasal murmur, and the falling second-formant frequency. The nasal is followed by a stop gap and by a stop release. The spectrum of the release burst seems to have a peak at around 2000 Hz—too low for an alveolar consonant. The place of articulation for the stop is too far back in the vocal tract.

There is a long pause between the two words *climbed* and *up*, and the /d/ on the end of *climbed* is not released into the vowel of *up*, as it would be for a hearing speaker. Rather, the word *up* begins with a glottal stop. The vowel formant frequencies are appropriate for /ʌ/, and there is a following silent interval corresponding to the voiceless stop consonant /p/. A brief noise burst corresponding to the /p/ release is visible. The release of the initial consonant in *the* appears to be a stop release (rather than a fricative), but the formant transitions in the following vowel (downward movements of F_2 and F_3) are consistent with a dental consonant. The formant frequencies for the vowel in *the* are in the proper range.

Between the words *the* and *hill* there is a silent interval, suggesting that a glottal stop was substituted for the /h/. The abrupt onset of the final vowel reinforces this observation. The vowel in *hill* begins with a second formant frequency that is not sufficiently high for the vowel /ɪ/. The second formant does not show a fall at the end of the word, as it should for the final consonant /l/, although the continued voicing through the word is evidenced for a final sonorant consonant.

The ratings given in Table 25.A show that this child produces 12/17 or 70 percent of the consonantal events with correct place of articulation, but only about 40 percent of these events with correct manner of articulation. Of the six vowels, only two are produced with correct place of articulation (rating of 2), and three of the vowels (all high front vowels) are produced with grossly incorrect articulation. The overall intelligibility of the speech of this child was 38 percent for words in read sentences.

An analysis similar to that just described has been carried out for other utterances produced by the same child, DK, in 10/76, i.e., almost one year earlier. The overall performance is similar to that for the sentence given in Figure 25.5: 67 percent correct actualization of events indicating consonant place, and 26 percent for consonant manner. Clearly, this child is especially deficient in producing correct voicing and frication, and in linking the sounds of one word with the sounds of the adjacent word. All of these deficiencies result in a lowered performance in the category manner of articulation and voicing.

We believe that, with sufficient experience, it will be possible to interpret spectrograms, perhaps in combination with careful listening and more detailed spectral analysis in selected portions of the signal, to yield a quantitative evaluation of the speech problems of individual deaf speakers. As more becomes known about the cues that are necessary for the identification of particular phonetic segments, it will be possible to make more precise estimates of which cues are not being effectively represented in the signal, and to relate these estimates to loss of intelligibility.

Automated Speech Understanding

Still another possible approach to the study of the relationship between intelligibility and the physical properties of speech—and one that has not been used in the past—involves the application of the technology that has been developed in the effort to provide computers with a speech understanding capability. We have commented on this possibility in another place (Nickerson & Stevens, 1977). When computer-based speech understanding systems are sufficiently powerful to understand a broad range of normal speech as well, or nearly as well, as human listeners, we believe they should be useful in helping to diagnose objectively what is wrong with defective speech, and how it would have to be changed in order to be made intelligible. This comment assumes that the speech understanding algorithms that will be most successful will utilize the same sorts of analytic and constructive processes to assign meaning to the speech signal as does the human listener. This may or may not prove to be a correct assumption, but it seems to be a reasonable one to make at this point in time.

Computer-based speech understanding systems are not yet sufficiently powerful to understand speech as well, or even nearly as well, as a human listener. Are they sufficiently far along toward that goal to be helpful in diagnosing speech problems and prescribing remedial training? We think perhaps they are, which is to say that we believe an explicit effort to apply them in this way would probably yield some useful results. Whether this would be a cost-effective effort at the present time, relative to other things that can be done, is not clear. As the costs of computing resources continue to drop, however, the application of automated speech-understanding in this way should become an increasingly attractive possibility.

Figure 25.7 shows the kind of output one part of one such speech understanding system can produce.[1] The program that produces this analysis is the Automatic Phoneme Recognizer, which is part of a larger system developed under a program of research on computer understanding of speech (Woods et al., 1976; Schwartz & Cook, 1977). The larger system includes several other components that would bring syntactic, semantic, and pragmatic information to bear on the problem of speech understanding. The Automatic Phoneme Recognizer does not utilize such information, but attempts to identify a

[1]We are indebted to Richard Schwartz for doing the analyses represented in Figures 25.7 and 25.8, and helping us interpret the results.

FIGURE 25.7
Output from the Automatic Phoneme Recognizer, given the utterance "Five boys climbed up the hill' spoken by a normal-hearing adult.

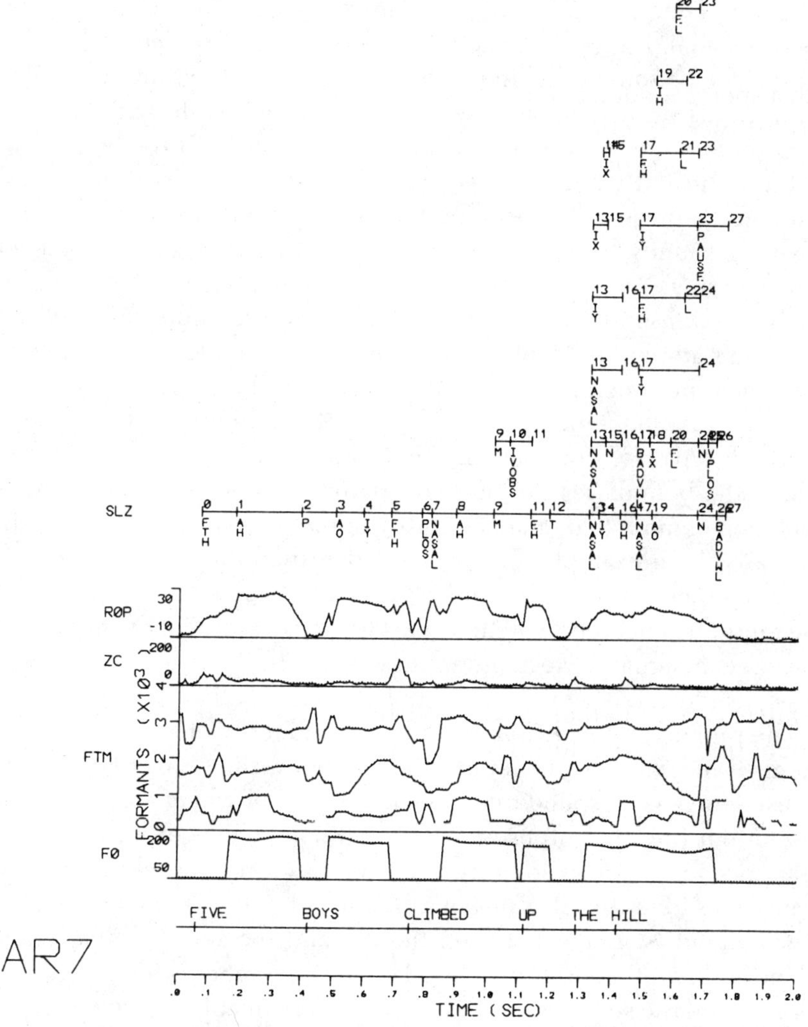

sequence of phonemes in continuous speech by using only that information that is explicitly contained within the speech signal.

The program uses a relatively small set of easily measured features to distinguish the phonemes. The feature parameters are adjusted to be appropriate for a speaker who is cooperative and talking at a "normal" rate. With such a speaker, it is capable of identifying about 60 percent of the phonemes correctly with its first choice. The speaker whose speech is represented in Figure 25.7 was an adult female with normal hearing. The utterance (indicated at the bottom of the figure) was "Five boys climbed up the hill."

The program is capable of performing a variety of analyses on the speech signal. Figure 25.7 shows the output from a selected subset of these. The bottom of the line on the figure shows the time scale. The utterance is printed immediately above the time scale with each tic mark on the line representing the approximate time of the beginning of the indicated word. The six plots immediately above the printed utterance represent, from the bottom up, the fundamental frequency of voiced sounds, the frequencies of the first three formants, the rate of zero crossings, and the energy in the pre-emphasized signal. The analysis represented by the top half of the figure is the result of the program's attempt to identify the phoneme sequence. To identify this sequence the program must do two things: (1) locate the boundaries between the phonemes, and (2) identify the phoneme between each successive pair of boundaries. When the program is uncertain as to where the boundaries lie, that uncertainty is reflected by the representation of more than one possibility in the output of the analysis. In the case of our example, the program identified the first nine boundaries unequivocally but was uncertain with respect to the location of the tenth. Its uncertainty with respect to how to segment the portion of the speech signal corresponding to the last two words became very large, as indicated by the number of alternatives that it proposed.

The program's conclusion regarding the identity of each of the segments is indicated by the letters directly below the segment numbers. These letters correspond to a code, the details of which are not essential for our present purposes. We should note, however, that the program does not always identify a segment as a unique phoneme and sometimes identifies it as one of a member of a class. For example, the 0th segment (segment between the 0th and the first boundaries) is identified as either an F or a TH. The sixth segment is identified as a plosive and the seventh as a nasal sound. Presumably as knowledge of the defining characteristics of individual phonemes is increased, more effective identification programs can be developed. There is probably a limit, however, to how far one can go toward identifying speech sounds strictly on the basis of local signal analysis and without resource to contextual and other cues. We know that the speech signal often does not contain the cues that are necessary to identify these components, and we hear them only because we infer them from the existence of other types of cues.

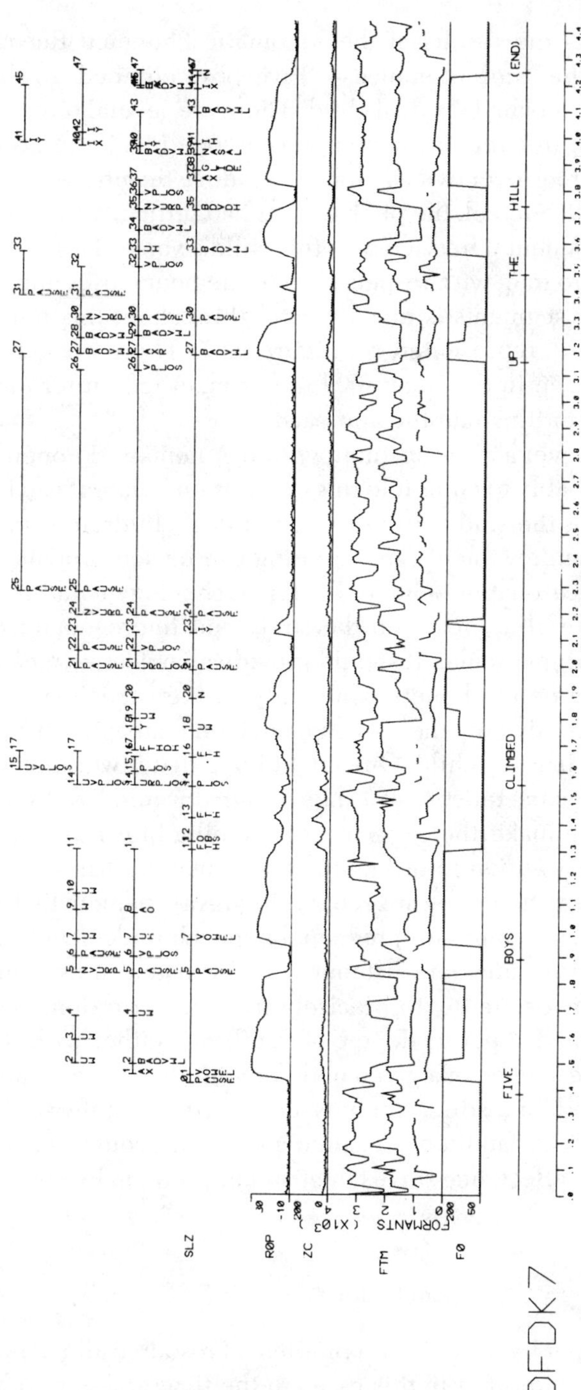

FIGURE 25.8

Output from the Automatic Phoneme Recognizer, given the utterance "Five boys climbed up the hill" spoken by a deaf child.

Figure 25.8 shows the results of the Automatic Phoneme Recognizer's analysis of the same utterance—"Five boys climbed up the hill"—but this time spoken by a deaf child. There are several obvious differences between this representation and the one in Figure 25.7. First, the deaf child took over twice as long to produce the utterance as did the hearing adult. Second, the pitch tracker had difficulty tracking changes in the fundamental frequency of this child's voice. Third, the uncertainty of the program with respect both to the boundaries and to the identities of the segments is much greater throughout this utterance than for the one represented by Figure 25.7. There are other things that can be seen in this analysis, but our main reason for presenting it is simply to illustrate the approach.

There is, we believe, a need to improve the Automatic Phoneme Recognizer and probably to tailor it to this application before it can be a very useful tool for the study of the speech of deaf children. Given that the necessary improvements and tailoring can be accomplished, however, it seems reasonable to hope that this technology could represent one more useful approach to the study and improvement of speech of the deaf. In particular, it should provide an objective means of assessing the degree of phonetic ambiguity in the speech signal, and it should help clarify how the speech of a given deaf child differs from that of a given hearing child. One might hope that it would help determine how the characteristics of a speech signal would have to be changed in order to make the speech more intelligible. Finally, it could represent the solution to one of the problems that has always complicated the task of assessing speech intelligibility, namely that of listener variability. In a computer program for speech understanding, what one has is a truly invariant listener that can listen to as many speech samples as is desired with precisely the same criterion. One need not be concerned about its degree of familiarity either with the characteristics of the speech of a given child or with the speech material that is being used for testing. Nor must one worry about the possibility of this degree of familiarity changing over the course of the listening session. In effect, one solves the listener problem by getting rid of the listener.

Conclusion

We began this paper by describing a problem of resource allocation. The resources to be allocated in this case are the time and energy of teachers and students, and the efforts of technologists to find ways to apply technology to help them accomplish their teaching and learning goals. We certainly have not solved the problem in this paper, but hopefully we have made a case for asserting that it is a critical problem, and one that deserves more attention than it has received from speech scientists who have an interest in facilitating the teaching of speech to deaf children. We have argued that an essential component of—if not the key to—solving the resource allocation problem is a better understanding of how intelligibility relates to physical properties of speech. We have described briefly several approaches that have been taken in the study of that relationship and have argued for more concerted efforts to undertake the kinds of analyses that would permit one to determine why particular utterances are unintelligible and what would have to be done to fix them. Finally, we have promoted the notion that computer-based procedures for producing or understanding speech may represent tools with some potential for fruitful application to this problem area.

REFERENCES

Ando, K. & Canter, G. A study of syllabic stress in some English words as produced by deaf and normally hearing speakers. *Lang. Speech,* 1969, *12,* 247–255.

Angelocci, A. A., Kopp, G. A., & Holbrook, A. The vowel formants of deaf and normal hearing 11- to 14-year-old boys. *J. Speech Hear. Dis.,* 1970, *29,* 156–170.

Cole, R. A., & Scott, B. Towards a theory of speech perception. *Psych. Rev.,* 1974, *81,* 348–374.

Cole, R. A., & Zue, V. W. Speech as eyes see it. In R. S. Nickerson (Ed.), *Attention & performance VIII.* Hillsdale, N.J.: Lawrence Erlbaum Associates, in press.

Flanagan, J. L. *Speech analysis synthesis and perception,* 2nd ed. New York: Springer-Verlag, 1972.

Hood, R. B. *Some physical concomitants of the perception of speech rhythm of the deaf.* Doctoral dissertation, Stanford University, 1966.

Houde, R. A. *Instantaneous visual feedback in speech training for the deaf.* Paper presented at the American Speech and Hearing Association Convention, Detroit, 1973.

Huggins, A. W. F. Speech timing and intelligibility. In J. Requin (Ed.), *Attention & performance VII.* Hillsdale, N.J.: Lawrence Erlbaum Associates, 1978.

John, J. E. J., & Howarth, J. N. The effect of time distortions on the intelligibility of deaf children's speech. *Lang. Speech,* 1965, *8,* 127–134.

Klatt, D. H. Acoustic theory of terminal analog speech synthesis. *Proceedings of 1972 International Conference on Speech Communication and Processing,* Boston. IEEE Catalog No. 72, CHO 596-7, AE, 1972, 131–135.

Levitt, H. Speech processing aids for the deaf: An overview. *IEEE Transactions on Audio and Electro. Acoustics,* 1973, AU-21, 269–273.

Magner, N. *A speech intelligibility test for deaf children.* Northampton, Mass.: Clarke School for the Deaf, 1972.

Markides, A. The speech of deaf and partially-hearing children with special reference to factors affecting intelligibility. *Brit. J. Comm. Dis.,* 1970, *5,* 126–140.

Metz, D., Schiavetti, N., & Sitler, R. *Toward an objective description of the dependent and independent variables associated with intelligibility.* Paper presented at the Institute of Speech Assessment and Speech Improvement, National Technical Institute for the Deaf, Rochester, 1979.

Monsen, R. B. *The stop consonants: Some ways that deaf children produce them.* Communication, International Congress on Education of the Deaf, Tokyo, Japan, 1975.

Monsen, R. B. The production of English stop consonants in the speech of deaf children. *J. Phonet.*, 1976, *4*, 29–41.

Monsen, R. Toward measuring how well hearing-impaired children speak. *J. Speech & Hear. Res.*, 1978, *21*, 197–219.

Nickerson, R. S., & Huggins, A. W. F. *The assessment of speech quality.* BBN Report No. 3486 prepared for the Defense Advanced Research Projects Agency, 1977.

Nickerson, R. S., & Stevens, K. N. Implications for the hearing-impaired of computer-related research in human communication. *J. Acoust. Soc. Am.*, 1977, *62*, Abstract.

Nickerson, R. S., Stevens, K. N., & Rollins, A. M. *Research on computer based speech diagnosis and speech training aids for the deaf.* Final Report on Contract No. 300-76-0116, BBN Report No. 4029, 1979.

Osberger, M. J. *The effect of timing errors on the intelligibility of deaf children's speech.* Doctoral dissertation, City University of New York, 1978.

Potter, R. K., Kopp, G. A., & Green H. C. *Visible speech.* New York: Van Nostrand, 1947.

Schwartz, R. M., & Cook, C. *Advanced acoustic techniques in automated speech understanding.* IEEE International Conference on Acoustics, Speech, and Signal Processing, Hartford, Conn., 1977.

Stevens, K. N., & Blumstein, S. E. Invariant cues for place of articulation in stop consonants. *J. Acoust. Soc. Am.*, 1978, *64*, 1358–1368.

Stevens, K. N., & House, A. S. Speech perception. In J. V. Tobias (Ed.), *Foundations of modern auditory theory, Volume II.* New York: Academic Press, 1972.

Stevens, K. N., Nickerson, R. S., Boothroyd, A., & Rollins, A. M. Assessment of nasalization in the speech of deaf children. *J. Speech Hear. Dis.*, 1976, *19*, 393–416.

Stratton, W. D. *Intonation feedback for the deaf through the tactile sense.* Thesis, Massachusetts Institute of Technology, 1973.

Studdert-Kennedy, M. The perception of speech. In T. A. Sebeok (Ed.), *Current trends in linguistics.* The Hague: Mouton, 1975.

Subtelny, J. D. Speech assessment of the deaf adult. *J. Acad. Rehab. Aud.*, 1975, *8*, 110–116.

Subtelny, J. D. Assessment of speech with implications for training. In F. Bess (Ed.), *Childhood deafness: Causation, assessment, and management.* New York: Grune and Stratton, 1977.

Viswanathan, R., Makhoul, J. I., & Huggins, A. W. F. *Speech compression and evaluation.* BBN Report No. 3794 prepared for the Advanced Research Projects Agency, 1978.

Woods, W. A., Bates, M., Brown, G., Bruce, B., Cook, C., Klovstad, J., Makhoul, J., Nash-Webber, B., Schwartz, R., Wolf, J., & Zue, V. *Speech understanding system: Final Report.* Final Report on Contract No. N00014-75-C-0533, BBN Report No. 3438, ADAO 35166, 1976.

PART VI

Personnel Preparation for Teaching Speech to the Hearing Impaired: Recommendations for Improvement

26

Personnel Preparation for Teaching Speech to the Hearing Impaired: Current Status and Recommendations

Joanne D. Subtelny, Penelope E. Webster, and Lee C. Murphy

One of the objectives of this Institute was to formulate recommendations to improve personnel preparation for teachers of speech, uniquely qualified to work with the hearing impaired. There are primarily two disciplines—academically termed Education of the Deaf, and Speech/Language Pathology—involved in this task, and there are definite differences in the training offered by these two programs. Because of this fact it became evident that information, opinions, and recommendations should be secured from both areas. To secure information we needed first to identify 25 professionals in personnel preparation from each area and, secondly, to develop and distribute an appropriate questionnaire. Two criteria were used to identify the professionals in personnel preparation: a large number of graduates at the master's level, and geographical location. After identification, a questionnaire was developed and distributed to each of the 50 professionals:

1. To define his or her academic background and personal perceptions of its adequacy;
2. To secure judgments of the competencies of students upon completion of a master's degree; and
3. To solicit recommendations to improve personnel preparation.

The questionnaires were addressed to directors of the programs in Education of the Deaf and to chairmen of Departments of Speech Pathology and Audiology. In the event program directors or chairpersons felt poorly qualified to respond, they were requested to forward the questionnaire to the one faculty member considered most knowledgeable and experienced in teaching speech to the hearing impaired.

Fifty questionnaires were mailed six months prior to the Institute. Of this number, 23 were returned from programs in Education of the Deaf and 24 from Speech/Language Pathology. In this writing our purpose is to report the results of the questionnaire in a meaningful way and to summarize the recommendations for improvement of personnel preparation. For reasons previously mentioned, responses were analyzed to facilitate comparisons between training programs and to maintain a sharp relationship between recommendations and their reference to a specific training program.

Educational Background of Respondents

The educational background of respondents expressed in terms of the highest academic degree obtained is reported in Table 26.A.

TABLE 26.A

Educational background of respondents in Education of Deaf and in Speech/Language Pathology expressed in percentage for the highest degree obtained.

Degree Area	Education of Deaf (n 23)	Speech/Language (n 24)	Combined (n 47)
Master's Level			
Education of the Deaf	30%	4%	17%
Education	4%	0	2%
Speech/Language Pathology	0	8%	4%
Audiology	0	4%	2%
Total with Master's Degree	34%	16%	25%
Doctoral Level			
Education of the Deaf	18%	0	9%
Special Education	35%	0	17%
Education	0	0	0
Speech/Language Pathology	9%	63%	36%
Audiology	0	13%	7%
Linguistics	0	4%	2%
Psychology	0	4%	2%
Instructional Technology	4%	0	2%
Total with Doctoral Degree	66%	84%	75%

TABLE 26.B

Summary of courses participated in by the respondents during their professional preparation. Course participation is expressed in percentages for respondents from personnel preparation programs in Education of the Deaf, in Speech/Language Pathology, and for the two groups combined.

Course	Educ. of Deaf (n 23)	Speech/Lang. Path. (n 24)	Combined (n 47)
Phonetics	83%	100%	91%
Speech Development	97%	92%	94%
Teaching Speech to the Deaf	96%	50%	72%
Acoustic Phonetics	17%	75%	47%
Language Development	91%	79%	85%
Linguistics	48%	33%	40%
Auditory Training	100%	88%	94%
Speechreading	96%	83%	89%
Diagnostic Audiology	57%	83%	70%
Hearing Aids	70%	67%	68%
Anat. & Physiol. Speech	91%	100%	96%
Anat. & Physiol. Hearing	100%	92%	96%
Speech Pathology	70%	92%	81%
Voice Disorders	52%	83%	68%
Disorders of Lang.	74%	71%	72%
Speech Science	57%	92%	74%
Clinical Practicum: Teaching Speech to Hearing Impaired	87%	71%	79%

Seventy-five percent of the respondents from combined areas of Education of the Deaf and Speech/Language Pathology had doctoral degrees. From Education of the Deaf programs, most doctoral degrees were in Special Education (35 percent) followed by: Education of the Deaf (18 percent),[1] Speech/Language Pathology (9 percent), and Instructional Technology (4 percent). From Speech/Language Pathology programs most doctoral degrees were, as expected, in Speech/Language Pathology (63 percent) with other doctoral degrees in Audiology (13 percent), Linguistics (4 percent), and Psychology (4 percent). Thirty-four percent of the respondents from programs in Educa-

[1]According to a report published in the *American Annals of the Deaf*, April 1979, there were only three or four universities or colleges granting doctoral degrees in Education of the Deaf as of September 1978.

tion of the Deaf and 16 percent of the respondents from Speech/ Language Pathology had terminal master's degrees.

To further describe educational background, respondents were asked to indicate courses they had taken in their own personnel preparation programs. To facilitate this, 17 courses were listed with space provided to report other pertinent courses. The results from this inquiry are reported in Table 26.B. Again, responses are expressed in

FIGURE 26.1

Academic preparation of respondents from programs in Education of the Deaf and Speech/Language Pathology, expressed in percentage (n 47).

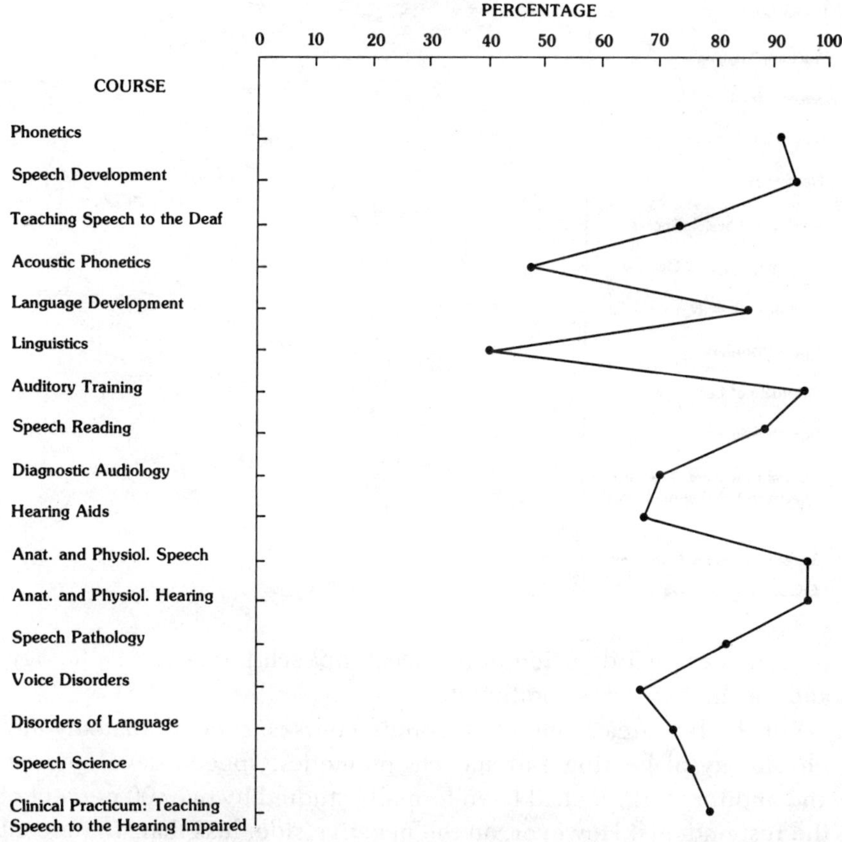

FIGURE 26.2
A comparison of the academic preparation of respondents from programs in the Education of the Deaf (n 23) and in Speech/Language Pathology (n 24).

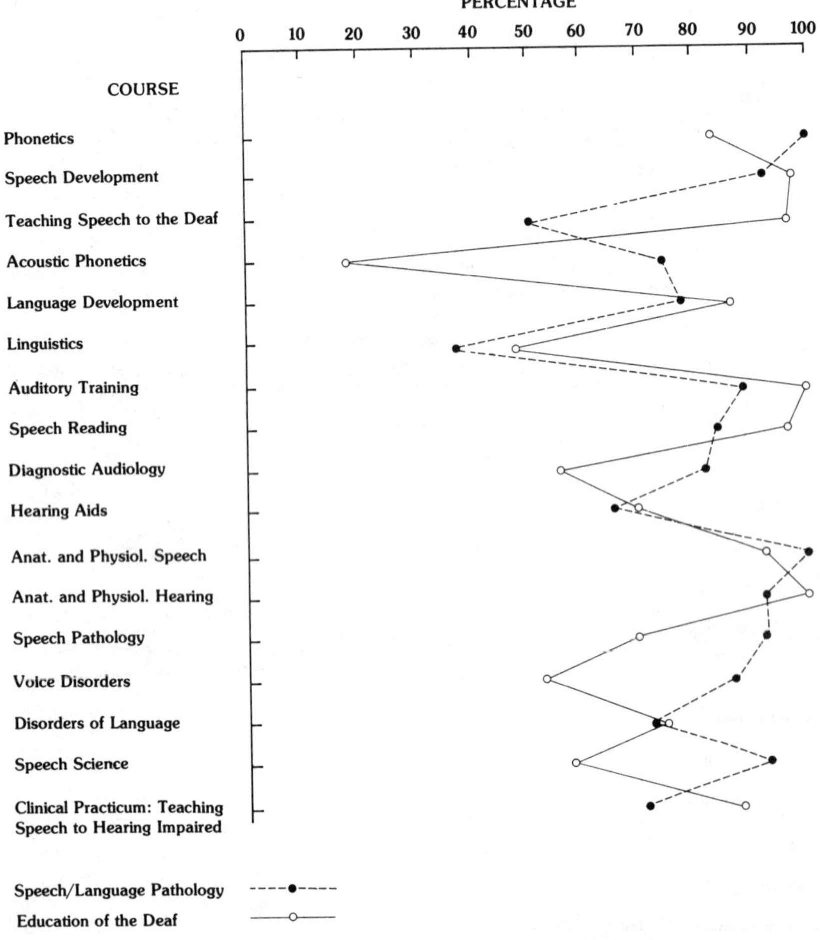

percentages for Education of the Deaf, Speech/Language Pathology, and for the two areas combined.

For the two areas combined, certain courses, such as anatomy and physiology of hearing and speech, phonetics, speech development, and auditory training had been formally studied by over 90 percent of the respondents. However, on the negative side, less than 75 percent of all respondents had taken courses in linguistics, acoustic phonetics, hearing aids, voice disorders, diagnostic audiology, teaching speech to the deaf, disorders of language, and speech science. Only 79 percent of the respondents reported that they had clinical practicum in teaching speech to the hearing impaired. These observations are graphed in Figure 26.1.

Differences in the educational backgrounds of the two professional groups working in personnel preparation are compared graphically and displayed in Figure 26.2. Perhaps the most significant difference is that only 50 percent of the respondents in Speech/Language Pathology had formal course work in teaching speech to the deaf while the analogous percentage for respondents from Education of the Deaf was 96 percent. In other areas, i.e., acoustic phonetics, diagnostic audiology, speech pathology, voice disorders, and speech science, the educational backgrounds of respondents in Speech/Language Pathology were stronger in comparison.

Respondents also listed "other" formal courses they had undertaken during their professional training. The most commonly listed "other" courses were: education of the hearing impaired (reading and other subject matter), language for the deaf, tests and measurements, articulation disorders, auditory disorders in children, and generative phonology.

Areas of Perceived Deficiency

Still another section of the questionnaire asked respondents to identify the areas of weakness in their own educational backgrounds. Responses to this introspective inquiry are reported in Table 26.C. In overview, the data suggest that respondents from programs in Education of the Deaf perceive fewer deficiencies in their own preparation than respondents from Speech/Language Pathology.

For the two groups combined, the major category of perceived deficiency was language, i.e., normal language development, linguistics, manual/simultaneous communication, language development and intervention with the hearing impaired. In the category of speech and voice, both groups (13 percent) perceived personal deficiency in speech training for the deaf. For respondents in Speech/Language Pathology, previous data indicated a low percentage of formal course work (50 percent) and practicum (71 percent) in the area of speech training for the deaf. Considering this academic and experiential background, the 13 percent level of *perceived* deficiency for speech/language pathologists seems very low.

TABLE 26.C

Identification of perceived areas of deficiency in professional preparation of respondents. Incidence is expressed in percentages for respondents from personnel preparation programs in Education of the Deaf, Speech/Language Pathology, and for the two groups combined.

Area of Perceived Deficiency	Educ. of Deaf (n 23)	Speech/Lang. (n 24)	Combined (n 47)
No deficiency perceived	35%	25%	30%
Audiology			
Clinical audiology	4%	4%	4%
Auditory training	4%	8%	6%
Hearing aids	0	13%	6%
Speechreading	4%	0	2%
Language			
Normal language dev.	13%	13%	13%
Linguistics	17%	21%	19%
Language dev. & intervention with hearing impaired	0	17%	9%
Manual/simultaneous communication	4%	8%	6%
Speech and Voice			
Speech diagnostics	4%	0	2%
Speech/voice science	17%	0	9%
Voice disorders	9%	0	4%
Speech training for deaf	13%	13%	13%
Phonetics	9%	0	4%
Acoustic phonetics	17%	0	9%
Miscellaneous			
Behavior modification	4%	0	2%
Curriculum development	4%	0	2%

Respondents from Education of the Deaf perceived their deficiencies primarily in areas of acoustic phonetics, speech/voice science, and voice disorders. Respondents from Speech/Language Pathology perceived few deficiencies in the speech and voice categories, but more deficiencies in audiology and language areas than were identified by respondents from Education of the Deaf.

Respondents' Ratings of Student Competencies

Three categories were established to secure judgments of student competencies upon completion of the master's degree: i.e., competencies were rated relative to knowledge, observational experience, and direct experience. This fractionated approach in rating was followed (1) to judge competency stemming from didactics independently from competency accrued through observation and/or direct experience, and (2) to facilitate further comparisons between personnel preparation programs in Education of the Deaf and in Speech/ Language Pathology.

Respondents reported their judgment ratings for each area using a 5-point scale ranging from 1 (no knowledge, observation or experience) to 5 (excellent). Intervening ratings of 2, 3, and 4 designated judgments of poor (inadequate), fair (adequate), and good (more than adequate), respectively. In analysis, ratings were totaled for each category to establish percentage of the total number of ratings made by respondents from both program areas.

Judgment Ratings of Student Knowledge

In Table 26.D, the distribution of judgment ratings for student knowledge upon completion of the master's degree is reported for each area of preparation. By considering the combined ratings of good and excellent, several generalizations can be drawn. Three areas of relatively strong knowledge were identified by both respondents. These were: phonetics, speech development, and language development. Two areas of relative deficiency were also identified by both groups of respondents. Less than 35 percent of respondents in both groups rated student knowledge of hearing aids and speechreading as good or excellent.

Superiority in knowledge as indicated by a much higher number of good and excellent ratings for graduates from programs in Education of the Deaf was indicated for the seven academic areas of child development, auditory training, speech training of the hearing impaired, principles and procedures in education of the deaf, psychology of deafness, sign language, and principles of curriculum development and evaluation. Superiority in knowledge is indicated for graduates from Speech/Language programs in other academic areas, namely, language disorders—assessment and remediation, assessment of speech and voice, speech pathology, and voice disorders.

In summarizing the judgment ratings of academic knowledge the

TABLE 26.D

Distribution of judgment ratings of student knowledge upon completion of a Master's degree in Education of the Deaf or in Speech/Language Pathology with data expressed in percentage.

Academic Area		No Knowledge	Poor	Fair	Good	Excel.	No Response
Child Development	Ed. Deaf	0	4	26	52	17	0
	Sp/Lang.	4	13	42	33	4	4
Anatomy & Physiol.—Hearing	Ed. Deaf	0	4	43	30	22	0
	Sp/Lang.	0	4	25	29	38	4
Anatomy & Physiol.—Speech	Ed. Deaf	0	0	48	35	17	0
	Sp/Lang.	0	0	17	33	46	4
Phonetics	Ed. Deaf	0	13	22	39	26	0
	Sp/Lang.	0	0	17	46	29	4
Speech Development	Ed. Deaf	0	9	13	35	43	0
	Sp/Lang.	0	0	25	42	29	4
Lang. Development	Ed. Deaf	0	0	17	22	61	0
	Sp/Lang.	0	4	13	38	42	4
Lang. Dis.—Assess. & Remediation	Ed. Deaf	4	9	30	30	26	0
	Sp/Lang.	0	0	13	42	42	4
Assess. Speech & Voice Disorders	Ed. Deaf	4	17	39	30	4	4
	Sp/Lang.	4	0	21	38	33	4
Hearing Eval. & Diagnosis	Ed. Deaf	0	13	43	39	0	4
	Sp/Lang.	4	4	38	33	17	4
Hearing Aids—Amplification & Assess.	Ed. Deaf	4	17	48	17	9	4
	Sp/Lang.	4	29	33	13	17	4
Auditory Training	Ed. Deaf	4	4	30	35	25	0
	Sp/Lang.	4	22	57	13	4	4

Speechreading	Ed. Deaf	4	8	50	17	17	0
	Sp/Lang.	4	22	52	13	9	4
Speech Training of	Ed. Deaf	4	4	17	35	39	0
Hearing Impaired	Sp/Lang.	4	42	25	13	13	4
Prin. & Procedures	Ed. Deaf	4	0	13	13	70	0
Educ. of the Deaf	Sp/Lang.	13	38	25	17	4	4
Acoustic Phonetics	Ed. Deaf	9	13	48	22	9	0
& Sp. Perception	Sp/Lang.	0	17	25	46	8	4
Psychology of	Ed. Deaf	0	4	22	52	22	0
Deafness	Sp/Lang.	17	21	29	25	4	4
Psych. Tests for	Ed. Deaf	4	22	43	17	13	0
Hrg. & Lang. Imp.	Sp/Lang.	13	38	29	17	0	4
Sign Lang.	Ed. Deaf	0	4	35	39	22	0
	Sp/Lang.	25	33	13	17	4	8
Linguistics	Ed. Deaf	4	9	22	39	26	0
	Sp/Lang.	0	21	29	33	13	4
Speech Science	Ed. Deaf	9	26	26	30	9	0
	Sp/Lang.	0	8	33	29	25	4
Prin. Curric. Dev.	Ed. Deaf	0	13	17	39	30	0
& Eval.	Sp/Lang.	25	33	21	17	0	4
Speech Pathology	Ed. Deaf	4	43	22	26	4	0
	Sp/Lang.	4	0	4	21	67	4
Voice Disorders	Ed. Deaf	4	48	30	13	4	0
& Therapy	Sp/Lang.	4	0	17	33	42	4
Total Academic	Ed. Deaf	0	0	22	57	17	4
Knowledge	Sp/Lang.	4	0	13	63	17	4

TABLE 26.E

Distribution of judgment ratings of student observations upon completion of a Master's degree in Education of the Deaf or in Speech/Language Pathology with data expressed in percentage.

Area of Observation		Judgment Rating*					
		No. Observ.	Poor	Fair	Good	Exc.	No Response
Evaluation of Hearing	Ed. Deaf	9	17	13	30	30	0
	Sp/Lang.	0	0	25	38	29	8
Hearing Aid Fitting	Ed. Deaf	17	39	30	9	4	0
& Evaluation	Sp/Lang.	17	13	29	17	17	8
Diagnosis	Ed. Deaf	22	22	30	17	4	4
Speech and Voice	Sp/Lang.	0	4	13	33	42	8
Articulation Therapy	Ed. Deaf	4	17	35	17	17	9
	Sp/Lang.	0	4	8	25	54	8
Voice Therapy	Ed. Deaf	22	30	22	22	0	4
	Sp/Lang.	0	8	21	21	42	8
Assessment of Language	Ed. Deaf	4	9	9	43	35	0
	Sp/Lang.	0	4	17	29	42	8
Language Therapy	Ed. Deaf	4	0	13	48	35	0
	Sp/Lang.	8	8	13	33	29	8
Speech Training of	Ed. Deaf	0	9	26	26	39	0
Hearing Impaired	Sp/Lang.	8	25	38	13	8	8
Auditory Training	Ed. Deaf	9	9	30	35	17	0
	Sp/Lang.	4	25	33	21	8	8
Speechreading	Ed. Deaf	9	17	43	17	13	0
	Sp/Lang.	13	25	33	13	8	8

Psycho-educ. Eval. of Hearing Impaired	Ed. Deaf	22	13	26	35	4	0
	Sp/Lang.	29	8	42	13	0	8
Educ. of Hear. Imp. (Procedures: Teaching Reading & Other Subjs.)	Ed. Deaf	4	4	4	43	43	0
	Sp/Lang.	33	29	25	4	0	8
Counseling the Hearing Impaired	Ed. Deaf	17	17	30	30	4	0
	Sp/Lang.	17	17	25	17	17	8
Counseling Parents of Hearing Impaired	Ed. Deaf	13	22	26	30	9	0
	Sp/Lang.	17	17	33	13	13	8
Counseling Classroom Teachers of Hrg. Imp.	Ed. Deaf	17	13	39	22	9	0
	Sp/Lang.	29	25	17	21	0	8
Curriculum Development & Evaluation	Ed. Deaf	0	17	17	35	30	0
	Sp/Lang.	33	25	21	13	0	8
Overall Rating	Ed. Deaf	0	9	35	39	9	9
	Sp/Lang.	0	4	50	33	0	13

*Descriptors for ratings are as follows: 1—No observation, 2—Poor (inadequate), 3—Fair (adequate), 4—Good, 5—Excellent.

TABLE 26.F

Distribution of judgment ratings of student experience upon completion of a Master's degree in Education of the Deaf or in Speech/Language Pathology with data expressed in percentage

Area of Experience		Judgment Rating					
		No Exper.	Poor	Fair	Good	Exc.	No Response
Evaluation of Hearing	Ed. Deaf	17	13	26	13	30	0
	Sp/Lang.	0	4	38	25	25	8
Hearing Aid Fitting	Ed. Deaf	30	35	30	0	4	0
& Evaluation	Sp/Lang.	17	29	8	21	13	13
Diagnosis	Ed. Deaf	17	30	22	22	4	4
Speech and Voice	Sp/Lang.	0	4	0	38	46	13
Articulation Therapy	Ed. Deaf	13	22	26	17	13	9
	Sp/Lang.	0	4	0	21	67	8
Voice Therapy	Ed. Deaf	26	26	22	17	4	4
	Sp/Lang.	4	4	13	33	38	8
Assessment of Language	Ed. Deaf	4	9	17	30	39	0
	Sp/Lang.	0	4	21	17	50	8
Language Therapy	Ed. Deaf	4	0	26	30	39	0
	Sp/Lang.	4	4	17	21	46	8
Speech Training of	Ed. Deaf	4	13	13	30	39	0
Hearing Impaired	Sp/Lang.	8	25	29	21	8	8
Auditory Training	Ed. Deaf	9	9	22	43	17	0
	Sp/Lang.	0	33	29	21	8	8

Speechreading	Ed. Deaf	9	13	52	13	13	0
	Sp/Lang.	4	29	29	25	4	8
Psycho-educ. Eval. of Hearing Impaired	Ed. Deaf	22	13	17	35	13	0
	Sp/Lang.	29	29	25	8	0	8
Educ. of Hear. Imp. (Procedures: Teaching Reading & Other Subjs.)	Ed. Deaf	13	0	9	30	48	0
	Sp/Lang.	33	38	17	0	4	8
Counseling the Hearing Impaired	Ed. Deaf	26	9	30	22	13	0
	Sp/Lang.	17	25	4	21	25	8
Counseling Parents of Hearing Impaired	Ed. Deaf	13	26	30	22	9	0
	Sp/Lang.	17	13	21	21	17	13
Counseling Classroom Teachers of Hrg. Imp.	Ed. Deaf	17	13	39	22	9	0
	Sp/Lang.	29	25	21	17	0	8
Curriculum Development & Evaluation	Ed. Deaf	4	13	17	26	39	0
	Sp/Lang.	50	13	21	8	0	8
Overall Rating	Ed. Deaf	9	17	26	30	13	4
	Sp/Lang.	0	8	38	42	4	8

following comments are supported. Respondents from both areas judge knowledge to be good or excellent in a few basic areas, but they also judge knowledge to be deficient in two critical areas. From a comparative viewpoint, knowledge of graduates from programs in Education of the Deaf was rated higher in academic areas highly specialized relative to the education and rehabilitation of the hearing impaired. On the other hand, knowledge of graduates from programs in Speech/Language Pathology was rated higher relative to assessment of speech, voice and language, and in academic areas focusing on varied aspects of communication disorders and rehabilitation.

Judgment Ratings: Observational Experience

The same criteria of good and excellent ratings was applied to indicate the distribution of judgments for quality of observations. These ratings are reported in Table 26.E. The ratings of respondents from both personnel preparation programs show a high incidence (60 to 70 percent) of good or excellent ratings in two areas, i.e., evaluation of hearing and assessment of language. In contradistinction, a comparatively low incidence (13 to 34 percent) of good or excellent ratings is observed in five areas: hearing aid fitting and evaluation, speechreading, counseling the hearing impaired, counseling parents of the hearing impaired, and counseling teachers of the hearing impaired.

Again, in comparison, ratings of observational experience for graduates from Education of the Deaf programs were higher for the highly specialized areas of: speech training of the hearing impaired, education of the hearing impaired, and curriculum development. The ratings of the observational experience of graduates from Speech/Language Pathology were higher for diagnosis of speech and voice, articulation therapy, and voice therapy.

Judgment Ratings: Experience

The data reporting judgment ratings of the direct hands-on experience of graduates (Table 26.F) reflects many of the findings already reported for student knowledge and observational experience. The findings do merit repetition, however, because the ratings of experience are perhaps most directly related to the teaching skill of the graduate after leaving the personnel preparation program.

Experience was rated good or excellent by 67 to 69 percent of the respondents from both areas in regard to assessment of language and language therapy. This rating for experience is, as would be expected, based on previously reported high ratings in these areas for knowl-

FIGURE 26.3
Distribution of respondents' judgment ratings of student experience upon completion of a master's degree in Education of the Deaf (solid line) and in Speech/Language Pathology (dotted lines). Ratings of experience are comparatively graphed for: Diagnosis Speech and Voice, Speech Training of Hearing Impaired, Voice Therapy, and Auditory Training.

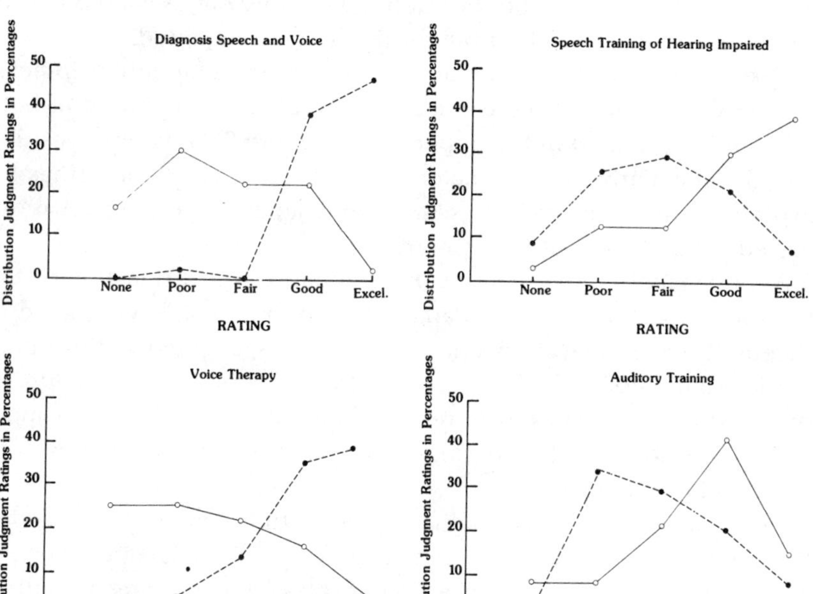

edge and observational experience. A very low incidence of good or excellent ratings (ranging from 4 to 38 percent) was reported for respondents from both programs for certain areas of experience. These areas included hearing aid fitting and evaluation, speechreading, counseling parents of the hearing impaired, and counseling classroom teachers of the hearing impaired. These ratings also may have been anticipated from the previously reported weakness in these content areas relative to knowledge and observational experience.

Some of the gross differences between programs of personnel preparation are best conveyed by graphs showing the distribution of averaged ratings for each content area in both programs. For example, the ratings for graduates in Speech/Language Pathology were higher relative to diagnosis of speech and voice and voice therapy as displayed in Figure 26.3 at the left. As a corollary, graduates from programs in Education of the Deaf were rated higher relative to speech training of the hearing impaired, as shown at the upper right. Graduates from both programs (lower right) showed a low incidence of excellent ratings for experience in auditory training—an essential component in any program of speech training for the hearing impaired.

The comparative low incidence of good or excellent ratings in hearing aid fitting and speechreading was revealed for graduates of both programs as graphed in the upper half of Figure 26.4. On the positive side, a comparatively high incidence of good or excellent ratings for experience in language assessment and language therapy was revealed for graduates of both programs.

Approximately 50 percent of the graduates from Education of the Deaf and Speech/Language Pathology were rated as having good or excellent experience in evaluating hearing as graphed at the upper left in Figure 26.5. However, gross differences in experience for the two groups of graduates were revealed for articulation therapy (upper right), education of the hearing impaired, and curriculum development and evaluation.

Less than 50 percent of graduates from both programs were rated as having good or excellent experience in the psycho-educational evaluations of the hearing impaired, counseling the hearing impaired, counseling parents of the hearing impaired, and counseling teachers of the hearing impaired. These findings have a particularly sobering effect since both evaluation and counseling relative to evaluations are highly important roles for the special teacher of speech within restricted or within mainstreamed environments (Figure 26.6).

In sum, in both areas the ratings of the relative adequacy of experience upon completion of the master's degree reflect a rather parallel profile of the ratings established for knowledge and observation. This finding is logical if one assumes that a previously established knowledge base and observational experience are prerequisites for good experience.

Respondents' Recommendations To Improve Personnel Preparation

In total, 106 recommendations were submitted by respondents. Of

FIGURE 26.4

Distribution of respondents' judgment ratings of student experience upon completion of a master's degree in Education of the Deaf (solid line) and in Speech/Language Pathology (dotted lines). Ratings of experience are comparatively graphed for: Hearing Aid Fitting and Evaluation, Speechreading, Language Assessment, and Language Therapy.

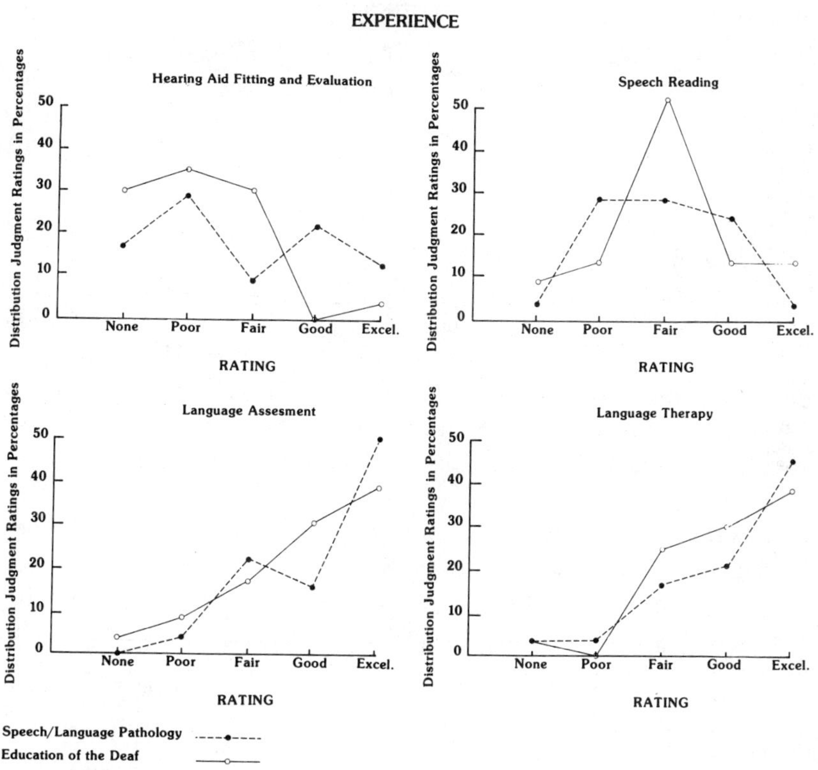

this number, the majority (60) were submitted from the area of Speech/Language Pathology. By far the highest number of recommendations from Education of the Deaf (n 19) and Speech/Language Pathology (n 17) called for more experience and a better academic background to improve procedures applied in teaching speech to the hearing impaired with varying degrees of loss. In this recommendation, specific items identified for emphasis included: use of amplification, auditory training, voice improvement, correction of supraseg-

FIGURE 26.5

Distribution of respondents' judgment ratings of student experience upon completion of a master's degree in Education of the Deaf (solid line) and in Speech/Language Pathology (dotted lines). Ratings of experience are comparatively graphed for: Evaluation of Hearing, Articulation Therapy, Education: Hearing Impaired, and Curriculum Development and Evaluation.

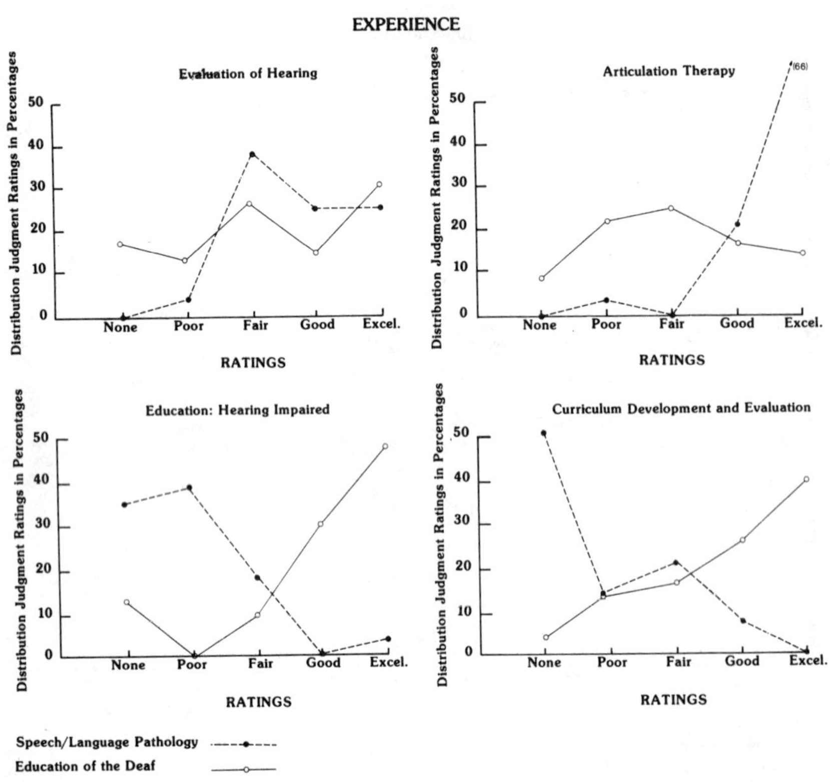

mental features, use of visual or tactile feedback in training, and operant conditioning.

More experience and improved academic background to diagnostically assess speech, voice, and speech perception was the second highest priority recommended to improve personnel preparation. Despite a high priority, the number of recommendations to improve diagnostic assessment was *much* lower (Education of the Deaf, n 6; Speech/Language Pathology, n 8) than the number of recom-

FIGURE 26.6
Distribution of respondents' judgment ratings of student experience upon completion of a master's degree in Education of the Deaf (solid line) and in Speech/Language Pathology (dotted lines). Ratings of experience are comparatively graphed for: Psycho-Educational Evaluation, Counseling: Hearing Impaired, Counseling Parents, and Counseling Teachers.

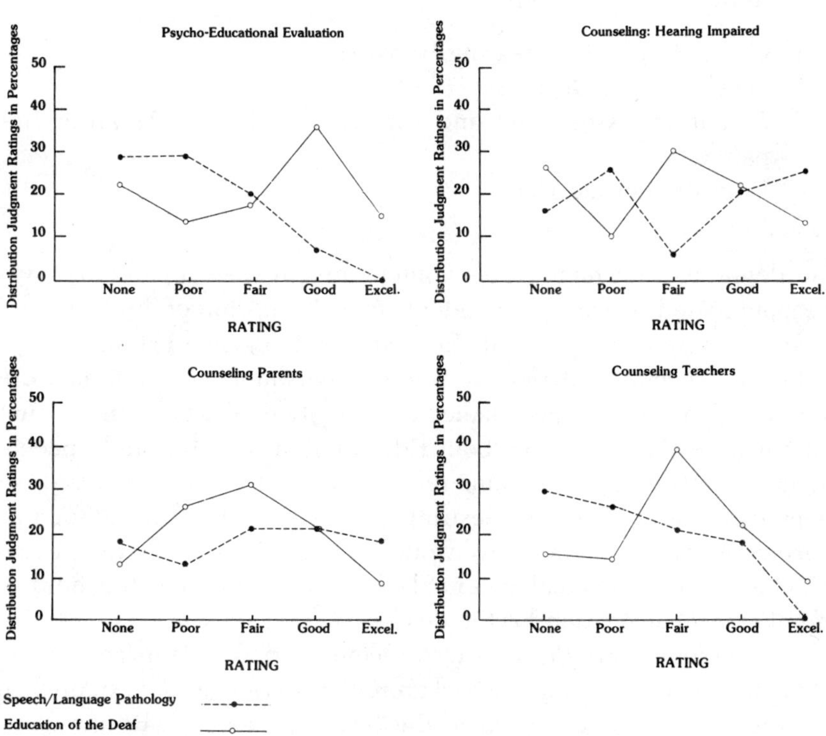

mendations to improve teaching procedures. The first two recommendations generally stressed the need for increased practicum or "more experience under excellent supervision" to facilitate learning and the development of skillful teaching. This need received much greater emphasis than the need for improvement in academic background.

A total of 46 recommendations were submitted to improve training in academic areas identified in order of priority as follows:

1. Speech and Language Development
2. Phonetics
3. Speech and Hearing Science
4. Acoustics
5. Sign Language
6. Information Theory

Five additional academic areas needing improvement were identified exclusively by respondents from Speech/Language Pathology programs. These included:

1. Counseling of the Hearing Impaired
2. Psychology of Deafness
3. Language Assessment and Intervention for the Hearing Impaired
4. Education of the Deaf
5. Linguistics

Academic improvement in the content area of speech pathology was recommended by some respondents from Education of the Deaf programs, but by no respondents from Speech/Language Pathology.

Several recommendations to improve personnel preparation were focused upon student acceptance and faculty credentials. In the first instance, respondents from both Education of the Deaf and Speech/Language Pathology programs recommended elevating standards of acceptance for applicants desiring preparation. Fulfillment of this recommendation theoretically would assure a better affective, experiential, and intellectual potential of students entering the field of aural/oral rehabilitation for the deaf.

Respondents in *both* areas also recommended higher faculty credentials relative to academic background, experience, and established expertise in training speech to the hearing impaired. Respondents from programs in Education of the Deaf added a further recommendation calling for in-service training of faculty relative to speech instruction and improved media to assist instruction. In these recommendations, it appears that both areas are acknowledging that *some* professionals in the business of preparing future professionals do not themselves possess the requisite skills they are trying to develop. In sum, the respondents seem to have made a tacit and honest acknowledgment of inadequate faculty credentials relative to the specialized task of speech training for the deaf.

Summary and Conclusions

According to the comparative data surveyed, the personnel preparation of speech/language pathologists provides greater breadth in diagnosis of communication disorders and in training to ameliorate communication problems with varied etiologies. This preparation also provides greater depth in the science and theory underlying disorders of communication. Although these features in preparation of speech/language pathologists are all positive, from a practical sense this preparation was judged to be less specialized than the preparation provided by programs in Education of the Deaf. In this sense, the graduates from programs in Education of the Deaf are perhaps better prepared by experience and training to remediate many of the communication problems encountered by people with both mild and profound hearing impairment.

In essence, respondents from both areas recognize certain areas of deficiency in the knowledge base, observational experience, and direct experience of graduates. Each program acknowledges certain strengths, but neither program judges its graduates to have good or excellent knowledge and experience in all critical areas required to effectively teach speech to the hearing impaired. For example, students prepared in programs in Education of the Deaf were rated comparatively weak in diagnostic procedures for speech and voice, speech science, and voice therapy. Students prepared in programs in Speech/Language Pathology were rated comparatively weak in language diagnosis and intervention for the hearing impaired, speech training for the hearing impaired, and in counseling hearing-impaired children and the parents and teachers of the hearing impaired.

In *both* areas of personnel preparation, marked deficiencies were indicated by ratings of student knowledge, observational experience, and direct experience. These deficiencies were identified in critical areas of hearing aid fitting, auditory training, speechreading, and supervised practicum.

It may be hypothesized that the educational or rehabilitative audiologist could fill *some* of the informational and experiential gaps in professional preparation and competence revealed by this survey. However, there is no objective assurance that audiologists are much better prepared to meet the multiple and diverse needs of the hearing impaired. It seems most reasonable to predict that students graduating from personnel preparation programs in audiology with the master's degree would also be rated exceptionally strong in some areas but also weak in other areas.

For many years, professionals involved with aural/oral rehabilitation have been recommending changes to improve personnel preparation, but little has changed on a national scale. Perhaps this fact may be partially explained by the heterogeneity in programs providing graduate and undergraduate training. It is hoped that results of this survey will contribute to a consolidation of recommendations and strengthen professional resolve to effect change.

All requisite knowledge and skills for effective speech teaching of the hearing impaired are not now provided by any single program of professional preparation. Specific areas in need of improvement have been indicated. If existing programs are not improved to meet current and future needs, an alternative solution may be indicated. One possible solution may be a revised program of preparation designed to uniquely prepare a communication specialist to work with the hearing impaired. The certification of this "specialist," to be endorsed by both authorizing bodies in Education of the Deaf (CED) and Speech/Language Pathology (ASHA), should perhaps require a written examination demonstrating academic competence and the successful completion of a clinical fellowship working with the hearing impaired under expert supervision, after completion of the master's degree.

Acknowledgments

The authors wish to thank all of the Institute participants from personnel preparation programs who gave generously of their time and thinking to critique their own training programs and to formulate recommendations for local and national improvement in personnel preparation. The authors also express appreciation to Jorge Samper, audiovisual specialist, for assistance in processing illustrations.

27
Recommendations To Improve Preparation of Personnel

THIS PORTION of the conference, as stated in the title, is concerned with recommendations for improving the preparation of personnel. Section 1, titled "Pre-conference Recommendations," contains the papers prepared by the panelists prior to the conference. At the conference, the panelists and chairman met to synthesize ideas and to develop a framework for discussion of the major issues of personnel preparation. The "Responses of Panelists and Participants" in this discussion are presented in Section 2. The material in Section 2 is categorized by topic as follows: (A) Recruitment of Competent Individuals Into the Field; (B) Establishment of Standards; (C) Preparation of Personnel; and (D) General Observations Related to Improving Speech. Since many of the points made by panelists in their papers could not be raised in the discussion because of time constraints, it is important that the comments be considered in the context of the full papers. Section 3 is titled "Summary and Recommendations of the Chairman." These recommendations reflect his perspective and, while he has drawn heavily upon the ideas of others, he assumes full responsibility for them.

—Milo E. Bishop, *Chairman*

Section 1
Pre-conference Recommendations

The following manuscripts were submitted by panelists to express recommendations to improve the preparation of professional personnel. In some instances the recommendations are made by describing current programs of training and by addending evaluative comments and further suggestions to improve the existing program. In other instances, specific suggestions to improve training are made without reference to a specific program.

Sister James Lorene Hogan
Fontbonne College,
St. Louis, Missouri

In 1960, Fontbonne College inaugurated its four-year undergraduate major in deaf education with what was then considered to be a well-planned speech curriculum. Since then that well-planned curriculum has undergone numerous revisions, the latest resulting in the contact speech curriculum.

Rationale

At the end of each academic year Fontbonne College faculty members, St. Joseph Institute cooperating teachers, and graduating student teachers majoring in deaf education are asked to evaluate the speech components of the deaf education curriculum. After reviewing the results of these evaluations over a period of years, we noted that each of the above-mentioned groups was identifying the need for more student contact with deaf children. All concerned agreed that it is necessary for the students to learn how to communicate with deaf children before these same students are expected to know how to teach communication skills (especially speech) to deaf children.

After exploring possible ways to provide more contact hours with deaf children, we decided that this would best be accomplished by practicum placements prior to student teaching and by providing more contact hours in conjunction with the speech courses. We also decided that there was a need for these two types of contact: speech-readiness and speech-practice experiences. Each of these contact experiences is now a part of the deaf education speech curriculum.

Sophomore Speech Contact Practicum

The first practicum, speech readiness, provides for 60 clock-hours of contact with deaf children in nonacademic activities (dorm, playground, sports, etc.). Each student is required to work with deaf children for a minimum of two hours per week (total 30 weeks) during the entire sophomore year. Most students have the opportunity to work with two groups of children whose communication skills are at different levels.

The primary purpose of this speech-readiness contact experience is to improve the students' communication skills with deaf children. As a part of this practicum, each student is expected to engage in the following speech-related activities: listening to deaf children's speech; identifying speech errors; asking the child to repeat unintelligible speech in a more satisfactory manner; and, finally, attempting to help the child (in a very global manner) to produce better speech through imitation when he/she is unable to make the desired correction unaided.

At the termination of this 60 clock-hour speech-readiness contact experience, each student must demonstrate improvement in communication skills in each of the areas identified above. Students failing to demonstrate proficiency in the speech-readiness skills are placed on probation at the end of the first semester. Students failing to improve their communication skills by the end of the second semester are dismissed from the program.

Junior Speech Contact Practicum

During the junior year each student is required to complete the junior tutorial practicum. This speech-readiness practicum provides a minimum of 30 clock-hours of contact with deaf children in classrooms under the direct supervision of certified teachers of the deaf. To enable students to come into contact with as many children as possible and also to observe different cooperating teachers, each student is placed with two cooperating teachers whose classes are functioning at different grade levels, with different levels of communication skills.

The primary purpose of this contact experience is to improve the student's communication skills with deaf children in academic settings. As part of the assignment, each tutor engages in the following activities: listening to the spontaneous speech of the children; listening to the improvements in speech when such are elicited by the teacher; becoming aware of each child's hearing loss and its effect on speech; observing the teacher in informal speech instruction within the context of an academic lesson and within a speech lesson; observing the teaching strategies and materials used in teaching speech; and, finally, attempting to model speech work after that of the teacher.

Upon completion of a minimum of 30 contact hours in the abovementioned activities, each student must demonstrate improvement in speech-readiness skills to the satisfaction of the cooperating teachers. Students failing to demonstrate such improvement are placed on probation. If the student fails to improve communication skills during the second semester, he/she may be dismissed from the program.

Speech Courses and Contact Experiences

Having completed a minimum of 90 contact hours with deaf children in the two speech-readiness practicums, students are now aware of their need to have both theoretical knowledge and technical skills in order to teach speech to deaf children. Consequently, students are not only ready but eager to take the two speech courses included in our curriculum.

In the first semester of the senior year all student teachers take the first course in teaching speech to the deaf. In this course current techniques and methods of teaching speech to deaf children are explored. The content of this course includes both technical information and theoretical knowledge needed to teach speech to deaf children. Five areas of special interest are discussed in detail: articulation, breath control, rhythm, accent, and phrasing.

As a part of this course, contact with deaf children occurs in the following ways: listening to audiotapes; viewing videotape speech demonstrations; and viewing live speech demonstrations. It is imperative that the students be given the opportunity to observe the actual teaching of speech to hearing-impaired children. Since the instructor of this course is a certified full-time teacher of hearing-impaired children, he/she is able to present model speech lessons together with materials that have been used successfully in teaching speech. Speech lessons and materials demonstrated are for children in preschool, primary, middle, and upper school.

First-Semester Student Teaching Contact

The third and last speech-readiness contact comes as a part of the first-semester student teaching experience. During the first semester, each student completes approximately 300 clock-hours of contact with hearing-impaired children. Because this experience occurs concurrently with enrollment in the first speech course, the students are not expected to be ready to teach speech in a formal manner. They are still in the process of learning both the theoretical and technical aspects needed to allow them to teach speech with any degree of proficiency.

As a part of this contact experience, however, each student is expected to improve those skills identified in the junior tutorial practicum. The student is expected to engage the children in speech whenever this is possible. At this level, most of the students feel comfortable in responding to the children's speech and in modeling correct production. Students are evaluated on their ability to identify speech problems. They are not expected to engage in formal speech lessons which would require the planning, preparing, and teaching of speech to the children in their classroom.

Second Speech Course Contact

The second speech course is a speech-practice practicum. Students are assigned deaf children to whom they provide different speech lessons each week. One of these children is in preschool or primary, and the other is an older student. The instructor of the course identifies speech problems and then assigns specific lessons relating to these problems for each week's practice sessions of one and a half hours. Students are now required to plan, prepare, and present original speech lessons using appropriate strategies and materials.

Each student is assigned a work station. The instructor of the course rotates from one student to the next, supervising each lesson, assisting the college student and child when indicated. In each contact session the student receives individualized supervision, immediate evaluation, and suggestions for improving future work.

To receive credit for this course each student must demonstrate the ability to: identify appropriate behavioral objectives for the lesson; prepare visual aids and use them correctly; establish rapport with the child; improve the child's speech; and modify original lessons in response to directions received from the course instructor. (The same instructor teaches both speech courses.)

Second-Semester Student Teaching Contact

This is another speech-practice contact which runs concurrently with the second speech course. Speech-practice experiences vary for each student teacher because these are governed by the type of classrooms in which the student teacher is placed. Those teaching in self-contained classrooms have different opportunities than those teaching rotating classes. Each student is expected to engage in as many of the following kinds of speech activities as placements will allow.

Informal Speech-Practice Contact: As a part of each content lesson (math, science, etc.) the student teacher should include some informal speech-practice work. Primarily, this will consist of identifying speech errors and encouraging children to correct errors using strategies presented by the teacher.

Formal Speech-Practice Contact: Whenever possible, the student teacher will engage in planning, preparing, and presenting speech lessons to individual children under the supervision of the cooperating teacher and/or the coordinator of student teaching. In addition to receiving help from these two persons, the student teacher will have an opportunity to discuss any problems that arise in teaching speech with the instructor of the speech course during the weekly speech sessions. Because all practicum placements are at St. Joseph Institute, and the instructor of the speech courses is a faculty member who knows the speech problems of each child being discussed, it is possible to give very specific help to each of the student teachers.

By the time this speech-practice contact is finished, each student will have engaged in over 700 clock-hours of speech-related contact with deaf children in eight different placements.

Summary and Conclusions

Institutions of higher education preparing teachers of the deaf must provide speech courses on how to teach speech to the deaf (including the principles, objectives, and strategies for effective speech teaching), as well as speech-related contact practicums in speech readiness and speech practice.

While specific and more detailed competencies may be identified as necessary for the teacher of speech, it seems the following more general ones would also be acceptable if we assume that each student has had sufficient contact experiences in speech-related practicums: ability to communicate orally with deaf persons; ability to identify speech errors; ability to teach deaf children speech using appropriate strategies; and the ability to present original speech lessons which relate to the speech needs of each individual child in the class.

To develop a contact curriculum similar to the one described above, it is necessary to have: students enrolled in the program for more than four semesters; close cooperation between the college/university and the school(s) providing the practicum experiences; hearing-impaired children available for speech-practice sessions after their school day; cooperating teachers, college instructors, and supervisors who are willing and capable to supervise and evaluate the speech practice of the student teachers; and, finally, college/university administrators who are willing to give credit for contact practicums.

It would appear that students graduating from teacher education programs having limited contact in speech-related experiences with deaf children are poorly prepared to engage in the difficult task of teaching speech to deaf children.

Arthur Boothroyd
Clarke School for the Deaf
Northampton, Massachusetts

Today's teacher of the hearing-impaired faces an almost impossible challenge. He or she must have theoretical knowledge and practical skills in several disciplines, each of which could absorb years of study. These include speech and hearing science, audiology, speech pathology, learning theory, psycholinguistics, and learning disabilities, in addition to counseling and academic subject matter. In short, the teacher of the deaf must be a highly sophisticated generalist.

The practical situation is far from the ideal implied by the foregoing. The profession of teaching the deaf seldom attracts young people with the potential to assimilate difficult concepts from a variety of disciplines and to synthesize them in ways which will lead to the development and improvement of intervention strategies. Personnel preparation programs offer only a cursory introduction to allied disciplines, and in-service training programs are sporadic, disconnected, and frequently narrow in outlook. Few schools have organizational structures which permit personnel and program development on a long-term coordinated basis.

Within this context, the topic of speech training and the preparation of speech teachers is but one of a series of difficult problems.

Who Is the Teacher of Speech?

Since the profession of teaching the deaf, as a whole, has failed to produce large numbers of competent speech teachers who have an adequate conceptual framework and effective diagnostic or teaching strategies, there is an increasing tendency to request the assistance of speech pathologists. They obviously have better preparation in their own discipline than do teachers of the deaf. Unfortunately, however, many speech pathologists come from programs that do not delve deeply into the special speech and language problems of the deaf. This leads to the danger of speech being learned as a motor activity without proper emphasis on its function in verbal communication. To return to the original question, Who is the teacher of speech?

Whoever would take on the responsibility of development, diagnosis, and remediation of speech in the deaf must, again, be a sophisticated generalist. There is at the present time no paper qualification which guarantees that its bearer has the necessary knowledge and skills for this difficult work.

What Training Is Required?

This brings us to the central issue, what is the nature of the training program which any individual must complete if he or she is to be an effective speech teacher? Some five training goals are obvious. One is a knowledge of normal speech physiology, acoustics, phonology, and development. A second is a knowledge of the effects of hearing impairment on these areas. An understanding of residual hearing and its potential and limitations as an input and feedback modality in speech development is a third. A fourth is an understanding of vision and touch as supplements to or substitutes for hearing. A fifth is the availability, possibilities, and limitations of instrumental aids to speech training. I would assume that these topics are already covered to greater or lesser extents in existing training programs.

But it is clear that course work alone is not enough. From my experience in this field I have come to realize that there are three key requirements for a first-class teacher, over and above the kinds of knowledge just listed. These are:

1. An intimate understanding of the relationship between speech, language, and conceptual thought and an ability to involve deaf persons in activities that provide intrinsic motivation for growth in all three areas simultaneously.

2. Specially developed listening skills that will permit the teacher to detect and identify speech problems without being misled by redundant information carried by speechreading, vocabulary, syntax, semantics, or situation. It has taken a long time for me to realize the

significance of this issue, but I have come to the conclusion that an effective speech teacher must have listening skills on a par with a professional musician or music teacher. These skills are acquired only by years of experience. This experience must provide opportunity for associations to be learned between known physiological deviations and their acoustic and perceptual correlates.

3. This brings us to the third component, which is apprenticeship. Effective speech-teaching skills cannot be developed through course work supplemented by short periods of practicum. They must be acquired slowly at the elbow of a master speech teacher.

Summary

The logical conclusions to be drawn from these comments are as follows:

1. More in-depth training must be provided to speech teachers, regardless of their professional qualifications.
2. The training of speech teachers cannot be viewed only as a preservice responsibility. Long-term, in-service training is required along an apprenticeship model.
3. The previous goal cannot be realized until the profession establishes a core of master speech teachers. Somehow it must "pull itself up by its own bootstraps."
4. None of the above goals will be realized until the image of the profession of deaf education improves to the point where it attracts a significant percentage of highly capable young people to its ranks.

Linda J. Rowe
John Tracy Clinic
Westminster, California

I have met, worked with, or heard about many deaf persons, children and adults, who feel that the poor quality of their speech is an unchangeable side effect of their deafness. This suggests that we as educators must focus our attention on the affective as well as the cognitive skills needed for effective speech teaching. Teachers must be able to instill in their students a zest for learning and a feeling that they can be successful no matter how difficult the task.

We can assume that the basic knowledge component in deaf education, which may differ slightly from program to program, is covered in every teacher preparation program. Can we make the same assumption about the component responsible for teacher attitude? How many teachers understand that the primary responsibility for a pupil's acquisition of new and difficult speech skills rests with the teacher? It is the teacher's enthusiasm, ability to motivate, skill in the presentation of information, and confidence in the pupil's ability to succeed that are the primary determinants of speech success with deaf children. Student teachers develop these skills by observation and practice. Therefore, in addition to the basic content presented to student teachers, we must provide a variety of practicum situations supervised by "master speech teachers." Student teachers must be helped to realize that the pupils' attitudes about speech and their possibilities for success are directly related to the teacher's attitude.

Accepting these ideas means shifting the focus of the teacher education program. Until now the concentration has been on providing students with factual knowledge. We must now add to this the demonstration of skills in the teaching environment and the demonstration of a positive attitude about the abilities of hearing-impaired children to learn speech. These facts in turn indicate a need for a new kind of teacher educator. We cannot be satisfied with a theorist whose last contact with children was 15, 20, or more years ago when he/she was a classroom teacher. We must have "master speech teachers" who work with children on a regular basis. These teachers must be able to transmit their positive feelings about deaf children and their abilities, as well as their speech-teaching skills.

In sum, we must: (1) continue to present strong basic knowledge components in teacher preparation programs; (2) develop new course components focusing on the development of positive teacher attitudes that will lead to improved pupil attitude and performance; (3) provide students with a variety of practicum situations; and (4) employ a new breed of teacher educator—"the master speech teacher."

Ann M. Mulholland
Columbia University
New York City

The competencies needed by those professionals involved directly with the language and speech development of the profoundly deaf child are many and varied. Yet, the manner by which such knowledge and skills are acquired has evolved serendipitously more often than by design. The considerable body of research undertaken during the past 15 to 20 years poses a formidable task in processing, selecting, and applying the results to the instruction of prelingually, profoundly deaf children. The requisite skills for speech instruction have been expanded significantly with the explosion of knowledge in linguistics, information processing, brain function, auditory perception, and learning.

The Professional Person

The process of developing oral communication skills depends upon a close personal relationship between instructor and learner, which, by its very nature, is an important variable in the child's development of language and speech. It is crucial that the criteria for selection of entrants to the field having this major responsibility be determined on the basis of the applicant's personal and professional integrity, capacity to be flexible, attitude of optimism relative to the potential of the deaf person, and conception of the deaf child as a human being of dignity and worth. One has but to examine the emerging studies of interaction analysis of adult/child communication to recognize the importance of this dyadic relationship.

At present, social forces seem to be attracting people to the field whose motivation is pecuniary rather than reflecting a commitment to education of the hearing impaired, whose vision of work in the field is romanticized, and whose admission to college has been based on an open-door policy. To improve the potential of applicants, it is recommended that the professional organizations in the field of deafness establish minimum standards for entrants into programs and require applicants to meet these standards.

Program of Study

The commonly designed curriculum in teacher education programs to develop competence in speech instruction includes what may be termed the scientific and the specific approach or method of instruction advocated by the teacher educators. In formulating the core courses, compartmentalization ensues, and the science is automatically separated from the art of teaching. To inculcate in students "the science of the art of teaching," it is recommended that the program first establish a sensory aids-to-communication laboratory where experiments may be designed to clarify and facilitate the comprehension of the knowledge and skills required in speech instruction. This might include simulation of hearing loss and study of speech perception with varying signal-to-noise ratios, with differing microphone placements, and with various parameters of speech acoustically manipulated. Other laboratory activities may include diagnosing speech errors from audiotapes and determining appropriate instructional steps from the critical viewing of videotapes.

Secondly, it is recommended that teaching experience under supervision be strengthened and intensified. Hands-on experience properly supervised is essential to the attainment of competence and the repertoire of skills which must be developed. While one might assume that during student teaching the student would have adequate opportunity to observe speech instruction and correction, teacher educators know that such does not necessarily occur. Yet, it is through such observations that the student may first understand how speech is integrated into the curriculum and the art and the science of teaching conjoined.

An analysis of graduates' responses to a questionnaire designed to determine projections for the Teachers College program has revealed that one common deficiency observed in the field is the lack of emphasis on speech. Other responses indicate that teachers need more supervised practica in speech and the use of audition. A rank order of the respondents' perceived gaps in knowledge revealed that speech teaching and tutoring were most commonly ranked at the top of the list. On the basis of results obtained from this questionnaire, it is recommended that practica for the development of the audio-vocal system be designated by the Council on Education of the Deaf (CED) in terms of minimum clock hours under supervision.

Second, it is recommended that these hours be specified possibly in addition to the clock hours of student teaching.

Third, it is recommended that sequencing and content of course work be studied and evaluated to determine the most efficient curriculum design for pre-service and in-service students.

Fourth, it is recommended that the first year on the job be considered an internship under the supervision of the university/college. This provision would enable graduates, particularly in integrated and resource programs, to be supervised by qualified professionals.

Certifying Bodies

In the writer's opinion, the role of the teacher of the deaf in self-contained settings or integrated settings is being fractionated by a variety of consultants. Many times these consultants, termed speech/language pathologists, audiologists, learning disability specialists, psychologists, or reading specialists, are not necessarily knowledgeable in the education of deaf persons. It seems that too many individuals have become "instant experts" on deafness, which is clearly observable in the teaching of speech. Speech instruction unrelated to the child's ongoing academic content violates recognized principles of learning. Speech instruction apart from the requirements of the total curriculum emphasizes compartmentalization and speech as a subject, not a tool. Synthesis of the child's developing audio-vocal system requires knowledge gained within the classroom.

It is recommended that the Council on Education of the Deaf:

(1) Revise its current standards to specify:

a) qualification of those involved directly in the assessment and instruction of hearing-impaired pupils (preschool to adulthood) by specialization such as: psychology, speech/language pathology, audiology, etc. Such qualifications should include supervised practica in self-contained settings and a prescribed competency level;

b) qualifications of personnel involved with adult or continuing education of deaf persons; and

c) a code of professional ethics.

(2) Initiate a major thrust toward having CED standards adopted by states, especially where qualifications may be much lower than the CED standards currently established.

At present there seems to be a definite national trend for states to adopt noncategorical certification in special education for all handicapping conditions. This has the effect of eliminating the specialized requirements for teachers of the deaf. As such, this trend warrants unified, immediate action to prevent further compromises in the education of the deaf child.

Eugene O. Mencke
The University of Oklahoma
Oklahoma City

Implicit, if not explicit, in this Institute is an assertion that a disparity exists between the teaching of spoken language to the hearing impaired, as the available information base would have it practiced, and its day-in, day-out pedagogical practice. The product of this disparity, presumably, is unintelligible speech—unintelligible even though good practice would predict otherwise (Ling, 1976). The literature (Ling, 1976; Northcott, 1971; Oyer, 1976) suggests that personnel who teach speech frequently lack the requisite commitment, knowledge, and/or skills; all of which lends credence to the need to examine and restructure personnel preparation programs.

Personnel representing one of three contrasting professional groups customarily accept a significant role in teaching speech to the hearing impaired. Among them, the teacher of the hearing impaired has traditionally assumed the primary role. More and more frequently, however, as mainstreaming under the Education of All Handicapped Children Act of 1975 (P.L. 94–142) is implemented in the public schools, the audiologist and/or speech-language pathologist becomes responsible.

Ling, Ling, and Pflaster (1977) have described and proposed new patterns of personnel types in Education of the Hearing Impaired. In response to the need for a variety of alternative management options to meet disparate individual requirements, other innovations in programs and in personnel types such as the teacher-clinician, the hearing therapist, or the educational audiologist have emerged (Alpiner, 1974; Forbes & Johnson, 1975; Healy & Jones, 1973; Ross & Calvert, 1976; Yater, 1978). Efforts generally are being made to spur the delivery of speech and hearing services to infants and their parents (Pollack, 1970) and to youngsters in the schools (Healy & Jones, 1973). All such innovations in personnel preparation and/or service delivery systems, not to mention traditional models, are equally vulnerable to the same familiar disappointments in spoken language achievement among the hearing impaired, unless more adequate standards of personnel preparation can be made to prevail.

The Problem: A Question of Standards

Whatever shortcomings exist in the skills of those who teach spoken language to the hearing impaired, they reflect, in a rather direct way, the accreditation and certificate standards defined by and for the professions involved. These standards, intended to provide the best assurance of quality services, have a substantial, and some say inordinate, impact on the shape of academic training programs. It can be argued that at least part of the explanation of the effectiveness, or lack of it, in teaching spoken language to the hearing impaired may lie in how well these standards assure that professional personnel can, in truth, provide the information and skills relevant to this task. Added to this is the fact that standards developed by professional groups, not having the force of law, may be further diluted by the hiring practices of state and local agencies which continue to recruit personnel of questionable competence for service in programs for the hearing impaired, among others.

In spite of how professional standards get to be applied in the marketplace, it is still helpful to examine the standards themselves since, presumably, they express the views of the professions about the kind and level of training required to do the job. What, then, it might be asked, constitutes the kind and extent of training required of those who teach speech to the hearing impaired?

The standards that bear most directly on the question are those defined by the Council on Education of the Deaf (CED) and the American Speech-Language-Hearing Association (ASHA). Explications of these standards programs have been widely disseminated by the respective certifying bodies (ASHA, 1975; CED, 1974). Time does not allow nor is it necessary to detail here the knowledge and competencies considered basic to the task in question. The literature (AOEHI, 1968; Ling, 1976; Northcott, 1971; Oyer, 1976) and the proceedings of this Institute have covered that ground very well. An examination of existing certificate requirements suggests that some of the knowledge and skills required are defined within each of the certificates in Audiology, Speech/Language Pathology, and Teaching the Hearing Impaired. The full range of competencies, however, may very well not be embraced by any one of them.

The certificate requirements for the speech/language pathologist, for example, stipulate extensive course work relating to the development of speech and language behavior, its disorders, assessment, and remediation; but only three semester hours of work need pertain to speech and language problems associated with hearing impairment. At the same time, the audiologist must obtain three semester hours of study in speech pathology and three in language pathology; but it is expressly stated that this work is to be directed to evaluation and management of speech and language problems which are not associated with hearing impairment. The teacher of the hearing impaired, on the other hand, is required to include no more than three semester hours of study in the areas of speech science and audiology—hardly a base from which to attain requisite competencies in auditory coding and recoding. On the practicum side, the speech/ language pathologist must acquire only 15 clock hours in assessment and management of speech and language problems associated with hearing impairment. By contrast, the audiologist, as well as the teacher of the hearing impaired, need obtain no specific training experience whatsoever in these areas.

When it is recalled that such standards are usually expressed in terms of minimal rather than optimal requirements, it becomes immediately apparent just where the central problem lies. To expect such personnel preparation standards to furnish practitioners who are minimally competent to assume primary responsibility for teaching spoken language to the hearing impaired is illogical. Personnel preparation programs usually train to minimum standards so that, as frequently happens, minimum standards become maximum. Minimum standards, in turn, regulate, although they may not necessarily define, the real quality of personnel admitted into a profession.

Some other features of certificate standards spill into the way in which personnel are trained to deal with the spoken language of the hearing impaired. First, while the array of knowledge and competencies specified for CED certification is impressive and comprehensive in scope, it can be contended that it may not be realistic. The guidelines specify a minimum of 30 semester hours of study and 250 clock hours of practicum in the broad context of preparing, at the undergraduate level, classroom teachers of the hearing impaired. It has been cogently argued that it would seem difficult to achieve, even minimally, the array of competencies implied by the CED standard with no more than 30 semester hours of study (Ling et al., 1977). This disparity, heightened by a burgeoning information base, has contributed to the mounting concern over the generally poor communication skills demonstrated among the more severely hearing impaired.

Secondly, each of the three certificate areas in question seems to be founded on the premise that their curricula cannot be combined effectively with the others into a single program of study and still retain the required depth of information. While the notion of a broadly trained "communicologist" has surfaced from time to time, it has not received broad support. There is the clear implication that the scope and level of knowledge and competencies cannot be accommodated within the usual time frame of a professional preparation program. Moreover, the broad range of faculty expertise and type and length of practicum experiences required to meet acceptable competency levels present difficult problems. While the arguments against the training of the "communicologist" or other generalist may be well founded, few would deny that the relatively limited interaction among audiology, speech/language pathology, and teaching the hearing impaired has, in effect, promoted a kind of professional insularity which conceives of the processes of speech, language, and hearing as mutually exclusive and independent entities.

A review of certificate standards suggests that professional personnel may be insufficiently grounded in important, basic, content information areas. If trained to prevailing standards, personnel preparing teachers of the hearing impaired may not have access to faculty with expertise in the areas of speech/language pathology or audiology and may, in fact, never be exposed in sufficient detail to these bodies of information. Similarly, personnel in the other two certificate areas may not be exposed sufficiently to content relating to education of the hearing impaired. In this connection, certificate standards in speech/language pathology and audiology specify only six semester hours of course work and 35 clock hours of practicum in the "other certificate area." A strong case can be made that, although depth of information is required to be professionally independent and effective, a greater sharing of information than now exists is both necessary and desirable. Regrettably, the three types of personnel preparation programs do not usually exist within a single academic unit where the necessary faculty, curricular, and practicum resources might be marshaled. Such an arrangement would be highly desirable, since it offers unique opportunities for interdisciplinary interaction in study and practicum activities as an integral part of the personnel preparation process. It is precisely here that mutual appreciation of the unique role of each professional area could be most effectively fostered.

It cannot be always assumed that the speech-language pathologist, the audiologist, and the teacher of the hearing impaired, when trained to their respective minimal certificate standards, are prepared to teach spoken language to the hearing impaired. This is not to say that competence for the task does not exist; it is merely in short supply. To the extent that professional standards affect the way in which this competence is defined and attained, they deserve a searching review.

A Response: Recommendations

Four specific recommendations aimed at improving personnel preparation standards for audiologists, speech/language pathologists, and teachers of the hearing impaired follow.

1. Our review of standards speaks to three unique, yet overlapping, professional roles with respect to the hearing impaired in general. One is that of a *classroom teacher* whose primary role is to provide educational services; another is a *communication skills specialist* whose primary role is the assessment and remediation of speech and language disorders; while the other, a *specialist in audition,* assesses auditory disorders and manages aural (re)habilitation. As different as these primary roles appear to be, all these disciplines share a common concern for the hearing-impaired youngster's competence in spoken language. This gives rise to potential problems of interdisciplinary interaction.

In this connection, it is difficult to accept the proliferation of new personnel types as being a viable solution to problems associated with personnel preparation and the teaching of speech. The contention is that the necessary personnel types already exist. They are the teacher of the hearing impaired, the speech/language pathologist, and the audiologist. The creation of a "communicologist," a "hearing therapist," or some other generalist represents a dilution of professional expertise and competence for the task and adds further to the already untoward confusion over professional roles.

There is an urgent need to evaluate and define the respective roles of the teacher of the hearing impaired, speech/language pathologist, and the audiologist as they relate to the teaching of spoken language to the hearing impaired. This should be done in a way that promotes the freest communication among the specialties and capitalizes on the special strengths of each group. The role of each specialty should be viewed as complementary rather than conflicting. Agreements on this major issue, particularly among all concerned national professional groups, would do much to define the goals of personnel preparation and training.

2. The national accrediting body representing the audiologist and

the speech/language pathologist should increase substantially the academic course work and practicum requirements related to teaching spoken language to the hearing impaired. These upgraded requirements should be incorporated into the certificate requirements at the earliest feasible time.

3. The national accrediting body representing teachers of the hearing impaired should adopt the master's degree as the minimum academic requirement in order to permit the attainment of competencies presently implied but seemingly not attainable within the present baccalaureate personnel preparation program.

4. There is a need for increased cooperation and joint efforts among the standards-developing and standards-setting bodies, particularly as they relate to communication skills development in the hearing impaired. To the extent that professional standards programs impact the training practices of academic institutions, and this impact is considerable, joint planning could do much to define more clearly training goals and practices.

In conclusion: The dimensions of speech, language, hearing, and their disorders in human behavior are myriad. What is presently known of the underlying principles and processes is undoubtedly overshadowed by the unknown. Nevertheless, progress is being made. Advances in the biological, physiological, sociological, and technological sciences continue to unfold. The degree to which these scientific advances can be made to benefit the severely hearing-impaired child in the acquisition of intelligible, albeit not necessarily normal, speech depends largely on the capacity of the professions concerned to apply them.

REFERENCES

Alpiner, J. Educational audiology. *J. Rehab. Audiol.* 1974, *7*, 50–54.

American Organization for the Education of the Hearing Impaired (AOEHI). *Competencies needed by teachers of hearing-impaired children.* Washington, D.C.: A. G. Bell Association for the Deaf, 1968.

American Speech and Hearing Association (ASHA). *Requirements for the certificates of clinical competence.* Washington, D.C.: American Speech and Hearing Association, 1975.

Council on Education of the Deaf (CED). Standards for the certification of teachers of the hearing impaired, 1972. *Volta Rev.*, 1974, *76*, 239–249.

Forbes, E., & Johnson, M. Bridging the gap between education and audiology. *Audiol. Hear. Ed.*, 1975, *1*, 12–54.

Healy, W., & Jones, S. *Project upgrade: Model regulations for school language, speech and hearing programs and services.* Washington, D.C.: American Speech and Hearing Association, 1973.

Ling, D. *Speech and the hearing-impaired child: Theory and practice.* Washington, D.C.: A. G. Bell Association for the Deaf, 1976.

Ling, D., Ling, A., & Pflaster, G. Individualized educational programming for hearing-impaired children. *Volta Rev.*, 1977, 79, 204–230.

Northcott, W. *Competencies needed by teachers of hearing-impaired infants (birth to three years of age) and their parents.* Doctoral dissertation, University of Minnesota, 1971.

Oyer, H. *Communication for the hearing handicapped: An international perspective.* Baltimore: University Park Press, 1976.

Pollack, D. *Educational audiology for the limited hearing infant.* Springfield, Ill.: Charles C Thomas, 1970.

P.L. 94–142: Education of All Handicapped Children Act of 1975. Washington, D.C., 1975.

Ross, M., & Calvert, D. R. Guidelines for audiology programs in educational settings for hearing-impaired children. *Am. Ann. Deaf*, 1976, *121*, 346–350.

Yater, V. Educational audiology. In J. Katz (Ed.), *Handbook of clinical audiology.* Baltimore: Williams and Wilkins, 1978.

Donald R. Calvert
Central Institute for the Deaf
St. Louis, Missouri

The urge to improve a large field of endeavor leads inevitably to the development of standards for performance. This is usually an attempt to bring *most* practice up to *best* practice. Standards guarantee nothing except the labor of new committees, site visits, and new forms to fill out, but they are the best device we have. For the purpose of improving the teaching of speech on a national scale, standards should encourage interdisciplinary efforts of teachers, speech/language pathologists, and audiologists. These three groups each have the fundamental background for teaching speech to hearing-impaired children, but none has standards that bear directly on the task of teaching speech, except for the minimal requirements of the Council on Education of the Deaf for teachers.

Rather than expand the present basic standards for certification in each of these three areas, I suggest a common body of standards specifically for teaching speech to hearing-impaired children which would be evidenced by a special certificate. Such standards may or may not be added to the competency of the individual professional. An audiologist, for example, who elected not to be involved in aural rehabilitation, preferring site-of-lesion testing in a medical setting, would be satisfied with the present Certificate of Clinical Competence in Audiology of the American Speech-Language-Hearing Association. But if an audiologist intends to work on speech for hearing-impaired children, either pre-service or continuing education would need to be expanded with specific work concerned with teaching speech to hearing-impaired children. This would hold for speech/language pathologists and for teachers, as well. Not all teachers of hearing-impaired children now have competence to teach speech even if they meet the present requirements of CED. This approach for the special added certificate avoids adding more and more to the already swelled curricula for professionals at the basic level.

One present standard actually *impedes* interdisciplinary efforts and should be looked at carefully. The Professional Services Board of the American Speech-Language-Hearing Association prohibits qualified teachers of hearing-impaired children from assessing or improving the speech of hearing-impaired children in a speech and hearing program accredited by the Board. It is a strange contradiction that a qualified teacher can work with a deaf youngster in a group in a school classroom but is not considered qualified if the point of contact is one-to-one in the room of a clinic. For the benefit of hearing-impaired children, this should be changed.

Section 2
Responses of Panelists and Participants

PANELISTS

Sister James Lorene Hogan
Fontbonne College

Arthur Boothroyd
Clarke School for the Deaf

Linda J. Rowe
John Tracy Clinic

Ann M. Mulholland
Columbia University

Eugene O. Mencke
University of Oklahoma

Donald R. Calvert
Central Institute for the Deaf

As noted in the introduction, the discussion focused around: (A) Recruitment of Competent Individuals Into the Field; (B) Establishment of Standards; and (C) Preparation of Personnel. Panelists' and participants' responses to each issue are provided separately below. Comments which did not fit into any of these categories are listed under the heading, (D) General Observations Related to Improving Speech.

The chairman opened the discussion with the following statement:

> It is the position of the panelists that for the most part professionals currently working with deaf students are not adequately prepared to facilitate the development of intelligible speech.
>
> The panelists also take the position that in general:
>
> 1. Speech development cannot be effectively facilitated by professionals who have not had formal preparation to work with deaf students;
> 2. Speech development cannot be effectively facilitated by professionals who have not spent considerable time associating with deaf students;
> 3. The intelligibility of a deaf student's speech will not meaningfully improve unless students are in an environment which requires the consistent use of speech in meaningful interactions.

Following these introductory remarks each of the three major categories was discussed. Each category was allocated 25 minutes and was opened with a brief introduction by two of the panelists. For the most part their introductory comments were extracted from their preconference papers. In providing the responses listed below, every effort was made to maintain the intent of what was said.

(A) Recruitment of Competent Individuals Into the Field

We know that there are a number of people teaching speech to the deaf who are not good teachers of speech. Good teachers result from well-qualified recruits. Excellent training alone is not enough. We must have trainees with high potential. In selecting trainees, the following issues must be considered:

1. Intelligence,
2. Analytical abilities, and
3. Synthetical abilities—the ability to take information from various disciplines and apply it to teach the deaf.

In considering intelligence as a factor, it was noted that a person should not be excluded from a training program because that person is too bright; however, gifted students sometimes do not have the required patience. They glide so easily through college that they don't learn about hard work nor do they see the challenge.

The vitality of student teachers should grow beyond their formal preparation. This requires a basic knowledge of the process of speech production, the ability to problem solve, and the ability to improve one's self without a mentor. Do we want candidates who seek "cookbook" approaches to teaching? This kind of candidate projects a poor self-image.

The admission process cannot be limited to a review of transcripts and references. Written evidence and demonstrated potential for achievement are also needed. In order to attract highly qualified applicants, we need to improve our recruiting materials and create an image that teaching the deaf is a challenge. We must seek to improve the quality of candidates by showing the challenge in speech training which is relevant to Special Education.

It seems that many prospective students enter our field for the wrong reason. They are interested in manual communication and when some applicants learn that we don't use sign language, they are actually disappointed. These applicants are reacting to what they see in the media and to what they read. We need to develop our efforts to convey the same aura relative to speech communication as a goal for the hearing impaired. Other teachers have entered the field to meet their own needs and encourage the dependence of parents and students on teachers. Such individuals should not be permitted to enter the profession.

We need to expand training programs which are noted for their excellence. We need assurance that potential recruits will be rewarded within the context of teaching and that our graduates will continue to have access to new knowledge.

People coming into education today may not be as highly qualified as recruits were in previous years. We will be drawing from a smaller pool of human resources. We should have in-service and pre-service recruiting efforts. We need to draw on competent people who are already in the schools. There is a great need for in-service training since a large majority of "regular" classroom teachers are the ones who will provide services to the hearing impaired. We must also look outside the field of Education of the Deaf to provide services for deaf children. We need to bring deaf adults into the teacher education programs in spite of the inherent challenges. While they may not be effective speech teachers, they can be effective role models and educators. In taking hard-of-hearing and deaf candidates into teacher training programs, we need to ensure the provision of jobs for which they are qualified.

We must look for persons who have the potential to become highly professional individuals. The teacher of speech is the one adult who must establish a communication environment to help the deaf child recognize the crucial importance of this skill. This teacher, however, is not only responsible for developing oral communication skills; he/she must also act as a "manager" in the other important variables of language and speech development. The professional must have this sense of managerial responsibility for the development of the total deaf child and accept this responsibility in a personable, flexible, and intelligent manner which enables the student to realize his/her potential.

There really is not one single list of criteria for recruitment. It is essential, however, that the candidate have an enriched background to bring to the study of speech, hearing, and education. We need to examine and where necessary change our own behavior as professionals to attract the kind of people we are seeking.

(B) Establishment of Standards

Regardless of how the marketplace regards professional standards, it is still helpful to examine them since these standards dictate the kind and level of skills that are required to do the job. The standards that are developed by the Council on Education of the Deaf (CED) and the American Speech-Language-Hearing Association (ASHA), as well as Public Law 94–142, exert an influence on audiologists and speech pathologists.

The full range of competencies necessary to teach the hearing impaired may not be guaranteed by any one certificate. Audiologists, speech pathologists, and educators of the deaf have similar training but with different areas of academic emphasis and practicum requirements. The problems in service delivery are compounded by mainstreaming placements of hearing-impaired children.

A joint ASHA-CED certificate is needed. It is time to stop the nonsense and stop fighting over territorial domains and begin to jointly provide services to hearing-impaired children and adults who do not receive any services. How well prepared are we to do this?

Usually training in the colleges and universities is geared to meet minimum standards, and thus these standards become the maximum. As a result, the preparation of personnel is not as strong as it should be. Some of this problem stems from a lack of qualified teachers in the training programs. If hearing-impaired youngsters are to learn and acquire the best possible speech, knowledge and skills from all three areas (audiology, education of the deaf and speech/language pathology) must be developed in candidates. When trained to their respective minimal standards, all teachers are not sufficiently prepared to teach speech and language to hearing-impaired children. Needed competencies are frequently in very short supply. In this regard, it is recommended that all speech pathologists be required to work with the hearing impaired because many of them will be involved with such teaching when they accept jobs. This recommendation would guarantee experience before entering the field. Although such experience is acknowledged as highly desirable, in some schools, the teacher of the deaf, who has a great deal of experience, is not allowed to teach speech to the hearing impaired because of certification requirements.

There is an urge to improve the field by raising the level of professional standards. In order to do this, training programs need access to the best practicum people. Researchers dealing with methods and equipment need to inform teachers concerning the application of fresh information.

The Council on Education of the Deaf (CED) has minimal requirements. Rather than expanding on present standards for teaching speech to the hearing impaired, a new certificate that limits entrance to the field is recommended. To illustrate, an audiologist may elect to not become involved with teaching speech. Such a person, however, could gain needed knowledge later through in-service training and thus attain certification.

One reason for developing a new certificate rather than expanding existing programs of certification is that we now have a vast array of new knowledge. The amount of information and skill required in professional training becomes a problem in terms of the amount of time available for professional preparation. As a result of the time constraints, students lack the ability to comprehend vital information.

Who is the person now certified to teach spoken language to the hearing impaired? It is not the teacher of subject matter. Standards should provide the best possible service and exert a positive effect on training programs. It can also be argued that the lack of effectiveness in teaching is a reflection of how well these standards assure professionals that they will have expertise and skills. We need the force of state and local laws to prevent the recruitment and hiring of incompetent personnel.

One of the many good things that has occurred at this conference is that we are all sharing this problem together. ASHA will be considering certification requirements relative to Aural Rehabilitation in the near future. In conference settings, people will be asked to respond to a short article in ASHA, "What do you think should happen?" In this way many interested people will have the opportunity to share their views and provide valuable input. We all seem to recognize the need to do something to establish and clarify standards for professional preparation and certification.

(C) Preparation of Personnel

There is no question but that there should be a certificate or credential available for those qualified in teaching speech. It seems that almost all of our teacher preparation programs are bound by certain external factors. Once we get through all the basic requirements of teacher training, we have difficulty including the things considered important in the area of speech training; we have no opportunity to examine different approaches and how they affect speech training. We don't have enough time to include parents, and yet the parents are the persons who will carry education on over into adulthood.

We need more practicum and more education if we are to develop qualified master teachers. Certification requirements are such that there are only so many hours for practicum. How much can one provide in a one-year program? Where does one get practicum sites? How does one expand practicum sites? What controls does one have? In some situations, students are limited by union contracts as to the number of hours spent in the schools doing student teaching. Thus, matters regulated by unions can become major problems.

We are very limited in setting up practicum by time constraints and lack of qualified master teachers. Instructors of courses in speech teaching should be persons who have worked with hearing-impaired children and who are able to supervise student teachers. Our greatest need is for specialists who can teach speech and can teach our student trainees how to do it. Research findings such as those presented at this conference should be shared with those who are actively involved in teaching speech to the deaf.

What kind of support will pull people from other areas into our discipline? How much time is realistic to be spent teaching in special fields? The kind and scope of education needed today cannot be accomplished in a one-year program. Two years is too short for specialization. We do not have enough time to expand what we want our students to learn about teaching the hearing impaired. Teachers in the classrooms must have educational backgrounds in Special Education. We must converse with our State Departments of Education and tell them that they are not giving us sufficient time to prepare teachers. The situation in personnel preparation is now such that there is a need to return to school for post-master's studies.

It could be said that there are many who are certified but not qualified. I guess the question should be raised: "How many students should be trained?" Do our students have enough practicum time with master teachers for teaching speech? The master teachers are torn between working with student teachers and working with their own students.

Another problem is that there are not enough master teachers to act as models for student teachers. In some situations, while we have tried to teach our students in a number of ways, hands-on experiences remain essential. All who work with the deaf need hands-on experiences, especially if they are to understand sensory development, equipment, and hearing amplification devices. Are we sure that we are making a contribution to the field by in-servicing the classroom teacher on speech practice, which is a matter that is absolutely necessary for the children?

It is not uncommon for audiologists to have limited experience with the deaf. Frequently audiologists have as much or more difficulty communicating their ideas to deaf people than deaf people have making their speech understandable. There are three or four things related to speech development and audiology that have not been mentioned. A good audiological report is crucial in providing speech training. Where does the school audiologist fit in? We need a lot more in-service training on amplification and use of hearing aids in the schools. It is also recommended that teaching preparation should place greater emphasis in general areas such as linguistics, reading, writing, and in development of the thinking process as well as in the area of speech.

What should come from this conference is some kind of joint proposal to ASHA and CED to develop training procedures that would involve close cooperation among the three areas of Speech, Audiology, and Education of the Deaf. This training process should also include some model practicum placements with supervision from all three areas.

(D) General Observations Related to Improving Speech

The topic of this conference is Speech Assessment and Speech Improvement. The emphasis at the primary education level has been fairly well addressed; however, there is a need to consider the fact that children grow up and have a need to maintain their speech skills once they leave the elementary and secondary levels.

Once the normal-hearing child talks, he continues it almost casually. The hearing-impaired child must practice. Although we have a system for developing and producing college students, we have no such system for maintaining the speech of the young deaf adult after he/she leaves school. This is good reason for teaching others how to assist in the maintenance of speech.

There is a consistent need over time for deaf adults to reinforce some of their own competencies. Even the most competent adult oralists should come for assistance periodically during their lifetime. There is a need to address continuing education as well as earlier developmental activities.

I think that in attempting to locate services, we need to be guided by competencies that are presumably required to meet specific needs. We should not be looking for this professional person or that professional person. If speech or language training is needed to help the hearing-impaired adult, then one should go to where such training is available. Unless one knows the need, one is not in a position to specify who should do it or who has the competence to do it.

One of the areas we haven't discussed is the crucial role that administrators play in the education of the hearing impaired. We need in-service programs for these administrators so they may be trained to promote speech development in day and residential schools.

I don't think we successfully apply information coming from research nor do we give sufficient consideration as to how the classroom teacher is going to apply new information. Research implications should be explained to the teachers. The classroom teachers are most important and they are the ones most neglected in our conferences.

Section 3
Summary and Recommendations of the Chairman

The issues of recruiting appropriate individuals into the field and of establishing standards have been adequately addressed by my colleagues on the panel. As chairman of this panel, I wish only to add my full concurrence with their observations regarding the significance of these two issues and urge that they be given appropriate attention by teacher preparation programs and by professional and certifying organizations. While there will be some overlap, it is the issue of personnel preparation on which I will focus my recommendations.

As noted earlier, the panelists took the position that for the most part, professionals currently working with deaf students are not adequately prepared to facilitate speech development. In summarizing and making my recommendations regarding improving personnel preparation, I should like to reflect on the panelists' recommendations from several different perspectives.

The first condition is related to the rapid acceleration in the amount of knowledge related to speech production and to the sophistication required to understand and apply that knowledge to developing speech in deaf children. My experience suggests to me—and I am confident the panelists would agree—that most new, as well as more experienced teachers of the deaf, are not aware of nor adequately prepared to apply new information.

From my perspective the answer does *not* lie in lengthening teacher preparation programs or necessarily in changing the emphasis. The demands on teacher preparation to include career education, social development, metrication, to name but a few, mitigate against such approaches.

The first step needed to improve teacher preparation programs is to upgrade the quality of what is presented. It is not reasonable to expect that the same person can adequately prepare teachers in educational theory, instructional development, career education, principles of teaching reading and math, and also teach language development, phonetics, acoustical phonetics, psychoacoustics, applied psycholinguistics, speech physiology, applied aural rehabilitation, etc.

This issue must be addressed in preparing courses for teachers in training. Courses need to be jointly designed by individuals current and sophisticated in the discipline and by individuals who have experience in the classroom. Collaboration can ensure that when information is synthesized and simplified it remains accurate and, just as important, it is relevant to what the new teacher will experience in the classroom.

The second step I recommend is for teacher preparation programs, certification agencies, schools, and teacher associations to recognize that completion of a formal program is the *beginning* of the individual's professional growth, not the end. This point, in my judgment, is the most significant issue needing attention. Let me provide three reasons why I feel so strongly about this point:

1. The amount of existing information which needs to be learned is too great to be acquired in one or even two years.
2. New information is being acquired at such an astounding rate that a person can be out of date within a few short years.
3. Learning requires a readiness. After graduation and with experience in the classroom, the need for and relevance of information become more sharply focused and the instruction takes on new meaning and importance.

I would recommend therefore that teacher preparation programs: (1) review their pre-service curricula to focus on the essentials which will provide a solid foundation upon which graduates can build; (2) develop in-service programs for teachers. For this recommendation to have real impact it will probably be necessary for certification agencies to require such in-service preparation as a means of retaining certification. Another practical suggestion is the institution of a one-year *supervised* internship before certification is granted.

Regardless of the approach taken, any effort to improve the effectiveness of speech training which focuses only on pre-service preparation is doomed to fail for the reasons cited above, plus one other very significant fact. As the job market for teachers continues to tighten, the trend toward low staff turnover will accelerate. The net result will be an even larger proportion of the teaching faculty who have not had the benefit of "improved" pre-service programs. To have any significant effect we must focus our efforts on in-service preparation as well as pre-service preparation.

Another condition significantly influencing what should be done is a shift in the environment in which deaf students are being educated. In recent years we have seen more and more deaf students being "mainstreamed" in their neighborhood schools. It seems certain that P.L. 94–142 will accelerate this trend for the foreseeable future. This can be both a blessing and a curse. It will be a blessing to the degree it provides an environment which requires students to meaningfully use their speech. It will be a curse to the degree it denies students access to professionals who: (1) understand that speech and language, while interrelated, are different; (2) recognize the significance of residual hearing in speech development; and (3) are prepared to work with deaf students in speech and language development.

It is beyond the scope of this discussion to argue the merits of mainstreaming. The fact is that it is becoming a prevailing condition and, as it continues, fewer deaf students will have a trained teacher of the deaf as their speech mentor. The issue we need to address is how can we ensure that personnel are prepared to meet adequately the speech development needs of deaf students who are mainstreamed.

To accomplish this it will not be possible to hold to the position that only teachers of the deaf are competent to teach speech to deaf students. Nor is it appropriate to assume that speech pathologists, audiologists, and language specialists are prepared to work with profoundly deaf students because they carry ASHA certification. Instead we must, as has been suggested above, find ways to work together and pool our resources in serving students. This, of course, will not be easily accomplished since it will require us, as professionals, and the organizations which represent us to set aside deeply indoctrinated parochial interests and to begin to recognize the professional worth of one another. Speech and hearing training programs will need to prepare their clinicians to work with the profoundly deaf and with their teachers. Teacher preparation programs will need to prepare teachers in training to capitalize on speech pathologists, audiologists, and language specialists as a resource. Regardless of the approach employed, in the end success will be limited by the availability of "master speech teachers" who can serve as role models and who can supervise others as they develop their skills.

From my vantage point it seems most likely that a cadre of "master speech teachers" will, for the most part, e hearing programs with the vision to offer cialty. Such programs will closely affiliat programs which will allow graduate st students in a manner suggested earlier grams will be careful to provide extensi supervision of qualified speech te speech specialists gain experience grams serving deaf students will n tradition and employ such individuals t velopment efforts and to in-service their teachers.

This is a time for boldness in our approach to the complex of facilitating speech in profoundly deaf children. Traditional ap proaches have at best been marginally successful with a few notable exceptions. Unfortunately the exceptions are more the result of personalities than they are the result of effective processes. If we are to gain significant improvements we must be willing to break with tradition and take significant risks. We must be willing to mend broken fences and to tear down others in the spirit of cooperation. We must stop expending energy bickering among ourselves and channel that energy into meeting the needs of deaf students.

—*Milo E. Bishop*